THE QUEEN'S PIRATE

IAIN GATELY was raised in Hong Kong and studied law at the University of Cambridge. He gained his PhD in literature from the University of Southampton. Iain is the author of one novel and five works of non-fiction, including *Rush Hour: How 500 Million Commuters Survive the Daily Journey to Work* and *The Secret Surfer*. He lives in Dorset.

Also by Iain Gately

The Secret Surfer

Rush Hour: How 500 Million Commuters Survive the Daily Journey to Work

Drink: A Cultural History of Alcohol

La Diva Nicotina: The Story of How Tobacco Seduced the World

THE QUEEN'S PIRATE

The Triumphant Life and Tragic End of THOMAS CAVENDISH, Elizabethan Privateer

IAIN GATELY

HEAD of ZEUS

First published in the UK in 2026 by Head of Zeus,
part of Bloomsbury Publishing Plc

9 7 5 3 1 2 4 6 8

A catalogue record for this book is available from the British Library.

ISBN (HB): 9781035917556; ISBN (EPUB): 9781035917563

Typeset by Six Red Marbles, India
Printed and bound in Great Britain
by Clays Ltd, Elcograf S.p.A.

MIX
Paper | Supporting responsible forestry
FSC® C018072

Bloomsbury Publishing Plc
50 Bedford Square, London, WC1B 3DP, UK
Bloomsbury Publishing Ireland Limited,
29 Earlsfort Terrace, Dublin 2, D02 AY28, Ireland

HEAD OF ZEUS LTD
5–8 Hardwick Street
London EC1R 4RG

To find out more about our authors and books
visit www.headofzeus.com
For product safety related questions contact productsafety@bloomsbury.com

To Ed, who taught me how to sail offshore and promised that, if I wrote this book, he'd read it.

Contents

Berehaven
Plymouth
Azores
Islands
Canary
Cape Verde
Islands
Cabo San Lucas
Barra de Navidad
Huatulco
Paita
Pisco
Arica
Salvador
Rio de Janeiro
São Vicente
São Sebastião
Davis's return route
Cavendish's return route
St He
Concepción
Port Desire
Port Famine
All ships return route (second voyage)
Cavendish's circumnavigation 1586–1588
Cavendish's second voyage 1591–1592

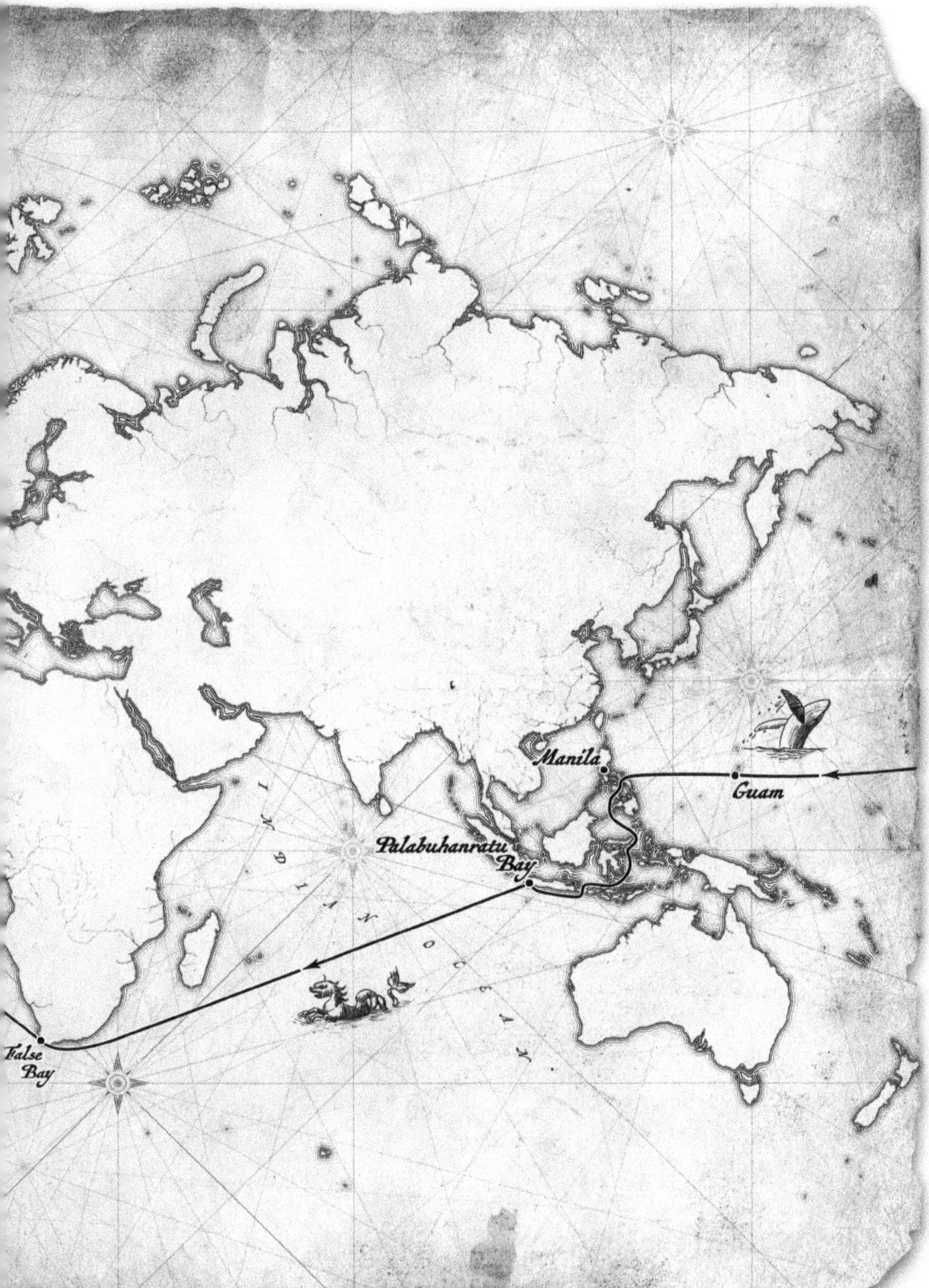

Manila
Guam
Palabuhanratu Bay
INDIAN OCEAN
False Bay

Introduction

Berehaven, Ireland

'The sea is a waving, wavering foundation, the wind's theatre for both comedies and tragedies.'
Samuel Purchas

ON THE MORNING TIDE OF 11 June 1593, the sailing ship *Desire* drifted into Berehaven on Ireland's southwest coast. She was the last to return of a fleet of five vessels that had left England to the sound of trumpets two years before. Now she was a floating wreck. Her sails had been blown to rags, and her decks were littered with fallen spars and tangled ropes. She had sixteen living crewmen, only five of whom had strength enough to stand up. They were the sole survivors of an initial company of seventy-four men who had sailed from Plymouth in the summer of 1591.

The *Desire's* anchors had been lost in a gale six thousand miles away, and her captain could only bring her to rest by running her aground. Irish labourers had been watching from the fields and, as soon as she was still, they climbed aboard to gather in the remnants of her sails and make her fast. They fled in horror the instant they'd secured the *Desire*. Her decks were littered with corpses whose intestines had burst out of their stomachs and scrotums. Beneath them, in her hold, was a coagulated mass of rotting penguins, whose flesh seethed with 'most loathsome and ugly' worms. The worms were eating their way through the *Desire*. According to a survivor,

> there was nothing that they did not devour... our clothes, boots, shoes, hats, shirts, stockings: and for the ship they did so eat the timbers that we greatly feared they would undo us, by gnawing through its side... at the last we could not sleep for them, but they would eat our flesh.

The *Desire* was a famous ship. Just under five years previously, she had tied up in the River Thames beside the Royal Palace of Greenwich in a very different state. On this occasion, her sails had been cut from damask and a giant standard sewn from Chinese silk and cloth of gold flew from her main mast. Her mariners were dressed in blue silk suits with gold medallions on heavy gold chains hanging from their necks. According to a Spanish spy, 'It was as if Cleopatra had been resuscitated. The only thing wanting was that the rigging should have been of silken rope.' As the *Desire* came into her mooring, she had 'fired off a great quantity of artillery', which, in the opinion of another spy, was 'a most beautiful sight'.

Her owner, Thomas Cavendish Esquire, gentleman, privateer and circumnavigator, had brought the *Desire*, which he'd had 'built up from the keel', to Greenwich to pay homage to his queen, Elizabeth I of England. After saluting her with cannon-fire, he'd staged a banquet for her aboard his ship in a cabin hung with 'marvellously rich' banners. They dined off solid gold plates, serenaded by the *Desire's* musicians. Elizabeth (spies reported) was in 'great good humour'. England was at war with Spain, and she boasted that its king 'barks a good deal but does not bite. We care nothing for the Spaniards; their ships, loaded with silver and gold from the Indies, come hither after all.'

The change in the condition of the *Desire* between her triumphant display in 1588 and her crippled state in 1593 reflected the altered fortunes of her owner. Thomas Cavendish, the youngest, most audacious hero of the Age of Discovery, a contemporary of Sir Francis Drake and Sir Walter Raleigh, had staked his inheritance, his social status and his life on perilous ventures in search of plunder and fame. He'd participated in the first English colonising expedition to Virginia in 1585; and had led his own fleet around the world a year later, returning to England after capturing the richest Spanish galleon afloat, 'victorious over elements and enemies, illustrious in wealth and honour'. However, in 1591, at the age of thirty, he had launched a final, fatal expedition, intended not only to privateer, but also to establish trade with China, which had been frustrated by treachery and mutiny. He died at an unmarked spot in the South Atlantic as his venture fell to pieces and his ships, including the *Desire*, returned without his body.

Cavendish's Spanish opponents called him a corsair – a pirate – and reacted to his depredations with a mixture of panic and fury. How could a youth 'of about twenty-two years, with a wretched little vessel of a hundred tons and forty or fifty companions' have disrupted their Pacific trade and beggared their colonies in Mexico and the Philippines, unless he was in league with the Antichrist? The Inquisition burned alive those of his crew that they captured, and news of his death was commemorated with *Te Deums* in three continents, to thank God for getting rid of him.

A portrait of this English hero and Spanish villain, painted when he was in his late twenties, shows an Elizabethan gallant, sumptuously dressed, rather than the brutal corsair his enemies feared and detested. Cavendish stands tall in his picture with his hands on his hips, holding the brim of a velvet hat with a jewelled cockade in the fingers of his right hand, while his left hand is draped over the pommel of a sword. A white lace collar around his throat is decorated with snowflake patterns, backlit by the crimson silk beneath. The collar tops a peascod doublet in candy-stripes of cream silk alternating with bands of embroidered cloth of gold. Above the finery, Cavendish's eyebrows are shaved pencil thin and his hair raised into a quiff. It's hard to imagine such an elegant individual burning ships and towns or cutting people's throats, until you look into his pale blue eyes, still luminous beneath the crackled varnish of his portrait, and see that Cavendish appears to be watching you from his young, lean face. His gaze is direct and, by some trick of the light, it seems that the eyes of a dead man live on in his picture and are scrutinising the stranger in front of them. The effect is both mesmerising, and chilling.

Thomas Cavendish was the most existential of Elizabethan heroes, aloof, calculating and motivated by opportunity and expediency rather than introspection, piety or prejudice. His principles – such as they were – derived from a medieval concept of honour that sanctioned both violence and theft, and glorified revenge. Nonetheless, he was feted in his own age. His triumphs were celebrated in ballads, and his fall was mourned by poets. His contemporaries considered his death to have been a model of fortitude in the face of adversity and named their sons after him. The Dutch followed in his footsteps, using his charts and pilots to establish themselves in Asia, and Cavendish's dream of sea-borne commerce between England and China proved to be prophetic.

Here, for the first time, is his story.

1

The Courtier

Suffolk, England

In September 1581, the twenty-one-year-old Thomas Cavendish was burning through his inheritance. He had just come of age and gained control over the estates that had been bequeathed to him. He'd had a melancholy childhood and a gloomy adolescence, and aimed to compensate himself now that he was rich and independent. Born into a family of wealthy and well-connected Suffolk gentry, Thomas was one of nine children. His infancy was punctuated by the deaths of his three elder brothers and one of his younger sisters, and his father had died when he was only twelve years old. He'd become the ward of his maternal uncle Sir Thomas, 2nd Baron Wentworth, after his father's premature death. Although Cavendish's guardian fulfilled his duties, steering him along the usual course for a young man of his social class by sending him to Cambridge University for a year in 1576, and thence to Gray's Inn to learn a little law,[1] Wentworth was a man of tainted honour, and Cavendish felt contaminated by association. The baron's long and mostly illustrious career had been stained by a single instance of gross incompetence. In 1553, Mary I had appointed him governor of Calais, England's last toehold in France, which it had held for over two centuries, and which Wentworth lost to a French army in 1558 in a siege lasting only seven days.*[2] The French captured Wentworth as well as Calais and kept him prisoner until he was ransomed by Elizabeth I. He retreated from court after this disgrace and became a staunch Puritan. A portrait from 1568 shows him as Thomas Cavendish would have known him. His clothing is austere – his doublet and hose are

* The defeat had shocked Mary so deeply that she'd claimed that, if her body were to be opened after her death, the word *Calais* would be found cut into her heart.

black, his ruff is minimal – and his expression is watchful, perhaps to give lie to the rumours that he'd been surprised by the French.

Once he'd received his inheritance, Cavendish rejected the puritanism that had cast a shadow over his adolescence, poured some of his wealth into his wardrobe and joined the exuberant band of courtiers who attended Queen Elizabeth at her palaces. No official ceremonies were required to be admitted to this enchanted circle. Cavendish was one of a number of young gentlemen with relatives among the privy councillors or with blood-ties to the queen who joined the royal entourage once they'd been presented. Cavendish and his fellow courtiers revelled in conspicuous consumption, spending fortunes on their clothing, their hats, their shoes, their jewels and their suits of armour. They aimed to lead as well as follow fashions, sporting both styles imported from Europe and those of their own devising. Edward de Vere, 17th Earl of Oxford, for instance, affected an Italian way of dress when he returned from a self-imposed exile in Tuscany after farting while 'making of his low obeisance to Queen Elizabeth',* and stunned the court with 'a little apish hat, couched fast to the pate, like an oyster'.[3] Sir Philip Sydney, meanwhile, (who was reckoned to be the finest English courtier alive, admired in Europe as well as at home) dazzled with a white silk peascod jacket, slashed and tufted, worn over black velvet trunk-hose embroidered with gold and a matching codpiece.

Cavendish and his fellow gallants also paid attention to the bodies beneath the finery, remedying natural defects with subterfuge. His friend Sir John Harrington, the queen's 'saucy godson', summarised the artifices necessary, including shoulder pads, deodorants and the tricks of small talk, to perfect themselves:

> We use much bumbastings and quiltings to seem fitter formed, better shouldered, smaller waisted, fuller-thighed than we are, we

* Elizabeth reminded him of his indiscretion when he returned from Tuscany. 'My Lord,' she said, unprompted, 'I had forgot the fart.'

> use perfumes both inward and outward to seem sweeter than we be; we use courteous salutations to seem kinder than we be; and sometimes graver and godly communications, to seem wiser than we be.[4]

Gambling was the favourite vice of these paragons of masculinity, and it was rampant at court. The queen and her privy councillors played at cards for money (Elizabeth cheated), the pot-boys shook dice for pennies and her courtiers bet on anything that moved, including random events – such as which one of two falling leaves would hit the ground first?

Thomas Cavendish was a natural-born gambler. He'd run up debts against his inheritance before he'd received it and increased his stakes once it was in his hands. In 1581, for instance, he wagered £1,000 on whether or not George Gifford, a gentleman pensioner of the queen, could walk to Constantinople.*[5] However, while such large, bold bets marked Cavendish as a thrill-seeker, within a year of becoming independently wealthy the excitement of laying wagers had paled. The kick faded once the bets had been settled, and Cavendish wanted more than transient excitement. He cast around for other channels for his money and energy, and found a role model and mentor in Walter Raleigh, a young captain of a good family who had borrowed £100 to make a splash at court. Raleigh's 'handsome and well compacted person', neatly trimmed beard, bright blue eyes and 'bold and plausible tongue'[6] had recommended him to Queen Elizabeth, who valued wit in her courtiers as much as the cut of their bumbasts, and she had made him her new favourite.

* Bets on feats of endurance were all the rage and were later satirised by the playwright Ben Johnson, whose character Puntarvolo, in *Every Man out of His Humour*, lays down stakes (at odds of five to one) not only for himself, but also for his dog and his cat, that they will walk to Constantinople and return to England.

Better educated than most of her councillors, fluent in Latin and Italian, Elizabeth was vivacious, quick-witted and erudite.[7] She danced every day, she loved hunting and both reading and composing poetry. Despite her responsibilities and the constant threat of assassination, she retained a sense of fun. She was a discriminate judge of company, who'd been flattered by the best wits in England, and she raised and rewarded those who caught her ear as well as her eye. She was bored by her previous favourites, who'd been elegant youths when she came to the throne in 1558 but had since grown long in the tooth, dull in their minds, and repetitive or evasive in their speech. She showered Raleigh with presents, gifting him Durham House (once the palace of the Catholic Bishops of Durham) as a residence and appointing him Master of the Stanneries, which provided him with a substantial income in tithes.

Raleigh put his new wealth into circulation. His shoes alone (which were valued at £600) cost more than ten skilled shoemakers earned between them in a year. His prodigality enchanted Thomas Cavendish and his peers. They envied Raleigh for his clothing, respected him for his experiences – he was a battle-hardened warmonger, who'd killed men with his sword and lance in campaigns in both France and Ireland – and admired his powers of self-expression. Raleigh was also known for his integrity, in that he never betrayed his roots. He was related to the great privateering families of the west of England and he participated or invested in the family business throughout his life.[8]

It was this aspect of his character that appealed most to Thomas Cavendish. Much of his own wealth was tied up in land and, like many of his class who had bets to make or clothes to buy, he was looking for opportunities to raise cash other than by collecting rents. Privateering, as espoused by Walter Raleigh, seemed ideal. It was a legal form of piracy. If a merchant lost a ship or cargo to hostile action, they could apply to England's Admiralty Court for 'letters of reprisal', which granted them the right to take shipping and goods to the value of their losses from their aggressors, and/or their countries of origin. The letters could be sold at a discount to professional privateers who would carry out retribution for a percentage of the takings. Privateering was also open to gentlemen, to whom it resembled jousting with ships as steeds instead of horses, and who believed that fighting at sea was as valid a path to wealth and fame as warfare on land.*[9]

Thomas Cavendish's ancestors had won their estates and privileges through warfare and oppression† and he decided to follow their examples, albeit by sea. He was motivated by glory as well as gain. Not just the gold, but the getting of the gold, inspired him. He wanted to exorcise the demons of his wardship under Wentworth and emerge from the shadow of shame. In 1584, Cavendish elected to throw his hand in with Raleigh, who was promoting a plan at court to establish a privateering base in America. Raleigh contended that war with Catholic Spain was inevitable, and that the best way to forestall conflict was to interrupt the flow of gold and silver her king, Philip II, received from his American territories by raiding his treasure fleets from a safe haven on the west coast of the Atlantic. Privateers could also be patriots.

Cavendish stayed close to his mentor as his plan evolved. First Raleigh applied to the queen for a patent to explore, exploit, settle and ultimately rule the entire east coast of America between Florida and Newfoundland. Elizabeth signed and sealed it on 16 March 1584, bestowing immense powers over unknown territories on her favourite:

* The precedent had been set by Edward III at the battle of Winchelsea in 1350, when he had ordered the pilot of his ship to 'set me against yonder Spaniard that is coming, for I wish to joust with him'. Quoted in Sir Julian Stafford Corbett, Drake and the Tudor Navy, With a History of the Rise of England as a Maritime Power (2 vols.) (New York: Burt Franklin, 1899) p. 20.

† A Cavendish had been Lord Chief Justice in the reign of Richard II, another slew Wat Tyler, leader of the peasants' revolt, in 1381; a third had played a conspicuous and gallant role at the Battle of Agincourt.

> We do give and grant to our trusty and well-beloved servant Walter Raleigh Esquire and his heirs and assignees ever after free liberty and license from time to time and for all times forever hereafter to discover search find out and view such remote heathen and barbarous lands Countries and territories not actually possessed by any Christian prince and to have hold occupy and enjoy... forever'.[10]

Once he had his patent, Raleigh launched a reconnaissance mission. Two ships captained by Philip Amadis and Arthur Barlowe crossed the Atlantic and spent six weeks exploring America, before returning to England in mid-September. Barlowe wrote a report of their findings, which Raleigh circulated among both courtiers and the City of London's merchants. The report was shameless propaganda, picturing Raleigh's new territory as an earthly paradise. When his ships had closed in on its shores, Barlowe reported, the air had been perfumed with sweet scents 'as if we had been in the middle of some delicate garden, abounding with all kinds of odoriferous flowers'.[11] Wafted by fragrant breezes, they had cruised the coast until they found an inlet where they anchored and rowed ashore.

Their landfall was covered with a tangle of grapevines, bursting with ripe fruit, so many, in Barlowe's opinion, that 'in all the world the like abundance is not to be found'. The land beyond consisted of a series of verdant islets, sheltered from the Atlantic by a barrier chain. The islets were graced with 'goodly woods, full of deer, rabbits, hares and fowl', and the woods themselves were composed of giant aromatic trees, including, 'the highest and reddest Cedars of the world'.[12]

This new Eden had people in it. When Raleigh's men established contact with the local Algonquin tribe, they found them 'very handsome... and in their behaviour as mannerly and civil as any of Europe'.[13] The Algonquin had proved eager to make friends and (for any merchants reading) were honest traders. They were 'most gentle, loving and faithful, void of all guile, and treason, and such as lived after the manner of the golden age'.[14] Barlowe imputed their fine characters to the fecund landscape, whose soil was 'the most plentiful, sweet, fruitful, and wholesome of all the world, which brought forth all things in abundance, as in the first creation, without toil or labour'.[15]

Fortunately, from the point of view of Raleigh's patent, the Algonquin were heathens, whose lands hadn't yet been claimed by any other Christian princes. None that Barlowe met had seen a white man or a European sailing ship before, and 'they wondered marvellously at the whiteness of our skins, ever coveting to touch our breasts'. If they had any faults beyond idolatry, it was an addiction to cruel and bloody wars that had 'marvellously wasted' the population so that the country had been 'left desolate' in some places, creating plenty of room for Raleigh to establish a settlement.[16]

Amadis and Barlowe brought back two Algonquin men, Wanchese and Manteo, to be taught English and to serve as ambassadors and interpreters on future expeditions. Raleigh used them as walking advertisements for his new venture and enlisted the scholar Thomas Harriot to transcribe their language and to teach them English. Raleigh was delighted with the results of his reconnaissance expedition. His scouts had found a site for a fort in America, had established peaceful relations with its inhabitants and had whipped up interest in the venture among both investors and influencers. His next aims were to get his patent ratified by Parliament, and to send a follow-up fleet of ships to build a privateering stronghold in his new possessions. He chose Thomas Cavendish to help him with both aims.

2

The Parliamentarian

London, England

Aᴛ ᴇʟᴇᴠᴇɴ ɪɴ ᴛʜᴇ ᴍᴏʀɴɪɴɢ of 23 November 1584, Queen Elizabeth and her court assembled at St James's Palace and processed to Westminster Abbey where they heard mass. The queen was carried on a gilded dais between two white horses, decorated with carvings of crowns, a lion and a dragon, all 'made with wonderful cunning'. After mass, she walked to the Parliament chamber in the Palace of Westminster and took her place on her throne. Her ladies-in-waiting knelt on the floor around her feet. The Lords temporal and spiritual – the barons and the bishops – sat back-to-back on four large woolsacks arranged in parallel rows perpendicular to the throne. Beyond the Lords, a rail ran across the width of the chamber, and MPs from the House of Commons crowded behind it to listen to Sir Thomas Bromley, the Lord Chancellor, as he set out the proposed business of the Parliament of 1584. Elizabeth, he told them, had summoned Parliament to raise 'subsidies' i.e. taxes, and to pass laws for her safety. These were nervous times. The subsidies were to pay for the army and navy in the anticipated war with Spain; and a law for her protection had been drawn up in response to several plots to assassinate her, which were expected to grow in number after Catholics everywhere had been instructed by Pope Pius V (who had declared Elizabeth to be thrice illegitimate – the bastard daughter of a Protestant whore) to pray for her death.

Thomas Cavendish was one of the new intake of MPs standing behind the bar in the House of Lords. He had been elected to represent Shaftesbury in Dorset. There had been no vote as such. Shaftesbury was a 'proprietary borough', owned by the Earl of Pembroke, who chose its MPs and wrote Cavendish's name on a blank indenture.* Pembroke was a friend and confidante of

* The procedure was common at the time. A third of the MPs assembled in front of the queen had been selected in a similar fashion, and very few of the others had been chosen by more than a dozen men.

Raleigh, who wanted to build a faction in the Commons to nod through the bill to ratify his patent for America, and Cavendish was one of his party. Cavendish was moreover a suitable candidate for Pembroke's borough, with distant family ties to the earl via the tangled web that bound the gentry together. His reputation, meanwhile, had improved since he'd taken Raleigh as his mentor – his name no longer featured in lawsuits for gambling debts, or in association with the young bloods he'd befriended when he'd become a courtier. Now (it has been suggested) he was taking lessons in mathematics and navigation at Durham House, Raleigh's London residence, rather than rolling dice.[1]

After Sir Thomas Bromley's speech, Cavendish and his fellow MPs trooped out of the House of Lords to the House of Commons. While Cavendish was accustomed to pageantry from his time at court, other members of the new intake were unsettled by the splendour and solemnity of the occasion and they disgusted veteran parliamentarians by 'making strange noises' and appearing 'out of all order'.[2] Meanwhile their pages and servants ran around and fought each other on the wide stone staircases and the Sergeants at Arms were called in to restrain them.

The House of Commons occupied the former Chapel of St Stephen in Westminster Palace. It had been deconsecrated after the Reformation, and its once sumptuous interior was now plain. Its decorated walls had been whitewashed, its stained glass had been replaced with clear panes and its statues levered out of their niches and smashed, though a pair of decapitated saints remained high up on the pillars behind the former altar. The chapel was small – only twenty metres long by eleven wide – and four hundred and sixty MPs crammed into it within touching distance of each other, resembling, from above, bees in a hive as the brims of their hats bobbed and jostled together in apparently random motion.

Once the MPs had settled, they elected a speaker. They chose John Puckering, MP for Bedford, a successful lawyer, described variously as 'very able' and a 'greedy grasper'.[3] The election was a sham. He had been selected in advance by the queen's Privy

Council and, once his name had been suggested, placemen told their neighbours to 'cry Puckering!' and did so themselves. To his credit, Puckering was honest about his priorities. After a ceremonial trip to the House of Lords, where Elizabeth confirmed him in his role, he explained to his fellow MPs that she 'well understood I was your mouth' but had told him that 'I was your mouth by her allowance'.

Puckering took his seat in the Speaker's chair on the altar step of St Stephen's and the MPs crammed in the ex-choristers' stalls in front of him. Proposed legislation was read out to them as bills, which they debated, amended, voted on and engrossed or rejected, before sending the successful bills to the House of Lords for approval. Some were of national importance, others trivial, involving small parcels of land or private debts. The complicated bills were allotted to committees, who took them off to debate and refine before they were presented to the house.

Cavendish was considered conscientious enough to be placed on a committee and, in between his committee duties, the whirl of formal activity and the shouting and barging of his fellow MPs, Cavendish met dozens of influential people. His mentor's faction included many notorious privateers such as Sir Francis Drake, Sir Richard Grenville and Sir George Carey, all eager for war with Spain and happy to embrace a new convert.

Raleigh's bill had its first reading in the Commons on 14 December 1584. It précised the terms of his patent and asked Parliament to confirm his rights to exploit his new lands on the far side of the Atlantic, which it named 'Windaganroza'. Although something of a mouthful, Windaganroza had an exotic and indeed authentic ring to it – just the sort of name, to the Elizabethan mind, that heathen Americans might give to their homeland. Raleigh later confessed that it was a placeholder, chosen from an encounter between his reconnaissance mission and the Algonquin: 'when some of my people asked the name of that Country, one of the savages answered *Wingandacon* which is to say,… you wear good clothes, or gay clothes'.[4]

The bill was presented to the Commons adorned with appealing arguments in its favour. A foothold in America, in a strategic location for preying on enemy ships, might also serve to propagate 'the knowledge of good and true religion' and so become a Protestant beacon of light in a continent groaning under the Catholic yoke.[5] At the same time, it could serve as a dumping ground for England's idle poor, where they could be 'trained in virtuous and Commodious Labour'. A committee was formed to consider Raleigh's bill, whose members were all privateers, military veterans or foreign policy hawks. When they returned the bill to the Commons it sailed through, attracting fewer comments than a 'A Bill for the maintenance of the Pier and Cobb of Lyme Regis in Dorsetshire'.

Cavendish knew that the evangelical and philanthropic sentiments that adorned the Windaganroza bill were window dressing. At the same time as it was being read aloud in Westminster, Raleigh was fitting out a second expedition to America in Plymouth and Cavendish had agreed to contribute a ship to the fleet. Soon he'd be sailing to and stepping foot on the semi-mythical land pictured to Parliament, where he didn't anticipate spending any time either proselytising or encouraging paupers to engage in labour. He was party to Raleigh's plans, had seen the preparations in train and knew from the resources being assembled that England's first colony in the New World would be a military venture, with more soldiers than settlers, no families, no idle poor and no priests. However, MPs were required to attend the House of Commons while Parliament was in session, and Cavendish drummed his fingers as it meandered through bills against moor-burning, against using sumac as a dye for clothes, and for the relief of the Hospital of Eastbridge in Canterbury. There were some fireworks amid the tedium: the Commons exploded over a bill 'against Jesuits, Seminary Priests, and such like disobedient Subjects'. Doctor John Parry, MP for Queenborough, spoke against it 'in very violent words', claiming it was 'full of blood, danger, despair and terror'.[6] War with Spain might well be on the way, but the bill would turn loyal Catholic subjects into traitors and carry England back in time to the religious executions of Elizabeth's siblings and predecessors on the throne.

Parry's speech was monumentally indiscreet. Religious freedom had been deemed too delicate a topic for the Parliament of 1584, and Parry had a questionable background, having spied for both England and the pope, acting at times as a double, and possibly treble agent. He was imprisoned in the Tower of London and, despite two public apologies to the Commons, the second of which they accepted, was condemned to death, and hung, drawn and quartered on 2 March 1585 in Westminster Palace Yard.[7] According to an eyewitness, 'when his bowels were taken out, he gave a great groan'.[8] Chunks of Parry's body were impaled on iron spikes above London Bridge, where carrion crows picked them to the bones.

The Parliament of 1584 was prorogued, or paused, on 29 March and Cavendish hurried away to his ship, the *Elizabeth*, a barque of 50 tonnes,[9] which was his stake in Raleigh's venture. He had financed her by selling five of his Suffolk manors – Stratton, Wenham Combust, Swaffing, Belton and Gapton – with the option of redeeming them 'by Lady Day 1586 at the "Faunte Stone" in the Temple Church at London'.[10] Cavendish's *Elizabeth* joined the rest of Raleigh's fleet in Plymouth, which comprised six other vessels – the *Tiger*, the *Red Lion*, the *Roebuck*, the *Dainty* and two pinnaces. The *Tiger*, the *Red Lion* and the *Roebuck* were privateers, and would be free to pursue their usual trade once they had landed their quotas of soldiers and colonists. The *Dainty* was a 'fly-boat' carrying provisions and passengers, and the pinnaces were miniature warships, with small cannon and shallow drafts, which could be rowed as well as sailed.

Queen Elizabeth had assisted her favourite's preparations while Parliament was still in session, ordering the Master of the Tower of London to give 'our trusty and well-beloved servant Sir

Walter Raleigh' (she had recently knighted him) four lasts of her finest corned gunpowder, enough to sink dozens of galleons.[11] In gratitude, Sir Walter renamed Windaganroza *Virginia*, and had a map drawn depicting his virgin queen ruling over a large chunk of North America, much of which was blank beyond its coast. Touched, perhaps, Elizabeth refused to let him go on his own expedition, which left the position of High Marshal vacant. Thomas Cavendish was chosen as Raleigh's stand-in for this key post. He would be the chief legal authority in Virginia, with the powers of life and death over its settlers.

Cavendish had some legal training from his time at Gray's Inn, and, as a gentleman, whose coat of arms gave him the right to bear arms, he had been taught how to use weapons from an early age. However, his new responsibilities were beyond his experience, and he sought advice from Sir John Smythe, a veteran of the Dutch wars from his home county of Suffolk. Smythe sent him several pages of handwritten notes, which told Cavendish how *he* would fortify, garrison and govern Virginia, if given a thousand soldiers. He assumed his troops would face, in the main, 'naked' (i.e. unarmoured) men equipped with stone-age weapons, and perhaps some Spanish infantry and cavalry. To counter these threats, Cavendish should ensure that half of his soldiers carried arquebuses, a musket with an effective range of a hundred paces, and to equip the remainder with swords, pikes, longbows and varying levels of body armour. As soon as Cavendish reached Virginia, his company was to build a pentagon – a pentagonal fort with gun emplacements on its corners.

Smythe continued with advice on the artificers to be included in the venture – an engineer, a traverse master, a physician, an alchemist and 'masons, Carpenters, makers of mud walls', before turning to the colony-to-be's officials and its governance.[12] He laid down ten laws for Cavendish to institute, together with penalties for those who broke them, including amputation of hands, public beatings and execution, with the caveat that a man accused of a capital offence should be tried before being punished.

Cavendish had plenty of food for thought when he joined the *Elizabeth*. The minor courtier addicted to gambling had become, to all appearances, a pioneer of empire. He was to be the first High Marshal of the first English settlement in America. Cavendish hadn't however given up on his wagers; he'd simply changed the game and the stakes. This time he was betting himself as well as his inheritance. On 9 April 1585, he captained his ship out of Plymouth, keeping company with the rest of Raleigh's fleet. Christopher Brooking, Plymouth's mayor, recorded its departure for 'Wingane Dehoy' (Windaganroza), noting it carried 'six hundred men or thereabouts'.[13]

3

The New World

Puerto Rico, Hispaniola

ON 19 MAY 1585, nearly six weeks after leaving Plymouth, Cavendish arrived at the Bay of Mosquetal, on the Caribbean island of Hispaniola.[1] Raleigh's fleet had been scattered by a storm off Portugal and Cavendish had been sailing alone for the past month. Mosquetal was the agreed rendezvous and, as he approached, a warship came storming out towards him, with colours hoisted and guns run out. It was the *Tiger*, the expedition's flagship, which had mistaken his *Elizabeth* at a distance for a hostile vessel, and had, in the words of her master, 'thought it good to weigh anchor and to go roome with' her.[2] As the *Tiger* closed in, her men recognised both the ship and her captain and 'for joy of his coming' the *Tiger* fired her cannon, saluting Cavendish 'according to the manner of the sea'. He deserved the compliment. He'd navigated the *Elizabeth* over three and a half thousand miles of ocean, enduring the 'force and violence of bad weather' as if he'd been a veteran.

It had been no easy transition from his previous life. Conditions aboard the *Elizabeth* were rough, and her accommodation was cramped. She was less than seventy feet long, broad at the beam and deep at the keel, and carried around sixty men – mariners, soldiers for the colony and a handful of gentlemen-adventurers. She bounced around on her tubby hull in heavy weather and leaked at the seams, and a scum of vomit, urine, rancid fat and dead rats sloshed through her bilges. Her constant motion, moreover, was alien to a landsman. Cavendish discovered that even in the flattest calm she'd rock gently from side to side or roll from end to end while her sails slatted against her booms and spars. First timers at sea, who were accustomed to standing still, had to grapple their way around the *Elizabeth* until they found their sea-legs. And she was never silent. The sea whispered and drummed on her hull and her oak beams creaked at every joint, while her ribs rasped and her masts juddered and groaned.

Seasickness was endemic. The poet John Donne, who suffered it himself on a privateering voyage, pictured the malady as an apocalyptic experience, which gave its victims a death wish while they endured it, and returned them to the world like the dead arising for the last judgement, fearing the worst:

> Some coffined in their cabins lie, equally
> Grieved that they are not dead, and yet must die.
> And as sin-burdened souls from graves will creep,
> At the Last Day, some forth their cabins peep:
> And tremblingly ask what news…[3]

Cavendish's surroundings were as disconcerting as the constant noise and perpetual motion aboard the *Elizabeth*. Once she'd sailed out of sight of land, with only the sea in every direction, she seemed lost in a wilderness of waves. Without a single feature to determine either distance or place, some novices on ocean voyages convinced themselves they'd never see dry land again and retreated to their cabins and prayed.

There had been more serious hazards than disorientation and seasickness. After the *Elizabeth* had passed into the Tropic of Cancer, the food in her casks had rotted, and the beer spoiled. Bowel disorders became endemic. Accidents moreover were common on such voyages. Mariners slipped from the rigging; soldiers fell down open hatches and, from time to time, a voyager would go insane and throw themselves overboard. While some found this claustrophobic, spartan and dangerous way of living hell, others thrived. In the month and a half it had taken to reach Mosquetal from Plymouth, Thomas Cavendish had travelled from a frozen spring in the depths of the Little Ice Age to the hot and humid tropics. He'd left the spectacle of courtly life, the comfort of his estates in Suffolk and the excitement of Parliament for a ship's cabin barely larger than a cottage parlour. The changes agreed with him. His body filled out, and his character strengthened.

❧

Cavendish needed to be tough to live up to the standards of Sir Richard Grenville, Admiral of the *Tiger* and General of the Virginia expedition. He'd first met Grenville in the House of Commons where Sir Richard had been one of Raleigh's Windaganroza faction, and Cavendish had seen the mannered version of the man. Grenville was a different creature in the Caribbean. He'd led a life of violence beyond Parliament, committing his first murder at the age of twenty when he stabbed a stranger to death in London. He'd since fought against the Turks as a mercenary, had soldiered for his queen in Ireland and had been a successful privateer. Grenville was said to be 'of so hard a complexion' that he would 'carouse three or four glasses of wine, and in a bravery take the glasses between his teeth and crush them into pieces and swallow them down so that oftentimes the blood ran out of his mouth'.[4]

Grenville had come out of retirement to lead the expedition to Virginia. He'd settled down in Devon in 1578 and had decorated his house, Buckland Abbey, with motifs that signified his withdrawal from chivalrous violence. A new frieze on the walls of its hall depicted:

> a knight who has retired from the world... turned his war-horse loose, hung up his shield upon the Tree of Life and, with a skull and an hour glass beside him... sits quietly meditating upon death and eternity.[5]

Officially, Grenville had buckled on his sword once more for the 'love he bore unto' his newly knighted cousin, Sir Walter Raleigh and from the desire 'to attempt honourable actions worthy of honour' again.[6] But old habits die hard. The 'Great Pirate' as the Spanish had known him in his earlier days of raiding intended to go privateering once he'd founded his cousin's colony. He chose his crew accordingly, starting with his pilot Simon Fernandes, a Portuguese pirate who hated the Spanish and had more sea miles under his belt than any other man in the eastern Atlantic.

The *Tiger* had reached the rendezvous in Mosquetal ten days before Cavendish, and her company had spent the intervening time building a new pinnace and fortifying the bay. The Spanish had spotted them at work and had sent a company of lancers to keep watch. Once Cavendish arrived, Grenville decided he had the strength to confront his watchers. He first attempted to parley with them and, when this failed, he burned his new fort and led the *Tiger* and the *Elizabeth* out to sea in search of prizes. He needed horses and livestock for Raleigh's colony and reasoned that he could force the Spanish to sell them to him if he had some of their ships to bargain with.

Cavendish got his first taste of privateering three nights later when they picked up two frigates. The closest was 'forsaken by the Spaniards upon the sight of us'[7] before they could fire a single cannon, and the crew of the other likewise took one look at the English ships and gave up without a fight. The second frigate was loaded with a 'good and rich freight' of cloth from Spain, and carried several gentlemen, who were rowed ashore and ransomed 'for good round sums'. Grenville put prize crews onto both frigates, sending one to collect salt from a nearby island, and ordering the other to keep company with the *Tiger* and the *Elizabeth*. His swift actions gave Cavendish a masterclass in privateering. Unarmed, or poorly armed, vessels wouldn't fight back – a show of force was enough to take them – and captives were better than casualties as they could be ransomed. Prizes meanwhile could be managed with skeleton crews until their cargos were disposed of, either by selling them locally, or sending them home. In this case, Spanish cloth was worth more in the Caribbean than on the other side of the Atlantic, and Spanish colonists would be eager to buy it back.

On 29 June, Cavendish sailed to the island of Hispaniola and anchored alongside Grenville off the port of Isabella, where they hoped to find a market for the frigate's 'rich freight'.[8] Isabella, named and claimed by Christopher Columbus in 1494, had been a lively entrepot until side-lined by subsequent Spanish conquests. The rivers of gold and silver that poured from Mexico and Peru had been diverted elsewhere and, by 1585, Isabella was a backwater, whose colonists survived by growing crops and rearing cattle to provision passing ships.

Although Isabella's commerce had stagnated, its strategic location had kept it alive as a guard post, and in 1577 an impressive stone fortress, the *Fortaleza Felipe*, had been built on a promontory near its harbour, whose cannon had a commanding field of fire over its bay. The *Fortaleza*, intended to deter or sink any foreign ships that tried to slip into the Caribbean, looked imposing against its backdrop of hills carpeted with dense green jungle, but its garrison was insufficient to defend its gates and man its guns.

Cavendish and Grenville anchored out of range, with their captive frigate on prominent display, and waited. Two days later, a message was rowed out to them from Isabella's governor, Don Rengifode Angulo. Don Rengifode wrote that he had learned from the captives they'd ransomed, who had since been brought to him, that they'd been 'well entertained' while in captivity and that there were 'many brave and gallant Gentlemen' on Raleigh's ships, who Rengifode would be honoured to meet.[9]

Rengifode appeared on the beach below the *Fortaleza* on 5 June with a retinue of 'a lusty Friar and twenty other Spaniards',[10] and a train of servants and African slaves. Once his people had settled, he signalled to Grenville and Cavendish, inviting them to come ashore. This act, under Spanish law, constituted treason. Rengifode was prohibited from trading (or indeed indulging in any form of communication) with foreign vessels and his duty, both as governor of Isabella and captain of its port, was to attack these interlopers and pass any prisoners he captured to the Spanish Inquisition, which would make public spectacles of their deaths. However, both the *Tiger* and *Elizabeth* mounted heavy cannon and the *Tiger* bristled with pikemen and harquebusiers. Rengifode was outnumbered and outgunned. He was a long way from Madrid and decided that offering hospitality to these visitors was safer than obeying orders and confronting them. There might also be the opportunity to buy back the frigates they had seized. And so he waited with his retinue on the shoreline, the gentlemen in velvet britches, steel breastplates and feathered bonnets, the lusty friar in a brown cassock, the soldiers in padded armour and the slaves wearing homespun trousers with straw hats.

Don Rengifode had a moment of doubt when his visitors climbed into their boats to be rowed ashore. The gentlemen among them were dressed in their best steel armour. Did they intend to impress, or to attack? However, their postures were relaxed, and as their boats approached the beach they made 'encouraging cries', which persuaded him he'd been right to invite them to land. His retinue advanced to greet the English, the gentry of either side exchanged courtesies, 'their inferior sort did also salute' their counterparts among the 'Soldiers and Sea men', and the tension dissipated.

Cavendish found this scene both novel and familiar. His first footsteps in the Americas, and his first face to face encounter with Spaniards, had been as charged with bluff and counter bluff as a hand of cards played for high stakes. He watched Grenville revert to courtier mode beneath the coconut palms and make small talk with Don Rengifode about 'the state of the Country, the multitude of the Towns and people, and the commodities of the Island' as if they had been dignitaries meeting at a European court, rather than officers whose countries were on the edge of war.

Once courtesies were complete, Grenville ordered his soldiers to cut down some of the trees behind the beach and build 'two banqueting houses covered in green boughs' on its sands, 'the one for the gentlemen, the other for the servants'. When these arbours were ready and tables had been laid, the Spanish and English of each caste sat down side by side. A banquet was rowed ashore and served to them on silver plate with the 'sound of trumpets and consort of music'.[11] Sunlight danced through the interlaced boughs, wine and beer flowed and the Spanish declared themselves 'more than delighted'[12] with the bucolic scene.

After feasting as a guest in the land he governed, Don Rengifode played host and arranged a sporting diversion for his visitors. In 'recompense of our courtesy', the *Tiger's* journal noted, he ordered that 'a great herd of white bulls and cattle be brought together from the mountains' and paraded near the shore. Three bulls were singled out of the herd 'to be hunted by horsemen' armed with spears. Don Rengifode provided mounts for every English 'Gentleman and Captain what would ride', including Thomas Cavendish. The 'pastime grew very pleasant for the space of three hours', the journal recorded, 'wherein all three of the beasts were killed'. Two of the bulls were finished off with lances and the third, which had waded into the sea to save itself, 'there was slain with a musket'.[13]

The following day, the Spanish and English re-assembled and Raleigh's men 'played the Merchants' with their new friends. They had an unusual shopping list. Rather than asking for tobacco, sugar or other commodities that were inexpensive in the Caribbean, but costly in Europe, they wanted livestock and horses, which were cheaper on the other side of the Atlantic. It was clear to Don Rengifode that they were buying supplies for a settlement in America. He sold them breeding pairs of horses, donkeys, cattle, goats, pigs and sheep, and the *Tiger* and *Elizabeth* departed for Virginia on 7 June 1585.

As soon as he judged it to be safe, Rengifode dispatched boats to other Spanish possessions in Cuba, Mexico and Florida, warning their officials that English corsairs had entered the Caribbean. His alarming news prompted an orgy of scribbling among its recipients, who sent letters to their king, Philip II, in Spain demanding reinforcements and complaining of neglect. The Council of the Indies, for instance, lamented to its most 'sacred Catholic royal majesty' that heretics had been able to trespass in his dominions, because of a 'lack of adequate care and protection' on his part, and warned if 'the arrogance of these corsairs remains unchecked, we will always be troubled'.[14] Other correspondents, unprompted, declared that no one had broken the royal prohibition on commerce with foreigners, even when threatened with death. Don Hernando de Altamirano, for instance, who'd been one of the ransomed captives, claimed that he'd been subjected to a mock execution to try to force his compatriots into trade. The English had placed a noose around his neck, he wrote, and had told his friends that he would be strung up unless they agreed to sell them cows and horses. To a man, they had rejected the proposal. It was better that Don Hernando died.

Before Philip's correspondents signed off with customary offers to kiss his hands and feet, they speculated about where Raleigh's ships might be heading with their breeding pairs of livestock. While the English had been open about their intention of founding a settlement, they had not said where. The southern end of the Caribbean was thought to be their most likely destination. According to Altamirano, 'special people had come from England on this fleet for the purpose of colonising Trinidad and Dominica'. But they also had 'two tall Indians' from the American mainland, who spoke English, wore decent clothes and were treated as equals, which suggested a different objective. Wherever they may be heading, it was evident that they intended to stay. As well as trying and failing to trade for livestock, they'd dug up 'many banana plants and other fruit trees', which they'd had the great good luck to find 'along the shore', rather than buying them by the dozen from Philip's treasonous subjects.[15]

Philip II, King of Spain, New Spain, Portugal, Naples and Sicily, Duke of Milan and Lord of the Seventeen Provinces of the Netherlands read his letters from the Caribbean in his austere suite of rooms at the heart of his new palace, *El Escorial*. Philip had overseen the construction from the ground up of this giant granite edifice, situated on a barren hillside thirty miles outside Madrid. Before the first stone had been laid, he'd walked around the hillside, sniffing the air and tasting the water in its streams before deciding this would be the place. He'd planned *El Escorial* to be a mausoleum as well as the nerve centre of his empire, and the bodies of his parents, Emperor Charles V and Queen Isabella, were disinterred from their respective resting places and reburied side by side in the Basilica San Lorenzo el Real – the great chapel at the heart of the palace – with half of their coffins under the altar and half 'under the priest's feet'.

Philip worked at a long wooden table piled high with correspondence from around the world – from Mexico, the Philippines, Cuba, Italy, the Netherlands, Peru and Portugal. He hated to delegate and spent much of his time dealing with trivia as well as matters of state, which exasperated his courtiers. According to Don Juan de Silva, who had served him both as soldier and councillor, 'His Majesty's brain, although it must be the largest in the world, like that of any other human being, is not capable of organising the multitude of his affairs without making some division between those that he should deal with and those that he cannot avoid delegating to others.'[16]

At fifty-eight, Philip was 'the most potent monarch in Christendom', with 'a command so wide that out of his dominions the sun can neither rise nor set'.[17] His motto, taken from a medal struck to commemorate his subjugation of Portugal in 1580, which had given him Brazil and Portugal's colonies in Africa and Asia, was *Non Sufficit Orbis* – The World is Not Enough.

In person, Philip was 'of less than average height… with broad shoulders and chest, and a large pale face'.[18] The pallor is visible in a full-length portrait from 1587, which shows him dressed in his favourite black. Philip's legs are long and thin, his torso compact and his full, sensual lips contradict the otherwise austere impression that the portrait conveys. His pale blue eyes have a slight squint and, if they shine with a sense of providence, they also radiate menace.

Philip was an ardent Catholic who rejoiced in the death of heretics. He attended the *auto-da-fés* of the Inquisition and waved his sword to signify approval as unbelievers burned to death. When he heard news of the St Bartholomew's Day Massacre in Paris in 1572, during which three thousand French Protestants were murdered and their bodies dumped in the River Seine, which ran red with blood, Philip confessed that he 'experienced one of the greatest pleasures that I have had in all my life'. The French ambassador, at a later audience, witnessed the afterglow. The massacre came up in conversation and Philip 'began to laugh, showing signs of extreme pleasure and satisfaction'.[19]

The English vexed him. Philip had endured an unpleasant marriage of convenience to Queen Mary I, Elizabeth's elder sister, in the 1550s, which had been tainted by a phantom pregnancy, a fatal illness, insolent courtiers and unenthusiastic crowds, who had made it plain that they did not wish to kiss his feet. And now, under his Protestant ex-sister-in-law, the country had become a danger to his subject nations in both Europe and America, spreading the stain of heresy and sinking his galleons. Sooner or later, he would have to strike out against Elizabeth, and England.

As the king read his correspondence from the Indies, he scrawled comments in its margins in frenetic, looping handwriting. In response to the letters from Isabella and elsewhere in the Caribbean crying out for protection, he ordered that troops and ships be sent from Spain to hunt down the trespassers in his dominions and exterminate them.

4

Virginia

East Coast of America

THOMAS CAVENDISH GOT HIS FIRST glimpse of continental America on 20 June 1585 as the *Elizabeth* and *Tiger* 'fell with the main of Florida'.*[1] They sailed north, hugging the coast, and he watched the land creep past to his left, its vegetation changing from jungle to woodland, from the exotic to the familiar. It was tricky sailing. Few English ships had passed this way, and the navigation was complicated by shallow banks and changeable winds. Three days later, according to the *Tiger's* journal, they were 'in great danger' of being wrecked 'on a beach called the Cape of Fear' whose shoals were already the graveyard of several Spanish galleons and French privateers.[2] Danger, however, was followed by plenty: 'The 24th we came to anchor in a harbour where we caught in one tide so much fish as would have yielded us 20 pounds in London: This was our first landing in Florida.' They were now in known waters, closing in on Virginia-to-be. Two days later, 'we came to anchor at Wococon'.[3]

The Wococon inlet was the gateway through an outer chain of islands to their destination in Pamlico Sound. However, it had a sand bar across its mouth and could only be entered at high tide. The pinnace went first, and bumped its keel on the bar, followed by Cavendish and the *Elizabeth*, which likewise 'struck aground' before clearing the obstacle and reaching the sheltered bay beyond. The *Tiger*, however, hung back. She drew more water and remained at anchor on the seaward side of the inlet, waiting for a better tide. On 29 June, Grenville tried to bring her in, but the waves picked up and threw her down on the bar. Atlantic rollers pinned her in place and pounded her hull, heeling her over at a vertiginous angle, and the cattle, pigs

* Florida was the Spanish name for the American coast and hinterland between Miami and North Carolina.

and other livestock on her decks were washed overboard and drowned. Her sails flogged, her spars shook, the waves roared in and her mariners feared that her keel might snap and split the ship. The *Tiger* took 'eighty-nine strokes' from the breakers before a rising tide lifted her off the bar and carried her to shore, where she was secured. It seemed miraculous that she still floated and an eyewitness attributed her salvation to the hand of God alone. She was, however, 'so bruised' from the grounding and the sea had poured 'so abundantly' into her hold that 'the most part' of the 'corn, salt, meal, rice and other provisions' she'd carried for the planned colony were spoiled.[4] The grounding made a deep impression on Cavendish. Riding at anchor in Pamlico Sound, sheltered from the noise and the force of the storm, the dramatic scene taking place a short distance away with the fate of the expedition in the balance had delivered a vivid lesson on the dangers of entering an unknown harbour in a deep-draught vessel. The most powerful warship in England might be impotent on uncharted coasts.

Cavendish spent his first week in Virginia at rest aboard the *Elizabeth* while the *Tiger* was repaired, and boats were sent out north and south to search for the rest of Raleigh's fleet. The *Red Lion*, *Roebuck* and *Dorothy* hadn't been sighted since the storm off Portugal and had missed the rendezvous in Hispaniola. Had they been wrecked, or were they simply lost? The searchers found the answers to these questions ship by ship. The *Red Lion*, commanded by Captain Raymond, an out-and-out privateer, was very much afloat. She'd deviated from plan as soon as she reached the Caribbean and sailed for Jamaica, where she'd had a savage, if inconclusive, fight with a French privateer, run low on rations, and had abandoned twenty soldiers destined for Virginia on 'the uninhabited North shore of the Island' before proceeding to the rendezvous. Upon arrival in Virginia, Raymond dumped thirty-two men (his share of the colonists at Croatan) north of Wococon and sailed away to hunt prizes among the defenceless fishing ships off Newfoundland. His colonists were rounded up by the search boats, but the soldiers he'd put ashore in Jamaica either starved to death or were eaten by the indigenous cannibals.*

The *Roebuck* appeared at about the same time as the *Red Lion's* colonists were collected. Although she was nominally a fly-boat, her captain, John Clarke, was as dedicated a privateer as Captain Raymond. Clarke's company included the notorious pirate John Challis, who'd been signed up for his sea-fighting skills and smuggling connections rather than his desire to plant a little piece of England in America. The *Roebuck* had also been prowling for prizes in the Caribbean, which had likewise delayed her arrival at the rendezvous. She was followed by the *Dorothy*, also late from choice rather than constraint, and it was rumoured that she'd participated in the *Red Lion's* fight with the French privateer off Jamaica.

Once all the ships in Raleigh's fleet had been accounted for, Grenville decided to investigate Pamlico Sound. Although Raleigh's exploratory expedition of 1584 had recommended Roanoke Island to the north as the ideal location for the new colony, Grenville wanted to check if there might be anywhere better nearby. His planning was guided by Manteo and Wanchese, the returning Indians, who'd impressed the Spanish in Puerto Rico with their clothing and were returning to their homelands. Manteo was from Cape Hatteras to the south, a member of the ruling family of his clan who'd joined Raleigh's scouting expedition as a volunteer when it sailed back to England in 1584. He had a friendly and open nature and had learned English during his stay in London. Wanchese, in contrast, was a warrior from Roanoke sent by his chief as a spy and kept his own counsel. Both men travelled ahead of Grenville to alert their respective clans of his arrival.

* With the exception of one named only 'Edward', who lived to be interrogated by Abbot Francisco Marques de Villalobos of the Spanish Inquisition. See Quinn (2016) p.165.

On 11 July, a flotilla of boats set off to explore the sound. Cavendish travelled in a pinnace together with Ralph Lane, the governor of the colony-to-be, and Thomas Harriot, the expedition's scientific adviser. Grenville took his seat amid a huddle of West Country gentry in a Thames wherry,* which had been ferried over on the *Tiger*. Two ships' boats completed the flotilla, which carried sixty men including gentlemen, soldiers, settlers, mariners and musicians. Cavendish and the other gentlemen wore their finery and their swords, as if they were being conveyed down the Thames to Greenwich to pay homage to their queen, the musicians sounded their trumpets and the soldiers were dressed for battle, carrying pikes and arquebuses. The boats flew banners, and whenever they paused their arrival was announced with music and their departure with cannon-fire.

The flotilla made slow going as it picked its way through the islets and sandbanks that littered Pamlico Sound. The mainland was delineated by a green wall of trees draped, as Amadis and Barlowe had promised, with grape vines. Patches of the virgin forest along the shore had been felled, offering glimpses of both the unexplored continent beyond and its inhabitants, who could be seen in the distance tending their crops against a backdrop of yet more trees, and an occasional column of smoke from deep inside the forest. The waters of the sound meanwhile were carpeted with edible wildfowl and crammed with fish. Traps had been staked across subsidiary channels to harvest this bounty, adding to the hazards of navigation.

Cavendish found his surroundings similar – on a larger scale – to the Orwell estuary in Suffolk where he'd grown up and where his family owned forests and fish weirs. There were the same shallow waters, big skies and ancient trees. It was as if the Orwell had been a child's version of Virginia, to give him a taste for the future. However, while the landscape was familiar, the people – disparate clans of the Algonquin Nation – looked very different. Rather

* A long, sleek type of rowing boat used in London as a water taxi.

than his Suffolk tenants wearing woollen clothing and dwelling in cob and thatch cottages clustered round a church with a spire, he saw Algonquin with painted bodies dressed in animal skins living in hamlets enclosed by stockades.

The sight of the 'Indians' going about their business on the fringes of a forest that stretched to the western horizon provoked mixed feelings in Grenville's flotilla. For its veteran mariners, Virginia was just another foreign coast to tell tales about and compare to 'savage' lands they had visited elsewhere – if they got home. It was not particularly alien in appearance and was thought to be free of wild elephants, endemic fatal diseases and bowmen shooting poison arrows. However, for the gentlemen-adventurers, soldiers and artisans who were there to found a colony, it was the place where they were to commence a mighty enterprise and which would be their home for at least a year. This wasn't an appealing prospect. Any hopes of even a modest self-sufficiency had been washed into the sea when the *Tiger* ran aground, and they knew that they would be colonising on short rations. There were also the Algonquin who outnumbered them, and on whose goodwill they would depend.

The flotilla's first stop was the village of Pomeioc. John White, official artist to the expedition, who travelled alongside Cavendish, painted a watercolour of the settlement. It shows a collection of wooden-framed houses covered with woven mats, some cosy, others tall and airy, encircled by a palisade of tree trunks whose tips have been sharpened into stakes. A bonfire puffs out smoke at the centre of the village, with men and women seated around it on mats. It looks a convivial place: some adults dance, others put their hands round each other's waists and wave to the artist, and warriors show off their skis and sledges. Children run among them, playing games. A dog, which the Algonquin kept both as pets and for the pot, stands by its master with its tail aloft.

While White studied the scene with an artist's eyes, the mariners and settlers in the boats looked to see if the women were beautiful, and the privateers among the company scrutinised both sexes for any signs of gold or silver ornaments. Thomas Cavendish also watched the Algonquin closely. As the expedition's High Marshal, he was duty-bound to control relations between them and his countrymen. Half of the ten laws in the advice on matters military that he'd been given in England were intended to discourage contact with 'Indians'. Any man who entered one of their houses should be sentenced to 'six months imprisonment'; the punishment for 'striking or misusing an Indian' was to be twenty 'blows with a cudgel in the presence of the Indian strucken', thus adding shame to pain; the price of theft was the loss of a hand; and death the penalty for violating a woman.[5] These draconian rules made sense from a tactical point of view. Although 'naked men' by European standards, the Algonquin were expert bowmen, masters of the forest, practised in fighting from their constant internecine quarrels and outnumbered the English, as far as they could judge, by at least ten to one.

The visit to Pomeioc was short and formal. Manteo and Wanchese acted as interpreters and intermediaries, and Raleigh's officers handed out presents before they departed. These included toys for the Algonquin children, and another of White's sketches of the journey shows the daughter of a chieftain, who clutches an Elizabethan doll with a look of rapture on her face.* The girl is naked bar a necklace and a kilt secured by a string around her waist, the doll wears a hat and is trussed up in a full-length dress with shoulder pads and wrist cuffs.

Cavendish's tour of Pamlico Sound continued with visits to other villages, including Aquascogoc, another palisaded settlement, and Secotan, where the flotilla moored, and he went ashore for a tour of the village, followed by a feast. Secotan was the largest hamlet he'd yet seen, and his fellow traveller John White recorded its features and curiosities in watercolour sketches. These included neat rows of tobacco, maize and sunflowers in its fields, and the interior of the village temple where the bodies of

* This faded snapshot from 1585 is now in the collection of the British Museum.

past chiefs, wrapped in shrouds, were laid out on its floor like sardines in a can. The Indians, White wrote in a caption to his picture, took great pains to preserve the corpses of their ancestors. After death, all the flesh was cut from their bones save the 'skin and hair of their heads'.[6] Their flensed skeletons were then sewn into buckskins, so that 'their form or proportions' were the same as they had been in life.

Such naked paganism was a shock to the godlier of the colonists in the flotilla, who didn't relish the prospect of living among heathens. Unlike the Spanish, who explored 'with the cross and with the sword', the English left their crosses at home. Raleigh hadn't equipped his expedition with a clergyman, and the colonists themselves would have to either manage or neglect the conversion of their neighbours themselves. Meanwhile, the flotilla's mariners had found that the Algonquin were, even by their own high standards, expert thieves. Masters of the night and silent movement, they swam or paddled out to the ships at anchor, looking for iron spikes and steel blades. On one raid, they took a silver cup belonging to Grenville. He and his company were hoping to find precious metals rather than to lose them, and he detached a punitive expedition under John Clarke of the *Roebuck* to raze their village and its crops. This was standard practice among privateers, but a questionable activity on an expedition that expected the Algonquin both to be its allies and to gift it land for a settlement. Cavendish chose not to intervene. Although the rules governing contact that he was expected to enforce were strict, they didn't prohibit reprisals, and the present action gave him the chance to gauge their tactical value. Might terror be a better ploy than diplomacy when dealing with new peoples?

After a week of exploration, Cavendish and the flotilla returned to their ships and sailed north for Roanoke, the site that had been recommended by Raleigh's scouting expedition. This small, narrow island, located just inside the Carolina Banks, was hidden from the sight of any punitive expeditions the Spanish might launch.[7] Even if it was found, Roanoke was protected by natural defences.

Encircled by water and marshes, its shores were beyond the range of cannon shot from any place that a hostile galleon could reach. The island moreover was blessed with a secure supply of drinking water and the 'many goodly woods' recorded by Barlowe, which could be felled for both timber and fuel. Most importantly, Roanoke was located in friendly territory. Granganimeo, the *Werowance*, or chieftain, of the local clan who'd established ties with Raleigh's reconnaissance expedition of 1584, lived on the island and the land for the settlers' fort was his present. He received Grenville's company as trading partners and friends, and Grenville reciprocated by hosting him aboard the *Tiger*. Barlowe had noted that Granganimeo had enjoyed wine when he'd first tasted it, and Grenville kept him topped up. However, the chief may have imbibed from policy as well as thirst. The English could be useful neighbours who might give his people swords as well as dolls one day, and it was well to humour them when they were in their cups.

Once Roanoke had been confirmed as the site of the new settlement, Raleigh's colonists started building. They laid a landing stage to ferry supplies from the ships, set up a forge, dug a sawpit, felled trees, excavated ditches and erected ramparts. The weather was temperate, the air wholesome and they worked quickly. Grenville was delighted with progress and, on 5 August, just over a fortnight after reaching Roanoke, he sent Captain John Arundel and the *Dorothy* back to England to tell Raleigh that Virginia had been 'possessed and inhabited' to her Majesty's use.[8] Arundel also brought the news that the colony would be more modest in its size than had been planned and would need to be resupplied as soon as possible.

However, while the settlers laboured, friction developed between Grenville and Ralf Lane, the colony's governor. Lane was a fifty-three-year-old military veteran who'd been called back from Ireland at both Queen Elizabeth's and Raleigh's requests to rule the new settlement. Although more rational than Grenville, he was equally irascible. Lane wanted as many men and provisions as possible for his garrison; Grenville was itching to cruise for prizes in the open sea and wanted to keep them for the *Tiger*. He had moreover, in one of his psychotic moments, threatened to string Lane up.

Thomas Cavendish had to mediate between them. He sided with Ralf Lane. It took a strong character to tell Sir Richard Grenville to his face that he could be wrong, and Cavendish stepped up to the mark. He succeeded in calming the antagonists and Lane was full of praise for him. The expedition's young High Marshal couldn't have behaved 'more faithfully, and more industriously in an Action' from 'ye first to ye last'.[9]

Grenville sailed for England on 25 August. He left the colony all his light boats, including the pinnace and his Thames wherry. In his eyes, he'd done his duty to Raleigh to establish a privateering base. Now its potential as such needed to be verified. Was Roanoke too far north of the path of the Spanish galleons from the Caribbean to attack them? How did the winds and the currents flow? The questions were answered favourably when he ran into a Spanish convoy near Bermuda. He singled out the *Santa Maria de San Vincente*, the 300-tonne flagship of the Santo Domingo Squadron of the annual treasure fleet, raked her with cannon and disabled her. He'd left his boats in Virginia, and led a boarding party over to the *Santa Maria* on a raft cobbled together from spare planks and seamen's chests, which 'fell asunder, and sunk at the ship's side, as soon as ever he and his men were out of it'.[10] Once he had secured the galleon, Grenville demanded that all the gold, silver and pearls listed on her register be handed to him immediately, and her officers and crew be strip-searched lest they'd hidden valuables in their clothes. The *Santa Maria's* main cargo of ginger, hides and sugar, meanwhile, was worth enough both to pay for the entire Virginia expedition and to turn a profit for its investors.

In Roanoke, however, the colonists were soon feeling the pinch. Lane had hinted at shortages in a letter to Sir Francis Walsingham that he'd sent back with Grenville, in which he'd made a virtue of necessity. He was happier, he'd claimed, to be surviving on fish and water while engaged in so glorious an endeavour than 'to live in the greatest plenty the court could give me'. The thought that the colony he governed might one day give America 'relief and freedom from the servitude and tyranny of Spain (being ye sword of ye antichrist of Rome and his Sect)' was further consolation for both a meagre diet and enforced sobriety.[11]

A fortnight later, Lane's tone had changed from cheerful self-denial to hot-headed fury. In his next letter to Walsingham, he told him that Grenville had 'demeaned himself, from the first day... at Plymouth, until the day of his departure hence'. Time and time again his 'intolerable pride and insatiable ambition' had endangered the venture.[12] Lane also brought up Grenville's threats of execution, telling Walsingham that he'd feared for his neck, and praising Cavendish, who had defied this monster of vanity and greed.

Cavendish probably carried this second letter with him when he left Virginia for England in September 1585. He spent his twenty-fifth birthday at sea and, over the course of the long return voyage, had time to consider the revelations and the lessons of Raleigh's expedition. It had taught him that it was no dream to sail from continent to continent and navigate a course over the thousands of miles of ocean. His world had expanded, and Cavendish imagined travelling even further. If the Americas were easy to reach, then why not Asia? He'd also encountered new worlds of behaviour. He'd feasted with Algonquin chieftains, captained English soldiers and sailors, and served under and stood up to a petulant and violent leader. He'd found the confidence to command, and his abilities had been both noted and approved by the expedition's other officers. He'd seen too that colonising was fraught with danger. A single accident so far from home could ruin its chances of survival. It appeared to be a lot of effort for little reward. From a gambler's point of view, the chances of succeeding in privateering far outweighed those of empire building. Meanwhile, Grenville's masterclass in taking merchant ships had impressed him. It seemed easier to capture a galleon than to found a colony. Cavendish was back in England by October 1585. Virginia had made a man of him: 'Thus fleshed and somewhat hardened unto the sea, immediately after coming home', he 'began to take a hand in a voyage into the south seas.'[13]

5

Throwing Land into the Sea

Grimston Hall, Suffolk, November 1585

WITHIN A FEW WEEKS OF his return to England, Thomas Cavendish retreated to his Suffolk estates and started work on the bold plan he'd conceived on his way back from Virginia. He had decided to bet his entire wealth – to 'throw his land into the sea'[1] – on an enterprise so risky that only two ships in history had succeeded in completing it: to sail west to Asia via the Americas and return to Europe round the southern tip of Africa, circumnavigating the globe in the process. He would attack Spanish shipping in both the Atlantic and Pacific, and trade for spices when he reached Asia. The key to this route was the Strait of Magellan at the toe of South America, which offered a passage between the two oceans. However, it had so evil a reputation 'that the very thoughts of attempting it were accounted dreadful'.[2]

The Strait was named after the Portuguese navigator Ferdinand Magellan, the first European to pass through it. Magellan had set out from Seville in 1519 with five ships carrying two hundred and seventy men. He had edged his way down the coast of South America, enjoying plenty in Brazil, and seeing off a mutiny in Patagonia before entering the Strait, which at that time existed only in rumour.[3] He had picked his way through it, then set off over the Pacific in search of China. Three years later, the *Victoria*, the last of his fleet still afloat, limped back to Seville under Juan Sebastian Elcano, who'd taken command after Magellan had been killed by the warriors of Lapu-Lapu in the Philippines. Elcano was one of only eighteen survivors. The *Victoria*, however, had twenty-three tonnes of spices in her hold, which compensated for the loss of the rest of the fleet, and indeed its first leader. She'd also proven that the route was feasible, if perilous. However, follow-up expeditions did not achieve so much. The next expedition to pass through the Strait, under García de Loaísa, a Knight of Malta, lost half of its ships in transit. Loaísa died in Mexico, and none of his fleet made it back to Europe. The Spanish had since explored the Strait from both its Pacific and Atlantic mouths, but the harrowing conditions they'd encountered each time had led them to reject it as a commercial route.

More than fifty years after Magellan had made his discovery, the English began to take an interest in his Strait. Sir Richard Grenville, among others, drew up plans for an expedition to traverse it, and to return to England via the 'Northwest Passage', a speculative route through the Arctic Circle. His premise was that the Americas were the remnants of the lost continent of Atlantis, which was said by the ancients to have been an island, and if there was a route around its bottom via the Strait of Magellan, then a similar passage must exist at its top.[4] Moreover, since the bands of longitude converged at the poles, England and China could be (according to his calculations) near neighbours. Grenville's plans were picked up by Francis Drake, a privateer from Devon who sailed from Plymouth in December 1577 with five ships and one hundred and sixty-four men, intending to reach the 'great South Sea'* through the Strait of Magellan. Once he'd passed into the Pacific, Drake aimed to attack unprotected Spanish settlements and shipping in Chile, Peru and Mexico, and to return to England via the 'Strait of Ainan', the name given to the eastern end of the as-yet undiscovered Northwest Passage.

Drake's journey across the Atlantic and down the coast of South America to his first obstacle was marked, like Magellan's, with dissent, lost ships and an execution. His fleet had been reduced to a single vessel – the *Golden Hind* – by the time he reached the Pacific and launched his planned raids. Thereafter, his luck changed. He found plunder wherever he touched land, and took a giant galleon named the *Cacafuego* (the 'Shit-fire'), which carried so much bullion that he ballasted the *Golden Hind* with

* Drake was the only named Englishman to have viewed the Pacific – from a tree, recovering from wounds suffered during a raid on the mule train carrying tonnes of silver ingots across the Panama isthmus.

silver ingots. However, when he sailed up the California coast towards Alaska to search for the fabled Strait of Ainan, he found a continuous and ever wilder landscape. Drake staked an English claim to the territories in California where he took on wood and water, christening them *Nova Albion*, then set off over the Pacific for Asia. When he reached the Spice Islands, he traded some of his captured silver for pepper and cloves, which were more valuable, pound for pound, and returned to England via the Cape of Good Hope, reaching Plymouth on 26 September 1580 with fifty-six men, and a hold full of silver, gold and spices.[5] Although he'd lost two-thirds of his company, his circumnavigation had made him very rich and opened English minds. Drake's prizes were valued at the stupendous sum of £120,000, the equivalent of half of Queen Elizabeth's annual income, from which she supported her courts, her navy and her armies.

The visible evidence of stacks of silver bars and sacks of spices being unloaded from the *Golden Hind* was supplemented by the stories that Drake and his crew had brought back with them. The wealth and weakness of Spain's kingdoms in the Americas were the stuff of dreams. On one occasion, they had found a man sleeping under a tree in Tarapaca in Chile with thirteen ingots of silver piled up beside him ('we took the silver and left the man'[6]); on another, Drake's men had intercepted a train of llamas carrying eight hundred pounds in weight of silver on their backs, guarded by 'a Spaniard and a boy'; and, while hunting for the *Cacafuego*, they'd picked up a barque with a cargo of spare rigging, and found that this miserable little vessel also carried eighty pounds in weight of solid gold, and a large gold crucifix 'with goodly great emeralds set in it'. Although these and other riches were on the other side of the world, Drake had proved that it was not out of reach. The odds might be long, but the prizes were enormous.

However, no English ship had followed Drake in the intervening years. The closest any had got to the Strait of Magellan was Brazil, where a 1582 expedition under Edward Fenton had run into a large Spanish fleet, sent from Seville to colonise and fortify the southern gateway to the Pacific. Fenton, described by a contemporary as a 'foolish flattering fretting creeper', was a master of indecision and, although he sank two galleons in his encounter with the Spanish, he'd turned tail.[7] He'd been spooked by the evidence that several thousand men were in transit to Patagonia, and that Spanish cannon soon would be guarding the Strait. Rather than pushing on south and wiping them out, Fenton decided instead to set himself up as King of Newfoundland and sailed north for Canada.

Fenton's news was still current while Thomas Cavendish planned his bold voyage. Although the probability that the Strait of Magellan had been fortified had increased the odds against an attempt to repeat Sir Francis Drake's triumphs,* Cavendish was undeterred. He had decided to make his bet and, within a month of his return from Virginia, was mortgaging his estates to finance his wager. He based himself at Grimston Hall, his ancestral home in Suffolk.

Situated on elevated ground overlooking the estuary of the River Orwell, encircled by a moat and surrounded by forests and pastures, Grimston was in sight of both Harwich and Ipswich, two great Medieval ports that specialised in trade with Europe and connected Suffolk to a wider world. Grimston had a history stretching back to the Domesday book of 1186, where it was recorded as *Grimestuna*, held by 'Udo from Count of Mortain; Roger Bigot and Ralph de Turlaville from him'.[8] The Hall had been in Cavendish hands since 1365 and Thomas had spent the first twelve years of his life there. In this ancient place, surrounded by the spirits of his ancestors, he formulated his plans to follow in the footsteps of Magellan and Drake. He seems to have inherited the vigour of his paternal grandfather, Sir Richard Cavendish, who'd been knighted on the battlefield while fighting against Scotland for Henry VIII, and threw himself into his preparations with a similar dynamism.

Cavendish turned to his near-neighbour Henry Seckford to help him turn his lands into cash to raise the stake for his wager.

* Queen Elizabeth had knighted him on the deck of the *Golden Hind* in 1581.

Thomas had known Seckford since his gambling days, when they'd celebrated their friendship by buying suits from an Italian tailor in Ipswich. Seckford was in his late forties at the time – a courtier-cum-merchant with a shady reputation. He'd been a member of the queen's household since 1558, serving as both Groom of the Privy Chamber and Master of Tents, Hales and Pavilions. He also managed – and was rumoured to have exploited – a contract to provision English troops in Ireland. In addition to his official duties, Seckford moonlighted as both a trader and a privateer. He financed merchant vessels to carry French and Spanish wines to Bristol and, when trade between England and Spain was embargoed in 1584, he loaded the same ships with cannon and sent them out hunting along the Atlantic coast of Europe, where the line between piracy and privateering was often blurred. Seckford crossed it when one of his ships attacked the *Maiden* of Denmark, 'without cause or provocation', a neutral vessel carrying a cargo of sugar and pig-iron, which, respectively, dissolved or sank in the encounter.[9] The master of the *Maiden* charged Seckford with piracy, and the cost of proceedings, together with losses in his trading, gave him both the time and the incentive to assist Thomas Cavendish in his quest for ready money.

Seckford arranged a number of transactions whereby Cavendish conveyed or mortgaged some Suffolk manors, including Grimston Hall, to him, his brother Gilbert Seckford and their associates for thousands of pounds. The transfers included not just halls and lands but also all the 'tenements, mills and knights'-fees, advowsons, gifts, and patronage of churches, rectories, vicarages, chantries, and chapels, tithes, oblations, pensions, portions, court-leets, view of frank-pledge, franchises, &c., thereunto belonging'.[10] These transfers, however, were not intended to be permanent, and gave Cavendish the option to reverse them – if he returned from his planned expedition – within three years. The clock started ticking in March 1586.

Once he had his money, Cavendish commissioned a new ship. Shipbuilding was a complex business: fighting ships were the most sophisticated machines of their age and required vast quantities of natural resources in their construction. Each one needed as many cannon as a fortress and more timber than a manorial hall. A good-sized privateering vessel consumed two hundred mature trees. Shipwrights toured the forests, looking for tall elms for keels, and thickset oaks with promising joints between their trunks and boughs whose natural shapes would match the stresses imposed on them when they became part of a new privateer.[11]

The process of turning lumber into a finished ship that would be balanced in the water under her masts was part art and part science. After the shipwrights had selected their trees, following clues in their shapes that only they could see, they drew plans for the new vessel, timber by timber. The skill of using 'paper instruments' to build a ship was pioneered by Mathew Baker, a master of the building and making of ships, whose designs were radical improvements on earlier generations of privateers. They sailed quicker, tacked faster and were better platforms for carrying broadside guns.

Baker was not only a skilled craftsman, but also a talented mathematician who'd studied the renaissance art of drawing in perspective, which was then rare in England. He was proud of his achievements in applying geometry to shipbuilding, noting that just as Pythagoras had cut the throat of an ox in sacrifice to Jove, god of gods, from pure joy after 'the finding out of the doubling of a square by the line diagonal… I say I have good cause to give our living and known God thanks for this invention so necessary for my… countrymen'.[12] Baker had a love as well as a care for the 'Art or Mystery' of shipbuilding, perceiving his creations in organic as well as geometric terms, and sketching his ideal fighting ship in the form of a galleon above the waterline and a pelagic fish beneath it.

Ships were built quickly once they had been planned on paper. A mid-sized privateering vessel could be completed in three months. The shipyards' hands laboured long hours – from dawn to dusk between All Hallows and Candlemas* and for the rest of the year from five in the morning until seven at night, six days per week. They worked from the inside out and were dwarfed by the vessels they shaped around themselves. First, they laid the keel as a spine, then added a giant timber ribcage, whose varying breadth marked the curves of their creation, bellying out amidships and tapering at both the bow and the stern. This skeleton was fitted with 'the strengthening structures of keelson, riders, knee timbers and internal wales',[13] some of which had first been seen in those shapes buried under the bark and branches of a living tree.

Privateering ships were built to fight as well as to sail and their frames were strengthened accordingly – both to counter the recoil of heavy cannon and to withstand the impact of enemy shot. Once these reinforcements had been made, a skin of planks was nailed onto the skeleton, the gaps between them caulked with tar and tow, and the decks fitted. After the hull had been completed it was graved and launched into the water where its masts were stepped and rigged and its gunports painted in bright colours. A suit of sails was cut, anchors, warps and chains were loaded, and the new vessel was ready to go to sea.

Thomas Cavendish used Drake's *Golden Hind* as the model for his new ship. His experiences in Virginia had taught him that he needed a nimble vessel rather than a floating fortress bristling with cannon but with too deep a draft to enter most harbours. His new ship also had to be a good sailor, able to stand up to both furious storms and pounding surf. The finished vessel, which Cavendish named the *Desire*, was about seventy-five feet long at the waterline, twenty-five wide at the waist and carried three masts. She was divided horizontally by three decks. The lowest covered her hold, where she kept her stores and ballast stones; the gun deck, where the crew slept, housed her cookhouse, forge, carpenter's stores and artillery; and the top deck was fitted with a tiered 'castle' on a

* Between 1 November and 2 February.

half deck running aft of the main mast, which held cabins for her officers and gentlemen. She was steered by a whipstaff, a vertical beam linked to the tiller below.

Once he had his flagship, Cavendish was a blur of activity. He bought two more vessels, the *Content* and the *Hugh Gallant*, both close in size to the little *Elizabeth* he'd captained to Virginia. The *Content* was to be a fly-boat, and the *Hugh Gallant* a landing craft. Next, Cavendish sourced his weapons. He equipped the *Desire* with seven demi-culverins on each side, which were the favourite heavy guns of privateers. Eight to ten feet long, each weighing two-and-a-half tonnes, demi-culverins fired a nine-pound iron ball with sufficient velocity to smash holes in the thickest of hulls. They were cast in iron or bronze, and the bronze variety were most sought after as they weighed less, had a longer lifespan and were less likely to blow up in the faces of their gunners. If, moreover, they did explode, they tended to bulge before they burst and so gave warning of their imminent demise, 'whereas an iron gun [would] fail catastrophically without warning'.[14] A third of the *Desire's* guns were bronze. Her sister ships were also fitted out with cannon, and between his three vessels Cavendish could call on demi-culverins mounted as broadside guns and bow and stern chasers, sakers (demi-culverins that fired a five-pound ball) and swivel-mounted 'murderers', which were used to spray grapeshot over the crews of enemy vessels at close quarters. All the large guns could fire bar shot (pairs of iron rods linked by a chain, which were used to sever rigging and masts), grapeshot (cannisters of musket balls and scrap iron, used to kill and maim), as well as cannonballs. So much artillery required hundred-weights of explosives and Cavendish had learned from Raleigh that quality mattered more than price. He purchased his gunpowder in London and bought enough to see his vessels through a small war.[15]

While he managed the complex business of fitting out his ships, Cavendish recruited the men he needed to sail and fight them.

This aspect of his venture required different skills to the logistics of procuring privateering ships and their artillery. Once again, he rose to the occasion and proved to be as good a judge of men as of cannon. His first targets were the survivors of Drake's circumnavigation, and he succeeded in recruiting a handful including Francis Pretty, a gentleman from Ely in Suffolk, to the north of Grimston. Pretty had kept a journal on Drake's expedition, which was filled with whimsical observations of natural curiosities such as coconut palms, as well as accounts of the skirmishes and sea-battles where he'd had to fight for his life. His character, like his writing, was governed by good humour, and Pretty and his fellow veterans would exert a calming influence over the expedition's neophytes.

Cavendish's next targets were pilots and navigators. He appointed Thomas Fuller, a privateer who knew the coasts of both Africa and Brazil, as master of the *Desire* and engaged the Oxford-educated Robert Hues, an expert in both mathematics and astronomy, to help him to manage his bearings and star sights. His skills would allow Cavendish to keep as precise a record as possible of his position and route. Hues had been to sea before, checking compass variations off Newfoundland, and wrote that he'd signed up for the new expedition 'purposely for taking the true Latitude of places'.[16] Always looking to shorten the odds, Cavendish gathered nautical charts as well as specialists, and 'carefully obtained every draft, map and chart that would be of use' on his venture.[17] Any information on any hazard or harbour on either coast of the Atlantic or the Pacific was better than none at all.

Once he had his experts and navigational charts, Cavendish recruited gentlemen-adventurers, who joined up for the chance of glory, a share of the profits and the prospect of paying off their debts. These men were easy to find, but hard to control. They did not expect to do anything beyond fighting, looting and perhaps a little gambling to while away the long days at sea in between. Moreover, they were loath to take orders and were capable of interpreting rational requests as grave insults. In contrast to both Magellan and Drake, Cavendish enlisted only a handful of gentlemen. Mercenary soldiers and their officers were also easy to come by. Demand for their services ebbed and flowed with the fortunes of the ongoing war in the Netherlands. When the Protestant rebels were on the back foot – as was the case when Cavendish was enlisting men – soldiers of fortune were happy to consider a long sea voyage. His recruits included three infantry captains with combat experience.

In contrast, mariners – the men who would sail his ships – were the hardest to recruit. Unlike landsmen, they knew how long the odds were against them ever returning home. Although Drake had kept his promise that 'the worst in this fleet shall become a gentleman', less than a third of his men had lived to enjoy it. They may have reached England with enough treasure to lift them into a different social stratum, but they also had to pass on news of dead husbands, fathers and sons to widows, orphans and mothers.[18] While some sailors *did* enlist in the expectation of adventures in strange new lands, fights with cannibals and Catholics and purses full of shining gold pieces, most went to sea for reasons of economic duress. The long frigid winters and brief cool summers that prevailed at the time had reduced harvests; fishing and trade were interrupted by pirates and privateers; and many of the crews who signed up for trans-oceanic expeditions chose to sail instead of starve.[19] Cavendish, however, had the advantage of a pool of experienced seafarers close to home and recruited a number of his company from Ipswich, a few miles upriver from Grimston Hall. These included Thomas Eldred, chandler and portman, who left a profitable business and his wife and children to embark on a journey to the ends of the earth. He also enlisted men from Weymouth, the *Hugh Gallant's* home port, who knew her and trusted her to bring them home.

Cavendish had his ships, armaments and company by May 1586, just seven months after returning from Virginia. He next applied his energy to another vital, if complicated, task: sourcing provisions for over a year at sea. Elizabethan seamen were prodigious eaters. The rations on navy ships, which were similar to those of privateers, gave them over 4,250 calories each per day that were washed down with a gallon of beer.[20] The bulk of the solids in their diet was composed of ship's bread and salted meat or fish. Their weekly menu had four 'flesh' days, on which they 'received either 2 lbs fresh meat, ½ lb salt beef, or ½ lb bacon. On the three fish days they had either a slab of dried cod or four herrings, plus 4 ounces of butter and ½ lb cheese.' For vegetables they had dried beans and peas. Provisions were bulky and heavy. One man's rations for a year required up to three tonnes of stowage.[21] Both food and drink were stored in wooden barrels of varying sizes, ranging from hogsheads for the beer to casks for the butter. The salt meat – chunks of either pork or beef, still on the bone – was carried pickled in brine. Its longevity was unpredictable – the contents of some barrels stayed edible for years, whereas others started rotting while a ship was still in port. The bread meanwhile (also called biscuit) consisted of large, hard discs, each the size of a dinner plate, which were baked ashore then packed into sacks by the hundredweight and ferried aboard. The last provisions to be loaded were the livestock: hens, pigs, goats and – if there was space – cows, and fresh fruit and vegetables.

Cavendish's supplies had cost him as much as his men, and he was running low on money. A thousand pounds more would get him over the line and he brought in a syndicate of City investors headed by the Admiralty Judge Dr Julius Caesar, who staked £50 each and enabled him to tie up the legalities of his proposed voyage. Laws governing privateering had been tightened in 1585, and Cavendish had to pay a bond of £2,000 to the High Court of Admiralty 'as a recognizance for "the good behaviour of his ship"'.[22] The bond permitted him '"by license of reprisal" to set forth to the seas one ship called the *Desire* of the Port of London… for the apprehending and taking whatsoever the ships goods and merchandises belonging the king of Spain'. The bond was to be forfeit if he committed any acts of piracy, or if he 'broke bulk' i.e. allowed goods to be taken from the *Desire*, or any prizes he might have captured, before 'a proper inventory was made before a vice-admiral or other officer'.[23]

Finally, after so many months of frenetic activity, planning, acquiring and judging, Cavendish was ready to launch his venture. He had his portrait painted by John Bettes the Younger in Moorgate while he readied his fleet on the Thames. In addition to capturing his youth, and the intensity of his gaze, the portrait featured an *imprese*, a picture within a picture, in its top right corner. *Imprese* were intended to convey the sitter's state of mind, or aspirations. Cavendish's showed the sun breaking through dark and billowing clouds, like the flash from the muzzle of a cannon. It had a motto in English above and a phrase in Latin beneath. First there were the lines:

> When storms of Strife shall banish light,
> Such Cloudy days are worse than night

followed by the image of the coal black sky and emerging sun and, underneath, painted in Roman capitals as if graven into stone:

> ERVMPIT ALIQVANDO E NVBIBVS IGNIS.*

Cavendish needed the queen's permission to leave England, which she granted in June 1586. He sailed immediately from the Thames to Harwich, where he stayed a fortnight, topping up on victuals and taking on men, and thence to Plymouth, which served as the launchpad for most English voyages westwards, where he boarded his company. He had a total of one hundred and twenty-three men, including gentlemen-adventurers, mariners, soldiers and their officers, and individuals with special skills – carpenters, coopers, blacksmiths, cooks, musicians, gunners, sailmakers and a barber

* 'FIRE SOMETIMES BURSTS FORTH FROM THE CLOUDS.'

surgeon. Each man carried the tools of his trade, his bedding, his personal weapons and his sea chest, in which he stored his clothes, with space set aside for plunder and pillage.

When the wind turned fair, Cavendish hoisted sail and Francis Pretty, embarking on his second privateering expedition to the great South Sea, recorded that they departed Plymouth on 'Thursday the 21 of July 1586 with 3. sails to wit, The *Desire* a ship of 120 tonnes, the *Content* of 60 tonnes, and the *Hugh Gallant*, a barque of 40 tonnes' with 'victuals sufficient for the space of two years, at the charge of the worshipful Master Thomas Cavendish of Trimley in the County of Suffolk Esquire, being our General'.[24]

6

From Plymouth to Sierra Leone

Western Atlantic

A FORTNIGHT AFTER THOMAS CAVENDISH had led his fleet out of Plymouth, destination unstated, the Spanish conquistador and explorer Pedro Sarmiento de Gamboa, returning home aboard a galleon from Brazil, spotted three sails on the horizon near the Island of Terceira in the Azores archipelago. The Azores were a mid-Atlantic staging post for galleons from the Americas, Africa and Asia, and were nicknamed 'the Isles of Pickery' by English privateers, who circled the waters around them like sharks, hoping to pick up a straggler from a treasure convoy, and sometimes ganging together to bring down larger prey, like a Portuguese carrack.*

As the sails closed in on him, Sarmiento identified them as belonging to three English corsairs carrying, he estimated, 'thirty-four pieces of artillery and 170 musketeers and arquebusiers'. He took stock of his forces aboard his own ship, which had had a difficult voyage, cursed by foul winds. Disease, hunger and anomie had done for half his company, and he was down to 'twenty inefficient men as a crew'. Sarmiento decided he could neither fight nor run. 'Without power either to resist or to escape', he confessed, he had no option but to surrender. He and his company were taken aboard the largest privateer, where they were body-searched for valuables, and some were stripped to the skin and 'tortured with fire and twisted cords in such a way that the ends of their fingers were maimed and broken'. 'This was done to make them say whether they carried silver or money.'[1]

The privateers were the *Serpent* and the *Mary Spark*, both owned by Sir Walter Raleigh, accompanied by a prize they'd captured a

* Carracks were thousand-tonne behemoths used by the Portuguese for their trade with the Far East. The value of their cargos could be several hundred thousand pounds.

few days before. John Evesham, aboard the *Serpent*, left a laconic account of their meeting. Raleigh's ships had been prowling the Atlantic 'not much respecting whom we took, so that we might enrich ourselves, which was the object of our expedition', when Sarmiento's galleon had appeared in the distance.[2] To be on the safe side, the *Serpent* had flown a false flag until her target was within reach of her guns, whereupon she'd hoisted the Cross of St George and opened fire. The galleon struck its colours, and Evesham watched her crew throw her cannon overboard as the *Serpent* closed in for the kill, together with a confetti of letters and her nautical charts. He skipped over the torture and pillaging that followed but noted that the prisoners included 'a Spanish gentleman named Pedro Sarmiento' 'who was governor of the straits of Magellan, whom we brought home to England, and presented to the Queen our Sovereign'.[3]

This chance meeting with Raleigh's privateering expedition was perhaps the best thing to have happened to Sarmiento in five years. He was indeed the governor of the Strait of Magellan, where he'd established two fortified settlements to guard the Strait against foreign shipping, and had been on his way back to Spain to report to King Philip on progress. His news might have disappointed his king. Although Sarmiento had founded colonies as instructed, and Spanish cannon now commanded the narrowest part of the Strait, his settlements were less populous than had been planned and would need to be resupplied until they became self-sufficient.

Sarmiento had many good excuses for achieving only a partial success, including monstrous weather, flighty colonists, mutinous friars, hostile Patagonians, a corrupt and venal co-commander and an abundance of bad luck. He'd endured years of hardships, including shipwreck and starvation while trying to carry out his duties, beside which being captured by an English privateer seemed a minor misfortune. As he lay in chains on the gun deck of the *Serpent*, he meditated on his condition and decided that he had plenty to be proud of. Despite constant setbacks, he'd left over four hundred settlers and two dozen heavy cannon to defend the

Strait. Any enemy ship that tried to follow Drake's footsteps would be in for a shock.

Sarmiento's unpleasant news reached England too late to send it after Thomas Cavendish, who was now far to the south. He'd had an eventful first fortnight under sail. Shortly after leaving Plymouth, he'd suffered the first casualty of his voyage when Mr Hope (by his title a gentleman-adventurer) had died aboard the *Desire* from wounds he'd received in a duel 'a little before he went to sea'.[4] In accordance with maritime custom, his corpse was sewn into a canvas shroud, a cannonball was placed between its feet and, after communal prayers, the package was slid overboard. The sailing had been fast and free after the body had been given to the Atlantic and Cavendish soon got the chance to try out his guns, when he crossed paths with a convoy of 'four great Biscayen ships'* returning from cod fishing off Newfoundland. According to NH, a military officer aboard the *Desire* who kept a journal of the venture, Cavendish decided on some target practice and rolled out his demi-culverins with gratifying results: 'we bestowed eighteen great shot,' NH recorded, and 'shrewdly tore the ship which we in the *Desire* assailed.'[5] The action, to NH's regret, was broken off prematurely. Night was falling, and Cavendish resisted the pleasure of taking his first prize lest he lose touch with his other ships in the dark. Besides, the clock was running on the mortgages on his estates, and fishing vessels carrying salted cod, worth – at best – a thousand pounds each, which would require prize crews to control and would also slow his pace, simply weren't worth his time. He sped on south, passing the Canary Islands at about the same time as Pedro Sarmiento arrived in chains in Southampton, not stopping until he reached the mouth of the Senegal River nearly three thousand miles distant from Plymouth, which he sighted less than a month after leaving the English Channel.[6]

* Spanish vessels from its Province of Biscay.

Cavendish had chosen Sierra Leone in West Africa as the first pit-stop on his course to the Strait of Magellan. The *Desire* was brand new; he'd not commanded his own fleet or so many men before and a short first leg gave him the opportunity to test both his ships and company before they reached enemy waters. Moreover, Thomas Fuller, his privateer master from Ipswich, knew the route to Sierra Leone and, after weighing its advantages as a destination (easy to find, plenty of fresh water, fruit and vegetables) against its limitations (warring indigenous tribes, endemic fatal diseases), Cavendish had decided it was perfect for his purposes.

His ships approached the African coast with caution. The winds were capricious, the air was filled with a tropical haze and the waters abounded with reefs and sandbanks. Although Fuller claimed to know Sierra Leone 'very well', he nonetheless took fresh soundings as he piloted Cavendish's fleet to the *roads*, or anchoring ground.[7] Soundings were a crucial element of Elizabethan navigation – more ships were wrecked on coasts than out at sea. They were taken by lowering a lead weight overboard on a cord that marked every fathom with a strip of canvas, which were tallied as the weight descended until it touched the seabed. It was an imprecise way of measuring depths – fractions of fathoms were judged by eye, and the line might be slanted away from the bottom by the motions of the ship or by currents and tides. The weight itself was coated with grease so that it brought up a sample of whatever covered the seabed. These particles and smears of sand, ooze and broken shells could be precise indicators of the ship's position.

Fuller recorded his findings in his rutter. 'Going unto Sierra Leona,' he wrote, 'having the cape East-northeast off you, 7 leagues off you shall have 22 fathoms brown sand. And hailing in you shall find very fair shoaling. You may be bold to borrow on the Southernmost: but take heed of a rock that lieth in the fair-way a good berth off the shore.'[8] The roads lay beyond the rock.

The *Desire* and her consorts came to anchor on 26 August. The shore close by was heavily wooded, and jungle continued inland to a line of hills, just visible in the distance through the hazy air.

For most of Cavendish's company, the land in front of them was a mystery – their first view of a new continent. For a few, however, it was a familiar scene. Sierra Leone had been linked by trade with Europe since the 1450s, when the Portuguese had brought blades, beads and horses to exchange for gold, pepper and slaves with the local tribes. They'd named it after the mountain range behind the coast, whose silhouette resembled a lion crouching and ready to spring, an impression enhanced by constant thunder, which rumbled and growled and roared around them during the rainy season. The Portuguese didn't stray far from their galleons, relying on hearsay as to what lay inland. They had no idea or indeed interest, for instance, in the provenance of the river in whose estuary they anchored. Alvis Cadamosto, writing in 1460, had declared 'This river, in the opinion of the learned, is a branch of the *Gihon*, which flows from the Terrestrial Paradise', which seems to have satisfied their curiosity.[9]

Portuguese knowledge of local topography remained misty for a century. There was less gold in Sierra Leone than they'd hoped to find, and the supply of slaves was complicated by local politics. Two warring tribes, the Sambeses and the Sapies, were locked in a generations-long battle for dominance. The Sapies were an agricultural nation, and the Sambeses were cannibals who lived 'most by the spoil of their enemies, both in taking their victuals, and eating them also'.[10] From time to time, the Sapies revolted against their oppressors and, when they were in the ascendant, they made slaves of their former masters and sold them in large batches to foreign traders. In contrast, when the Sambeses ruled, slaves were kept for the pot and were only available in smaller lots. Such uncertainties decided the Portuguese against building a fort and exploring upriver as they had done elsewhere in Africa, and their trade with Sierra Leone became ad hoc. A galleon would turn up from time to time – several some years then none for a decade – pick up a cargo of slaves and a few tonnes of pepper and leave before it lost too many crew to the fevers that plagued the coast.

English merchants began trading with Sierra Leone a century after the Portuguese. They too were after gold, spices and slaves, and also found the risks to be high. Although they'd started well, in 1555, Thomas Wyndham had returned to London with fifty pounds of gold and eighty tonnes of pepper (but less than a third of his original company) their luck hadn't held, and for a decade the Sierra Leone trade was reduced to 'the sale of miscellaneous items' such as tin pots, lumps of iron and horses' tails 'to miscellaneous Africans'.[11]

When the English had tried their hand at slaving, their luck had followed a similar trajectory. At first, it had seemed all promise: in 1564, Sir John Hawkins had conducted a campaign of terror in West Africa, leaving with four hundred victims that he sold to the Portuguese in Brazil for a huge profit. He returned to Sierra Leone three years later with more ships and snatched another five hundred Africans, in his own words, 'partly with the sword, partly with other means'.[12] This time, however, Hawkins couldn't dispose of his victims in the Americas, even at gunpoint. The mood had changed since his last visit, when Spanish officials had been happy to trade covertly. All commerce with Protestants had been banned outright, two of Hawkins's ships were destroyed by the Spanish in San Juan de Uloa, and he returned to Plymouth with only fifteen men left out of the two hundred who'd sailed with him. His voyage of shame was the last English slaving venture to Africa of the sixteenth century. The market for slaves in the Americas had been closed to Protestants, and there was no demand for them in England.

Although trade with Sierra Leone declined, it became a popular destination with privateers, who might lurk there incognito while planning raids on the opposite side of the Atlantic. There was less chance of running into enemy scouts or warships than in the Canary or Cabo Verde archipelagos, and plenty of firewood, drinking water and fresh fruit. Sir Francis Drake had visited Hawkins's old anchorage in Sierra Leone on his circumnavigation, and Edward Fenton had followed him several years later. Fenton fretted and procrastinated during his visit, which was characterised, like the rest of his expedition, by indecision, bad decisions and continual quarrels among the factions in his company. He vacillated for days before dropping anchor while his mariners died of scurvy and his merchants panicked as the woollen kerseys and other trade goods in his ships were saturated by the incessant rain. He also made a mess of diplomacy. News of his appearance in Sierra Leone reached the Islamic Kingdom of the Wolofs to the north, whose ruler, King Fattema, sent him presents, including a monkey and an ivory tusk. In return, Fenton dispatched a length of red kersey, a cask of gunpowder and a dress and mirror for the king to give to whichever of his queens he loved the best. His gifts were accompanied by a letter expressing the hope that both commerce and friendship might flourish between Fattema's dominions and England. However, instead of waiting for a reply from the most potent ruler in West Africa, Fenton decided to leave at once for Brazil, or perhaps St Helena, to establish a kingdom of his own.[13]

Cavendish anchored just inside the mouth of the Senegal River almost four years to the day after Fenton had left. The rainy season was in full swing, and it poured in torrents every dawn and dusk while the air throbbed with thunder and the sky was split by lightning bolts. No other English ship had visited since Fenton, and there was a degree of apprehension aboard the *Desire* over what they might find. Would King Fattema of the Wolofs emerge from the jungle to greet them, waving Fenton's letter? Would the cannibal Sambeses or the agrarian Sapies be dominant? There was also the risk that a Portuguese or Spanish warship might be loitering nearby. Cavendish had not been long at rest before two Africans paddled out to tell him that a giant vessel with tall masts was indeed moored out of sight around a bend in the river. He ordered the *Hugh Gallant* to haul anchor and investigate. She sailed a dozen miles upstream but saw nothing and, when she took soundings, found that the waters were too shallow for a galleon. If there was anything upriver, it was too small to trouble them.

After this scare had passed, Cavendish sent a landing party of soldiers and gentlemen, including Francis Pretty, the gourmand who'd sailed with Drake, to take the lie of the land. Pretty and his companions were met as friends by the Sapies – the peaceful cultivators who were then in the ascendant – and they 'played and danced' together 'all the forenoon'.[14] The fun, however, was interrupted by the discovery of a Portuguese sailor hiding in the bushes – surely a spy – who was bound tight* until he confessed who he was and why he was hiding. His name was Emmanuel, and he was a caulker from Lisbon. Emmanuel told Cavendish that there *had* been a galleon upriver, which had wrecked itself on a shoal, and that the Sapies had massacred his shipmates and stripped the vessel.[15]

Cavendish had hoped for a peaceful reception from the tribes of Sierra Leone, who could be dangerous enemies. Although they didn't have firearms, their arrows were tipped with fatal toxins. In 1567, Hawkins's slavers had laughed at the 'pin-prick' wounds they caused, until the venom had begun its work. According to an eyewitness, 'The strength of the poison was such that it caused their jaws to shut' and, although the victims tried to 'keep open their mouths with a wedge', most went mad with horror and died in pain within two days.[16]

Cavendish decided to confront and neutralise this threat at once. He called seventy of his company to arms and led them ashore at dawn to attack the Sapies' 'towne' – a large, circular village surrounded by a mud wall that enclosed a hundred or so houses. Its inhabitants fled into the forest and fired arrows at Cavendish and his soldiers as they broke down the wall, burned some houses and pillaged the remainder as best they could. We 'took what spoil we would, which was but little', confessed Pretty, before turning his quill to the layout of the village, which he had

* A form of torture. The victim was tied up with cords and wire, and the bonds were tightened until the excruciating pain persuaded them to tell their inquisitors the truth.

admired while he sacked it, noting that it had been 'marvellous artificially builded' and kept 'wonderfully clean'.[17]

It seemed to have been an easy victory. Cavendish took his men back to the ships, and the Sapies kept away from the shore. However, when the *Desire's* crew rowed in to wash their clothes in fresh water the following morning, they were ambushed. Prevailing notions of hygiene required clean garments rather than scrubbed bodies and, time after time, mariners were ambushed at watering places after they'd laid down their arms and turned their backs as they crouched to launder their clothes. Fortunately, a carpenter had gone 'into the wood to do some special business'. Spotting the concealed warriors, he'd hoisted his britches and raised the alarm just as they fired a volley of poison arrows. William Pickman, a soldier from the *Desire*, was hit in the thigh. He tore the arrow out of his flesh, but its venom had entered his bloodstream and 'wrought so that night, that he was marvellously swollen, and all his belly and private parts were as black as ink, and the next morning he died'.[18]

Thereafter, Cavendish's company and the Sapies kept their distance. The mariners gathered lemons on shore under an armed guard, collected oysters from the mangrove swamps and fished from their rowboats. Cavendish landed again and carved his name on a boulder at the watering place beside that of Francis Drake, which England's first circumnavigator had cut there six years before.[19] Perhaps he felt touched by destiny when he saw their names together. He sailed for Brazil on 6 September 1586.

7

Port Desire

Brazil

THE NEXT LEG OF CAVENDISH'S venture was to Rio de Janeiro, two-and-a-half thousand miles across the Atlantic from Sierra Leone. It was a moon-shot to most of his company. Africa, although it had been strange, appeared in the Bible and had some cultural familiarity. Brazil, however, was part of a New World, which had existed only in legends of Atlantis prior to 1492. Very few Englishmen had visited it and returned. Most of what was known about Central and South America came from European sources, selected for translation in accordance with prevailing tastes. The most popular of these focused on the brutality of the Spanish and Portuguese in their conquered lands, and the barbarity and paganism of the tribes they oppressed. Bartolomeo de Las Casas's *Brief Account of the Destruction of the Indies*,[1] for example, was a catalogue of infamies featuring Spaniards cutting Aztecs in half to test their swords, and feeding pregnant women to their dogs. English readers had also been enthralled by André Thevet's *The New found world, or Antarctike* (translated in 1568), which offered a lurid eyewitness account of the first European footsteps in Brazil, highlighting in eye-popping detail false prophets, devil worshippers and warring tribes of cannibals who fought to enslave and consume each other.[2]

The journey to this wonderland took seven weeks. Cavendish lost the trade winds within a few days of leaving Africa and spent his twenty-sixth birthday in the doldrums, a band of still seas between five degrees north and south of the equator. He didn't reach the equator until 30 September, and his fleet was soon becalmed again. The fresh food he'd taken on in Sierra Leone rotted in the hot, damp air, and scurvy appeared among his company. Its symptoms were physical exhaustion, hair loss, bulging eyes and 'spongy, purplish bleeding gums', from which the teeth were easily dislodged. Its cause was unknown, but, if its sufferers could be put ashore before it took too strong a hold, they usually recovered, albeit with gaps in their jaws and permanent baldness. Finally the trade winds switched on, the sailing became fast and free and Pretty recorded that on 'the last day of October running west-southwest about 24 leagues from Cape Frio in Brazil', they 'fell in with a great mountain which had a high round knop on the top of it standing from it like a town'.[3] This was the unmistakeable *Pao de Azucar* – the Sugar Loaf mountain – that marked the Portuguese settlement of Rio de Janeiro. It was a flourishing place, built on sugar cane and slavery. Merchant ships from Lisbon were regular visitors, and *pataches* – fast-sailing dispatch boats – kept Rio in touch with the Caribbean to the north and Argentina to the south.

Although Rio was bursting with fresh provisions, Cavendish kept hull down over the horizon once its towering landmark had been identified. He planned to stay in Brazil for at least a fortnight and wished to do so incognito. Now was not the time to show his hand. Guided by Stephen Hare, an officer of the *Desire* who'd visited Brazil with the *Minion* of London in 1581, he chose the bay of St Vincent on the Island of San Sebastian as a hideaway. It was a secluded place, invisible from Rio, with all the resources that he needed to get his ships ready for the Strait of Magellan. Cavendish had a long list of tasks: a forge was set up to make new hoops for his casks, men were dispatched to take on water and cut firewood for the galley, and his carpenters assembled a pinnace that had been ferried over from Plymouth in kit form.[4] This ten-tonne craft, which could carry a score or more armed men and could be rowed as well as sailed, would be essential for both scouting and raiding once Cavendish reached the Pacific.

However, before the pinnace had been completed, his expedition was discovered in its hiding place. A week into his stay at St Vincent, a canoe appeared in its bay, carrying a Portuguese merchant at its prow and paddled by six naked slaves. If Cavendish killed them out of hand, they would be missed, and he called the canoe over to the *Desire*. He deputed Hare, who spoke Portuguese, to explain that his ships were peaceful merchantmen, hoping to carry out a little business. Fortunately, the canoe's passenger recognised Hare from his visit on the *Minion* and agreed to carry a letter to an English Catholic based near Rio, which asked him to sell them provisions. The subterfuge bought Cavendish enough time to finish his pinnace and his other tasks, and he sailed south for the Strait of Magellan on 23 November 1586.

He stood offshore for the first week of his journey. The last English expedition to visit these waters had been Edward Fenton's, who'd dwelt on both the size and potency of Spanish forces ranged against him in Brazil when he wrote an apologia for his failed voyage. He had claimed that a large and well-armed naval squadron had been stationed in the South Atlantic 'purposely sent to fight with us or to take us, where they should meet or find us'.[5] Fenton's advice was still current when Cavendish had left Plymouth, and he proceeded on the assumption that there might be enemy galleons waiting ahead.

As Cavendish pushed on south the night sky changed and most of the familiar constellations used for navigation vanished. Even the Great Bear, which Homer described in the *Odyssey* as 'ever circling' sank behind the northern horizon.[6] Meanwhile the stars appeared in new patterns in his direction of travel, and the Southern Cross flamed higher and higher in the sky. Once he was below forty-five degrees south, where the odds of meeting a Spanish squadron were low, Cavendish closed back in on land. His chart for the South Atlantic had little detail for Patagonia beyond an outline of its coast.[7] There were a few stray place names for bays and inlets, some of which may have been speculative, with gaps of a hundred miles or more between them.

He planned to make a final pit-stop before the Strait, and it seemed that he had only one choice. His chart had a cluster of detail around Port St Julian in latitude forty-nine degrees south, where both Magellan and Drake had found a safe anchorage and replenished their ships. It had, however, an evil aura. When Francis Pretty had visited Port St Julian with Drake in 1578, the first sign of human activity he'd seen was a gibbet, erected by Magellan over fifty years before to display the severed limbs of mutineers, whose bones lay in untidy heaps at its foot.[8] Drake's carpenter turned the gibbet's timbers into souvenir goblets, and the malign spirits that seemed to rule Port St Julian infected his expedition. Drake had claimed that Thomas Doughty, one of his principal gentlemen, was a witch, and executed him for treason after a show trial. Pretty had witnessed Doughty's decapitation and had admired his calm, noting that he'd 'laid his head to the block' 'in a quiet sort of way'.[9] After the axe had fallen, Drake had ordered the head to be held up by its hair and shouted 'Lo! this is the end of Traitors!' to his company, before continuing to the Strait.[10]

Might there be an alternative to Port St Julian? Cavendish scoured the coast as he continued south, looking for an inlet that could lead to a natural harbour, and scanning the sea for run-off – clouded water stained brown – that would indicate an estuary nearby. On 17 December, he spotted a minor feature on that vast and empty shoreline, a steep bluff that marked a slender opening in the cliffs, only seven hundred metres wide at its narrowest point, with a deep-water channel in its centre and a safe anchorage beyond. It was the mouth of an unexplored river that snaked inland through an arid red desert towards distant mountains. To the north, a range of jagged hills crinkled with ravines cast its shadows over the water. There were rock stacks covered with bird colonies in the harbour, and two large islands at its entrance. There were no signs of human habitation. Cavendish christened his discovery – which no Englishman had visited before – Port Desire, after his flagship, and wrote its name onto his chart.[11]

Francis Pretty was much taken by the new anchorage. He spotted a 'wonderful great store of seals' on one of its islands, of 'a wonderful great bigness', whose heads and forequarters were covered with rough hair so that they resembled lions with bristling manes. He joined a victualling party sent by Cavendish to collect some for provisions, and found the adult 'sea-lions' were so large and strong that it was 'as much as 4 men are able to do to slay one of them with great coal-staves'. Muskets were no use, for the animals didn't seem to feel the bullets, making straight for the water after being shot and diving out of reach, as if they'd been surprised rather than wounded. In Pretty's opinion, the sealions repaid the effort required to club them to death for they made 'wonderful' eating, especially their pups, which were 'hardly to be known from lamb or mutton' either 'boiled or roasted'. He found other gastronomic treats in Port Desire, including a 'great store' of penguins, which lived underground in burrows like rabbits and were, likewise, 'very good meat'.[12] Such abundant wildlife – which had no fear of man – was received as a gift from God. After they'd been at sea for months, subsisting on rotting salt meat, rancid salt fish, biscuit infested with weevils and stale beer, Elizabethan mariners considered all the creatures they encountered to be fair game.

Port Desire had a large tidal range, and Cavendish seized the opportunity to clean, grave and trim his ships. Their hulls had grown skirts of weed over their months at sea, and their planking was studded with barnacles and patterned by the calcined spirals left by marine worms that had burrowed inwards. He grounded the *Desire* at high water so that she rested on one side, her masts were hauled downwards, and the exposed flank was scrubbed and burned clean of marine growth. Damaged planks were replaced and caulked. Once her hull was sound, it was graved, or coated with 'a mixture of tallow, soap and brimstone'.[13] This both made her a quicker sailer and acted as a barrier to infestation. At the next high tide, she was re-floated, beached on her other side and the process repeated. Meanwhile the ballast in the bottom of her hold, consisting of stones ranging in size from cobbles to footballs, was taken out to be washed clean by the tide, then re-stowed and sprinkled with vinegar. The provisions were also shifted to balance, or trim, her. Once they had finished the *Desire*, Cavendish's company turned to the *Content* and the *Hugh Gallant*. It was arduous work, but the labour was compensated with boundless chunks of seal, supplemented with a variety of seabirds. The military minded NH, who limited himself to two paragraphs when describing Cavendish's voyage from Sierra Leone to Port Desire, was moved to a brusque expression of rhapsody at the cornucopia. There were 'gulls, puets,* penguins, and seals in abundance, to all our comforts and great refreshing'.[14]

The only drawback to Port Desire was its lack of drinking water. The harbour was brackish, and the nearest pure source welled up from the ground some distance from the anchorage in 'a very faire green valley at the foot of the mountains'. While they worked on the ships, Cavendish's company shuttled between the beach and the spring to fill their casks and launder their clothes. Although the land around seemed deserted – no fires, no distant glimpses of 'Indians' flitting among the shadows of the mountains – they were being watched. When John Gage, mariner, and 'a boy named Lutch' wandered off to wash their linen on Christmas Eve 1586, they were ambushed by dozens of tribesmen. Gage was shot through the knee with an arrow, and Lutch was wounded in the shoulder. Cavendish called for a boat, loaded it with soldiers and rowed for shore. When he jumped out, the attackers sprinted away at a startling speed. According to Pretty, who'd landed with his general, they were 'as wild as ever was a buck or any other... beast: for we followed them and they ran from us as it had been the wildest thing in the world'.[15]

Magellan had christened the indigenous tribes he'd encountered in the region *Patagonians* after the wild man *Patagon* ('Bigfoot'), engendered by 'the most monstrous beast... there is in all the world' and a human woman, who starred in his favourite courtly tale, the *Primaleon*. Cavendish knew Magellan's tale and once *his* Patagonians were out of sight, he had a footprint left by a fleeing warrior measured. Pretty recorded it as being '18 inches long'.

Cavendish was almost done in Port Desire. His ships had been spruced up, their casks had been filled and, once he'd marked his chart with bearings radiating out from its harbour,[16] fixing its location for future visits, he took his fleet back to sea, steering

* Lapwings.

for the Strait. The winds blew steady and fair and, two days later, they sighted, Pretty reported, an island 'much like unto Eddystone', which he recognised from his last visit as being close to their objective. On 3 January 1587, the *Desire* breasted a 'great white cape, then a low beach which marked the opening to the "dangerous Strait of Magellan" '.[17]

8

Port Famine

The Strait of Magellan

FOUR DAYS AFTER CAVENDISH'S SHIPS had sailed into the Strait, they were spotted in the distance by Tome Hernandez, Captain of the Guard at the Spanish City of *Rey Felipe*, one of the settlements that Pedro Sarmiento had founded in 1584. Hernandez shouted to his companions that he'd seen 'ships which were coming into the Strait'. Night was falling and they hurriedly lit a fire and signalled with torches to the sails on the horizon 'for it was supposed that they were Spanish'.[1] Their signals were answered, and each flash of light out at sea was balm to minds ravaged by malnutrition and a murderous environment. The happy and prosperous country in which they'd once lived *did* exist and *had* sent an expedition to rescue them, for the City of *Rey Felipe* that they were supposed to be defending had failed. The substantial settlement Sarmiento had established of several hundred colonists – men, women and children – with a timber and stone church, a central storehouse '100 paces long, with thick and lofty forts of oak and beech timber', and six cannon in fortified emplacements manned by professional gunners had been abandoned.[2] All but a handful of its settlers had starved or frozen to death, or had been murdered by Patagonians.

At dawn the ships were closer, and Tome Hernandez ran along the coast, waving a white shirt to catch their attention. A rowing boat pulled out, made its way to shore and beached beside him. His elation gave way to fear. The occupants of the boat weren't Spaniards. 'Who are you?' he shouted and was told in Spanish that they were English and that they were going to Peru. The interpreter in the boat then asked if Hernandez and his companions, who had caught up with them, would like to be taken there? Hernandez repeated the offer of salvation to his fellow survivors, but it was too much for their fragile condition. They warned him that the Lutherans would throw them into the sea as soon as they had them in their clutches. This unhappy delusion made them forget the misery of their present circumstances, and they declined the invitation. The interpreter gave them a second chance, saying 'they might as well embark because those on board were better Christians than them' but Hernandez alone climbed into the rowing boat and came face to face with 'General Thomas Candi'.[3]

Cavendish had crept into the Strait, expecting (from the information that Fenton had brought back to England) to find it fortified by his enemies, who might open fire on his ships at any and every cape he rounded. He'd kept to the centre of the channel – Fenton's captains and chaplain had calculated that, if the Spanish had occupied the narrowest part of the Strait, which was three miles wide, and the range of their cannon was less than a mile from each coast, then there would be a mile-wide path in the middle that they couldn't reach. The signals from shore had puzzled him. Were the lights trying to lure him into range, or onto rocks? When daylight returned, his fears were allayed. Hernandez and his companions presented, even at a distance, a pitiable spectacle. NH, otherwise a hot-blooded man of action who seems to have regarded the Spanish as his mortal foes and the voyage as an opportunity to chastise them, was moved to sympathy at the sight of these 'poor starved Spaniards travelling overland'.[4]

Cavendish questioned Hernandez when he got him to the *Desire* and learned that Sarmiento's cities in the Strait had fallen apart. Neither guns, nor galleons, were waiting ahead. Hernandez told him that, as food had run out at the Cities of *Rey Felipe* and *Nombre Deus* (the second settlement founded by Sarmiento), the colonists had shuttled back and forth between them, dying in their dozens en route, until less than forty out of four hundred were left. Most of the survivors had spent the past winter scavenging along the shoreline 'picking up shell-fish'. The pickings had been slim, and they'd had to work singly, keeping sufficiently far apart 'so as to be able to support life'.[5] At night, they huddled together in tiny huts. When spring had arrived, just eighteen – fifteen men and three women – remained. Their last and only option for survival had been to trek back overland towards the entrance of the Strait, where they could watch for both Sarmiento, whose return had been expected daily ever since a storm had torn his ship off her moorings three years before, and for resupply vessels from Spain, which had been promised to them when they'd signed up for the New World. As Hernandez and his companions had hobbled along the coast, they'd picked their way around the emaciated corpses of scores of soldiers frozen in various states of decomposition who'd been lost along the trail the year before. They were down to thirteen when they'd sighted Cavendish's ships and signalled to them.

This, from Cavendish's point of view, was wonderful news. The cannon that he'd expected to face had been abandoned, their gunners having 'utterly perished for hunger', and the gate to the Pacific Ocean was open. The wind was on the beam, and he weighed anchor immediately. The odds had shifted in his favour. His ships were newly graved, his crews were glutted with sealion pups and an obstacle he'd included in his calculations back in Grimston Hall had vanished.

Although traversing the Strait of Magellan was the shortest stage of Cavendish's planned route, its hellish reputation argued that it should be approached with caution as much as daring. The Strait zigzags across the bottom corner of South America from the Atlantic to the Pacific, with specific hazards at every turning. Some stretches are hemmed in by glaciers and granite cliffs; others are so deep that a ship could lower an anchor a hundred fathoms without finding the seabed. The Atlantic and Pacific send storms through the Strait in their seasons, the topography of the land accelerates their respective squalls and its few known havens could become death traps for sailing ships in the space of minutes if the wind turned foul. Its dangers were personified by Tome Hernandez, who was emaciated, dressed in rags and not entirely sane when Cavendish took him on board. The Strait of Magellan was 'not fit for Christians to inhabit', and it was no place to linger.

The winds continued fair and light, and Cavendish pushed on towards the Pacific, sailing by day and anchoring at night. Thomas Fuller took soundings as the fleet progressed, recording its course and the distances sailed in his rutter in his usual terse style, laying down a trail of white pebbles for future voyagers:

> Item, from the second narrow unto the islands that be called Elizabeth, Bartholemew, and Penguin islands, the distance is 5 leagues, and the course is Southwest and Northeast: the islands being distant a league and a half the one from the other.
>
> Item, from the said island unto Port Famine is 16 leagues: the course is south-south-west and north-north-east.[6]

Port Famine was the name Cavendish had given to the City of *Rey Felipe*, which he reached on 9 January 1587.[7] Sarmiento's settlement was a charnel house. Pretty was one of a shore party sent to investigate and described its neat lines of streets, its church, gun emplacements and gibbet, and the rotting bodies that surrounded them. Starvation was perhaps the worst death that Pretty could imagine, and the scene stirred him to reflect that, while man proposes, God disposes: the Spanish had tried to close the Strait so that 'no other nation should have passage through into the South Sea saving only their own: but as it appeared, it was not God's will so to have it'. Their victuals ran out and they 'died like dogs in their houses, and in their clothes, wherein we found them still at our coming'.[8]

The settlers had buried their cannon while they'd still had the strength, and Cavendish's men dug up six excellent guns, three of bronze and three of iron, which they carried away. As soon as they had loaded these prizes, he raised anchor. Port Famine had horrified his company. NH spoke for them all, admitting that they 'were glad to hasten from this place, for the most noisome stench and vile savour wherewith it was infected, through the contagion of the Spaniards' pined and dead carcasses'.[9]

Favourable weather soon carried them out of range and Cavendish was halfway through the Strait before it turned. Rather than trying to force his way against it, he anchored his fleet and waited until he had a favourable breeze. As the wind blew alternately fair and contrary, he hopped from bay to bay along the Strait, naming as he went. At Elizabeth Bay, he suffered his first casualty since leaving Brazil, when 'Grey, a carpenter by his occupation' passed away from unknown causes and was 'buried there in that Bay' – the furthest south an Englishman had ever been interred.[10]

After a series of vistas of 'craggy rocks and monstrous high hills and mountains', the landscape opened up into 'champain' country to the south – a fertile plain intersected by a broad river. Cavendish paused and sent a boat to explore. Its crew got their first glimpses of the Tierra Del Fuegians, reputed to be giants among giants, who came to the riverbank to parley with them. NH thought them 'of reasonable stature' but no more; Pretty too was underwhelmed by their physiques and shuddered at their diet: 'They were men-eaters and fed altogether on raw flesh, and other filthy food.'[11] He also noted that they had tipped their spears with Spanish 'knives and pieces of Rapiers', evidence – to his mind – that they had killed and eaten some of Sarmiento's settlers. These 'Savages' made signs of friendship to Cavendish's men and 'used all the means they could possibly to have allured us up further into the river'.

Tome Hernandez had met and fought the 'Savages' several times over the course of his *via dolorosa* in the Strait. In his opinion, there was no point in trying to befriend them as they were born with cruel hearts and were masters of duplicity. He told Cavendish that 'they intended deceit, and to form an ambuscade'.[12] Cavendish heeded the warning, recalled his boats, loaded them with arquebusiers and sent them back in. NH was one of the shooting party and recorded the ensuing skirmish as if it were target practice. When the tribesmen emerged from their hiding places and massed together at the point where they expected

Cavendish's men to land, 'we gave the first onset, every shot of us chose his man; and by that means slew some, and hurt more'.

Cavendish continued his bay-hopping for several days, until he met with the tempests he'd been warned to expect from the instant he had entered the Strait. 'Filthy foul weather', and 'rain and vehement stormy winds which came down from the mountains' prevented him from advancing further.[13] He was forced to kedge in an exposed spot and deployed his 'best anchors and cables' to get a hold on the seabed. The *Desire's* anchors were huge in proportion to her size, with cables as thick as an arm. Pretty fretted as they groaned under the strain, for, if a line had snapped, 'we had been in great danger to have been cast away, or at least famished'.[14] The second risk, in Pretty's mind, was the greatest. Cavendish's ships were bottled up for a month in this unprotected bay, and his company supplemented their rations – like Sarmiento's late colonists – by scavenging for mussels and limpets in the chilly rockpools, and shooting 'the fowls of the air' that had been driven onto land by the 'continual rainy weather'. Finally, the wind turned fair, they hoisted anchors and, on 23 February, NH recorded, 'we passed out of the Strait into the sea called by MAGELLAN, mare pacificum, "the Peaceable or the Calm Sea"'.[15] Cavendish was through the Strait.

The 'Peaceable' Pacific was also known as the Spanish Lake. The subjects of the Vice-Royalties of Peru and New Spain shipped goods, priests, soldiers, slaves and silver up and down its western coast in unarmed boats. Their carelessness was legendary. Drake's *Golden Hind* had been the only English ship to have reached the Pacific before Cavendish's fleet, and the wealth and stories she'd brought back about Chile, Peru and Mexico had inflated their riches to mythical proportions. The sailing was easy, Spanish holdings were crossed with rivers of gold and scattered with unguarded heaps of silver ingots, provisions were bounteous and the wine was good. Every year, moreover, the Spanish sent a pair of treasure galleons to Manila in the Philippines, which returned with luxuries from China. If Cavendish could find and take one of these it would be the ultimate prize.

It had been nearly a decade since Drake's visit, and Cavendish had calculated that the Spanish Americans might have forgotten his depredations. They believed the back gate through the Strait had been locked and did not dream that they might be attacked from any other direction. He knew from Hernandez that they hadn't sent supply ships or any other vessels to check on progress in the Strait and trusted that their indifference would enable him to take them by surprise. Expectations were equally high among his company, especially after their relatively easy transit, and they hoped to sail into a dream world of defenceless enemies laden with bullion, gemstones and other imagined plunder.

These illusions were doused when the Pacific belied its name and sent Cavendish a series of gales as he sailed north into the Roaring Forties, a belt of strong, persistent and contrary winds, which had held Drake back for a month in 1578, and had wrecked many Spanish ships that had tried to cross them. Although the *Desire* passed through the Forties without mishap, the *Hugh Gallant* was trapped. Francis Pretty was aboard and recorded that he'd had to work her pumps with the mariners, expecting 'every hour to sink, our barque was so leaky, and ourselves so… weakened with freeing it of water, that we slept not in three days and three nights'.[16]

After her leaks had been stopped, the *Hugh Gallant* caught up with Cavendish, who was waiting at anchor at Santa María, a picturesque, star-shaped island off the coast of Chile at 37° South. The season was autumn, and the climate pleasant with steady, cooling breezes. Santa María's beauty was enhanced by clear evidence of cultivation. Unlike the wild country Cavendish and his company had seen in Brazil and Patagonia, jungle had been replaced with fields and terraces of fruit trees.

Cavendish led a party of seventy armed men ashore in several boats. He aimed to make a show of force. Little was known about the indigenous cultures in the region, or the extent to which they'd either resisted or been subjugated by the Spanish. It was impossible to tell if he'd be met with arrows or steel lances. In the event, he was greeted with provisions when he stepped onto dry land for the first time in weeks. 'There came unto us the country people', NH recorded, 'who intreated our General [T. Cavendish] very well, and presented him with many sorts of meats. For there we had at our commandment, Spanish wheat, potatoes, hogs, hens, dried dog fish and divers other good things, to our contentment.'[17] The 'people of the country' were Mapuches who had been converted to Christianity by the Spanish 'with the cross and with the sword', enslaved and forced to both cultivate and accumulate provisions for their masters' ships. So complete was their subjection that, according to Pretty, 'they dare not eat a hen or a hog themselves'.[18] Believing Cavendish to be a Spaniard, they gave him everything he asked for, and Pretty recorded tasting his first fresh meat since leaving Penguin Island in the Strait, his first fresh fruit and vegetables since Brazil and 'wheat and barley… as fair, as clean, and every way as good as any we have in England'. There were, moreover, exotic delicacies including 'cades full of potato roots, which were very good to eat'. Best of all was the sheer volume of food available, including 'as many hogs as we had salt to powder'.

However, the Mapuches of Santa Maria were ready to shed their yoke, and their *Lonkos*, or chiefs, declared as much to Cavendish when he invited them to dine aboard the *Desire* and told them that, rather than being a Spaniard, *their* oppressors were *his* enemies. It was customary to entertain foreign dignitaries of unknown status by getting them drunk, and he 'provided great cheer for them, and made them merry with wine'. The *Lonkos* opened up in their cups and revealed that the Araucanians, their fellow Mapuches on the mainland, had resisted the Spanish conquistadores, defeating them in battle after battle and driving them out of their territories for, according to Pretty, 'these Indians are marvellous desperate and careless of their lives to live at their own liberty and freedom'. They also indicated 'as near as our General could perceive, that if we could go over unto the main land unto Arauco, that there was much Gold'. Cavendish resisted the temptation. Although well-armed, his force was small, and the chance of finding 'much Gold' was outweighed by the risks of getting involved in a protracted war against the Spanish. At sea the odds were stacked in his favour; on land they were against him. He was in the Pacific to privateer, and it was time to make a start. He returned his fuddled guests to shore and departed Santa María after loading all the fresh provisions he could carry, leaving, to Pretty's regret, 'marvellous great store behind'.[19]

9

The *Nao*

Luzon, Philippines

WHILE CAVENDISH WAS ENTERTAINING THE Mapuche *Lonkos*, the Spanish galleon *Santa Ana* was being refitted at the Cavite yard in the Philippines for her forthcoming voyage to Mexico. The *Santa Ana* was a Manila galleon, or *Nao*, built to sail the longest trade route on the planet. Every year she navigated thousands of miles across the Pacific and back, carrying silk, porcelain, spices and Asian luxuries to Acapulco on her eastward leg, and silver, gunpowder, priests and colonists on her return journey to the Philippines. Cavite was the *Santa Ana's* home port, where she'd been built in 1584 by a diverse group of craftsmen – Spanish shipwrights, Chinese carpenters and Filipino artisans and labourers. She'd been framed with tropical hardwoods including teak and molave, which were, according to the historian Fray Casimiro Díaz Toledano, 'the best that can be found in the universe', and she was sheathed with planking from the Lanang tree,* which was believed to be cannonball proof: smaller projectiles lodged in its grain, and large shot bounced off it and into the sea.[1]

The *Santa Ana* was robust rather than fast. She had a typical galleon shape to her hull, whose silhouette resembled a recumbent crescent moon. The horns of her forecastle and sterncastle rose up from her back, vestiges of the days when naval warfare was dominated by clashes between floating fortresses and the ship with the taller battlements usually won the day. These appendages caused serious windage, however, limiting her ability to manoeuvre and sail. She was also slowed by her swollen belly, which accommodated her enormous hold, and her stability was compromised by the tiers of cabins in her castles for her officers, gentlemen, priests and merchants, and their servants, concubines and slaves.

* *Shorea astylos.*

The *Santa Ana* spent two months in the Cavite yards, during which time she was checked over and made good from stern to stem. Once her hull and spars had been repaired, she was rigged with Manila hemp, fitted with new sails made from cloth woven in Ilocos and fastened with ironwork forged by Chinese blacksmiths who'd taken up residence in Manila. While she was being readied for sea, her officers and men were selected. Thomas de Alzola, an experienced and resourceful mariner, was appointed her captain and Alonzo de Valladolid, a master of Pacific navigation, was chosen as her pilot. However, few of her other officers were of the same calibre. Many had got their posts through nepotism. A well-connected thirteen-year-old, who might never have been to sea and have no experience of command beyond ordering family slaves to do his bidding, had a better chance of becoming an officer on a *Nao* than an intelligent and accomplished veteran. Once appointed, their position allowed them space in the ship's hold, which their sponsors and families filled with goods for private sale. These placelings were immoral as well as underqualified and avaricious. When a visiting bishop was introduced to some examples of the caste, he dismissed them as 'ungodly people, guilty of sins of the flesh, and of other offences' that were too ugly to specify.[2]

The mariners who sailed the giant ship beneath this collection of adventurers and parasites were, like their captain and pilot, experienced and competent. They were a mixture of Spaniards, Portuguese, Malays and Filipinos. Most carried a bolt of silk or a parcel of ivory combs in their sea chests, hoping to profit from the voyage as well as earn their wages. Finally, the company of the *Santa Ana* was topped up with members of the clergy, including Don Juan de Almendrales, the Canon of Manila. These men of God also carried items of trade in their cabins and in the hold, and their slaves were sometimes transported for resale rather than to perform menial duties for their owners or the Church when they reached Acapulco.

A single voyage either way on a *Nao* could lift a priest, mariner or officer from poverty to affluence, and the *Santa Ana* transported as much undeclared cargo as the goods listed on her manifesto. Her official lading, valued at five million pesos, consisted of bolts of silks, satins, damasks and brocades woven with threads of silver and gold, chests of spices, crates of porcelain and boxes of silk stockings and fretwork Chinese fans in tortoiseshell and ivory.[3] She was fitted with three great strong-boxes bound in iron with double locks, which stored small items of great value: velvet bags of pearls, golden coins in leather satchels and crystal flasks of musk and civet, whose secretions were, ounce for ounce, the most valuable items onboard.[4]

Once the *Santa Ana* had been crammed with hundreds of tonnes of luxuries, she took on her weaponry. This consisted of a pair of muskets, a flask of gunpowder, a handful of spears and eighteen swords. Although she'd been fitted with cannon when built, they had been left behind in Mexico on her last voyage. She could carry more cargo without the weight of her guns and, besides, it was understood that the Strait of Magellan had been sealed by Pedro Sarmiento.

On 'the eve of St Peter's Day' 1587, the *Santa Ana* sailed for Acapulco.[5] Immediately prior to her departure, 'a procession of chanting friars' had gifted her an effigy of her patron saint, while she was saluted by a 'salvo of seven guns' fired from Manila's ramparts. The archbishop of the city blessed her as she slipped her moorings, and prayers for her safety were offered up in every church.[6]

The *Santa Ana* planned to follow the route to Mexico that the Spanish had pioneered in 1565, after they had deciphered the system of circulatory winds in the North Pacific. The winds were seasonal, and she and her fellow *Naos* waited for the *Vendaval*, the southwestern monsoon that arrived in the Philippines in May or June before departing. The first leg of their route was its most complicated. They had to thread their way through the *Paso de Acapulco*, a narrow passage that ran through a 'Labyrinth of

Islands, eighty leagues in length and very dangerous'.[7] Although the scenery was beautiful and the sea blue and clear, the passage was packed with hazards, including coral reefs and submarine volcanoes. When the moon was full, currents ran through it with such force that Gemelli Careri, an Italian traveller who made the journey on the galleon *Santisima Trinidad*, was 'Astonished, and Trembled to see the Sea have a Motion like Water boiling over a hot Fire'.[8] It often took a month to complete this short stretch of the voyage.

Once a *Nao* was clear of the *Paso de Acapulco*, she would beat north towards Japan in search of the westerly winds and the east flowing Kuroshio current that would carry her over the Pacific. This leg of the voyage was haunted by the legends of the *Rica de Plata* and the *Rica de Oro* (the *Island Rich in Silver* and the *Island Rich in Gold*), which had been discovered somewhere to the east of Japan in 1565 but had not been seen since. As their names implied, both islands were believed to be composed of precious ores. According to one version of the legend of their discovery, 'A Galleon sailing from Manilla for New Spain... was drove by Tempest upon an Island. The Storm having removed and thrown away all the Earth around the ship's stove... they took some from the Island to replace it. When the Galleon came to Acapulco, this Earth being removed they found under it a Mass of Gold, which the violent Heat had melted and separated from the Earth.'[9] Such stories, and the slight chance that *Rica de Oro* and *Rica de Plata* might exist, like the mythical islands of courtly tales, inspired the Spanish to send a series of fruitless expeditions in search of them.

The *Nao*, however, were required to steer a course away from these phantom atolls; and the next stage of their route to Mexico, leading east into the Pacific, was as hazardous – if less consistently so – as the *Paso de Acapulco*. If they'd been slow on the first leg, their course took them through the western Pacific tropical cyclone belt during the typhoon season, and over the Pacific Ring of Fire,*

* A tectonic belt studded with volcanoes.

whose few and rocky islands, surrounded by deep water, were hazards rather than sanctuaries should a tempest materialise. On calm days, meanwhile, the *Nao* attracted a retinue of sharks, which ate everything that fell overboard. This section of the journey was named 'the graveyard of Doña María de la Jara', after a young woman who had become so depressed by what she thought to be her limited prospects of reaching Mexico alive that she committed suicide by jumping into the sea.[10]

The third leg of the route, seven thousand miles across the Pacific and 'the longest from land to land on our globe', was the easiest to sail.[11] The winds were steady, and the galleons ploughed on over the swells, often on the same tack for weeks at a time. The Pacific took between two and four months to cross. In slow years, rations rotted and, as they ran low, competition for them emerged from swarms of 'little Vermin' called *gorgojos* (weevils), which fed and bred in the ship's biscuit 'so swiftly that in a short time they not only overrun cabins, beds and the very dishes the Men eat on, but insensibly fasten on the body'.[12] There were also 'several other sorts of Vermin of sundry Colours, that suck the Blood' and an 'Abundance of Flies' that fell into 'dishes of Broth, in which there also swam worms of several sorts'. Meanwhile diseases spread among the passengers, including a 'universal raging itch… Berben, which swells the Body and makes the Patient die talking' and scurvy.[13] Teenaged officers could become balding, crippled and toothless by the time they reached Acapulco, and rich at the price of appearing middle-aged. Those who died en route were consigned to the sea and the waiting sharks.

Although Spanish navigators were the best in the world at measuring longitude,[14] it was still an imprecise art and they relied on dead reckoning for most of this leg of their route, and also the appearance of '*señas*' or signs of land as they approached America. The *señas* started to emerge nearly a thousand miles out to sea. The first were 'aguas malas' – shoals of Portuguese man o' war jellyfish – described as 'large as the head, round and violet coloured, with a crest in the middle like a lateen sail'. The next *señas* to appear, encountered up to three hundred miles off the coast of California, were sealions, which were regarded with affection, as being proof that the *Nao* might only be days away from landfall. According to one traveller, they were 'frolicsome' animals with 'Head and Ears like a Dog and a Tail like that they paint Mermaids with'. The final *señas* were '*balsas*' – rafts of matted vegetation, inhabited by small fish named *lobillos* ('little wolves') that flitted over the *balsas* 'like monkeys' before diving back into the sea.[15] A day after observing the *lobillos* at play, the galleon's company might expect to see California on the horizon.[16]

The appearance of the *señas* was greeted with jubilation. The passengers, haunted by the deaths among their company during the passage, and bored of short rations and shark fishing, indulged in a *Fiesta de las Señas* 'to the sound of drums and trumpets', 'in gratefulness for the approaching end of our so wearisome voyage'.[17] The *Nao* usually made landfall around Cape Mendocino in California, where they turned south. They kept out to sea both to avoid the dense fogs that often blanketed the American coast and which were in themselves another *seña*, and the risk of being struck by lightning, which the galleons seemed to attract. The *Nao Espiritu Santo*, for instance, was hit by two bolts in twenty-four hours, which killed or wounded eleven men and left many more so stunned that they 'were speechless and unconscious all that day'.[18]

After rounding Point Conception, the galleons travelled through the Santa Barbara channel and followed Baja California all the way to Cabo San Lucas. From here onwards, they were in well-charted waters. Sailing conditions were usually clement and their pilots knew where to pull in for firewood, fresh food and water. The *Nao* were often met by *pataches* (dispatch boats) from Mexico on this last leg, which carried stores of victuals and took off any seriously ill passengers, ferrying them to the nearest port to recuperate.

The arrival of a *Nao* was anticipated in Acapulco for months ahead. Investors fretted over the safety of the silver they'd advanced on the goods in its hold, and parents, partners and children anticipated being reunited with their loved ones. A Manila galleon could return at any time between August and December. Tension mounted if she was late in the season. Would she make her patrons rich, or reduce them to rags? Were the wanderers she carried still alive, or would the people waiting for them soon be dressed in mourning?

10

Decimation

Chile

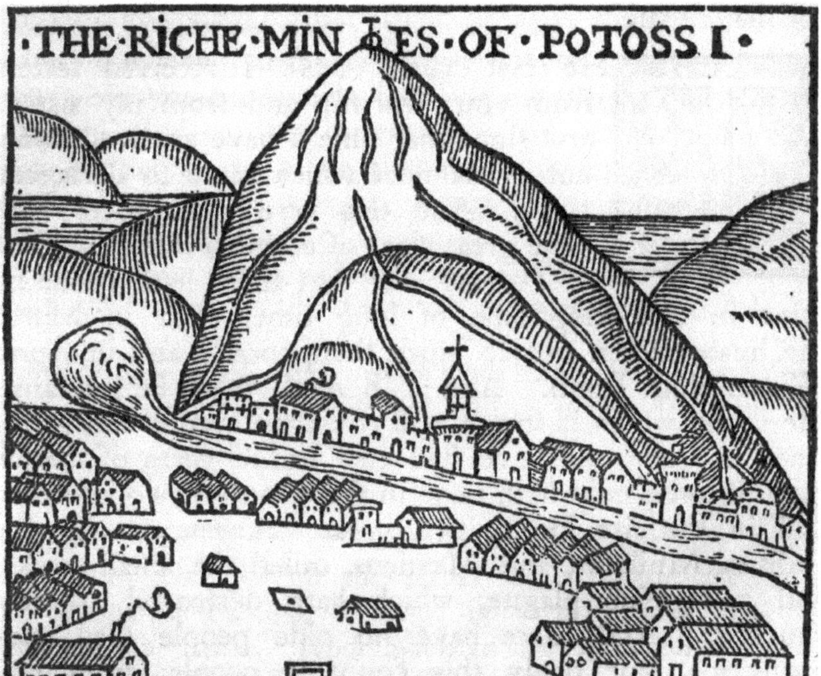

AT THE SAME TIME AS the *Santa Ana* was being made ready for her voyage to Mexico, Thomas Cavendish edged his fleet up the Chilean coast, sailing by day and lying to the wind or anchoring at night. As soon as the land bent away to the east above him, he stood out to sea. When he had planned his voyage in Grimston Hall in 1586, this part had been, of necessity, vague. There was very little reliable information available in England on the Pacific coast of South America. Drake alone had reached it and had fixed the latitude of only a handful of harbours on its thousands of miles of shoreline. He'd taken gold and silver at some of these, and Cavendish hoped to do the same. Although his licence from Queen Elizabeth limited him to 'taking whatsoever the ships goods and merchandises belonging the king of Spain', it did not restrict him to the high seas. Ships in harbours, and the ports that defended them, and the people who supplied these, were all fair game. 'Ships' included anything that floated, from a galleon to a canoe. Hence his plans had anticipated shore raids as well as sea fights, and above all the importance of surprise. If Cavendish could appear at every harbour he attacked like a bolt from the blue, then the odds would remain in his favour, however many times he rolled the dice.

His first target was the Port of Arica, the shipment point for bullion from the vast Potosí silver mine in the Bolivian hinterland. Arica lay another thousand miles to the north, and he needed to collect water and provisions along the way. Without a local pilot, Cavendish had to rely on a few known places and chose the Bay of Quintero as a pit-stop, which Pretty had visited with Drake in 1579. Pretty had recorded that its Indians were friendly, there was plenty of sweet water and the sloping pastures around it teemed with cattle. There was also the chance of finding a prize: Drake had picked up a ship at anchor nearby carrying '25,000 pesos of very pure and fine gold of Valdivia'.[1]

Cavendish closed in on Quintero through a coastal fog on the morning of 30 March, a fortnight after leaving Santa María. When the air cleared his company were delighted to see the promised cattle grazing on the hills nearby. They also spotted a herdsman asleep on the brow of the hill who woke up, caught his horse and galloped off to raise the alarm. When he realised his fleet had been detected, Cavendish called thirty soldiers to arms and hurried ashore. He had to intercept the lookout before he spread news of his presence. However, by the time he'd landed, he was already too late. 'There came 3 horsemen with bright swords', who pulled up just beyond the range of his arquebusiers.[2] Drawn swords, glinting in the sunshine, signified hostile intent. Cavendish sent Tome Hernandez, flanked by two guards, to tell the horsemen they were Spaniards, travelling from the Strait of Magellan, and in need of firewood. He also dispatched a dozen soldiers to creep round behind them. But Hernandez betrayed him. Against all notions of honour, which expected prisoners to keep their parole, Hernandez sprinted over to one of the horsemen mid-parley, climbed up behind him and galloped off. Pretty, usually the most equable of men, was incandescent at this ungallant behaviour. He had spent time with Hernandez – their common interest in food may have drawn the epicure and starving man together – and the desertion seemed doubly base. It was a crime against friendship as well as honour. He railed in his journal at the 'deep and damnable oaths' that Hernandez had made 'continually to our General and all his company never to forsake him', and his promise to die beside Cavendish 'before he would be false'.

Hernandez had been aboard the *Desire* since January. He'd counted her cannon, knew the size of her company to a man and could also provide an accurate account of Cavendish's other ships. In order to have any hope of surprise, Cavendish now had to catch him, the herdsman and the three horsemen. But he had only foot soldiers to hunt mounted men and had no idea of the lie of the land. He returned to the *Desire*, and sent reinforcements ashore under Captain Havers, whose tasks were to eliminate the

Spanish, and to find their settlement and burn it to the ground. Pretty was among the raiding party and was much taken by the abundance of the countryside through which they marched. There were numerous herds of 'cattle, of kine and bullocks', a 'great store of hares and conies, and plenty of partridges and other wild fowls'. They travelled more than seven miles inland, to the foot of a mountain range, but didn't spot another soul. When Havers led them back to the ships in the evening, they met with 'many wild dogs' along the way.[3]

The dogs weren't feral – the Spanish were planning an ambush and had let them loose. Hernandez had been ridden straight to Alfonso Campofrío de Carvajal, Corregidor of Santiago, a fifty-three-year-old conquistador who'd helped to win the territory that he governed with his lance and his sword.[4] A veteran of the Araucanian wars, infamous for their brutality (the Spanish burned their captives alive, the Araucanians killed theirs by cutting them into pieces slowly, starting with their fingers and toes, and turned their skulls into drinking cups), Campofrío was ready for a fight. When Hernandez told him that Cavendish's force 'was but small' and 'wonderfully weak', he assembled a force of lancers and positioned it around a lagoon that held the only source of sweet water in Quintero Bay.

Campofrío struck the next morning as soon as Cavendish's men had rowed ashore to fill the ships' water casks and to indulge their ill-fated obsession with washing their clothes. Pretty watched as 'almost 200 horsemen' 'came pouring down from the hills', surrounded a dozen of his crewmates at the watering place, forced them to surrender and carried them off. When the soldiers Cavendish had sent as guards came to their senses and started shooting, the lancers drew out of range and melted away. Pretty was shaken at how suddenly it had begun and ended, and, though he claimed that at least two dozen of the lancers had been killed, he didn't stay ashore to take a body count.[5]

NH, who took no part in the action, was also shocked. Cavendish's company had been careless, and had been punished for it: 'The 1st of April, we had ten of our men slain and two taken captive by the Spaniards: which great misfortune lighted on our men through their great recklessness, and want of circumspection; being suddenly surprised by the enemy, when they little thought of him.'[6]

Pretty listed the names of the casualties in his journal, together with their places of origin and, in some cases, their occupations. They came from all over England – mariners from Newcastle and Cornwall, privateers from Dorset and soldiers from London, all taken far from home by their European enemies, in a place no one in Europe had known existed a century before.

However, according to Spanish sources, none of the men listed by Pretty as 'slain' died on the spot. All twelve were taken alive, and nine were executed shortly afterwards. They were given the opportunity to convert to Catholicism before they were strung up, which some accepted, and their executioners were commended for saving their souls, if not their necks. The three survivors, William Stephens, Thomas Lucas and William Hilles, a teenager, were dispatched to the Viceroy of Peru to be examined by the Inquisition. Once he'd disposed of his captives, Campofrío sent letters to Peru and Mexico by both sea and land, alerting them to Cavendish's presence and advising them to mobilise at once. His resolution and heroics* were immortalised by Fernando Álvarez de Toledo, an Andalucian Cavalier, in his epic work *Araucana*, which also named a handful of Campofrío's companions and praised their fighting skills:

> Campofrío, Pasten, and the Blacksmith…
> Broke enemy heads,
> Like skilled reapers harvesting corn.[7]

* In the first battle involving Protestants on Chilean soil.

The ambush at Quintero cost Cavendish a tenth of his company. It both shifted the odds against him and taught him how vulnerable he could be on land. Even at the outer limits of their far-flung empire, the Spanish were deadly fighters, whose lancers could pick off his soldiers at will if they caught them on open ground. Cavendish moreover had no idea of how many might be waiting for him at the few harbours marked on his chart. He was over eight hundred miles from Arica and still had to replenish his stores. He chose Moro Moreno as his next target. Located at the midway point between Quintero and Arica, Moro Moreno was known to have an island across the mouth of its harbour, where he might establish a stronghold. He reached it a week later, anchored the *Desire* within cannon range of the shore and led an armed party onto land. NH found the 'Indians' they encountered ashore to be submissive and thought their town 'base and rude'.[8] They'd been ravaged into submission by Campofrío's fellow conquistadores and had assumed that Cavendish and his company were their overlords. Pretty was struck by their timidity: 'They are in marvellous awe of the Spaniards, and very simple people, and live marvellous savagely.' These fearful Indians showed Pretty around their village, which was too haphazard for his liking. The houses were built out of sticks, and their diet was 'raw fish, which stinketh most vilely'. He was, however, impressed by their ingenuity and craft, embodied in their 'canoas', which were assembled from hides, inflated 'like unto bladders' with quills, stitched together with sinews and paddled far out into the ocean to fish for giant tuna.[9] Pretty was also taken by their graves, one of which was dug up for his inspection. It contained the body of a warrior laid out in preparation for the afterlife with his canoe and weapons. NH too examined the funerary goods. Quintero was still raw in his memory. Although death was part of a soldier's trade, it hurt to see men lost without a fight and to believe that their bodies had been left to rot in a wasteland.

Moro Moreno marked a turning point in Cavendish's fortunes. His stock of alcoholic drinks was running low, and Elizabethan crews languished without them. They were capable of mutinying over bad beer, let alone no beer, or an inebriating substitute. Fortunately, the *Content*, which had split from the fleet in search of supplies, had 'entered into a bay where a great deal of wine of Castile was buried in *botijas* in the sand, to the quantity of some 300 tuns' awaiting collection by a Spanish vessel.[10] *Botijas* were large clay jars, resembling Roman amphorae, which were used to carry oil, wine and drinking water along the Pacific coast. The *Content* loaded as many as she could carry and caught up with her sister ships off 'a town called Arica', where she found Cavendish in action against the Spanish.

La Muy Ilustre y Real Ciudad San Marcos de Arica ('the Most illustrious and Royal City of Saint Mark of Arica'), founded in 1541, was situated at the head of two lush valleys that cut through the Atacama Desert. It was the shipment point for silver from the Potosí mine, then the largest and the richest in the world. Potosí was fabulously productive, exceeding even the expectations of conquistadores reared on the *Enchantments of Amadis*. Its seams of ore had been worked for centuries before the Spanish arrived. According to Inca legend, Potosí had been discovered and named when a warrior pulled a bush out of the ground on the slopes of a lone mountain shaped like a pyramid and found silver nodules tangled in its roots. 'For the Incas, silver was thought to derive from the tears of the moon goddess Mama Kilya',[11] and the presence of this sacred metal on so prominent a landmark lent it a spiritual aura. The Spanish also venerated Potosí, which they named the *Cerro Rico* (the 'Rich Mountain') after fictional examples in courtly tales. The city that grew up at its base declared on its coat of arms: 'I am rich Potosí, treasure of the world, king of all mountains and envy of kings.' Its reputation had spread as far away as China, where some of its production ended up, and where it was known as the *Jiyi* Mountain, which was reputed to be covered with trees 'on which golden beans grow all by themselves', and whose roots wound themselves around rich seams of silver.[12] The tonnes of bullion Potosí produced were ported down to Arica on the backs of llamas, mules and slaves once a year, and were shipped from there to Mexico or Panama and eventual dispatch to the Philippines and Spain.

Cavendish had hoped to take Arica by surprise, and had launched a dawn attack with the *Desire*, the *Hugh Gallant* and his pinnace on 'a great ship and four barques' anchored by its harbour. He captured one barque very quickly and sent his smaller vessels closer to shore for the others. Arica's harbour was protected by a fort, whose gunners opened fire as soon as they came into range. Pretty recorded the action from the deck of the *Desire* and was impressed by their accuracy. They 'made three or four very fair shots at the pinnace as she was coming in', which threw up plumes of water around her, missing her 'very narrowly' with one of them.[13] When the pinnace reached the 'great ship', a galleon of a hundred tonnes, her crew abandoned her, diving overboard and swimming to shore. A prize crew was put aboard, who cut her anchor cable and sailed her out to sea. Cavendish and the *Desire* meanwhile captured the other three barques, which were also abandoned by their crews. These were his first prizes – the first vessels he'd taken as a privateer. Guided by the lessons he'd learned from Sir Richard Grenville off Puerto Rico, he had acted quickly, with maximum force, and with much the same result.

Cavendish assembled his trophies just offshore and had them searched. They all had empty holds – no silver, nor anything else of value, not even provisions. It was as if they'd just been unloaded. It looked as if he'd lost the element of surprise, and that Campofrío's warning messages from Quintero had arrived ahead of him. His company also believed that the Spanish had been forewarned. They'd stripped their ships and 'conveyed all their treasure away', Pretty recorded, and 'buried it before we were come near the town' 'for they had heard of us'.[14] There were other signs they had been anticipated. The *Desire's* lookouts had sighted the tips of lances poking out over Arica's battlements and a company of infantry forming up behind banners on the beach. It appeared to Cavendish that he would have to fight if he went ashore, and his men were still twitchy after Quintero. He decided to hold back: 'Our General,' Pretty wrote, 'saw there was no landing without loss of many men: wherefore he gave over that enterprise.'[15]

Cavendish missed a fortune. According to a Spanish witness, there had been no advance warning and, when Arica's lookouts first saw his ships on the horizon, all the silver produced by Potosí that year was stacked along the dock and the beach beside it, ready to be loaded onto the waiting vessels. At the news that unknown ships were approaching, every man in Arica had run to the mounds of silver and carried them to the fortress ingot by ingot. Meanwhile the women of the town had made banners and pennants out of their 'gowns, wimples and shawls', which they'd hoisted on broomsticks behind the battlements and paraded towards the beach so that Cavendish's company would mistake them at a distance for companies of lancers and musketeers.[16]

The deception had worked, and Cavendish remained a little offshore, pounding Arica with his demi-culverins. Although he couldn't take the town, he still had its ships. He sent 'a boat on shore with a flag of truce',[17] offering to exchange the largest vessel, intact, for any of his men who might have been spared death at Quintero. He was haunted by their loss, and a hundred-tonne ship was a handsome ransom for a handful of soldiers. But, rather than being guided by the rules of war, the spirit of chivalry or the chance of a bargain, the Spanish refused. Their hands were tied, they told him. They had been forbidden by their king 'on pain of death' to trade with the enemy, or to ransom any prisoners. Their intransigence infuriated Cavendish. He resumed his cannonade while his company ransacked his prizes. He decided to keep one, naming it the *George*, as she'd been taken on St George's Day, torched the others and left their smoking wrecks in Arica's harbour.

Cavendish hurried north. If the silver wasn't in Arica, it could be at sea ahead of him. He also had to run down the warning ship or ships that he believed had alerted Arica, which may have sailed on to other ports. The next stretch of his course followed the coastal rim of the Atacama Desert. It was a dangerous seaboard to navigate without a pilot. Safe anchorages were hundreds of miles apart, and the rock reefs and subsea pinnacles that abounded close to shore were washed by giant swells driven by onshore winds. It was a coast that demanded caution rather than haste. However, shortly after leaving Arica, Cavendish had another stroke of luck. His pinnace captured a *patache*, whose crew comprised three Spaniards, an elderly Dutchman and a Greek.[18] This odd assortment refused to explain the purpose of their journey and Cavendish, bitter that he had failed to ransom his captured men, had the Spaniards tortured with thumbscrews* 'at several times with extreme pain', to find out why they were at sea. He also put the Dutchman through a mock execution: a noose was fastened round his neck, and he was 'pulled up a little from the hatches' at which one of the men in thumbscrews confessed that they'd been sent from Quintero to Lima with letters to the viceroy warning that English corsairs were on the loose. He claimed the letters had been jettisoned before their *patache* was intercepted, but Cavendish burned the boat rather than wasting time in searching it. While interrogating his prisoners, he discovered that George, the Greek, had been her navigator and was 'a reasonable pilot of all the coast of Chile'.[19]

After destroying the *patache*, Cavendish thought he was ahead of the news at last. He also, thanks to George, had detailed information about where he might find food, water and wood, even in the absence of a secure harbour. George guided him to

* Thumbscrews were a simple but effective instrument of torture – a miniature vice, consisting of two bars of iron or wood connected with a threaded bolt, topped by a nut or handle that could be wound down to force them together. The thumbs of the victim were placed between the bars and the top bar slowly screwed down with enough force to crush their bones. They could cause intense pain in a matter of seconds, and lifelong damage if wound tight.

the village of Paraca at the southern end of Pisco Bay, where the sea was too high to anchor, but when Cavendish sent a boat ashore it picked up useful provisions – 'figs, pomegranates, and pomegranate wine'.[20]

With expert advice to hand, Cavendish split his fleet, sending the *Content* to hunt seals at a rookery on a nearby island, and his other ships to patrol the sea-lanes in search of prizes. The hunting was good. On 13 May, Pretty recorded, 'we took with the *Hugh Gallant*, being but sixteen men of us in it, a great ship which came from Guaianil… of the burthen of three hundred tuns'. To their disappointment, her cargo was nothing but 'timber and victuals' so they took her foresail and provisions, sank her tender, kidnapped her pilot, Gonzalo de Ribas and a slave called Emmanuel, and left her, with twenty-two crewmen still aboard, 'seven leagues from the land very leaky and ready to sink'.[21]

Cavendish was also catching prizes. The *Desire* took two merchant ships, one loaded with wheat and boxes of marmalade, the other with Indian handicrafts, Chinese silk, goat skins from Cordova, white soap, clarified pig fat and other Spanish luxuries and delicacies for homesick conquistadores. Neither vessel offered any resistance, and the morale of his company soared with these easy pickings. The merchantmen also carried a good stock of provisions, including molasses and 'one or two thousand' live hens.[22]

They were the first really valuable prizes Cavendish had captured. Pretty estimated that the larger of them would be worth £20,000, nearly twice the cost of Cavendish's expedition, 'if it had been in England or in any other place of Christendom where we might have sold it'.[23] But there was nowhere to dispose of the boats or their cargos. Cavendish now knew from his experiences at Quintero and Arica that the Spanish would fight him when they could and would never trade with him. He took his prizes to a desolate anchorage, stripped them of their most valuable goods 'and burned the rest, ships and all'.[24] The 'men and women that were not killed' were set ashore to fend for themselves until a Spanish vessel passed by.

This run of successes at sea bolstered the confidence of Cavendish's company, and he resumed his attacks on land. His next target was Paita in Peru. Paita was a staging post on the silver run between Potosí and Panama, where ships carrying European luxuries, like the ones he'd recently taken, paused on their voyage south, and the silver ships from Arica, travelling in the opposite direction also put in. On 20 May, Cavendish anchored in its harbour and led a raid ashore with sixty men. It was a brilliant success. According to NH, who participated in the assault, they drove 'about three hundred persons' out of Paita 'who fled with bag and baggage' into the hills. Although the colonists left a hundred of their servants and slaves behind them, gathered under 'a bloody ensign', a blood red flag symbolising that they would fight to the last man and give no quarter, they were dispersed with cannon-fire and Cavendish gave his men free rein to pillage the abandoned town.

The right of pillage was normally limited to the personal effects of the crew and passengers of captured vessels. Mariners were licensed to keep whatever they could find and charged around prize-ships, threatening prisoners and breaking into chests, hoping to secure any portable valuables before their messmates. On the occasions that the privilege was extended to people and their possessions on land, they would exercise it to the full and, once they'd stripped people of their wedding rings and emptied their cupboards, they would take the sheets off their beds and the window frames and doors from their houses. These could be tossed overboard if they found better pillage elsewhere, and had a market in English ports, should they return. Cavendish's company were spoiled for choice in Paita. Its warehouses were filled with 'five or six thousand pounds' worth of goods, and its terrified citizens had left twenty-five pounds in weight of silver behind when they took to the hills. While Cavendish was impressed by the ferocity of the pillaging, he had to caution his men not to 'cloy themselves with burdens' lest the Spanish recovered their nerves and counterattacked. Pretty approved his prudence 'for they were five men to one of us: and we had an English mile and an half to our ships'.[25]

The timorous inhabitants of Paita stayed in the hills behind their town while it was stripped and watched Cavendish burn it to the ground, together with the remaining goods in its warehouses, once his company had finished pillaging. As a final flourish, he set fire to 'a barque riding in the road' and sailed away in high spirits.[26] Morale had been restored among his company, his ships were stocked up with staples and delicacies, including spiced pig fat, marmalade and wine, and the cargo that he'd snatched from his prizes was worth enough to cover the costs of his voyage. From now on, he was operating at a profit. His next target was the shipyard on the Island of Puna two hundred miles to the north.

11

Puna

Ecuador

CAVENDISH APPROACHED PUNA AT DAWN on 25 May 1587 and announced his presence by cannonading and sinking the *San Jeronimo*, a 250-tonne galleon anchored in the channel between the island and the mainland.[1] Puna guarded the mouth of the Guayas river, which led to the port of Guayaquil, a major transhipment point for trade goods and silver bullion. Its shipyard was one of the most important in South America, turning out galleons like the *San Jeronimo* for the *Armada del Sur*, a squadron of fighting ships responsible for protecting Spanish trade along the Pacific coast, and Cavendish intended to destroy as many of them as he could. Moreover, his new captives had told him on the journey from Arica that there was also the prospect of finding gold in Puna. They had explained that the island was semi-independent from the Spanish, reflecting its former status under the Incas, and its present ruler, an Ecuadorian *Cacique*, or chief, named Don Francisco Tomala, was married to a 'marvellous fair' Spanish woman and possessed of a treasure worth a hundred thousand crowns.[2]

After dispatching the *San Jeronimo*, Cavendish sent his soldiers ashore at the point 'where the lord of the Island dwelt'.[3] They found that Don Francisco had fled with his wife and treasure, and the villagers who lived around his mansion had followed him when they saw the galleon sinking. The soldiers wandered through the *Cacique*'s deserted and 'sumptuous' house, which was 'marvellous well contrived with very many singular good rooms and chambers', and galleries offering 'a stately prospect into the sea on the one side, and into the Land on the other side'.[4] The mansion contained 'a marvellous great hall' and 'a very great storehouse at the one end of the hall', packed with materials for cleaning and repairing ships, including *botijas* of pitch for caulking, and was surrounded by rich gardens and lush pastures. Although only three degrees south of the equator, Puna's climate was tempered by both the Humboldt current and the cool winds that flowed up from Chile. The *Cacique*'s herb beds grew rosemary, thyme, melons and green vegetables, and his orchard was filled with orange, lemon, pomegranate and fig trees. His pastures meanwhile were crowded with cattle, 'sheep very fat and fair, great store of goats, which be very tame, and are used continually to be milked' and an 'abundance of pigeons, turkeys and ducks of a marvellous bigness'.[5]

The façade of Don Francisco's house formed one side of an elegant plaza, facing a 'large and great church'. He had converted his people and their slaves to Catholicism, and this was their temple. Pretty admired the 'five bells hanging in a belfry at the church's "nether end" ', and 'an high altar with a crucifix', when he stepped inside.[6] Church bells were cast from the same bronze as cannon, and could be melted down and repurposed as handsome and durable guns. They were removed from their seats, the altar torn down, its crucifix snapped and the church and hundreds of houses around it were looted then razed.

Once he'd cleared the ground, Cavendish set up camp in the *Cacique*'s mansion and got repairs to his ships underway. A forge was built in the plaza to hammer out nails, and sails were spread out to be patched and stitched. Puna had a large tidal range, and the *Desire* was beached so that her hull could be scrubbed. It had been five months since she was last graved, in Port Desire, and she was encrusted with marine life from both tropical waters and the Pacific Ocean. She was hauled on ground, her keel burned and scraped clean of its hitchhikers and her hull pitched and tarred. Her rigging and tackle were renewed with ropes taken from the *Cacique*'s private store, and from the half dozen prizes Cavendish had stripped and burned since passing through the Strait of Magellan.

While his mariners were busy scouring and replacing planks, ladling tar and hammering tow into seams, Cavendish took the pinnace and sailed over to the mainland in search of the *Cacique* and his treasure. At his landing point, he found four *balsas* (coastal boats) laden with plantains and bags of meal. According to Pretty, 'our General marvelled what they were and what they meant'. They looked like provisions for Spanish troops and Cavendish realised that the boats might be there to supply a force of soldiers that could be already advancing against him. His men had captured a local man (who was being used as both interpreter and guide) and Cavendish had him bound tight, commanding him 'to speak upon his life what he thought these Balsas should be'.[7] The guide tried to distract Cavendish by promising he could lead him to Don Francisco's gold, but, when threatened with his life again, he confessed that the *balsas* were intended to carry sixty local men to reinforce the nearby town of Guayaquil 'where two or three of the king's ships were on the stocks in building' and there was a garrison of a hundred armed men.[8]

Pretty was impressed by Cavendish's composure when he learned that the Spanish had mobilised. 'Our General,' he recorded, 'not any whit discouraged either at the sight of the balsas unlooked for, or for hearing of the threescore soldiers not until then spoken of, with a brave courage animating his company in the exploit' advanced at once. Night was falling as Cavendish entered the forest beyond the shore. He came across a recently abandoned campsite with meat still 'boiling and roasting at the fire' – but the Spanish had vanished. The next day, he searched a neighbouring island, where he discovered the gilded leather hangings from the *Cacique*'s palace, and more ship's tackle and stores, but no signs of either his foes or the missing treasure. When Cavendish returned to the *Desire*, he was met with bad news. Emmanuel, the Spanish slave captured by the *Hugh Gallant*, had deserted and fled to his masters in Guayaquil. Not only, it seemed, had the Spanish been forewarned of his presence, they would also now know the precise strength of his fleet.

Emmanuel brought his news to Geronimo de Reynosa, Corregidor of Guayaquil, a conquistador from the same mould as Alfonso

Campofrío in Quintero. Once the slave had given him a detailed account of Cavendish's forces, and revealed their vulnerability ashore, Reynosa mustered Guayaquil's soldiers at the 'vespers of San Bernabe' and dispatched riders to summon reinforcements from the nearby City of Quito. Quito sent a squadron of cavalry by return, led by the *Hidalgo* Juan de Galarza, a 'hot-headed youth', who held up Reynosa's advance by arguing over precedence. Galarza claimed his command, granted by the Royal *Audiencia* in Spain, overruled that of Reynosa, who held a lesser mandate from the Viceroy of Peru, and demanded to be in charge. But haste was of the essence, and the two commanders reached a compromise: they would ride together, but each would lead his own men. They proceeded to the mainland opposite Puna and posted spies over the water to watch Cavendish's camp. At 2 a.m. on 2 June, the joint force of three hundred men crossed to the island, 'marched with all necessary silence' to the wharf beside Don Francisco's mansion, waited for the English to wake up and attacked in a pincer movement. Galarza, who 'felt the blood of heroes running through his veins', led the charge. 'Juggling arquebus, rapier and royal standard', he 'fearlessly cut through enemy lines' and claimed (with the assistance of a handful of companions) to have killed more than twenty heretics.[9]

Cavendish's men were driven back to the sea and were only saved from greater slaughter by the bravery of Zachary Saxie, a soldier from the *Desire*, who sacrificed his life to buy time for his comrades to retreat to the cover of the ship's cannon. Zachary held the entrance to the safe path to the beach with his halberd, a cross between a spear and a battleaxe, and killed two of his attackers while keeping the rest at bay. The halberd was a versatile weapon, capable of disembowelling a charging horse, smashing through its rider's armour and beheading him. But it was also heavy. Zachary had to pause to catch his breath in the equatorial heat and, when he stood still, was gunned down. He had a quick and honourable end 'for a shot struck him to the heart' and 'feeling himself mortally wounded cried to God for mercy, and fell down presently dead'.[10] He was one of nine Englishmen to die on Puna. Three more,

Walter Tilliard, Edward Smith and Henry Aseley, were captured and sent to Lima to be dealt with by the Inquisition. For a second time since passing through the Straits, Cavendish's men had been ambushed and decimated.

Reynosa dispatched a point-form account of his victory to the Viceroy of Peru, noting that 'the battle lasted two hours', after which the enemy had retired 'with great haste to the sea', and 'there died more than thirty English… three were taken alive'.[11] Although he exaggerated the deaths by a factor of three, his prisoners were real enough. His force also shot holes in Cavendish's pinnace, burned the sails that had been laid out in the plaza for mending, knocked over the forge and stole its tools, and broke up the water casks and *botijas* that had been landed to be filled.

Reynosa was rewarded for his decisive leadership and personal bravery with an *encomienda*, which guaranteed him the forced labour of a fixed set of 'indians' and their offspring for two of his own generations. Other men involved in this glorious action also petitioned for reward, including Galarza, who was granted another generation of oppression over the inhabitants of his *encomienda* in 'Guano, near Riobamba'. Recompense however was neither sought nor offered to Emmanuel, whose daring escape had made the ambush possible, and who remained a slave.

Both Pretty and NH gave accounts of the action in their journals, which differ markedly from their enemies' versions. Pretty recorded a brutal initial onslaught, which had caused panic among his fellows as they retreated. Robert Maddock, 'being a snap-hance', had shot himself through the head with his arquebus while trying to board the rescue launch, and two other men had drowned.[12] But, once the survivors had been evacuated, Cavendish had bombarded the Spanish with his demi-culverins and sent soldiers ashore to counterattack under the covering fire. According to Pretty, they killed nearly fifty of their enemies* and forced the

* Reynosa claimed that he lost only two men but did not include Indians and slaves on his casualty register.

remainder back to their landing place on the other side of the island. NH, meanwhile recorded that the Spanish 'ran away like greyhounds', and considered the action to have been a triumph, despite the casualties.[13] Cavendish had lost men, but he'd won the field and, rather than lapsing into shock and shame as they had done after the ambush at Quintero, his company had stayed resolute and had avenged their dead friends by rampaging through the island and burning its principal town 'to the ground, having in it to the number of three hundred houses'.[14]

After the town had been razed, Cavendish sent out foraging parties to strip the countryside of its fruits, both vegetable and animal. They carried 'goats, hogs, hens, figs, oranges, lemons, besides other wholesome herbs in great quantity' back to the ships, then 'made havoc' of the 'fields, orchards and gardens'.[15] He stayed in Puna for three more days, while the *Content* was hauled aground and graved 'in despite of the Spaniards' and the pinnace that Reynosa had damaged was repaired and trimmed.[16] Cavendish sailed for Mexico on 5 June and, 'for a farewell' NH recorded, 'we first set four of their ships on fire, whereof one was of 200 tonnes, the rest of a 100 apiece: being all upon the stocks a building. We also fired another of 400 tonnes, called the Great Saint Luce, riding before the town to be mended.'[17]

Although Puna had felt like a triumph, the fortunes of the expedition were in the balance. While Cavendish had already taken enough goods in value to turn a profit, and his ships were in fine shape with ample supplies of provisions, wine and gunpowder, he was running low on manpower. Nearly a quarter of those who had sailed with him from Plymouth were now either dead or in the hands of the Inquisition. He could seize all the treasure afloat off New Spain, but he was still most of the way around the world from home. Without enough men to crew his ships and fight, he had little chance of getting them back to England.

His only hope of replacing his casualties was to find recruits among his captives. But few so far had been willing privateers, and some had been traitors, including Thomas Hernandez and Emmanuel. Since he couldn't rely on picking up fresh and trustworthy crew, Cavendish decided to concentrate his forces on the *Desire*, the *Content* and the *George*, and to scuttle the *Hugh Gallant*. She'd been a fine sailer, one of only a handful of ships in history to have threaded the Straits of Magellan. She'd taken a galleon of eight times her tonnage and had proved her seaworthiness through tempest after tempest. Francis Pretty had spent some of the expedition aboard her and mourned her end. The *Hugh Gallant* was sunk at her mooring and Cavendish led his remaining ships towards Mexico, crossing the equator on 12 June 1587, and holding his course 'northwards all that month'.[18] His next target was Acapulco, the American terminus of the Manila galleons.

Cavendish kept offshore, trusting in the speed of his ships to outsail any warning vessel that might have been sent after him. By the beginning of July, his fleet was off Guatemala and passed in sight of an erupting volcano, which was a thing of wonder to NH, who'd never before witnessed such a prodigy of nature – 'an hill that burneth continually!' Once he was abreast of Mexico, Cavendish turned back towards the coast and spotted fresh prey as he closed with land – 'a new ship of the burthen of 120 tonnes' – which he captured without a fight. Her skeleton crew of seven were taken aboard the *Desire* while she was searched. Her hold was empty, and Cavendish's company stripped her of her sails, ropes and firewood, pillaged her thoroughly, set her ablaze and cast her adrift.

Cavendish questioned his prisoners to determine whether they had any useful skills or might make trustworthy privateers. He was in luck. His haul included a Frenchman from Marseilles named Miguel Sanchez who 'was one of the best coasters in the South sea'.[19] Cavendish took Sanchez on as a pilot, and he became a very willing member of his company. He brought news as well as expertise. 'This Miguel Sanchez,' Pretty recorded, 'was the first man that told us news of the great ship called The Santa Ana.' He told them that she was reckoned by the Spanish to be 'the richest ship in the world', and that she was expected in Acapulco at any time from September onwards.[20]

Although there had been rumours in England of the Manila galleons, and the incredible value of the cargos they carried from Asia to Mexico, no Englishman had ever seen one. Were they like the Portuguese carracks, thousand-tonne floating fortresses bristling with cannon? And if not spices, then what was in their holds that made the Spanish, accustomed to shipping tonnes of bullion around the world, catch their breath?

Cavendish stood back out to sea when he learned Sanchez's news. This was the sort of prize he had imagined when he'd plotted his voyage at home in Suffolk. She might even compare with the *Cacafuego,* the galleon that Drake had taken off Mexico, which had carried so much silver that her crew renamed her the *Cacaplata* ('shit-silver') after Drake had emptied her hold. Cavendish calculated that, if he could be in Acapulco by early August and neutralise its shipping, he would have a clean run at the *Santa Ana*, whatever she might be.

As he raced up the coast, Cavendish intercepted a *patache* whose crew abandoned ship and rowed away. She was searched and found to be 'the ship of *adviso*, to give warning of us, sent from Lima to the coast of New Spain'.[21] He burned her and left her crew in their rowing boat far offshore, confident now that he was ahead of the news – at least by sea. Guided by his new pilot, Sanchez, he followed the Spanish shipping lanes and, on 26 July 1587, just over a year after leaving England, he came to anchor in ten fathoms of water in the river of Copalita, two leagues from Acapulco. That night he sent in his pinnace with thirty armed men, and they attacked at dawn.

Acapulco's horseshoe-shaped bay, sheltered by the *Sierra Madre de Sur* on three sides, was the best natural harbour on the Pacific coast of Mexico. Direct trade with the Philippines had made it rich, and it was an impressive ghost town when Cavendish's raiding party reached shore. According to NH, its inhabitants 'ran away at the sight of our little pinnace'.[22] They found over a hundred houses, several churches and a 'custom-house… very fair and large' – all of them abandoned – when they landed. The custom house was loaded with valuable, if bulky, goods – '600 bags of anile to dye cloth; every bag whereof was worth 40 crowns, and 400 bags of cacaos (cocoa); every bag whereof is worth ten crowns'.[23]

Cocoa was a novelty. Chocolate was unknown at the Elizabethan court and Pretty, the first Englishman to describe both its raw ingredient and flavour, wondered at its value in his journal. How could something 'very like unto an almond, but nothing so pleasant in taste' 'go among them for meat and money'? 'For 150 of them are in the value one rial of plate in ready payment.' After tasting and deprecating cocoa, Pretty re-joined his fellows as they 'spoiled' Acapulco.[24] Cavendish kept the anile, cocoas and some Castilian wine, and gave the town to the flames. He then turned to a 'fully laden barque of 50 tonnes' anchored in the bay, which had been deserted by her crew, carrying yet more 'cacaos and anile'.[25] Cavendish had enough of both commodities and, after giving his company time to pillage the barque, he prepared to torch her too. However, he was interrupted by a Spaniard on the shoreline who 'came down out of the hills with a flag of truce' together with the rest of the townsmen. The man waving the white flag was the owner of the vessel and he wanted to buy her back. Cavendish sent a boat to row him out to the *Desire* and listened to his proposals. In between offering a ransom, the owner explained that cocoa was used to make a stimulating drink, which the Spanish adored.

Cavendish wasn't interested. Both times he'd attempted to ransom his men he had been rejected out of hand – it was too late now to start negotiating. The Spanish would not take ships in exchange for lives, and the suggestion that he might accept their gold for an insignificant barque was insulting both to the memory of his lost crew and his own status as a gentleman. He returned the flag-waver to land and burned his vessel alongside the town 'for company'.

After immolating Acapulco, Cavendish took up station offshore and spent the next fortnight on the lookout for incoming vessels, whether prizes or *advisos*. After he'd judged the coast to be clear, he pushed on, hugging the shore and picking up provisions as he went. He had another stroke of luck when he reached Puerto de Navidad, where his landing party captured a messenger asleep in a house near the port, who carried 'letters of adviso concerning us'. They killed his horse, 'took his letters... set fire on the houses, and burnt two new ships of 300 tonnes apiece, which were in building there on the stocks'. [26] Cavendish was now certain that he was ahead of any warnings of his presence. He also, thanks to Sanchez, knew the dispositions of the settlements along the coast and, when circumstances permitted, paused to destroy them.

Cavendish continued to pick up fresh provisions from both the mainland and offshore islands as he progressed up the coast. The wild food was spectacular: NH celebrated the capture of 'a she tortoise which had about four hundred and odd eggs in her; which eggs we ate, and found them to be good meat'; and Pretty rhapsodised over the iguanas they slaughtered 'at a little Island called Sant Andrew', which were 'a kind of Serpents, with four feet, and a long sharp tail, strange to them which have not seen them; but they are very good meat'.[27] Cavendish also stocked his ships with seals, parrots 'as big as hens' and firewood. By mid-September, he'd reached Mazatlán Bay, just south of the Tropic of Cancer. He anchored by an island in the bay to grave and trim his pinnace, which had become 'wonderful leaky with worms', and to take on fresh water.

While the pinnace was hauled down and scrubbed clean, a Spanish prisoner named Domingo, taken alongside Miguel Sanchez, was sent ashore under guard to wash the company's linen. As soon as his guard turned his back, Domingo dumped the laundry, took to the sea and 'swum to the mainland, which was an English mile distant' where he raised the alarm and the Spanish sent cavalry to patrol the coast.[28] Their lancers appeared while Cavendish's men had landed nearby and were trading for fruit and fish with the local tribe. NH was ashore, and confessed that, at that instant, we were 'in great danger of our enemies'.[29] Cavendish called them back to his ships and considered whether he should attack or sail away. He needed fresh water and needed it in a hurry, and the only other source he knew of was more than ninety miles back down the coast.

It was now mid-September, and the *Santa Ana* might appear any day. Sanchez had told him that that she would make her landfall off California and follow the coast home and Cavendish decided to take up station at Cabo San Lucas, on the southern tip of Baja California, and wait for her there. Without fresh water, however, he would lose his chance. As he stood on the beach deliberating whether to land at Mazatlán and drive off the lancers, or to push on and risk running dry, a prisoner named Flores was, according to Pretty, inspired by God 'to make a motion to dig in the sands'.[30] Cavendish realised at once that Flores was trying to tell them that fresh water seeped into the sea under the beach. The same thing happened in Suffolk near Grimston Hall. 'Our general,' Pretty recorded, 'having had experience once before of the like, commanded us to put his motion in practise, and in digging three foot deep we found very good and fresh water. So we watered our ships, and might have filled a thousand tuns more.' In Pretty's opinion, this was a timely miracle. Like the rest of Cavendish's company, his thoughts were fixed on the great galleon due imminently off California, and if they'd had to turn back to fill their casks 'we might have missed our prey'.[31]

Cavendish and his company were on tenterhooks when they reached Cabo San Lucas, whose stark rock pinnacles reminded Pretty of 'the 'Needles at the isle of Wight', and took up station. The *Desire* and the *Content* spent three anxious weeks 'beating up and down the headland of California' with lookouts at their mastheads, scanning the horizon to the north and west.[32] Day after day, the shimmering line of water that marked it remained unchanged as the sea altered colour with the passage of the sun. Then, on 4 November 1587, 'between seven and eight o'clock of the morning' the trumpeter of the *Desire* 'going up into the top espied a sail bearing in from the sea... whereupon he cried out with no small joy to himself and the whole company, A sail, a sail!'[33]

12

California Dreaming

Santa Cruz, California

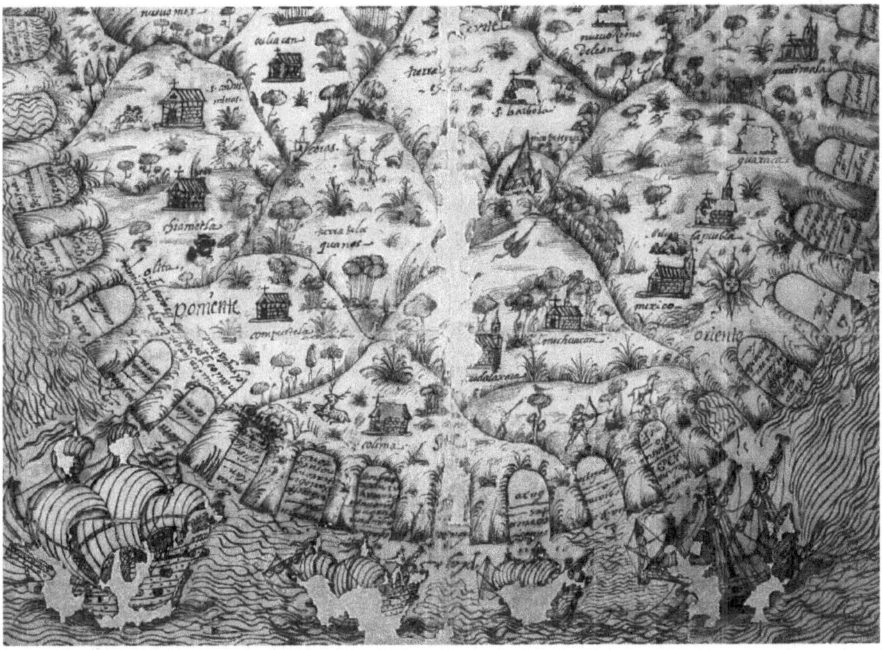

WHILE THOMAS CAVENDISH AND HIS company were digging for water in the sands of the Islas De Mazatlán, Captain Pedro de Unamuno, commander of the Spanish fighting ship *Nuestra Señora de Esperanza*, had been searching for the Californian coast in the fog hundreds of miles to the north. On 7 October, he'd sighted land or what he thought was land but, he recorded, 'it was not clear, inasmuch as the land was covered with a thick mist, we were not certain that it was land which had appeared'. That night his vessel nearly crashed into a small island that was only detected when it was 'within an arquebus shot' of the *Esperanza's* hull. Had 'we not been keeping a good watch', Unamuno confessed, 'we would have been lost this night'.[1] The following morning, the fog lifted and he saw a ridge of hills to the south whose tallest peak was marked with three pine trees. As the visibility continued to improve, a bay ringed with woods appeared at the foot of the hills. The 'smoke of many fires' rose in columns through the trees and drew vertical lines in the air. Unamuno called a council of his officers and asked if they agreed that they should drop anchor and explore.

The *Esperanza* had left the Philippines at the same time as the *Santa Ana* and had continued via Macao into the Pacific on a voyage in search of the *Rica de Oro*, the Island Rich in Gold, and the *Rica de Plata,* the Island Rich in Silver. After steering zigzags over the sectors of ocean where these wonders were said to be located, Unamuno concluded they were phantasms cooked up by starving explorers, whose minds had been further deranged by the claustrophobia induced from living in wooden boats in the midst of limitless seas. The *Rica de Oro*, he stated, did 'not exist, but somebody in hearsay ordered it drawn on his chart', and the *Rica de Plata* likewise was a myth: 'we earnestly endeavoured to sight this island. We could not find it, and we believe that it does not exist.'[2]

Unamuno had been instructed to proceed to California after searching for the phantom islands and scout for safe havens on its coast where the *Nao* might shelter from heavy weather and reprovision en route to Acapulco. The *Esperanza* carried soldiers and priests to claim any likely spots for both Spain and Catholicism, including Padre Martín Ignacio de Loyola, nephew of Ignacio de Loyola, founder of the Jesuit order. Padre Martín was a minor celebrity in his own right in the Catholic world, who had travelled around the globe by land and sea in search of souls to save. He was accustomed to both hardships and reluctant converts and, when Unamuno took counsel as to whether or not to land on the Californian beach that had appeared through the mist, Padre Martín sensed an opportunity to proselytise. 'Carrying a cross in his hands', he led a party of soldiers ashore.

They were struck at once by the potential of the country around them. There were tall straight trees, 'suitable for masts', and enough firewood to fuel a city. The bay meanwhile was crowded with 'a limitless quantity of fish of different kinds'. There was also 'a good sized river' of sweet water, whose sandy banks were pockmarked with footprints. The landing party looked up at this reminder that there were people in this Eden and noticed Indians spying on them from a hill. Soldiers were sent after them but they 'were naked and fleet' and vanished into the landscape.[3]

Unamuno explored inland over the next three days, finding many signs of human habitation including deserted villages, smouldering fires, forest trails and more footprints, sighting Indians in the distance, but never more than one or two at a time. He decided to claim this unknown and apparently abandoned land for Spain and, after planting a cross, cutting 'branches from the trees' and performing the 'other customary ceremonies', he named the spot where he stood the City of St Lucas.* Diego Vásquez Mexia, an infantry sergeant, was elected as its first mayor,

* Now Morro Bay near San Luis Obispo.

and Unamuno and his company rowed back to the *Esperanza* for supper.

However, when they went ashore to their new city the next morning, they were ambushed by hundreds of warriors of the resident Salinan tribe. As Unamuno led a column of soldiers into the country, the Salinans attacked its tail. Three men 'wounded with many arrow and javelin wounds' stumbled towards him spouting blood, followed by Felipe de Contreras, who'd removed his chainmail coat because he'd felt too hot and had been hit 'with a javelin which went entirely through his breast'. Contreras died at his leader's feet.[4]

Unamuno ordered his men to close ranks and retreat as the Salinans pressed down on them. He evacuated his company with difficulty and withdrew to the *Esperanza*. He assembled his officers and priests and told them that, in his opinion, the City of San Lucas was too good a discovery to leave in hostile hands. Although they lacked the manpower and time to convert or exterminate the Salinans, they might instead try to make peace with them. They also needed to fill their water casks, and the company wished to wash their clothing. His audience acquiesced and Padre Martín, cross in hand, led a troop of soldiers ashore to conciliate Spain's new subjects while Geronimo de Vallejada, the ship's barber, took a detachment to the river, laden with laundry and empty barrels.

The Salinans were waiting and, once the watering party had spread out their washing, they struck. Vallejada and his men had only one sword between them and the warriors showered them with arrows, stole their clothes and were closing in with their spears, when the soldiers under Padre Martín returned to save their barber. At Martín's insistence, they fired their muskets over their opponents' heads, who retired to the hill above the bay where they regrouped and shouted out their defiance, raising 'a great outcry, making many gestures and jumping from one place to another'.[5]

This seemed an opportune moment to attempt peace. Padre Martín sent Vallejada and two companions into the no-man's land between his soldiers and the Salinans, carrying a basket of ship's biscuit. They crossed halfway with the gift, placed it on the ground and took a few steps back. The Salinans sent three warriors to examine the offering. Padre Martín gestured that they should taste it. The biscuit had been loaded in Macau and had deteriorated over many months at sea. The warriors took a mouthful each and ran back to their chiefs. They lived off fresh salmon, berries and wild game, and the present tasted like poison. Once this news had been shared, the Salinans organised themselves into three bands, opened fire with their bows and charged at the Spanish again.

Unamuno's company kept their chainmail on after the loss of Felipe de Contreras and the Indians shot 'many arrows without doing our men damage'. At first Padre Martín would not allow the soldiers to shoot back, until the rain of arrows became too much for him. He declared that the Indians were 'being arrogant' and gave permission to return fire. His troop obliged 'and wounded some and compelled them to withdraw'.[6]

Once they had driven off the Salinans, the shore party rowed back to the *Esperanza*, where Unamuno held council once again. There seemed no point to staying on at the City of St Lucas. The indigenous were dangerous, they'd run low on gunpowder, they had three badly wounded men to tend to, a 'scanty' supply of medicines and the weather was changing. Autumn was settling in, and with it came the foggy calms that haunted the Californian coast during that season.[7]

The council agreed with Unamuno, and he sailed for Acapulco on 11 October. By 2 November, he had reached Cabo Corrientes, where, for the first time since leaving Asian waters, another sail cut across his course. He headed straight towards it, hoping that it might be the *Santa Ana*, but, as he closed, he saw the ship it belonged to was too small. It was an *adviso*, sent to warn both the *Esperanza* and the *Santa Ana* that an 'English corsair was on that coast'. Her instructions were to sail 'as high as latitude 25°, north of Cabo San Lucas', to intercept the Spanish ships and to tell them to 'avoid the enemy by standing out to sea'. Unamuno gave the *adviso's* crew sufficient ship's biscuit and rice to feed them for six weeks and she hastened towards Baja California.[8]

The *Santa Ana* had had a trying journey over the Pacific. She'd been slowed both by her heavy cargo and light winds, provisions had run low and some of her company had died from scurvy. The survivors numbered 'about one hundred Spaniards, men and women; and another sixty' Filipinos.[9] All aboard were eager to touch land after four and a half months at sea. They had passed through all the bands of *señas,* from the man o' war jellyfish to the playful *lobitos* frisking on the *balsas* of vegetation that had been flushed offshore and were expecting to see dry land every hour. On 4 November, a smudge appeared on the horizon. Captain Tomas de Alzola sent a lookout up the mainmast who sighted not land, but a sailing ship. His company rejoiced, as this must be the *Esperanza*. Alzola shouted up to the lookout, asking if he saw any more sails, and the reply was yes, another ship had appeared. It was judged to be about twenty miles away, and its hull was below the horizon.[10] The buoyant mood aboard the *Santa Ana* continued. The *Esperanza* was sending a launch across to greet them. Perhaps she had linked up with an *adviso*? But, as the sails grew closer and they could see them in more detail, they spotted 'white and red flags and standards on the leading ship' and realised that they were English.

Cavendish and his company on the *Desire* had been jubilant when they'd heard their trumpeter cry 'a sail, a sail' from the masthead. Thomas Fuller had raced up the rigging and confirmed the 'happy news' that a Spanish galleon was in sight. Cavendish immediately ordered his 'whole company to put all things in readiness'.[11] The demi-culverins were loaded, and pikes, halberds and swords were sharpened and distributed. The gentlemen pulled on their armour, and the musicians readied their instruments while Cavendish set a course to close in on the *Santa Ana* from the windward. After three or four hours of manoeuvring, he caught up with his prey. The vast black ship towered over the *Desire*. She was a forbidding sight with her tall masts and castles, a pointed beak beneath her bowsprit and a row of gunports on a level with the *Desire's* main deck. Cavendish reckoned he'd have only one chance at her before the ports opened and the cannon were rolled out to annihilate his crew and fell his masts. He sailed to within point-blank range of the *Santa Ana* and gave her 'the broadside with our great ordinance, and a volley of small shot'.[12] As clouds of gun smoke enveloped both vessels, Cavendish ran the *Desire* alongside the galleon and his soldiers readied to board her. He staked everything on his first assault. Here was the prize he had gambled his estates for, and he sent forty of the sixty men remaining on the *Desire* into action.

Although Alzola had only had a few hours to prepare his ship for the onslaught, he'd done his best with his limited resources. The *Santa Ana* sat far higher in the water than the *Desire*, and any boarding party would have to scale her hull to reach her decks. He'd improvised his defences around this advantage, installing horizontal nets to hinder attackers and vertical wooden barricades to shelter defenders on her gunwales.[13] His mariners meanwhile had carried ballast stones up from the hold and piled them on deck to tumble down onto boarders. Once the *Santa Ana* was ready, Alzola called her company to arms and inspected their weapons. Only eighteen men had swords and shields. In terms of firearms, he found a total of two arquebuses with enough gunpowder for one and a half shots each. There was also a stock of spears and pikes for dealing with boarders. However, rather than being dismayed by the odds against him, he later claimed that his principal emotion had been contempt for his adversary when the *Desire* closed in. 'It was seen,' he recorded, 'that it was the admiral's ship of an English corsair and thief named Don Tomas Candiens of Tembley, a small man of little age.'[14]

Antonio de Sierra, a cavalier aboard the *Santa Ana*, watched the *Desire* approach and deliver her broadside. Cavendish had placed all of his men on her upper deck, 'sounded the bugles and trumpets, and fired six pieces of artillery at us with which they penetrated our main mast whilst others struck the ship at the waterline'. After the opening salvo, Cavendish 'pulled alongside at the bowsprit' and sent twenty men across it, then withdrew. De Sierra led the defence. We 'went at them', he testified, 'and we killed five English and wounded six' and, when 'they saw the battle was against them, the wounded and the others threw themselves into the water, leaving three of our men dead'.[15]

Meanwhile twenty more of Cavendish's company had tried to scale the hull of the *Santa Ana*, which curved outwards above them before sloping back in towards her deck. The Spanish tumbled down 'an innumerable sort of great stones' as they started to climb, which, according to Francis Pretty, present in the action, 'they threw overboard upon our heads and into our ship so fast' that the attack was repulsed 'with the loss of 2 of our men which were slain, and with the hurting of 4 or 5'. Those who dodged the rain of stones the size of footballs and reached the top were met with 'lances, javelins, rapiers' as their enemies rose up from their barricades, and they too were turned back.[16]

Cavendish could not afford to lose more men. He now knew that the *Santa Ana* didn't have any cannon, so he tacked away, reloaded his demi-culverins, sailed back in and gave her another broadside, raking her 'through and through to the killing and maiming of many of their men'. Once the thunder of his guns had died in their ears, Cavendish sent Miguel Sanchez, the renegade pilot from Marseilles now delighting in the role of an English privateer, to see if he could bring the Spaniards to terms. Sanchez climbed to the top of the *Desire's* stern-castle and harangued them in their own language. 'Demons,' he cried, 'why are you acting as the devil's own? Why do you not ask for mercy now, for when you get to the point where you will, it will not be given.'[17]

When no white flags appeared, Cavendish encouraged 'his men afresh with the whole noise of trumpets' and the *Desire* gave the

Santa Ana 'the third encounter with our great ordinance and all our small shot'.[18] This final pounding settled the matter. The *Santa Ana* had lost her main mast, her fabled cannonball-proof Lanang planking had failed to live up to its reputation and she was holed several times below the waterline.

Alzola couldn't fight back. The *Santa Ana* was incapacitated, and his men 'were discouraged because they had no arms nor artillery to damage the enemy'. If his ship had still carried the weaponry she'd been launched with, 'the enemy would have been damaged and surrendered as the Santa Ana was a fortress, and the men were capable with arms'.[19] He also had to think of the women and priests he carried, who honour demanded should be preserved. According to Pretty, the end came quickly: 'thus discomforted and spoiled, and their Ship being in hazard of sinking,' Alzola 'sent out a flag of truce and parlayed for mercy.'[20]

Alzola lowered his sails and standards and had Pedro Bravo de Paredes, the senior merchant on the *Santa Ana*, rowed over to the *Desire* to negotiate terms. Paredes lacked the *sangre fría* of his captain. Once aboard, he fell on his knees, offered to kiss Cavendish's feet and begged for clemency.

This craven display was met with 'mercy and humanity'.[21] Cavendish didn't wish to waste time with courtesies – he had his prize and wanted to know what she was worth. He told Paredes that he pardoned the Spanish for fighting him, promised them their lives and ordered that the *Santa Ana* now send over her captain, her pilot and her inventory. As soon as they were delivered to him, he sat down and read the inventory. He was staggered by the official value of the galleon's cargo, which included 'a hundred and twenty thousand pesos of gold', and hundreds of tonnes of 'silks, satins, damasks, with musk and divers other merchandize'.[22] There were also bags of pearls, flasks of civet and musk oil, and bezoar stones and rhino horns. Together, their stated worth was over five million pesos, which made her the most valuable vessel ever taken by a single privateer, worth more than Drake's famous prize. It was fabulous wealth, and Cavendish knew that the inventory was likely an understatement of the *Santa Ana's* true value, for her undeclared cargo could be worth as much again. He detained Alzola and five other hostages on the *Desire*, posted guards and a prize crew on the *Santa Ana*, and sailed for a nearby anchorage at Agua Segura to loot her at his leisure.

13

The Richest Ship in the World

Agua Seguro, Baja California

On 7 November, Cavendish was rowed over to the *Santa Ana* and assembled his captives on her deck. He ordered them to deliver up their personal holdings of gold and to bring him the contents of their chests and strong-boxes, whose keys he confiscated. Anyone who tried to hide anything, he told them, would be executed on the spot. According to Alonzo, 'everyone brought forth' 'gold, perfume, musk and pearls, which was a great deal and of great value'. Antonio de Sierra recorded that 'six thousand taels in gold' were taken from one merchant alone. Cavendish placed the gold in a large sea chest, which 'took an entire day to load'. The next morning, he landed most of his captives, who were searched for hidden valuables as they left the *Santa Ana* 'with such severity that they were not permitted to take out a single pin'.[1]

Cavendish behaved like a gentleman to the galleon's passengers once they had been pillaged. He put them ashore beside 'a fair river of fresh water' surrounded with plenty: a 'great store of fresh fish, fowl and wood, and also many hares and rabbits'.[2] To supplement the abundant wild food, 'Our General', Pretty recorded, also gave them 'great stores of garbanzos,* dried peas and wine'. Cavendish provided for their shelter as well as their stomachs. The sails of the *Santa Ana* were rowed over to be turned into tents, and he landed enough wooden planks 'as should be sufficient to make them a barque'. He then turned to looting the official cargo of his prize.

Francisco Mangabay, a Filipino servant of Alonso de Valladolid, one of Cavendish's hostages, who'd been kept aboard the *Santa Ana* as a menial to work her pumps and stop her sinking, testified that the looting had been a model of efficiency.[3] Cavendish had kept both a poker face as he'd worked his way through the ship's inventory and a tight rein on his company. First, he'd ordered

* Chickpeas.

Alzola to reveal the hiding places of the official strong-boxes. Alzola had led them to the iron-bound and double-locked chests, which were carried onto the quarterdeck, broken open and their contents divided into three shares – two for Cavendish, and one for his company. The gold was weighed out with scales before distribution to ensure equity. Sierra, who was watching, valued the contents of the chests at six hundred thousand pesos – far more than their stated worth on the register. When the distribution finished, Cavendish told his company: 'Now you are rich. For two years now we have been sailing and we have not found anything like this'.[4]

The sheer size of the haul – more wealth than any of them, gentry included, had ever seen in their lives, unless they'd witnessed a coronation, elated them. The mariners who'd sailed and fought their way from England to the Pacific coast of Mexico were now each as wealthy as a country squire, however small their shares. Even so, rancour arose and according to Pretty 'many of the company fell into a mutiny against our General, especially those which were in the *Content*'. The *Content* had joined the *Desire* in Agua Segura after the *Santa Ana* had been captured and the *Desire's* crew, who'd lost friends and spent blood for the prize, were furious that the latecomers were to receive equal shares. As tension grew between them and the shouting changed from insults to threats, Cavendish calmed them down and restored his authority by staging an execution.

Fate had presented him with the ideal candidate. His hostages on the *Desire* included Don Juan de Almendrales, Canon of Manila, who had travelled on the *Santa Ana* with a Japanese boy, named Cosmus, as his attendant. During the fight for the ship, Cavendish's men had separated the boy from his master and lover, for he was also Almendrales's catamite. The priest flew into a passion and, according to Mangabay, 'he fought and insulted the Englishmen' for taking Cosmus away.[5] Once a hostage, the heartbroken Almendrales made more trouble for himself. He told his guards that Spaniards were far braver than Lutherans and, if they'd been on equal terms, not a single Englishman would have stood a chance against them. 'For saying this,' Mangabay noted, 'he was put in chains.'[6] Next, the priest threatened to stab one of the *Desire's* pilots as he lay ill, by which time Cavendish had had enough of his provocations and, when his men grew fractious, he seized the opportunity to get rid of this troublemaker. It helped that Almendrales was a priest. His company remembered the companions they'd lost to ambushes along the coast of Chile and believed that any taken captive would be burned by the Inquisition. An intolerant cleric was a perfect scapegoat, not least of all because he seemed to be bent on martyrdom.

Almendrales was rowed from the *Desire* to the *Santa Ana* and strung up 'from the foretackle'. When the priest's feet stopped kicking, his body was thrown overboard. His death reminded Cavendish's men of both their duty to obey and their common purpose. According to Pretty, the malcontents 'were after a sort pacified for a time' and they returned to plundering the *Santa Ana*.[7]

The galleon's passengers watched from the shore as their belongings were inspected and either transhipped to the *Desire* and the *Content* or tossed overboard. Cavendish's company hacked open chests and cut into bales of Chinese brocades with axes and swords in search of any hidden gold, committing, according to Alzola who'd invested his life's savings in the voyage, 'destruction and inhumanities never before seen in the manner of infidel Lutherans'.[8]

The looters could afford to be wasteful. The *Santa Ana* carried ten times as much cargo as Cavendish's ships could load, even after they'd cleared out their ballast stones. Once their holds were full, Cavendish encouraged his company to throw the remainder – hundreds of tonnes of Chinese luxuries worth millions of pesos in Mexico or Europe – into the sea. The bulk of the jettisoned goods were rare and precious fabrics that had been intended to dress courtiers, the higher ranks of Catholic clergy, and courtesans, duchesses and effigies of the Madonna. Shantung silks with shifting iridescent hues and brocades and damasks shimmered underwater as they sank into the depths. The waste was lamented by NH, whose account of the seizure and sacking of the *Santa Ana* was otherwise brief and to the point. She 'was one of the richest vessels that ever sailed on the seas,' he recorded, 'and was able to have made many hundreds wealthy if we had had means to have brought it home'.[9] But the means weren't there. Cavendish barely had enough men for his own ships, let alone a skeleton crew for his huge, lumbering, damaged prize.

Cavendish finished loading and trimming his ships on 17 November – Accession Day – the most important date in an Elizabethan courtier's diary. In London, it was celebrated with the Accession Day Tilts, at which the country's nobles and knights fought each other in jousts to commemorate Queen Elizabeth's coronation. Cavendish was still part-courtier at heart and marked the event with due decorum. At daybreak, 'our General commanded all his ordinance to be shot off' while his men fired their arquebuses and cheered. After nightfall, 'we had many fireworks and more ordinance discharged, to the great admiration of all the Spaniards… for the most part of them had never seen the like before'.[10] Cavendish then sent his hostages ashore, together with nine prisoners he'd picked up in engagements along the coasts of Chile, Ecuador and Mexico, and four women from the *Santa Ana* who each were presented with a solid gold plate worth five hundred pesos.

However, Cavendish kept some of his captives. The Japanese boy Cosmus, together with another named Christopher, were retained to act as interpreters when Cavendish reached Asia, as were three young Filipinos, and an African who spoke Arabic.[11] Cavendish also held the *Santa Ana's* pilots – Nicholas Rodrigo, who had sailed to China, Japan and the Philippines, and Alonso de Valladolid, who knew the route across the Pacific Ocean, together with his servant Mangabay.

By 19 November, Cavendish was ready to leave. He signed the register of the *Santa Ana*, and presented it to Alzola, telling him through a sinister, one-eyed interpreter that 'the writing in the English language was a receipt in satisfaction of the entire Registry'.[12] He had won the wager he'd backed with his estates and the receipt served as an acknowledgement of his winnings. Cavendish followed up with a rare speech and, while his words have been distorted by translation and memory, they were uncompromising. He declared he was an 'enemy of the King of Spain who was at war with England, he sailed to rob and do harm, did not wish to allow peace to those in the King's domains'. He would also cause such damage as he could by sea.

After stating his position, Cavendish spoke about honour. He pointed out that, while the Spanish treated English prisoners 'with much harshness and cruelty', he had not done so 'because he was a gentleman'. Instead, he reminded Alzola, *he'd* cared for his captives properly and spared them their lives. Cavendish's words about principles were as pointed as his declaration of war. He'd tried and failed to ransom his lost crewmen, but, rather than taking vengeance by murdering his Spanish prisoners, he'd observed European standards of courtly behaviour and indeed the rules of war. He wanted glory as well as wealth, and he wanted his glory to be burnished by his conduct. He signed the *Santa Ana's* register, as Thomas Cavendish of Trimley, as if he wished to spread the fame of his native parish in Suffolk as well as his own name.[13]

At 'about three o'clock in the afternoon', Cavendish ordered his company to burn the *Santa Ana*.[14] Alzola watched from the deck of the *Desire* as 'In the manner of infidels and enemies of the Catholic Faith',[15] they hacked down her masts and rigging, and set her alight. The flames danced across her decks from stem to stern and burned through her anchor cable. The blazing wreck drifted into shore and impaled itself on a rock reef, hissing smoke.

Cavendish then gave Alzola 'a royal reward' and had him rowed ashore together with more weapons for self-defence against the 'Indians' native to Agua Segura. Mangabay recorded that Cavendish left them an additional 'five arquebuses, ten swords, one lance, a small sack of gunpowder and some bullets', a more formidable arsenal than the *Santa Ana* had carried when she'd departed Manila.[16] As night approached, Cavendish hauled anchor, fired one of his culverins as a parting salute and the *Desire* 'set sail joyfully homewards to England with a fair wind'.

The *Desire* sailed alone. A few hours after her departure from Cabo San Lucas, just as night was falling, she 'left the *Content* astern… which was not yet come out of the road'.[17] According to Mangabay, the parting was deliberate. Cavendish took all the Pacific pilots into the *Desire* and set off for the Philippines; while the *Content* made a course for the Strait of Ainan, the Pacific entrance to the fabled Northwest Passage, which Drake had sought but failed to find so many years before.

The marooned company of the *Santa Ana* watched as 'the tyrant' Cavendish vanished westwards towards the sunset.[18] The remains of their ship continued to burn for four days, until all that was left of her was submerged. They were a long way from help. The nearest Spanish port was hundreds of miles away, and only a handful of friendly vessels passed by Cabo San Lucas each year. It might be months until they were found. Meanwhile there was no known overland route to safety. The terrain was arid and barren, the hinterland unexplored and the natives were said to be 'Caribis' or cannibals. In the event, any chance of friendly relations was spoiled when they 'seized an Indian man and woman who were bathing in the lake of fresh water and carried them away with them. The man jumped overboard with some irons on him' and drowned, but the witness 'did not know what happened to the woman'.[19]

The fear of being eaten before their provisions ran out was foremost on their minds, and the *Santa Ana's* company spent their first days of isolation building defences round their camp. Once these were complete, they ventured out at low tide to look at the wreck of their ship. She was lying just below the surface of the water, with fish darting through the charred vestiges of her ribs. When Alzola inspected the *Santa Ana*, he saw that part of her keel was intact, together with a yard or so of planking along one side of her hull. He realised it might be possible to salvage enough to build a ship to carry some, or all, of them to Acapulco. The prospect of escape filled his company with purpose. Eighty men waded out to scavenge the wreck. They pulled out its ballast and collected the iron spikes and nails, 'which had fallen inside due to the fire'. After four days of frantic work, Sierra recorded that 'the keel was clean, and at high tide it was afloat'.[20]

They punted the remnants of the galleon to shore beside their camp and built a new ship around them using salvaged materials, and the tools and planks that Cavendish had given them. They cut sails from the *Santa Ana's* canvas, shaped a mast and rudder, and after thirty-six days stranded at 'that desert port and place of war', 'Commending themselves to the Divine Majesty', they sailed for Mexico on 11 December 'with that piece of a ship'.[21]

The makeshift vessel proved seaworthy. A fortnight later, Alzola reached 'Christian lands at the Port of Santiago in the Province of Colima' in Mexico.[22] He took on water, 'put ashore eleven sick passengers', then sailed on to Acapulco, the *Santa Ana's* intended terminus, which he reached on the eve of 29 December 1587. His heroism went unremarked at his destination. The compelling tale of his fight against adversity, and the fact that he had saved a hundred and ninety lives from starvation or cannibals, were of little interest to the inhabitants of Acapulco, many of whom had invested heavily in the *Santa Ana*, and the appearance of her charred remains, patched into an ungainly barque, was striking visual proof of their losses. The survival of their relatives, friends, employees and slaves was small consolation for millions of pesos' worth of missing goods. They raged against Cavendish, that Lutheran spawned by Satan, who had both broken their fortunes and insulted Spain by exploiting her weaknesses. The shock was psychological as well as financial. What if Cavendish came back every year? Who would defend them? They seethed with anger that the *Santa Ana* had been allowed to leave the Philippines without any arms, even though they had been responsible for removing her cannon. They sent frantic letters to their king in Spain, bewailing their losses and begging for protection. And they squabbled among themselves over the ownership of both the tiny fraction of the *Santa Ana's* cargo that Alzola and his company had managed to salvage when they'd raised her wreck, and the flotsam they'd gathered when the tides washed ashore a few of the items that Cavendish's men had tossed overboard.

The possessions that survived the disaster included a handicapped slave, described as 'the black man named Francisco with two toes less on one foot, with a good body and face and two signs in his face from the land of Mozambique' who had belonged to Almendrales (the hanged priest) and who was sold at auction for two hundred and sixty-one gold pesos.[23] The proceeds, less expenses and a commission of four per cent on the sale, were remitted to Spain and constituted the entire profits to the owners of and investors in the last voyage of what had been 'one of the richest vessels that ever sailed on the seas'.[24]

14

Islands

Guam, Marianas Archipelago

AFTER LEAVING THE *SANTA ANA* in flames off Baja California, Thomas Cavendish spent the next forty-five days at sea. Thomas Fuller noted in his rutter that this leg of the *Desire's* journey to the east was more than five and a half thousand nautical miles, all of it across open ocean.

> Item, From the cape Santa Clara unto the islands of the Ladronnes, the course is West and by South, East and by North, and the distance between them is 1850 leagues.[1]

Such was the monotony, neither NH nor Francis Pretty wasted much ink on it in their journals. However, a few glimpses of life aboard the *Desire* during the weeks at sea were provided by Pedro Hernandez de Saldana, a Portuguese 'grommet', or trainee mariner, who Cavendish had taken out of the *Santa Ana,* and who focused on the mundane, noting only that the ship was kept in good order and communal prayers were said each day.[2]

Guided by his captive pilots, Nicolas Rodrigo and Alonso de Valladolid, and driven by a fair and constant wind, Cavendish made landfall on 3 January 1588 at Guam, a mountainous island at the southern end of the Marianas archipelago. This chain of volcanic peaks had been named the *Islas de Los Ladrones* ('The Islands of the Thieves') by Magellan, whose ships had been the first European vessels to visit them, indeed perhaps the only vessels of any kind to reach them for several hundred years. They were inhabited by the Chamorro people, an Austronesian clan who had migrated from southeast Asia around 2000 BC.

The Chamorro made a favourable first impression on Magellan's company. According to Antonio Pigafetta, gentleman-chronicler of the voyage:

> These people live in liberty and according to their will, for they have no lord or superior; they go quite naked, and some of them wear beards, and have their hair down to the waist. They wear small hats, after the fashion of the Albanians; these hats are made of palm leaves. The people are as tall as us, and well made: they adore nothing, and when they are born they are white, later they become brown, and have their teeth black and red.[3]

However, these libertarians did not understand the concept of private property and, when they progressed from petty theft to stealing the tender from Magellan's flagship, he drove them off with gunfire, landed his soldiers and burned their settlements. Spanish ships visiting the islands forty years later had similar experiences. Miguel López de Legaspi had dropped anchor in Guam in 1565 and, after letting his men ashore, fights had broken out and one of his mariners had been murdered. He'd taken instant reprisals, burning a Chamorro village and hanging 'three disabled prisoners' 'upon the spot'.[4] Although the Spanish had since claimed the archipelago for King Philip II, christening it the Marianas in honour of his queen, mariners still knew it by Magellan's name – the Islands of the Thieves.

Cavendish's *Desire* was the first English ship to reach Guam. The fleet boats of the Chamorro, laden with food, shot out to meet her as soon as she appeared in the offing, and Pretty cheered them on. After six weeks at sea, he craved fresh fare, and the sight of so much of it skimming towards the ship opened his heart towards its ferrymen. The islanders, he wrote, were admirable people, who wore their hair long, sailed naked and were evidently well fed – with 'marvellous fat' bodies. They were as tall as they were stout, 'bigger ordinarily of stature than the most part of our men in England'.[5]

The Chamorro drew up alongside the *Desire* as she coasted along, offering plantains, coconuts, yams and fresh fish to trade. They were after iron in exchange and her company attached nails and knives to cords and fishing lines and lowered them to their boats. The islanders removed the offerings and tied a yam or a bundle of plantains to the same cord. They were desperate to trade. They hadn't seen another European vessel for several years and had no idea if it would be two months or as many decades before the next one arrived. Although they'd learned from hard experience not to trust their visitors, a metal blade could transform a life and the Chamorro kept pace with the *Desire*, crowding 'so thick about' her that she shattered two of their boats as she ploughed on with her course. Pretty was impressed by how little these accidents disturbed them. Unlike most English seamen, who couldn't swim and consigned their souls to their maker if they fell into deep water, the islanders were 'excellent swimmers and divers' and the men who'd been driven naked into the blood-warm sea simply swam to another canoe.

Pretty was also struck by their boatbuilding skills. The Chamorro made their swift little ships – outrigger canoes seven or eight yards long with a single lateen sail – 'without any edge tools', and with a craftsmanship that rivalled 'any that we had ever seen'.[6] These simple craft, moreover, could sail 'as well right against the wind' as before it. Pretty regretted, however, that their elegant lines had been marred by the carved wooden idols 'like unto images of the devil' that decorated their upturned prows.

Cavendish didn't intend to halt at Guam. It was merely a waypoint on his course to the Philippines. He was happy to pick up provisions from the Chamorro while still under sail, but, once he'd fixed its position on his chart, he was in a hurry to press on. He had enough fresh water and firewood for the next leg of his journey, Guam was not known to contain anything of value and, besides, the reputation of the islanders preceded them. His company, once they'd struck their bargains, were as quick to condemn the morals of their counterparts as Magellan and Legaspi. NH painted the Chamorro as 'thievish and treacherous' and, while (like his shipmate Pretty) he acknowledged that their canoes were 'admirable to behold for their swiftness in sailing', he expressed no regrets that two of them had been crushed into splinters under the bows of the *Desire*.[7] The islanders, meanwhile, became ever more frantic when they realised that she wasn't stopping, continuing to crowd round her. When they became a nuisance rather than a source of both food and entertainment, even Pretty turned against them. 'These Savages followed us so long,' he recorded, 'that we could not be rid of them; until in the end our General commanded some half dozen arquebuses to be made ready.' Cavendish was in a hurry, and the Chamorro were in the way. He himself fired the first gun and, according to Pretty, scored a direct hit. The rest of his shooting party were poorer marksmen. Their targets were used to firearms, and were 'so yare and nimble, that we could not discern whether they were killed or no', for they dived into the sea as soon as they saw the muzzles flash.[8]

Guam marked the end of the longest leg of Thomas Cavendish's planned circumnavigation. The Marianas archipelago delineated the eastern rim of the Philippine Sea, and he was now within a few weeks' sail of the source of the treasure piled in the *Desire's* hold. He had achieved his first two objectives in the eighteen months since he'd left Plymouth, and now it was time for the third. He wanted to discover the mechanics of the China trade; to make alliances with the tribes and nations he came across in Asian waters and establish the foundations of future commerce. If he, and by extension England, could create a base in the Far East from which they could both operate against Spanish and Portuguese shipping and trade in silks and spices, it would alter the balance of power in Europe.

Cavendish headed west from Guam and, despite 'scant winds and some foul weather', covered nearly a thousand miles in the next eleven days. On 14 January, after 'lying at hull with our ship all the middle watch', the *Desire* 'fell in with a headland of the isles of the Philippines', which marked his arrival in Asian waters.[9]

Cavendish had made the fastest, and probably healthiest, crossing of the Pacific that had yet been recorded. It had taken him only fifty-six days and he hadn't lost a single man. Magellan, in contrast, had required close to four months just to reach Guam, by which time twenty of his company had died of scurvy. The remainder, according to Pigafetta, survived on 'old biscuit reduced to powder, and full of grubs' that stank and tasted of the droppings rats had deposited after 'eating the good biscuit'.[10] When the biscuit ran out, both officers and mariners ate the rats, which were worth their weight in silver while they lasted, and then they started on the leather fittings of the ship's rigging. When Magellan sent his first boat ashore at Guam, the starving invalids in his crew had begged the landing party 'that if we killed man or woman, that we should bring them their entrails' to eat, 'as they would see themselves suddenly cured'.[11]

On 15 January 1588, the *Desire* dropped anchor off the Philippine island of Capul, at the entry to the Strait of San Bernardino. There were no Spanish settlements on Capul, whose principal indigenous people, the Abaknon, had taken refuge there from the Moslems in the thirteenth century 'since they already had a God in whom they believed and they did not want to change'.[12] The Abaknon were named after their first king, Abak, who had led the exodus and had introduced rice as well as his native deity to the new homeland.

Cavendish arrived at Capul when its weather was most clement. The breezes were steady, rainfall light and the temperature below its searing summer peaks. Once the *Desire* had come to rest, an Abaknon *Cacique* paddled out to greet her at the head of a fleet of canoes carrying green coconuts and yams. As ever, Pretty was well disposed towards the bearers of food and was impressed by the *Cacique*'s tribal scarifications, which were 'carved and cut with sundry and many strakes and devices all over his body', representing mystical links to the cosmos.[13]

Unsure if the chief was friend or foe – clearly, he was used to European ships and might be subject to the Spanish – Cavendish took him into custody. Assisted by the Filipino youths he'd taken from the *Santa Ana*, Cavendish established communications, decided that the Abaknonian was no threat and persuaded him to summon his fellow *Caciques* to trade. Messengers sped away on their outrigger canoes and a short while later the other chiefs appeared, accompanied by a little armada carrying 'hens and hogs'. These were offered for sale rather than as gifts, and Pretty recorded the prices: 'they took for every hog (which they call *Balboye*) eight rials of plate, and for every hen or cock one riall of plate.' Every man on the *Desire* had money to burn, and they enjoyed an idyllic day riding at anchor 'doing nothing but buying roots, coconuts, hens, hogs, and such things as they brought, refreshing ourselves marvellously well'.[14]

While Cavendish's company feasted, the prisoners he'd taken in America plotted their escape. The Abaknon could be bribed to carry messages to the Spanish in Cavite, now only a day's sail away. Alonso de Valladolid, the Spanish pilot from the *Santa Ana*, wrote a warning letter to his compatriots, informing them of the tragedy he had witnessed in Baja California, and cautioning them to get their galleons and defences in order. He hid the letter in his sea-chest while he waited for an opportune moment to send it ashore.

He was betrayed by Nicolas Rodrigo, the Portuguese pilot that Cavendish had taken alongside Valladolid. Rodrigo had decided to cast his lot in with Cavendish and conferred 'with our General in secret' before leading him to the hidden letter. Cavendish opened it and read it aloud. After issuing his warning, Valladolid had begged his readers to rescue him. Cavendish, he told them, was down to a single ship and if they could surprise the *Desire* at anchor 'they should dispatch her', for she was lightly manned, and her 'men but weak'. Finally, Valladolid pointed out that, if they let the *Desire* escape, 'within few years they must make account to have their town besieged and sacked with an army of English'.[15]*

Captives were expected to behave honourably until they were ransomed. Spying, and attempting to make direct contact with the captor's enemies, were forbidden. Valladolid had not only

* Valladolid also gave away the destination of the *Content* in his letter, which, he wrote, 'was gone for the North-west passage, standing in 55 degrees'.

sinned against honour but had also aimed to disclose Cavendish's weaknesses. If the Spanish knew how few men he had left, and how much treasure he was carrying, they might be ready to brave his guns, and the odds would be on their side. After interrogating Valladolid, and deciding he was both guilty and expendable – Rodrigo was a better pilot for the next leg of his expedition – 'our General willed that he should be hanged which was accordingly performed the 16 of January'.[16]

The *Desire* spent nine days at anchor off Capul while her sails were repaired, and she stocked up with provisions and filled her casks. Francis Pretty, well fed and content, was fascinated by the Abaknons, whose men had the novel custom of inserting nails through the ends of their penises: 'every man and man-child among them hath a nail of Tin thrust quite through the head of his privy part ... which is driven through... when they are young, and the place growth up again, without any pain to the child: and they take this nail out and in as occasion serveth.' Pretty and his crewmates bought a penis-nail as a souvenir, previously the property of 'a son of one of the kings which was the age of ten years'. When he questioned the Abaknon about this unusual custom, they explained that it had been introduced 'at the request of the women... who finding their men to be given to the foul sin of Sodomy, desired some remedy against that mischief'. Their inventiveness in adornment, however, was spoiled by their religious beliefs. 'These people wholly worship the devil,' Pretty noted, 'and often times have conference with him, which appeareth unto them in most ugly and monstrous shape.'[17]

On 23 January, Cavendish made ready to leave. He summoned the Abaknon chiefs and made a speech. He told them that he and his company 'were English men, and enemies to the Spaniards and thereupon spread his Ensign and sounded up the drums, which they much marvelled at'. In reply, the Abaknon promised him that 'both themselves and all the islands there about to aide him, whensoever he should come again to overcome the Spaniards'.

Cavendish then ensured that they were paid in full for the provisions they had delivered to the *Desire* and, according to Mangabay, gave each chief a bonus of eight pesos, telling them 'that they were coming back in two years so they should know and remember their flag'.[18] The bonuses were received with joy, as was the news 'that we were enemies to the Spaniards', and the islanders 'rowed about our ship to shew us pleasure'. To signal his departure, Cavendish 'caused a saker to be shot off, whereat they wondered, and with great contentment took their leaves of us'.[19]

Francisco Mangabay escaped from the *Desire* shortly after his master, Valladolid, had been executed. He hurried to Manila, carrying the alarming news of the loss of the *Santa Ana* – which hadn't been heard of since she'd sailed from Cavite seven months previously – and the presence of her destroyer in the Philippines. A debate arose among the *Audiencia* of Manila, a council composed of its royal officers and senior clergy, over how to respond. The Bishop of Manila, Fray Domingo de Salazar, argued that they should assemble an overwhelming force from their ample resources of ships and men, hunt down the Lutheran and take vengeance on him. Others in the *Audiencia,* however, favoured caution, not ready to trust the evidence of a slave. Although only one small, if heavily armed, ship had appeared, who could be certain that she wasn't simply a scout at the head of a large English fleet?[20]

As the debate raged, and no action was taken, Cavendish closed in on Manila. He too was faced with a dilemma: while he wanted to make his presence known by performing at least a token act of aggression, he didn't want to be drawn into a fight with the Spanish. He lacked enough men to be sure of winning and had too much to lose if he played his hand wrong.

The opportunity to make a nuisance of himself without taking too great a risk appeared just short of Manila Bay when a Spanish frigate crossed his path, and he ran her down. She sailed into a patch of calm water, furled her sails, 'banked up with her oars' and made a dash for the shallows.[21] Cavendish sent a boat after her crewed by a dozen armed men, which chased her into an estuary, where she was lost. As they searched for her, they encountered a native craft carrying a Spaniard, who they kidnapped. However, the estuary was full of sand banks and shoals and, as they picked their way around it, at times having to leap overboard and push their grounded boat clear of a hazard, 'there shewed upon the sand a band of soldiers' bearing 'an ensign having a red cross like the flag of England'. A detachment of this force manned the hidden frigate and rowed out to attack Cavendish's men, who retreated to the protection of the *Desire's* cannon.

Cavendish would have counterattacked and obliterated so small a threat had he met it earlier in his expedition, but he could not risk anything in his current circumstances. Instead, he sent a letter ashore, threatening to return with fire and sword and take his vengeance. The letter was caried by Lope de Arjoma, the Spaniard his men had kidnapped on their foray. Arjoma was, according to Pretty, 'a very simple soul' who had spent much of his life in a hospital on account of his [mental] handicap and was so tongue-tied that he 'could answer to very little that he was asked'.[22] His limitations made him, from Cavendish's point of view, an excellent bearer of unpleasant news: he was both impossible to question, and a symbol of bad luck.

Arjoma handed Cavendish's letter to Manuel Lorenzo de Lemos, the *capitane* of the Panay yard, where the *Santa Ana* had been built, and where a new Manila galleon, the *Santiago*, was taking shape on the stocks. The *Santiago* was almost complete, lacking only a few essential iron fittings for her rudder, and Lemos had assembled and armed his shipyard workers to defend her. This makeshift force with its improvised banner was the 'band of soldiers' that Pretty had recorded as having forced Cavendish to withdraw his men.

Lemos forwarded the letter, together with a modest summary of his own achievements, to the *Audiencia* of Manila, where it caused both fury and angst. Ink wells boiled as officials, priests and merchants scratched letters to King Philip in Spain, fulminating against the Lutheran corsair who'd struck at his empire on both sides of the Pacific, enumerating their losses and begging for protection. The sack of the *Santa Ana* had been 'one of the worst disasters that this land has suffered'. 'The loss has caused great poverty and distress in this city, and among its inhabitants and soldiers'.[23] Impoverishment and sorrow were compounded by the presumed deaths of relatives and friends, who'd been abandoned by a monster amid cannibals on a savage coast.

The damage to Spanish honour, however, had been even greater. Cavendish had vaunted in his letter that, as well as destroying the *Santa Ana*, he'd 'left the coasts of Peru and Nueva España utterly ruined'. He had also boasted that he'd strung up Almendrales, the Canon of Manila, as evidence that his cause was sanctified by his faith. Finally, he'd threatened to 'return soon to drive us all hence, and to destroy the nest that we have made'.[24] He would bring enough gunpowder to blast their town into the sea. To rub salt into their wounds, Cavendish had accompanied words with actions and, 'In testimony of his prowess and our misfortune', had hung some of the 'silks, brocades, and gold discs which he had seized as plunder' from the *Santa Ana*, along the rail of the *Desire* as he sailed through Filipino waters.[25]

The Bishop of Manila was particularly bitter over Cavendish's depredations. In a letter to King Philip, he grieved that

> an English youth of about twenty-two years, with a wretched little vessel of a hundred tonnes and forty or fifty companions, should dare to come to my own place of residence, defy us, and boast of the damage that he had wrought… The belief here… is that God is chastising us for our sins, and is making us the laughing-stock of other nations, who have all hitherto stood in such fear of us.[26]

After expressing his distress, the bishop turned to recriminations. He repeated the points he had made in the debate among the *Audiencia*. The Spanish had substantial forces in and around Manila – more than enough to capture a small and undermanned privateer – yet they had done nothing. These forces had been withheld, the bishop told Philip, after the *Audiencia* had concluded that the *Desire* – despite all the evidence to the contrary – might be the lead ship of an English fleet heading their way, and that it was better to sit tight rather than commit themselves, in case they woke up to find that the horizon was studded with the sails of rapacious heretics and they had nothing left to fight them with. Lemos, who also wrote to Philip, was of the same opinion as the bishop and listed the resources that could have been deployed against a man he'd driven off with a troop of workers from his shipyard. The Philippines, he told Philip, held 'six settlements, one master of camp, thirty five captains, three galleys, and three ships with high freeboard, the smallest of which is of three hundred tonnes burden, besides many frigates and native ships, powder and weapons, and four hundred soldiers' – more than enough to run down a little English privateer.[27]

As a ray of hope in an otherwise sombre picture, Bishop Salazar told his king that he doubted that Cavendish could make his way home either quickly or safely. He was seconded by other correspondents, who noted that the course ahead through Indonesian waters was full of hazards. Although Cavendish's skill at navigation had been impressive when crossing the Pacific, this was attributed to his affiliation with the Antichrist rather than the expertise of his captive pilots who – it was presumed – had refused to assist a heretic. He was sure to be wrecked as he tried to find a way into and across the Indian Ocean.

15

A Terrestrial Paradise

Lombok Straits

THOMAS CAVENDISH LEFT PHILIPPINE WATERS on 29 January 1588, and the *Desire* spent the following month picking her way south through narrow channels between coral reefs, with fickle winds and hot and humid airs. Thomas Fuller's sailing rutter is crammed with frequent course changes and warnings of 'shoal-water' and 'great currents'.[1] Meanwhile, the 'extreme heat and intemperateness of the Climate' rotted the provisions and sickness spread among her company. The first to die was John Gameford, a cooper by trade, followed by the valiant Captain Havers, who had led the rearguard action at Quintero. Havers passed away on Ash Wednesday from 'a most fervent and pestilent ague, which held him furiously some seven or eight days, to the no small grief of our General'.[2] His body was 'shrouded in a sheet', prayers were said, cannon were fired and he was 'heaved overboard with great lamentation'. Many others in the company 'fell marvellously sick, and so continued in very great pain', as the *Desire* inched down the coast of Borneo towards the Lombok Straits.

Cavendish had decided not to risk sailing to the Spice Islands, which lay to his east. Although he might trade his silks there for nutmeg and pepper, his company was now too reduced in number, and the survivors too ill, to stake his winnings on a diversion through dangerous waters. The last English vessel to travel that course had been Drake's *Golden Hind*, who'd impaled herself on the Mulapatia Reef, south of Peling Island. To lighten her, Drake had ordered three tonnes of cloves and eight cannon to be thrown overboard, representing 'as much wealth' (according to Francis Pretty) 'as would break the heart of a miser to think on it'.[3] Instead, Cavendish elected to sail to the Lombok Straits, the gateway to the Indian Ocean. There was the possibility of acquiring gemstones on his chosen route, which might compensate for any missed opportunities with spices and, as importantly, the chance to make contact with regional potentates and establish alliances that could be built upon in future voyages.

The *Desire* passed through the Lombok Straits on 1 March and dropped anchor 'under the South west parts of Java Major'.[4] Cavendish knew he was in Moslem territory and, when he led a landing party ashore, he included the African slave he'd liberated from the *Santa Ana* who could speak 'Morisco' (Arabic). Before he touched land, he chanced upon a fishing boat, which he hailed and his interpreter managed a conversation with its crew. Once communications had been established, Cavendish asked where he might find fresh water, and was given directions to a nearby source. He then told the fishermen to pass the message to their ruler that he had come to trade for provisions, and 'for diamonds, pearls, or rich jewels', for which Cavendish would offer 'either gold or other merchandise in exchange'. He loitered off Java, waiting for an answer, and a week later several canoes paddled out to the *Desire*, laden with fresh fruit, and an invitation from the Rajah of Balamboam, who ruled the region, to sail a little way up the coast to a port where he could be received with due decorum. Cavendish complied and, as he stood in for the port, he was met by a flotilla of canoes, with a royal canoe at its head carrying the Rajah's vizier. The vizier gestured to the craft astern of him and explained that he had brought token offers of food and drink and would return with as much as they might need in four days' time. The fresh provisions were received with the usual pleasure, and the alcohol with especial interest. Cavendish's company was working its way through the heady Spanish wines they'd taken from the *Santa Ana*, and there was always room aboard for a new alcoholic beverage. The Javan Arak* stunned them. It was 'as strong as any aqua vitae, and as clear as any rock water', and quickly became a favourite tipple.[5]

Cavendish invited the vizier aboard the *Desire* and had him serenaded by his musicians when he stepped onto her deck. The

* Palm wine.

vizier was an imposing figure, wearing 'a piece of dyed linen cloth folded up like unto a Turk's turban' round his head, and nothing else but a sarong. His bare chest was 'carved with the broad arrow upon it'. He carried a message of friendship from the Rajah, and Cavendish banqueted him 'most royally' 'with the choice of many and sundry conserves' and 'wines both sweet and other'. While they were feasting, Cavendish told his guest that he and his company were English traders who had 'been at China' – a white lie that gave a provenance to the spoils of war in his holds – and that they were travelling 'to discover' new lands and new peoples.[6] The vizier explained that there were already Europeans in his master's dominions – two Portuguese factors, who dealt in spices and who would be able to give him a proper account of the Raja and his kingdom – and promised to summon them.

The vizier spent the night on board the *Desire* and Cavendish put on a show at the change of the watch, commanding 'every man in his ship' to load their arquebuses and fire a volley.[7] The noise of over forty weapons crashed out, accompanied by the simultaneous roar of a saker. The spectators' ears rung as flames shot from muzzles and lit up the night, and gun smoke shrouded the decks of the *Desire*. Cavendish's audience were mesmerised by this shrewd demonstration of firepower, which 'was no small marvel to these heathen people'. Although familiar with European ships and weapons, they'd never before seen so great a concentration of firearms in a single ship, nor so prodigal an expenditure of gunpowder.

The following morning, the vizier returned to his master with a favourable opinion of the strange vessel that had appeared within his territory. The Rajah responded by sending his own canoes to the *Desire* after the promised four days had elapsed, 'so deeply laden with victuals as they could swim'.[8] His gifts included 'two great live oxen, half a score of wonderfully great and fat hogs' and hens, ducks, geese, eggs, citrus fruit, salt 'and a great store of wine and aquavitae'. The flotilla was headed by the royal canoe carrying the vizier and the Portuguese traders he'd summoned, who sat together cross-legged beneath a silk awning.

Cavendish welcomed the royal party aboard. The traders were a gift from heaven. They could tell him what inroads the Portuguese and Spanish had made in Java, the disposition of local rulers towards them both, the loyalty – or not – of the Portuguese to their Spanish overlords and help him to judge how easy or difficult it might be to establish an English presence in the East Indies. His company, meanwhile, studied the traders when they climbed onto the *Desire*, 'for we had not seen any Christian that was our friend' for eighteen months. Both 'were of middle stature, and men of marvellous proper personage'. In Pretty's opinion, they dressed 'very decently, only their bare legs excepted'. They wore loose jerkins and hose stretching from the waist to the ankle with 'very fair and fine white' lawn over-shirts, ornamented 'with falling bands on the same'. The traders explained that they'd adopted this mixture of eastern and western costume for both personal and political reasons: it was then Lent and they were practising self-mortification, hence the bare feet, and the rest of their clothing marked them out as men of consequence in Java.[9]

Cavendish treated his guests 'singularly well, with banquets and Music' then sounded them out.[10] It transpired that the traders hated the Spanish, who they believed had subjugated their own country. They were equally pleased to see friendly faces, and wanted news of Portugal, even if it was nearly two years old. What had happened to Don Antonio, the pretender to the Portuguese throne, who they recognised as their king? Was he still alive? The Spanish had told them he was dead. Cavendish allayed their fears: Don Antonio was living in exile in England with an 'honourable allowance' from Queen Elizabeth. In return for this welcome news, the traders promised Cavendish that, if he could bring a fleet of ships like the *Desire* back to Java, he could be sure of finding support among both local rulers and Portuguese expatriates. Together, they could drive the Spanish from the region.

The traders also talked about Rajah Balamboam, who had granted them permission to trade in his dominions. He was 'a man held in great majesty and fear' they said, the stern but just ruler of a significant amount of territory, and husband to a hundred wives.[11] The Rajah was a hundred and fifty years old, and it had been a combination of his great age and marital duties that had prevented him from meeting Cavendish in person. The traders told other stories about the customs of the land, which Pretty, who loved the exotic, noted down. When a Rajah of Balamboam died, he learned, his spouses would gather together, the chief wife would throw a ball into the air and the wives would commit mass-suicide on the spot where the ball landed. Each killed herself with a *Kris*,* 'as sharp as a razor', which she drove into her heart, and together the dying wives bathed 'themselves with their own blood' and fell 'grovelling on their faces' to 'so end their days'. 'This thing is as true', Pretty added, 'as it seemeth to be strange.'[12]

The Rajah's warriors were equally devoted and fanatical. If any failed him, for whatever reason and even if their motives had been pure, they were decapitated immediately. Hence, they preferred the uncertain risk of death in combat to the certainty of being killed for disappointing their ruler. If they were pierced by a sword or lance, they would run themselves onto the weapon, so as to reach their enemies with their *Krises* and annihilate them while hastening their own deaths. Their zeal appealed to the gentleman in Pretty, who also believed in dying for a good cause. One day these warriors might be England's allies.

After entertaining the vizier and the Portuguese, Cavendish sent them away with generous presents, gifting the traders 'some church ornaments and other valuable articles' from Peru.[13] He saluted his guests' departure with three demi-culverins, which was probably as many of his heavy guns as he could fire at one time with his much-reduced crew. He also gave the traders letters to

* A traditional dagger with a wavy blade, 'both a weapon and a spiritual object'.

Portuguese officials in Malacca before setting a course across the Indian Ocean for southern Africa.

One of his letters reached Manuel de Sousa Coutinho, Portuguese Viceroy of India, who shared its contents in a letter of his own to King Philip II. Cavendish had stated, Coutinho told Philip, that he had come to explore the region and seek out opportunities for commerce. Unlike Cavendish's previous missives, there were no threats to return with fire and the sword. When the traders were questioned by the auditor of Malacca about their encounter with the interloper, they confirmed that Cavendish had played the diplomat rather than the warmonger: 'it was ascertained that the purpose of [his] coming was none other than trade, exploration, and prizes'. Cavendish had, however, 'asked particularly' about the principal European settlements in 'Aceh, the straits of Meca and Malacca, and their fortifications', indicating interests beyond commerce alone. Finally, the traders had reported that Cavendish had been plain as to his next moves. According to Coutinho, he'd 'lay his course to the island of Santa Helena, following the course taken by the Portuguese vessels'. Although Coutinho didn't demand galleons and armies for protection like Philip's other Asian correspondents, he implied their need. 'Pray God he come not hither again,' he concluded, 'as an example for the daring of others—although the interest they have in doing so is so great, that I fear this navigation cannot be stopped without much trouble.'[14]

'The rest of March and all the month of April,' Pretty recorded, 'we spent in traversing that mighty and vast sea, between the Isle of Java and the main of Africa.'[15] Although he made only a couple of pages of entries in his journal over that period, his vocabulary was changing. The gentleman-adventurer from Ely with more sea miles under his belt than all but a handful of men then living was learning how to sail. The *Desire* was shorthanded, and her cargo so valuable to every man on board that it was no time to stand on ceremony. Nautical terms crept into Pretty's journal, as did a greater awareness of the motions and management of the ship. He was no longer thinking like a passenger. The sailors also taught him how to observe 'the heavens, the Crosier or South-pole, the other stars, the fowls, which are marks unto the Seamen of fair weather, foul weather, approaching of lands or islands, the winds, the tempests, the rains and thunders, with the alterations of tides and currents'.[16] His progress in matters maritime is evident in his description of the Cape of Good Hope on the southern tip of Africa (sighted by the *Desire* after nine weeks at sea), which reads like an excerpt from Thomas Fuller's rutter:

> The 16. day of May about 4. of the clock in the afternoon the wind came up at East a very stiff gale, which held until it was Saturday with as much wind as the ship could go before: at which time by six of the clock in the morning we espied the promontory or headland called the Cape de Buena Esperanza, which is a reasonable high land, and at the Westermost point a little off the main do shew two hummocks, the one upon the other, and three other hummocks lying further off into the sea, yet low land between and adjoining unto the sea.[17]

After rounding the Cape of Good Hope, Cavendish steered a course northwest, aiming for the island of St Helena, arriving on 8 June, following what now seemed to Pretty to have been a routine voyage of a mere fifteen hundred miles.

The *Desire* was the first English ship to reach St Helena. This small island with lush valleys and barren mountains, formed by the caldera of an extinct volcano, had been uninhabited when the Portuguese chanced upon it in 1502, and they had kept its location a secret from their competitors and enemies for over eighty years. St Helena was the perfect staging post for their *carracks*, the vast galleons used in the spice trade, travelling home from Asia. It had protected anchorages, sure supplies of fresh water, and timber for repairs and fuel. The Portuguese introduced pigs, goats, partridges and pheasants to the island, planted terraces of fruit trees in its valleys and seeded the ground between them with garden vegetables and herbs. St Helena's volcanic soil was gloriously fecund, the trees and vegetables seemed to cultivate themselves, and the hogs multiplied in the foothills of its mountains while flocks of goats occupied their flanks and summits. The Portuguese forbade settlers, lest they proliferated like the other introduced species and ate the island clean. And, since they did not expect visitors, this Eden was left unguarded. It had no permanent residents – when a ship passed, it would put a handful of its sick ashore and pick up any men who'd been beached by previous ships and since recovered their health.

When Cavendish landed on the northwest of St Helena, he found a small chapel and thirty or forty empty houses, 'built to lodge the Portuguese on their coming from the East Indies'. The only inhabitants were four invalids, who tended the vegetables and cleaned the houses and church. Out of habit, Cavendish's men 'beat down the altar and cross that stood in the chapel', before dispersing to harvest the island's bounties.[18] For the first time since leaving Plymouth, they did not have to trade or fight with strangers to obtain their food. The orchards around the deserted settlement were laden with ripe fruit including familiar European varieties that they hadn't tasted since Puna. There were figs, oranges, lemons and pomegranates, all 'planted carefully and very artificially with very pleasant walks under and between them', lined with beds of melons, radishes, parsley, basil 'and many special good herbs' all watered by a clear brook of pure water.[19]

Cavendish's company thought St Helena a 'terrestrial paradise' and passed a week killing game and picking fruits and melons. The partridge were as big and tame as hens, and almost as easy to shoot. The goats meanwhile traversed the hills in herds 'almost a mile long'. Some of the alpha males were the size of mules, each 'with a mane like a horse and a beard hanging down to the very ground'. Although they were swift and surefooted, capable of climbing up cliffs so steep 'that a man would think it a thing impossible for any living thing to go there', 'We took and killed many of them for all their swiftness'. The feral pigs, meanwhile, were 'very wild and very fat, and of a marvellous bigness'. Although they too were flighty, they were traced to their wallows and shot as they 'laid in the mire'.[20]

Cavendish took observations while his men indulged themselves and marked St Helena onto his chart together with a compass rose beside it, showing bearings to the Cabo Verde islands and Sierra Leone to the north, and Brazil and Patagonia to the west and south.[21] The island was a wonderful self-regenerating storehouse of provisions, and it was perfectly placed to either resupply a fleet, or to capture carracks returning from Asia. Although small and a long way from any other land, St Helena stood in the course of the trade winds and, now that Cavendish had fixed its latitude, he was confident he could return. He'd also learned that the carracks usually stopped there every May.

Once the *Desire* had been loaded with provisions, firewood and drinking water, she sailed for England on 20 June 1588. Her crew left a bucket and a sword behind, which were found eleven months later by mariners from the *Santa Cruz*, a carrack of sixteen hundred tonnes, on its way back to Lisbon.[22] The Portuguese were mystified. Had these items been left as messages? Were they, together, a single coded message? After considering both their symbolic and metaphysical significance, they could only agree that the bucket and sword had not been left by accident and – if nothing else – were proof that St Helena was secret no more.

Cavendish had a following wind all the way to the equator, which the *Desire* crossed on 4 July. She took a further week to pass through a band of light and variable breezes before she picked up the trade winds, and stood out for the Azores, which were sighted on 24 August. Cavendish had travelled over thirty-three thousand sea miles, and less than a thousand remained. He was close to winning the gamble he'd made when he had left England two years before. If the benign conditions continued, he could reach Plymouth in a fortnight. The *Desire* was sound, he had plenty of provisions, drinking water and alcohol, enough powder and shot to see off any hostile vessel, and the speed to outrun an enemy galleon should they cross paths.

A week's sail away from Plymouth, Cavendish hailed a Flemish merchant ship that, NH recorded, 'told us the joyful news of our Fleet's good success against the huge army of the Spaniards'. This was wonderful, if puzzling information. What fleet had overcome which Spanish army? Although Queen Elizabeth had given Cavendish permission to leave England partly on the understanding that he would perform his patriotic duty of harrying the Spanish in distant waters, he hadn't expected to come home to all-out war. His company too were dreaming of returning to the country they'd left in 1586, albeit fixed in time exactly how they'd left it, with their wives still faithful and children still living, rather than to a battle zone.

Two days later, Cavendish got more news from a privateer out of Southampton under Captain Clarke, who had just taken a Brazilian prize. Clarke told him the story of the 'invincible' Spanish Armada carrying an army of invasion, which had been defeated and driven into the North Sea, and the ships' companies celebrated the English victory together with drinks: 'We took some refreshing of them', NH wrote, which was 'recompensed with treble courtesy'.[23] On the *Desire*, however, the general exultation was shaded with disappointment. Her company realised that their achievements had been eclipsed by recent events, and that they would not be the only mariners in England with stories to tell.

16

The Will of God

English Channel

The news that Cavendish and his company heard from Captain John Clarke was as startling as it was unexpected. That July, the Spanish had assembled an immense fleet of a hundred and thirty-seven ships, including two dozen thousand-tonne galleons, carrying nineteen thousand soldiers, hundreds of cavalry horses and siege trains of heavy cannon to blow holes in the walls of London, and had set sail for England's south coast. This Armada had intended to pass up the Channel, link up with an army under the Duke of Parma, which was waiting in Flanders, and launch a combined amphibious assault on Kent.[1]

On 20 July, while Cavendish was in transit from St Helena to the Azores, the Armada had appeared off Cornwall. It had been met by the largest fleet that England had ever assembled, commanded by Lord Charles Howard of Effingham, and composed almost equally of Royal Navy ships and English privateers. Howard was a veteran courtier who had served his cousin, Queen Elizabeth, by land and sea and who Cavendish knew personally from his gambling days. Described as 'Personable, vain, brave, courtly, prodigiously nepotistic, and acutely sensitive to perceived assaults upon his dignity', Howard was also absolutely trustworthy, thorough, if cautious, and accustomed to commanding both soldiers and warships.[2] He was a stickler for form, believing that even naval battles should be started with due chivalry. He'd opened proceedings by issuing a formal challenge to the Duke of Medina Sidonia, commander of the Armada, by sending the barque *Disdain* to perform the nautical equivalent of throwing down the gauntlet.

Medina Sidonia's fleet was drawn up off the coast of Devon and downwind of Howard in a *lunula* formation, resembling a waning crescent moon with trailing horns. Its largest warships and transports cruised in close formation at its centre, sailing so near to each other that, according to an Italian mercenary aboard a galleon in their midst, 'you could hardly see the sea… The masts and rigging, the towering sterns and prows which in height and number were so great that they dominated the whole naval concourse.' This astonishing spectacle 'caused horror, mixed with wonder' in the eyes of its beholders.[3]

The *Disdain* performed her role of challenge-bearer with suitable composure, sailing between the horns of the *lunula* and firing a single shot at the *Rata Santa Maria Encoronada*, a galleon twice her size. Medina Sidonia, also a stickler for form, signalled his acceptance of Howard's challenge by hoisting his battle flag, a consecrated banner decorated with the arms of Spain, images of Christ Crucified and the Virgin Mary, and the legend *'Exsurge, domine et vindica causam tuam'* ('Arise, O Lord, and vindicate thy cause'). Once the courtesies of war had been completed to his satisfaction, Howard led his fleet into the attack. He opened fire on the nearest galleon at a range of three hundred paces and the smoke from his broadside followed its projectiles in a dense grey cloud. After firing his culverins, Howard held his course, and the next ship in the English line behaved the same way, shooting at long range, then standing off to reload.

Medina Sidonia was shocked by this ungallant conduct, protesting (in his letters) that the English had discharged their cannon then darted away 'without attempting to grapple', which, in his mind, was the only honourable way to behave.[4] There was glory in choosing to fight a powerful enemy on his own terms. His flagship, the *San Martín*, was a floating fortress whose storeyed forecastle and towering aftercastle took up three-quarters of her deck. He'd loaded both fore- and aft-castles with musketeers and arquebusiers and had also posted three hundred marksmen on the decks and in the rigging. The castles were stocked with grappling irons attached to coils of rope that were used to hook enemy vessels and draw them in, and with pikes, spears, swords, shields, pistols and daggers for hand-to-hand fighting. The gundeck meanwhile sported 'ship smashers', heavy short-range cannon that fired huge projectiles and went off with so loud a roar and so much smoke that both the gunners and their targets were blinded, deafened and stunned. If only the English would do the right thing, then God would give him strength to do the rest.

This first encounter between Howard and Medina Sidonia was watched by crowds from the Devon coast, who saw a puzzling struggle partially shrouded in gun smoke, pricked with red flashes from the mouths of cannon, their sound arriving as a rumbling wave. Despite the distant thunder and lightning, nothing cataclysmic happened. There were no dramatic sinkings and only one of the distant ships, the galleon *San Salvador,* caught fire. The *lunula* kept its shape and continued eastwards up the Channel, while Howard's fleet followed on its heels.

Fighting continued in a sporadic and inconclusive fashion for several days. Howard's ships used up their shot, and the Armada continued its progress along the Channel, averaging about two-and-a-half miles per hour. Howard sent desperate messages ashore, begging for more ammunition. The people rallied round, scoured their farms and villages, and sent him leather bags of scrap iron and plough chains to feed his weapons.

On 25 July, Sir George Carey, governor of the Isle of Wight, reported that he'd seen 'both fleets becalmed about six leagues' to the south of his island.[5] Medina Sidonia had reached his first objective. However, Howard succeeded in preventing him from entering the Solent, the channel between the island and the mainland where the Armada could anchor and attack either coast, by setting a trap using the thousand-tonne *Triumph*, his largest warship, as bait. The *Triumph* lured Medina Sidonia towards the Owers Bank, a notorious set of shoals to the east of the Solent, and, although Medina Sidonia managed to tack his ships before they were wrecked, the wind was now blowing him away from the Isle of Wight. He sailed for Calais in France, where he could link up with the Duke of Parma, commander of the invasion force he was to convey to England, rather than trying to turn the *lunula* around.

Howard followed the Armada to Calais and brought his fleet to rest 'a long culverin shot apart' from Medina Sidonia's fleet.[6] He decided to deploy 'hell-burners' – fireships – to drive the galleons from their anchors. He bought, on the queen's account, eight privateers that were stuffed full of combustibles, sprinkled with gunpowder, their cannon double-shotted, then set alight and loosed against the Armada after nightfall. Carried by the tide and a faint west breeze, these apparitions sent a wave of fear through the Spanish. 'Eight ships with artificial machines on board', the officer Pedro Calderón recalled, 'came towards us all in flames, burning furiously in the bows, with the mainsails and foresails set and the rudders lashed.'[7]

But Medina Sidonia had anticipated Howard and had set up a curtain of frigates between their fleets. Working in pairs, the frigates would tow any fireships clear as soon as they approached. He told his captains that, if a fireship got through the defensive curtain, they were to slip and buoy their anchors, stand out to sea and return to their marks once the danger had passed. The frigates succeeded in diverting the first two hell-burners, but the other six kept on coming. Some galleons crashed together in their hurry to slip anchor, and the *Rata*, which had received the *Disdain's* opening shot, was disabled and driven ashore. Chaos ensued, and Medina Sidonia spent the rest of the night and the following morning rounding up his fleet.

After the Armada had regrouped off the port of Gravelines in western Flanders, Howard attacked again. This time his ships closed to within a hundred and twenty paces before firing their cannon, and this time they hit their targets. Like Cavendish, Howard found the effect of his artillery was magnified as the distance to its targets diminished. Pedro Estrada, aboard the *San Marcos*, watched as Don Felipe de Cordova was hit by a cannonball 'that struck off his head and splashed out his brains'. A further twenty-four sailors on his ship perished in the same broadside. Calderón meanwhile was dazed by the weight of iron flying through the sky: 'so tremendous was the fire that over two hundred balls' 'enough to shatter to pieces a rock' struck his ship 'killing and wounding many men, disabling and dismounting three guns, and destroying much rigging'.[8] When the bombardment was at its most intense, Medina Sidonia took to his cabin, which had been padded with woolsacks to absorb the shrapnel and flying splinters, while priests stalked his flagship's deck, 'crucifixes in hand, confessing and absolving the dying'.[9] His company, meanwhile, shouted out to their opponents 'that they were cowards' for failing to grapple with them 'and, with opprobrious words, reproached them for their want of spirit, calling them Lutheran chickens'.[10]

The battle off Gravelines drove the Armada downwind of both Calais and its rendezvous with the Duke of Parma. While most of its galleons were still afloat, many had lost both masts and rigging and had been holed by gunfire in the action. Their hulls had sprung further leaks where they'd been pounded by cannonballs and been stressed by the shock of firing their own guns. Casualties mounted in the days after the fighting as wounds turned gangrenous. Everyone was hungry and thirsty. The provisions shipped in June, some already months old, were dwindling and rotting. Their water, from the same source, was foetid, and much of their wine had soured.

In this fragile condition, the Armada was forced into the North Sea by mounting winds from the southwest, which exploded into gales, and drove it north, north, always north towards Scotland. Off Newcastle, Medina Sidonia ordered his ships to throw the cavalry horses and mules that they were carrying overboard, as there was neither food nor water for them. A German vessel crossed their tracks and reported 'sailing through a sea filled with swimming mules and horses'.[11]

Howard tailed Medina Sidonia to the Firth of Forth, then withdrew south where his ships were pinned in harbours by the 'most violent storm as ever was seen at this time of year'. He too was running out of provisions. Sir Thomas Heneage, who'd learned 'by the news' of the deprivations in the fleet, reported that 'my Lord Admiral was driven to eat beans', and other officers to drink their own urine.[12] The mariners, moreover, hadn't been paid, and were falling ill. On 10 August, Howard wrote to Baron Burghley, the Lord High Treasurer of England, telling him that 'Sickness and mortality begin wonderfully to grow amongst us'. 'It would grieve any man's heart,' he continued, 'to see them that have served so valiantly to die so miserably.'[13]

The privateers in his fleet took matters into their own hands and slipped away as soon as they could. Captain John Clarke was at sea by mid-August, and the cargo of sugar on the prize he'd taken just before meeting Cavendish on 24 August more than compensated his company for their recent hardships.

17

The Return of the *Desire*

Atlantic, Western Approaches

THE STORM THAT HAD TRAPPED Howard's ships in port was followed by a series of storms worse yet than any others in that unusually tempestuous 'Year of the Eights',*[1] which caught the *Desire* when she was just a few days' sail away from Plymouth. Both Francis Pretty, who'd now nearly sailed around the world twice, and NH were stunned by its violence. It was as if fate had placed a last obstacle on their path to fame. Pretty recorded 'a terrible tempest which carried away most part of our sails'; NH that they'd suffered 'as terrible a night as ever men endured'. Although the winds had shredded the *Desire's* canvas into rags, they made 'as good shift as we could with certain old sails we had' and limped on the starting point of their expedition. Cavendish reckoned that he'd 'endured more hazard and trouble in two nights upon our coast than in his long navigation'. After this final ordeal, 'The 9 day of September 1588', Thomas Fuller wrote in his rutter, 'we arrived… in the haven of *Plymouth* in safety, by the gracious and most merciful protection of the Almighty, to whom therefore be rendered immortal praise and thanksgiving now and for ever. Amen.'[2]

Two years and two months previously, Cavendish had sailed from Plymouth with three ships and one hundred and twenty-five men, dreaming of gold and glory. The forty or so survivors on the *Desire* had realised their dreams. All were rich enough to buy themselves a tavern or a manor. The rest of their companions had

* The advent of 1588, the 'great wonderful and fatal year of our age', had been anticipated and feared since 1496 when Regiomontanus, the German mathematician and stargazer, had noted that it would be riven with dangerous astral conjunctions, marked by portentous Christian numerology, and promised turmoil.

died far from home or languished in dungeons on the other side of the world, prisoners of the Inquisition.

The survivors had had a lifetime of adventures on their circumnavigation. They'd fought cannibal tribes in Africa and Patagonia, the Spanish by land and sea, and had been wounded by flint arrows, lead slugs and steel blades; they'd eaten sealions, penguins, parrots, potatoes and iguana; they'd smoked tobacco and drunk chocolate and Arak; they'd burned ships, churches, houses and huts; they'd thrown enough silk to dress a coronation into the Pacific; they'd witnessed prodigies of nature, including volcanoes spewing fire into the sky and an earthquake that shook the sea beneath their ship; and they'd met, clashed and traded with a greater variety of cultures than they could have dreamed existed before they'd set off around the world.

The day he reached Plymouth, Cavendish sent a letter to Lord Hunsdon, Chamberlain to the Queen, summarising his achievements. It was a true vaunt, in the chivalric sense, enumerating feats of arms, acts of war and prizes won. 'It hath pleased the Almighty,' Cavendish wrote, 'to suffer me to circumpass the whole Globe of the World.'

> In which voyage, I have either discovered or brought certain intelligence of all the rich places of the world that ever were known or discovered by any Christian.
>
> I navigated along the coasts of Chile, Peru, and New Spain, where I made great spoils. I burnt and sunk nineteen ships, great and small. All the villages and towns that ever I landed at, I burnt and spoiled.[3]

For these paragraphs alone, the letter was gold. The English had not only seen off their enemy in home waters but had also struck at them in the most distant parts of their empire. Cavendish moreover had sunk more Spanish ships than Lord Howard's fleet. He'd also taken more prizes, including the fabulously wealthy

Santa Ana: 'being one of the richest of merchandise that ever sailed on those seas.'

Cavendish elaborated a little on his discoveries, which might be followed up both to England's advantage and the discomfort of her enemies:

> From the Cape of California, being the uttermost part of all New Spain, I navigated to the islands of the Philippines, hard upon the coast of China: of which country I have brought such intelligence as hath not been heard of in these parts. The stateliness and riches of which… I fear to make report of; least I should not be credited. […] I sailed along the islands of the Moluccas; where among some of the heathen people, I was well intreated. Where our countrymen may have trade as freely as the Portuguese… From thence, I passed by the Cape of Good Hope and found out, by the way homeward, the island of Saint Helena, where the Portuguese use to relieve themselves. And from that island, GOD hath suffered me to return into England.

His words were shocking news for King Philip and his Spanish and Portuguese subjects. Their trade in both Mexico and Asia was threatened, and their secret station mid-Atlantic had been discovered. Hunsdon recognised the propaganda value of Cavendish's letter, and had it translated into French and published in a pamphlet that also covered the Armada's losses in Ireland.

News of Cavendish's return sped along the south coast of England. On 12 September, Sir George Carey, an avid sponsor of privateers, wrote to his sister that 'We have a rich ship come into Plymouth. A young gentleman, one Mr Cavendish, who hath been at the West and East Indies, and hath been absent this 2 years and 6 weeks, is returned very rich; chiefly laden with silks; he hath musk and civet great store, some gold, and other goods.'[4] The news spread from England to Holland: James Digges wrote from Flushing to Peregrine Bertie, Thirteenth Baron Willoughby de Eresby, the English commander in the Dutch provinces, to tell him that 'Mr. Cavendish is back with only one ship, another having become separated from him during a storm, and two pinnaces being sunk for want of men. He is said to have brought greater riches than Sir Francis Drake did, and much of it gold bullion.'[5]

Meanwhile, the pamphlet with the French translation of Cavendish's letter to Hunsdon had reached Paris, where it was read by Don Bernadino de Mendoza, King Philip's ex-ambassador to England. This was the first the Spanish had heard of Cavendish's depredations – the furious letters describing his outrages in both Mexico and the Philippines had yet to reach Spain. The pamphlet put Mendoza in a quandary. He'd been posted to Paris to foment discord among the French by pitting Henri III, King of France against Henri, Duke of Guise, and had succeeded in taking his hosts to the brink of civil war. However, he'd been less than honest with his own king about the performance of the Armada. While its galleons were being wrecked in Ireland, he'd written to Philip telling him that the plan to invade England had been a brilliant success. The Lutheran Jezebel's best ships were decorating the seabed of the Channel, Sir Francis Drake had had his leg shot off and was either dead or in chains, Medina Sidonia had linked up with the Duke of Parma, the Catholics of England had risen up in support of their saviours and Elizabeth had abandoned her palace for the safety of an army camp.[6]

However, as the number of eyewitness accounts of Spanish losses and English celebrations mounted and reached Philip from other sources, Mendoza had had to adjust his narrative and confess to his king that the triumph he'd pictured had been a disaster. It was a good time to bury bad news, and Mendoza forwarded the pamphlet containing Cavendish's vaunts along with other printed matter that commemorated an English victory in the Narrow Seas. He added, in a short letter that followed:

> 'The booty brought back by Cavendish consisted of raw silks and spices, the value of which the English estimated at 1,000,000, but

as these goods are bulky, and the ships small, it is impossible that the value can nearly reach a half of it.'[7]

Philip also learned about Cavendish from Marco Antonio Messia, a Genoese working as a Spanish secret agent in London. In a long letter covering goings-on in the capital, Messia told the king that English privateers:

> 'will be encouraged by the coming of a gentleman named Cavendish, who three years ago sold some property of his and fitted out three ships which he took to the Straits of Magellan. He has now returned, very wealthy with gems, gold, and silver, to the value of 3,000,000 crowns, though others say only one million, which I deem more likely. But if it be only half that amount, it is quite enough to encourage others to seek similar adventures.'[8]

Meanwhile, news of the new circumnavigator rippled out across Europe. All of its trading nations were hungry for details of both the voyage and the discoveries it might have made, which their spies and diplomats did their best to supply. The Venetian ambassador in Paris, for instance, reported that Cavendish had returned with 'great wealth and also some natives from India, who they say accompanied him of their own accord through a desire to see the Queen'.[9] The Asians were a curiosity to the Venetians. Any matter that might help or hinder the spice trade piqued their interest. Since the natives weren't slaves, what could they be? Messengers? Hostages?

However, while his fame spread, Cavendish was immobilised in Plymouth and spent his twenty-eighth birthday on a sickbed. He was gravely ill with an unknown malady and had been further weakened by the burden of responsibility he'd carried for the previous two years. Cavendish was recognised by his men as an inspirational commander who led by example, but the extra energy he'd put into every engagement had wasted him. His condition is apparent in his cramped and blotched handwriting. In a letter sent on 8 October, nearly a month after his return, to Sir Francis Walsingham, principal secretary to Queen Elizabeth, Cavendish confesses that 'Of late, I have not been very well' and to reinforce the point his next word is blurred, as if he was beaded in sweat and shaken by a fever. 'At this present I thank GOD I am much better than I was,' he continues, although his writing shows that his quill was trembling, though 'not yet in such perfect health but that I mean to use the help of the physician' that Walsingham had sent to him 'for whose coming unto me, I am most heartily bound unto your Honour'.[10]

Once he'd thanked Walsingham, Cavendish proceeded to business. Rumours of the value of his prize had been growing, and he wanted Elizabeth's closest adviser to know that he was being scrupulously honest with the customs officers, with whom he'd agreed to pay a duty of five per cent on the *Desire's* cargo. This amounted to £900, implying that it was worth £18,000. However, the figure included neither the hundred and twenty thousand gold coins Cavendish had taken from the *Santa Ana* nor the many valuables that had been carried off the *Desire* before the customs officers had inspected her.

There were also, he told Walsingham in his letter, 'some things that I have kept from their sight for special causes', which he intended to 'make known' to him as soon as he reached London. As well as concealing some of his finds from customs, Cavendish advised Walsingham that he had gathered information of the greatest importance on his circumnavigation, of national interest, which 'shall not be known but unto your Honour', and could only be delivered face to face.[11]

After several weeks recuperating, Cavendish sailed the *Desire* round the south coast and into the Thames Estuary. On 12 November, he moored her at Greenwich by the royal palace, where the queen had commanded his presence. When he'd left England in 1586, he'd been on the periphery of her court, and now he was to be at its centre. Cavendish revered Elizabeth and had demonstrated his devotion to her in both action and word. He'd commemorated her Accession Day just under a year before with fireworks and a cannonade off Cabo de San Lucas, with only the miserable, marooned company of the *Santa Ana* for an audience; and his vaunting letter to Hunsdon had ended with a graceful submission of both his achievements and his person to his sovereign, 'For at this day, she is the most famous and victorious Prince that liveth in the world'.

He gave Elizabeth a memorable show. Flamboyance was the watchword at court, and Cavendish had both appreciated and practised it as a minor courtier. The *Desire* arrived in Greenwich under damask sails, with a standard sewn from pure silk and cloth of gold flying from her main mast. Her mariners wore blue silk suits and gold medallions on heavy gold chains around their necks. According to a Spanish spy, 'It was as if Cleopatra had been resuscitated. The only thing wanting was that the rigging should have been of silken rope.'[12] As the *Desire* came into her mooring, Cavendish 'fired off a great quantity of artillery', which, according to another spy, 'was a most beautiful sight'.[13]

After the thunder and lightning, he staged a banquet for Elizabeth aboard the *Desire* in a cabin 'hung with cloth of gold and silver' and 'marvellously rich' banners.[14] It was an exceptional privilege to be her host, all the more so for the intimacy of the surroundings. They dined off gold plate, serenaded by the ship's musicians. One Spanish spy reported that the queen was in great good humour, and 'she boasted more than I could repeat', while another claimed she had bragged that 'The king of Spain barks a good deal but does not bite. We care nothing for the Spaniards; their ships, loaded with silver and gold from the Indies, come hither after all.'[15]

The dinner was a triumph. Popular fame followed a queen's welcome and ballads describing Cavendish's exploits and his visit to Greenwich were rushed into print. Elizabethan ballads provided both news and entertainment, covering subjects ranging from deformed babies in the shires to momentous current events and the latest evolutions in theology.[16] They also celebrated the acts of the famous, or notorious, and people even commissioned ballads about themselves so as to be part of the news. They were printed in heavy black type on one side only of a single sheet of paper and were often decorated with a woodcut of an image appropriate to their theme – a buxom milkmaid, a public execution, a galleon in flames.

Cavendish was a prime subject for ballads. He'd chastised the Spanish and taught them that they did not own the Pacific Ocean, he'd robbed vain noblemen and cruel overlords of their luxuries and gold, and had made an appropriately splendid display before his queen. He was celebrated in not just one, but three, new tunes:

> A ballad of Master CAVENDISH'S Voyage, who by travel compassed the Globe of the World, arriving in England with abundance of treasure;
>
> A new Ballad of the famous and honourable coming of Master CAVENDISH'S ship, called the *Desire*, before the Queen's Majesty at her Court at Greenwich the 12th of November 1588, &c.'; and
>
> Captain ROBERTS – His Welcome of good will to Captain CAVENDISH.[17]

All three were being sung in London within weeks of his triumph at Greenwich. The balladeers who hawked them for a penny each on street corners, in markets, at fairs, in alehouses and taverns, and any other places where people gathered, formed their own tier in the Elizabethan underclasses, one rank above beggars. They were celebrated for their diversity in both appearance and performance. Their numbers included the blind, old, physically disabled and insane, as well as alcoholics and healthy young apprentices. Their voices were equally varied. Some sang with 'as harsh a noise as ever cart-wheel made';[18] others were renowned for their pure and sweet tones; the 'snuffling throat' of a celebrated 'noseless ballad woman' aroused pity; and the Barnes brothers of St Paul's Churchyard who roared out 'such adulterous ribaldry as chaste ears abhor to hear', one brother 'in a squeaking treble, the other in an ale-blown base', were cheered as they performed.[19]

The churchyard of St Paul's Cathedral, where the Barnes brothers sang, was the epicentre of the London book and ballad trades. Printers' shops faced onto it, there were book stalls in its centre, and booths sold pamphlets and ballads both alongside the cathedral's walls and crowded round its doors. Old St Paul's Cathedral was a huge gothic edifice, characterised by a long slender nave and double rows of flying buttresses. It had an odd, crippled appearance – like a man 'struck with the dead palsy on one side'[20] – having lost its spire to a lightning strike in 1561, which was presumed to have sprung from the fist of God, angry at the constant parade of vice that desecrated His house. The spire had burst into flames as it fell, melting the cathedral's bells and its lead roof, which spattered molten metal onto the marble floor. The internal damage was still visible and the spire still missing in 1588, and the nave was still crowded every morning 'foot by foot and elbow by elbow' with 'the knight, the gull, the gallant, the upstart, the clown, the captain, the apple-squire, the bankrupt, the scholar, the beggar, the doctor, the idiot, the Puritan, the cut-throat' and merchants, prostitutes, and foreign spies hoping to overhear the indiscretions of a courtier.[21] The crowds exchanged news and rumours, and bought and sold and cheated with the same enthusiasm and indifference to sanctity that they'd shown before the thunderbolt had struck the cathedral.

The name Cavendish was on many of their lips. Details continued to emerge of his circumnavigation, and the familiars of St Paul's also guessed at what he might attempt next. As well as great wealth, he'd brought back emissaries from Japan and the

Philippines. Could he be planning a return voyage to Asia? Other rumours had him teaming up with Sir Francis Drake and Sir John Norris for a raid on the West Indies.

Meanwhile speculation continued over the value of the treasure he'd carried home. Estimates were falling. According to the Spanish spy who'd reported on Cavendish's triumph at Greenwich, 'the treasure he brings does not approach in value what they said, but it is asserted that more value is attached to a new invention, or easier mode of navigating, which he has devised'. The declining value was passed on to Mendoza in Paris, who told King Philip that 'Cavendish's booty shrinks in value daily, but the English still estimate it at 500,000 crowns'.[22]

Whatever its true value, it was enough to disrupt London's foreign exchange market. The surplus of both gold and Spanish coin drove their prices down. 'Cavendish must have brought great riches,' a spy reported, 'for they are coining new broad-angels,* and gold is cheaper here than ever it was. Spanish pistolets, which four months ago were worth 12 reals 11 maravedis, will not now pass for 11 reals 24 maravedis, in consequence of the great abundance of them here.'[23]

Further evidence of the real worth of 'Cavendish's booty' appeared when his crew flaunted their new wealth. They had left England dressed in homespun and had returned wearing silk suits and gold chains. Even the lowliest of them was now a wealthy man. The apprentice Richard Casey, for example, received £200 worth of 'silk, gold, and other commodities'. This vast reward made his former master, the shipwright Thomas Greaves, jealous as it was more than his own business was worth, and he sued Casey for a share, on the basis that, as an apprentice, both Casey and his work belonged to his master. Greaves won the case. Masters, the Hight Court of Admiralty decided, 'should have the gain of their

* A gold coin with the image of the Archangel Michael slaying a dragon on its obverse face.

apprentices' voyages which they bring up, instruct and furnish to the sea'. [24]

The officers of the *Desire* also received life-changing sums. Nicolas Rodriguez, Cavendish's Portuguese pilot turned privateer, was now rich enough to represent himself as a great merchant from China, and as such also attracted the attention of Spanish spies. According to Messia, he visited Don Antonio, the English-backed pretender to the Portuguese throne, and gave him 'a great present of damasks and brocades, and other fine things from China' where he claimed to have been 'established for 30 years'. Rodriguez's activities were also reported on by the spy codenamed David, who likewise represented him as a peaceful merchant rather than privateer turned patriot: 'With Cavendish there arrived a Portuguese from China, a very rich man, who has made Don Antonio some presents, and tells him that if he sends to India and China he will obtain help.'[25]

As Christmas approached, business in London gave way to recreation and Cavendish returned to Suffolk. Before leaving, he sent the queen a dazzling Christmas gift to keep his name in her mind. Elizabeth expected valuable presents from her councillors and favourites and was happy to receive large sums of money from any who'd run out of ideas. Cavendish's gift was disproportionately generous for his station and was entered into her register of jewels as 'One cup fashioned like a scallop… of agate garnished with gold, set with pearls, diamonds, and rubies… the cover having in the top thereof two antique horses of agate'.[26]

When Cavendish reached his native county, he was feasted in Ipswich, which had supplied him with men and provisions for his circumnavigation, and whose inhabitants took an intense local pride in his achievements. The town chamberlains were ordered to provide a 'cragge of sturgeon', two large marzipan cakes and 'gallons of hippocras' for a banquet staged for their prodigal son.[27] These delicacies were marks of esteem. Hippocras, spiced wine loaded with sugar, was deemed suitable for 'feasts royal'. Sturgeon, meanwhile, vast primitive fish that spawned in England's rivers, were reserved for the queen and the laws required that only she could permit others to consume their 'superior' flesh.

Ipswich had other circumnavigators to welcome home, including Thomas Fuller, Master of the *Desire*, who'd mapped out her route in his rutter, and Thomas Eldred, the former tallow chandler. Eldred resumed his business when he returned and commemorated his circumnavigation with a carved oak overmantle for his house, whose panels framed a triptych of oil paintings, representing his voyage. One shows the *Desire*, her masts streaming pennants of the Cross of St George, her cannon poking through the gunports in her hull and looking very brave and warlike. Another has a portrait of Eldred, dressed in a black jacket with a snowy lace collar and matching cuffs. He appears both enthusiastic and alert as he gazes at the sky above and beyond the picture, holding a navigational instrument to his right eye. He has an appealing face, with large ears, bright eyes and an expression of rapture – as if he was a believer within sight of God. The legend beneath the paintings states:

> Thomas Eldred went out of Plymouth 1586 July 21 & sailed about the whole globe and arrived again in Plymouth ye 9 of September 1588.
>
> What can seem great to him that hath seen the whole world and the wondrous works therein, Save the Maker of it and the world above it?[28]

Cavendish returned to London in January 1589 to find that he had become the subject of books as well as ballads. As speculation over his treasure subsided, which was agreed to be worth about £125,000, or about half the annual income of Queen Elizabeth, from which she paid for her courts, her navy and her army, increased interest was shown in his discoveries, especially those relating to China. Although China was acknowledged to be large, powerful and fabulously wealthy, little was known about it beyond

Marco Polo's partly fictional account of his travels, circulated in Franco-Venetian[29] in 1300 and not published in English until 1579. Cavendish, in contrast, had brought back tangible information about the country, including 'a large map' of the mythic kingdom, marked with cities and annotated with comments on its inhabitants and organisation. The annotations described a nation far larger and more populous than any in Europe, whose army alone numbered '7,923,785 horse and foot' – nearly twice the size of the entire population of England and Wales.[30]

London's merchants had been trying – without luck – to establish direct trade with China for over a century. Amongst the other information that Cavendish had brought back about the country was the exciting news that its merchants travelled with a 'great store of gold... which they traffic and exchange for silver, weight for weight.'[31] It was an opportune moment to revive interest in the matter, and they sponsored the writer Robert Parke to translate Juan González de Mendoza's *History of the Great and Mighty Kingdom of China* into English. Mendoza's *History* contained descriptions of China, its people and its customs that had been written by sixteenth-century visitors, who focused on detailing their observations rather than inventing wonders. Parke dedicated his translation:

> TO THE RIGHT WORSHIPFULL AND FAMOUS GENTLEMAN, M. THOMAS CANDISH, ESQUIRE, INCREASE OF HONOR AND HAPPY ATTEMPTES.[32]

He commenced his dedication with compliments to Cavendish's daring and valour, then turned to trade. Cavendish, he believed, had discovered the route to a 'notable' market for English cloth, especially kerseys.* If this discovery was exploited, Parke suggested, it would heap even more glory on Cavendish and move 'many

* Kerseys were bolts of woollen cloth dyed in neutral colours and were England's principal export.

thousands of English subjects to pray for you, and to love and honour your name'. The wealth generated, moreover, would 'relieve more of the poorer sort, than all the hospitals and alms houses can or may, that have been built in this realm, since the first inhabiting thereof.' After offering Cavendish the prospects of earning the prayers of England and the gratitude of its paupers, Parke turned to his sponsors' message: China was ripe for exploitation and, if Cavendish would attempt another voyage, London's merchants would pay for it. They did not envisage him repeating his circumnavigation, but rather that he would reach the Far East via the Northwest Passage. Parke then elaborated on the merchants' interest in this as yet unsailed course. There was 'one special reason that giveth an edge unto their desires, proceeding from the late [recent] worthy attempts of that excellent and skilful pilot M. John Davis', who had already made an 'exact description' of the route 'four hundred leagues further than was ever hitherto thoroughly known'. According to Parke, Davis's discoveries and geographical theories had made a particular impression on William Sanderson, one of the wealthiest merchants in England, who was ready to support Cavendish 'even this year again, for the final perfection of so profitable and honourable a discovery'. Money was no object – Sanderson was ready to commit 'a far greater portion than in reason would be required of any other man of his ability'.[33]

This was food for thought. Cavendish was having trouble with Julius Caesar, one of the small investors in his circumnavigation. Sole judge of the High Court of the Admiralty, Caesar had sent a florid welcome to Cavendish while he was still at Plymouth, which celebrated his endeavours and thanked God for answering his prayers that the voyager might return safe, sound and wealthy. Caesar was a venal man in a venal age and was looking forward to receiving his profits on the £50 he'd invested. He wrote a series of increasingly discourteous letters filled with vague threats to Cavendish, who ignored them. The prospect of being able to launch an expedition such as Parke had sketched out, which would not give rise to such petty vexations, was intriguing. William

Sanderson was well known throughout London, in courtly as well as mercantile circles. He'd backed other voyages, and his pockets were deep. John Davis, meanwhile, the 'excellent and skilful pilot' recommended by Parke, had connections to West Country privateers, and if Cavendish didn't know him already, he might yet have heard of him.

18

The High Road to China

London, England

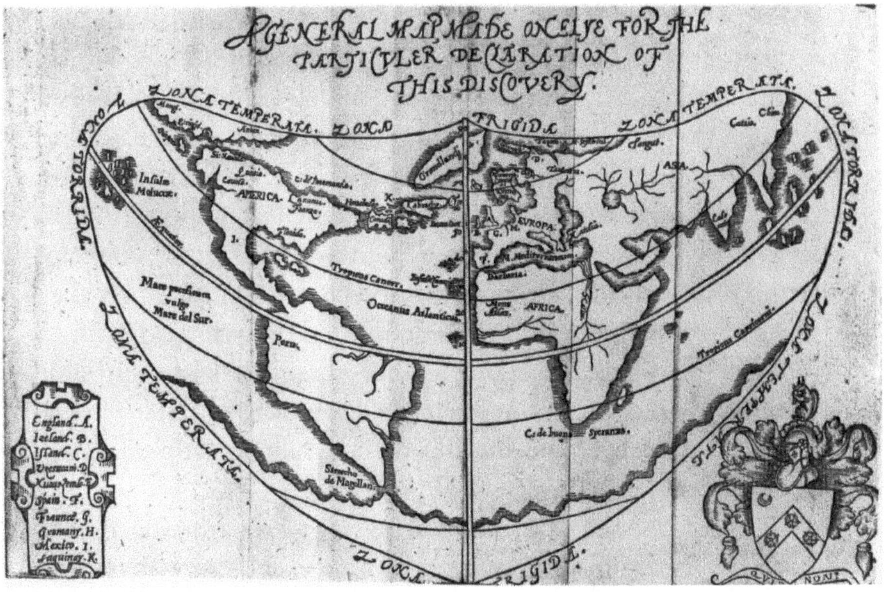

❦

JOHN DAVIS HAD BEEN A mariner since his youth and had built himself a name as a 'man well-grounded in the principles of the art of Navigation'. He came from Sandridge in Devon, upriver from the port of Dartmouth, which had a reputation as a nursery for seamen that stretched back to Geoffrey Chaucer's *Canterbury Tales*.[1] By the time that Thomas Cavendish had moved from Cambridge University to London, studied a little law, shown himself at court and taken up gambling, Davis had thousands of sea miles behind him. He inspired trust in the men who sailed with him. He looked every inch the mariner with a strong, compact build, large, soulful eyes, a curling moustache and a patriarchal beard. His character had other dimensions – Davis was a fervent Protestant Christian with a 'strong sense of providence' who believed in the power of prayer: God would intervene and protect the faithful when they petitioned his assistance. He was educated as well as devout, a competent mathematician and scholar, fluent in Latin and able to apply the principles of geometry to practical matters. Finally, Davis had a touch of the mystic to him, having claimed in his youth that he could converse with angels.

Davis was obsessed with the Northwest Passage (the speculative trans-polar sea route between English and Chinese waters) and had led three expeditions in search of it. At the same time that Cavendish had been exploring Pamlico Sound in 1585, Davis had been dodging icebergs in the fog off the coast of Greenland. Meanwhile, in the summer of 1587, when Cavendish was raiding Peru and Chile, Davis had been pushing even further north before turning his search to the Canadian coast.

Davis's fixation with the Northwest Passage, which he believed that he was predestined to find, had been planted and nourished by two men: Sir Humfrey Gilbert and Dr John Dee. Sir Humfrey, a courtier, soldier and coloniser, was convinced that both Classical philosophy and travellers' tales from the Dark Ages proved that a direct route to China through the Arctic Circle must exist.[2] In 1576, he'd published a pamphlet, *A Discourse of a Discovery for a new Passage to Cathay*, which set out his proofs. America, Sir Humfrey contended, on the authority of the Greek philosopher Plato, was all that remained of Atlantis, the 'incomparable great Island' larger than Africa and Asia combined which had lain beyond the Straits of Gibraltar in the direction of the sunset, before most of it had been 'swallowed up with water' six centuries before Plato's time, 'by reason of a mighty Earthquake, and streaming down of the heavenly Floodgates'.[3] However, even at its greatest extent, Atlantis had been an island, and so could be sailed around, and therefore its American remnants must be encircled by navigable seas.

Sir Humfrey's proofs were corroborated by Dr John Dee, the celebrated mathematician, alchemist and stargazer who'd served as astrologer to Queen Elizabeth.* Imposing in appearance with high cheekbones, intense brown eyes and a very long pointed beard, which he tucked into the top of his robe, Dee was famed for his learning throughout Europe. He deployed Neoplatonism, geometry and the Old Testament to prove the existence of a Northwest Passage. The physical world, Dee believed, was governed by proportion and 'Everything in the earth had a counterpart or a counterweight'.[4] This harmony was divinely sanctioned: according to the prophet Isaiah (Isa. 40:12), God had 'weighed the mountains in scales and the hills in a balance' and since there was water around the southern end of the Americas, there had to be an identical seaway to the north.

Dee had known Davis since his teens, when he'd employed him as a scryer to help him communicate with angels. While encouraging his supernatural gifts, Dee had also taught Davis the principles of celestial navigation and had convinced him once

* Dr Dee had been entrusted to determine the most auspicious day for Elizabeth's coronation.

and for all that God had built a balanced world for humanity's benefit, with habitable continents that could be circumnavigated. The pupil's belief had become more fervent than his master's. In Davis's opinion, 'If any man be persuaded to the contrary of this truth' (that the Northwest Passage existed), 'he shall do himself wrong in having so base an imagination of the excellency of God's creation.'[5] Davis had also developed an independent theory of why the passage might be ice-free in polar latitudes. Its warmth, he contended, derived from excessive salinity in those regions, and 'salt being by its nature linked to the element of fire generates heat'. Moreover, 'Since hot and cold, being opposites, cannot exist in the same place', pack-ice had to give way to warm and salty seas.[6] He'd tested his theory, with mixed results, on all three of his voyages north.

Davis's expeditions had been sponsored by the Merchant Adventurers of Exeter, the 'chiefest and wealthiest men' in Southwest England, whose signatures could commit as much money to a venture as an earl, and dispatch men and ships to the ends of the Earth. However, their enthusiasm and generosity had diminished with each successive venture.[7,8] Although Davis had named and claimed new lands and feasted on roast polar bear on his first voyage, and his men had played football with the Inuit tribe in Greenland during the second, China remained out of reach. Davis had moreover encountered 'a most mighty and strange quantity of ice, in one entire mass' in 1586, 'so big as that we knew not the limits thereof' which lay across the supposed route to the Northwest Passage. He'd spent thirteen fruitless days trying to sail around it and, after a short spell of exploring, had been driven home by 'Mighty tempestuous storms' and the pleas of his men that he should not, through 'over boldness', 'leave their widows and fatherless children' to give him 'bitter curses'.[9]

Davis's second expedition had, however, turned a profit. During a break in the weather off Labrador, his company had caught hundreds of large cod with bent nails tied to cords. Salt cod had a ready market, and indeed a black market all over Europe, and, in 1587, Exeter's merchants had decided to back Davis for a third time.[10] The emphasis was to be on fishing rather than discovery. They funded three ships, two to catch cod and one for exploration. These were the venerable *Sunshine* (a small barque of fifty tonnes) which Davis had captained on his previous voyages, the *Elizabeth* of a similar size and the pinnace *Ellen*. The *Ellen* was a mere twenty tonnes and 'clincher'* – the planks of her hull overlapped each other rather than being laid flush – which the superstitious members of Davis's company believed would bring them bad luck. The ships were to sail to Greenland in convoy, where the *Elizabeth* and the *Sunshine* would peel off to Newfoundland and the fishing grounds, leaving the *Ellen* to Davis for exploration.[11]

Davis led his three ships out of Dartmouth on 19 May 1587, the same day that Thomas Cavendish was preparing to attack Paita in Peru. Although the Merchant Adventurers had driven a hard bargain, any opportunity to complete his discoveries was better than none. He had faith in both his God and the path that he believed had been chosen for him.

However, *Ellen* (the clincher) disappeared on his first night at sea. The weather had been too mild to sink ships and Davis, aboard the *Elizabeth*, suspected that she'd run away. He turned back, found her with a broken tiller, sent carpenters to help with repairs and, once she could be steered again, resumed his course. Davis was accompanied on the voyage by the merchant John Jane, who'd sailed on his other expeditions. Jane was convinced that the lacklustre performance of the *Ellen* was an omen. 'We went forward,' he confided to his journal, 'hoping that a hard beginning would make a good ending, yet some of us were doubtful of it, falling in reckoning that she was a Clincher; nevertheless, we put our trust in God.'[12]

* Clinker.

The bad luck continued. The *Sunshine* sprang a leak in stormy weather six days out from Dartmouth and was forced to heave to. While her crew rummaged in the bilge, shifting her ballast to heel her to one side and expose the hole in her hull, the sea gushed through it and they had '500 strokes at the pump in a watch'.[13] When the weather eased, they found and stopped the leak in time for a fresh crisis: the *Ellen* spread her sails in light winds and lost her main mast. The *Elizabeth* took her under tow and the expedition limped on while repairs were made. This incident enraged Jane. Although the clincher had been 'much bragged of by the owner's report before we came out of England', at sea she 'was like a cart drawn with oxen'. And this was the vessel that had been set aside for exploration. Her performance also alarmed Davis, who asked Peerson, the *Ellen*'s steward, who knew the ship inside out, if her hull was 'staunch', i.e. sound. If not, he would have to sail back to Dartmouth and might miss the arctic summer while finding a replacement for her. Peerson calmed his fears, telling Davis that the little *Ellen* 'was as sound and as staunch as a cup'.[14]

As Davis crept towards Greenland, the weather changed from fair to 'fog and rain'. The dispiriting conditions sparked mutinous thoughts in the crew of the *Sunshine*, who wanted to break off immediately to go fishing in Newfoundland. Their master confessed to Davis 'that he was afraid his men would shape some contrary course while he was asleep'.[15] Davis was forced to board her and call her crew to order, lecturing and threatening them until 'they were content to bring us to land, which we looked for daily'. A little less than a month after leaving England, the lookouts spotted 'very great and high mountains' on the horizon. Two days later, 'being in the latitude of 64°', Davis brought his ships 'to an anchor among many low islands'.[16] As had been the case in his last voyage, Inuit tribesmen paddled out to meet him with seal skins to trade, 'crying "Il y a oute"' and his mariners 'played the merchants' with them.[17]

Davis had carried a pinnace in kit form with him from Dartmouth and, once his fleet's anchors had been laid, its pieces were rowed ashore to be assembled. The *Sunshine* had agreed to stay with him until the pinnace was complete and, with time on his hands, and no longer fearing a mutiny, her master kidnapped an Inuit, 'a very strong young lusty fellow' aiming to take him back to England and exhibit him for money when he returned from fishing.*

The hostage's kinsmen returned during the short hours of the night for revenge. Rather than attacking the fleet with their kayaks and walrus spears, they tore off 'the two upper strakes of the pinnace' and had to be driven back with a round from a saker before they ripped her apart. Jane had been outraged by the impudence of the Inuit and had hoped to see them to 'run away without legs' when the shot reached its target. However, after the smoke cleared, he was disappointed to 'perceive never a man hurt, but all having their legs could carry away their bodies'. When Jane wondered how the saker had missed the Inuit, he was told that its gunner, for both humanitarian and commercial reasons – 'fearing to hurt any of the people, and regarding the owner's profit' – had spared all concerned the expense of a cannonball and had fired a blank charge instead.[18]

The confrontation spooked the crews of the *Sunshine* and *Elizabeth*, who felt that they had done their duty as far as exploration went. On 21 June, Davis transhipped to the *Ellen* and his fleet split. When he stepped aboard the clincher, he found she was no longer staunch. Her pilot John Churchyard told him 'that the good ship which we must all hazard our lives in' was filling up so quickly that the men were working non-stop at her pumps. According to Jane, 'This disquieted us all greatly, and many doubted to go in her.' It was a grim scene: a small, ill-starred boat in frigid waters with a frightened crew off an alien coast.

Davis realised that, if he did not win their confidence at once, his search for the Northwest Passage would be over. He spoke to his company, and Jane recorded that he offered them the

* This had been a profitable strategy for past English explorers.

options of death or glory, and that the chance of the latter had won them over: 'At length our captain, by whom we were all to be governed, determined rather to end his life with credit than to return with infamy and disgrace, and so being all agreed, we purposed to live and die together, and committed ourselves to the ship.' They pumped the *Ellen* dry, stopped the leak and Davis got underway again. He followed the coast of Greenland north, keeping between ten and thirty miles offshore. He wanted to avoid the Inuit, but the distance didn't deter them, and they paddled out to sea in their kayaks to trade. They craved iron above all else and, although far from land, would 'sell their boat, coats, or anything they had', for needles, nails and bracelets.[19] Jane, who had no love for 'Indians', deigned to trade with them nonetheless and made a fabulous bargain, exchanging an iron knife for a spear tipped with a piece of 'Unicorn's horn'. This curio was not only rare and valuable but also evidence that the Inuit had trading links, albeit tenuous, with both the Moghul Empire and China, for 'there being no Unicorn in any part of Asia', Sir Humphrey Gilbert had declared in his *Discourse of a Discovery*, 'saving in India, & Cathay'.[20]

On 30 June, Davis took observations at both noon and midnight. It was the height of the arctic summer and the sun remained above the horizon twenty-four hours a day. He calculated he'd reached 72° 12' north, a personal best, and named the tall cliffs that rose sheer from the sea in front of him 'Sanderson's Hope' after the city merchant.

But Davis got no further. He was headed by gales when he tried to pass Sanderson's Hope and was forced to turn west across Baffin Bay. He made a virtue out of necessity – perhaps he'd been looking in the wrong place and the entrance to the Northwest Passage lay above Canada rather than Greenland? However, a hundred and twenty miles out to sea, Davis found his route blocked by 'a mighty bank of Ice'.[21] The wind prevented him from sailing around its top and he followed it south, looking for a route through it. After searching for four days, a gap was spotted in the ice wall, and his company rowed the *Ellen* into a trap. They'd entered the Middle Pack of Baffin Bay, which forms a shattered archipelago of icefloes and icebergs, in places a hundred miles wide. From the deck of a fragile wooden ship, it seemed both beautiful and sinister. The ice around the clincher had been carved into fantastic shapes by the winds and waves, and its colours changed with the angle of the sun. Translucent peaks became mountains of amethysts and rubies as the light passed through them, and these phantasmagoria creaked and groaned when they were forced together by the elements.

A few miles after sailing through the gap in the ice wall, Davis found his course obstructed by a second rank of icebergs. As the wind and current compressed the Middle Pack, the walls both in front and behind closed in on the *Ellen*, slowly yet visibly, like the jaws of a vice. There was no way back through the gap where she'd entered, which had been squeezed shut.

Davis kept a level head. No emergency at sea could faze him. The air – he thanked God – was still; he turned the *Ellen* south. She was rowed along the eastern ice pack, in search of an exit. After forty-eight anxious hours, Davis found an opening and the *Ellen* escaped. He was sufficiently chastened to attribute her salvation to divine assistance rather than personal skill, confessing that it had been only 'by God's help' that 'we recovered the open sea'.[22]

After clearing the Middle Pack, Davis had turned back for Greenland, aiming to find a safe anchorage where he could wait for the ice to dissolve. He was optimistic that this process would be over in less than a week. Jane seconded him: 'the sea continually beating it, and the sun, with the extreme force of heat which it had always shining upon it would make a quick dispatch.' However, when Davis reached Greenland, he found the shore ice-bound, the water too deep to drop anchor and the sea so high that it threatened to smash the *Ellen* against the coast. It was no place to linger while waiting for the Middle Pack to dissipate. He sailed back towards the walls of ice and, when the wind shifted in his favour, turned north, hoping to pass around the top of them into salty, balmy, arctic waters, and locate the passage of his dreams.

The clincher, however, resorted to her old tricks and sagged off her heading, while the current carried her towards yet more icebergs. Davis had to adopt a zigzag course as he ran from foul winds and evaded floating mountains. On 19 July, he sighted land again, and with it a familiar landmark – Mount Raleigh on Baffin Island, which he'd discovered and named on his last expedition. Once he'd reached Canada, Davis turned south, looking for a promising opening in the coast that he'd noted in 1586 and marked as a candidate for the mouth of the Northwest Passage. Twelve hours later, he found it. The air was clear, visibility excellent and he judged it to be fifty miles wide. He named it Cumberland Sound in the expectation that it had sea at either end.[23] Its entrance, meanwhile, was sufficiently imposing to announce a channel between two great oceans, and commensurate in size, perhaps, with Davis's dreams of how it should appear.

He sailed into Cumberland Sound at midnight. With mounting excitement, he followed it north and east for a hundred and eighty miles, anchoring eight days later 'among an huge number of isles'. It was just the sort of topography he had expected to find – Atlantis breaking up into islands as the seabed fell away into a deep passage between two oceans – and, as if to confirm his suspicions, a 'great whale', a creature of the open seas, 'passed by us and swam West'.[24]

Just as the evidence was screaming to him that he'd realised his quest, Davis had to tear himself away. It was nearly August, when he'd been ordered to reunite with the *Sunshine* and *Elizabeth* off Newfoundland and return home. With regret bordering on anguish, Davis turned his back on Cumberland's Isles, as he'd named the little archipelago where he was anchored, and made sail for his rendezvous with the fishing vessels. He was heartened, however, by a spell of hot weather that coincided with his departure from Cumberland Sound. Here was further proof that it was the gateway to the warm band of waters that circled the North Pole.

As Davis hastened towards his rendezvous with the fishing vessels, he passed yet another candidate for the Northwest Passage: 'we crossed over the entrance or mouth of a great inlet or passage', he wrote, which was as wide as Cumberland Sound where, to his 'great admiration', he found '8 or 9 great races, currents or overfalls, loathsomely crying like the rage of waters under London bridge, and bending their course into the said gulf'.[25]* Only a link between oceans could generate such turbulent flows. Jane, in contrast, confessed in his journal that he'd found the overfalls, which had whirled an 'Island of Ice' past the *Ellen*, frightening rather than thrilling. The giant iceberg was 'carried very forcibly with the set of the current faster than our ship went', and such hazards would be impossible either to detect or avoid in fog or darkness. Jane's thoughts, like the rest of Davis's company, turned towards home. God had already saved them twice, stopping the clincher from sinking back in June, and delivering them from the Middle Pack. Besides, rations were low and they were feeling the pinch.

Davis continued to search for the *Sunshine* and the *Elizabeth*, coasting down Newfoundland without finding any 'kind of mark, token or beacon', which they had promised to leave 'on every headland'. It was clear that they'd either been lost or had hurried back to England. However, while the *Ellen* was picking her way between a group of islets, looking for signs of the fishing boats, Davis was faced with another challenge. His ship hit a submerged rock and sprang 'a great leak'. As the sea gushed in through her overlapping planks, a storm arrived and the *Ellen* had to be patched up while the wind roared through her rigging and waves slammed against her hull. Davis was content to accept that these difficulties had been sent to test him, entered survival mode and turned his ship towards home.

* The Hudson Strait.

The storm was followed by another tempest, 'not very outrageous' in Jane's jaded opinion, who could now only think of his stomach. He was touched by paranoia, obsessing that the few rations left were being hoarded and devoured by Peerson, the *Ellen*'s steward who'd declared her to be staunch, and who now 'was so insatiable that the allowance of two men was scant sufficient to feed his greedy appetite'. Jane's fears were aggravated by their shortage of both fuel and water for the journey back to England – 'having in our ship but little wood, and half a hogshead of fresh water'.[26]

Davis, however, who seldom acknowledged the demands of his stomach, found the voyage plain sailing with little to comment on in his traverse book beyond his daily position, the course steered, and being chased by a Spanish warship. He reached Dartmouth on 15 September, having once again performed outstanding feats of seamanship. He'd navigated the ill-starred clincher to the furthest point north yet reached by an Englishman, had sailed into and out of the Middle Pack, and had discovered two more candidates for the western end of the Northwest Passage. Remarkably, he hadn't lost a single man on the voyage.

The Merchant Venturers of Exeter were unimpressed. This was the third time that Davis had claimed to have found the passage – almost. Meanwhile the *Sunshine* and the *Elizabeth* had both failed to catch any cod, and between them had lost a bale of kersey, which was mourned by these men who lived by the wool trade as if it had been a chest full of pearls. Whether the master of the *Sunshine* made a profit from his kidnapped Inuit, or Jane from his chunk of unicorn horn, was not recorded in their minutes.

However, there was no doubt in Davis's mind that he'd found the entrance, or entrances, to the sea-road to China. All the signs had been clear – the mild air, the overfalls, the whale swimming west. The floating mountains and walls of ice he'd observed, he decided, had fallen off the land and had drifted as they melted. Thorough as ever, he'd made precise charts of his discoveries and now knew that, if he could find sponsors for another expedition, he should sail directly for Newfoundland and then head north, instead of wasting time on Greenland.

The day after Davis landed, he scribbled a letter to William Sanderson in jubilant tones: 'With God's great mercy I have made my safe return in health, with all my company,' he announced. 'I have been in 73 degrees, finding the Sea all open, and forty leagues between land and land. The passage is most probable, the execution easy.'[27]

Davis had been cultivating Sanderson as a sponsor for years, assuring him in 1587 that he was certain the passage must be 'in one of four places' and that 'this voyage may be performed without further charge, nay, with certain profit to the adventurers, if I may have but your favour in the action'.[28] Sanderson believed in Davis. He too was convinced that a Northwest Passage was there for the finding. He'd invested in Sir Martin Frobisher's previous voyages to Canada and had backed Davis in the past. When Thomas Cavendish returned from his circumnavigation, both Sanderson and Davis sensed an opportunity. Cavendish had proved his excellence as a navigator as well as a privateer and might be persuaded, financially, to join the search for the Northwest Passage, albeit from west to east via the Strait of Ainan, as its supposed Pacific entrance had been named.

19

Natural Prizes

Westminster Hall, London

Cavendish was distracted from his thoughts of a second circumnavigation by the Parliament of 1589. The Earl of Pembroke had once again made Cavendish an MP, this time for Wilton, another of his private boroughs. Parliament had been summoned, as in 1584, to raise subsidies to pay for the conflict with Spain, and Pembroke and his fellow borough-owners had once again stacked the House of Commons with warmongers and privateers.[1] This time, Cavendish had been chosen for his experience rather than his potential. Sir Walter Raleigh's protégé had now seen more of the world than his mentor. Parliament opened on 4 February 1589, and once again Cavendish stood beyond the bar at the 'nether end' of the House of Lords to hear Sir Christopher Hatton, Chancellor of the Exchequer, set out the rules of engagement. Hatton drew their attention to Elizabeth's 'gracious disposition to peace, and her great wisdom in preserving the same', and listed the benefits that England 'enjoyed by her government', including 'her great Conquest over the Spanish late wonderful Army or Fleet on the Seas'. The King of Spain, however, remained 'bent against this Kingdom'. Before long, Elizabeth's subjects might require Her protection again. England needed to be 'prepared and furnished against all Events' with ships and soldiers and the money to feed them and pay them. Sooner or later, the 'inbred malice' of Philip II would stir him to launch a second armada.[2]

While Hatton spoke, Cavendish could see his younger sister Anne, one of Queen Elizabeth's maids of honour, seated on the ground beside the throne. This was a signal distinction. The greatest families in the land schemed to have their daughters chosen to be maids of honour, who were the surest route to the queen's ear, serving both as Elizabeth's bed mates and her dancing partners as well as being her personal attendants. Cavendish's extravagant Christmas present had been acknowledged.

Once Parliament had been opened, the Commons settled down to business in St Stephen's Chapel, overlooked by its headless saints. The subsidies bill was approved with little debate and scarcely a murmur of protest. Only Henry Jackman, MP for Calne, had dared to mention the 'heavy burden of taxation already laid upon the country', and had cautioned against 'setting a precedent "dangerous both to ourselves and our posterity" by voting double subsidies once the immediate threat of invasion had already been averted'.[3] After voicing his doubts, and remembering, perhaps, the fate of 'that villainous traitor' William Parry in 1584, Jackman duly voted for the bill, which was passed up to the House of Lords. England's peers and bishops assented to it without hesitation. Sir Christopher Hatton had made the case for fresh taxes – what more was there to add? Indeed, the Upper House dedicated more of its time to bills against horse stealing, house-burning, informers and for the 'Reformation in excess of Apparel'.[4] This last was a perennial favourite in the Lords: commoners must not be allowed to dress like gentry. They should be confined to wearing 'puce or other sad colours' lest they be mistaken for their betters.

Parliament was dissolved in late March, and Cavendish dashed back to Suffolk to redeem the lands and manors he'd mortgaged to finance his circumnavigation. He was pressed for time: some of his contracts had terms of two-and-a-half years, which were about to expire, and he had to redeem them in person at specific places. A mortgage on the holding of the manor of Chasers in Levington, for instance, had to be repaid before 'the Feast of the Annunciation' on 25 March 1589 at the market cross in Ipswich.[5]

Cavendish used Henry Seckford to help him unwind the transactions that they'd arranged together in 1586. In April, he regained full ownership of Grimston Hall, his ancestral home, together with its dependant manors of Stratton and Seabridge in Levington. By mid-May, he had reclaimed everything he'd staked. He decorated Grimston with some mementos of his voyage, planting a minion cannon with an octagonal barrel muzzle-down at the entrance to its drive,[6] and seeding an Ilex tree in its grounds.[7]

He was back in London the next month, aiming to tie up the loose ends of his expedition.

Thomas Cavendish had kept many of the rarer spoils that had been locked in the *Santa Ana's* iron-bound chests for himself. Although he'd divided her gold openly on her deck, he'd put the little flasks of pungent oils and the velvet bags holding the desiccated glands of various animals to one side, many worth at least their weight in gold, knowing that his company had no idea of their value. These treasures were, however, hard to sell in volume without depressing their prices. Cavendish had, for example, a year's supply of civet musk and only an expert could move so much without glutting the market. He met with the merchant Hugh Morgan, a prominent member of London's Worshipful Company of Grocers, to arrange the disposal of his private booty. The Grocers were 'engrossers' rather than dealers in fruit and vegetables. Their guild controlled the spice trade in the City, ran much of its foreign exchange market and held various monopolies in imported goods, which its members exploited to *engross* their wealth. Apothecary to the queen, Morgan was one of England's 'Wisest and best merchants'.[8] A natural scientist as well as a capitalist, he corresponded with other experts across Europe and, whenever he came across anything worthy of note in the animal and vegetable kingdoms, he shared his news.

Cavendish gave Morgan plenty to write about. A few days after their meeting, Morgan sent a letter to Carolus Clusius, the foremost natural scientist in Europe, listing the curiosities 'The eminent Cavendish' had for sale. These included 'three thousand units of oriental musk with an enormous value', forty units of civet with a pungent smell and 'three rhinoceros horns and three bezoar stones of a white colour from Peru'.[9] The bezoar stones were probably the first that Morgan had touched. Exceptionally rare, they were believed to be antidotes to any poison and were in high demand among princes and other potentates at risk of assassination. In antiquity, the best bezoars had come from Persian goats, which, it was believed, were fond of eating poisonous snakes that they hunted down in caves, stunned with their breath then trampled to death. It was a risky business, and the goats were often bitten before they subdued their prey. To counteract the venom, injured animals retreated to the nearest river. Once cooled by its waters, they ate the healing herbs that grew along its banks, whose juices combined with the snakes' venom inside their bodies to form bezoar stones. These treasures, which were either worn on the body or consumed in powdered form, worked as charms against every poison. They were also thought to restore flagging vigour: some authorities claimed that only elderly goats attacked snakes 'because their poison somehow brings their strength back'.[10] When bezoars were discovered inside llamas in Peru, they were judged to be almost as good as the Persian variety. A genuine bezoar was worth ten times its weight in gold, and the three that Cavendish owned were similar in size and shape to doves' eggs. In contrast, Queen Elizabeth's bezoar stone 'set in gold hanging at a little Bracelet of a flagon Chain', was no larger than a pea, and had been worn down with use.[11]

After listing the valuable exotica that Cavendish had brought to him, Morgan told Clusius about the botanical wonders that had been produced at the meeting – white nutmeg, samples of pepper including *piper longum*, and eight pounds in weight of seeds. There was a market in London for exotic plants as well as musk oil and calcified hairballs. Collectors and dealers invested in privateering voyages, paying advances to their officers and surgeons to gather specimens of any plants or substances they came across that might have nourishing, therapeutic or aesthetic qualities. Although not all of the expeditions they sponsored returned and most of the samples that these brought back were dead or spoiled, a few valuable finds had defied the odds. These had included tobacco, tulips, maize and cocoa. Cavendish's surgeon had been responsible for collecting seeds on the circumnavigation and, in addition to those presented to Morgan, had taken another batch to James Garet, a City apothecary based in Lime Street.[12] This batch included potato seeds from Peru, which Garet planted in his garden. No one had grown a potato* in England before and Garet, who also corresponded with Clusius, sent him updates on the progress of his plants. By January 1589, they were developing tubers, and Garet took the risky step of eating these. Potatoes cultivated from seeds were a genetic lottery, prone to throwbacks to their toxic ancestors, and could kill a man, whether raw or cooked. Fortunately, Garet's tubers weren't vegetal revenants, and he reported to Clusius that they were 'earthy' in taste and seemed 'very nutritious'.

Thomas Cavendish visited Garet shortly after England's first recorded potato harvest. He brought Miguel Sanchez, the pilot from Marseilles he'd picked up off Guatemala, to the meeting, who'd lived in Peru and confirmed to Garet that the potatoes were genuine. Sanchez also gave Garet some culinary advice, explaining that the Incas either boiled them in soups or roasted them 'in the ashes of a fire'. After recipes had been discussed, Cavendish showed Garet a new spice, star anise,† that he'd brought back from Asia, which was unknown in England. Star anise originated in China, where it was used in traditional medicine 'as a stimulant and expectorant, to relieve flatulence, to increase libido and as a tea to cure rheumatism'.[13] He gave Garet some of its seeds, and Garet enclosed samples in another letter to Clusius. The new spice was an exciting discovery. If a place could be found for it in Galenic medicine and/or European cuisine, it could make fortunes for its cultivators. 'It has a strong aromatic flavour,' Garet told Clusius, 'as you will see when you taste it.'[14]

Cavendish also brought one of each of the Filipino and Japanese youths he'd liberated from the *Santa Ana* to the meeting. When Garet had asked them to name the new spice in their own languages, both had called it 'damor'.[15] He then asked Christopher,

* *Solanum tuberosum.*

† The dried seed pods of the *Illicium verum* tree.

the Japanese youth, to scribble down the name and noticed that he wrote in a radically different fashion to Europeans – from top to bottom rather than left to right, and using squiggles instead of letters. This was so startling that Garet enclosed a sample in his letter and became the first Englishman to describe Japanese calligraphy.

Indeed, Christopher and Cosmus, the two Japanese lads of 'very good capacity',[16] were the first of their nation to reach England and became minor celebrities in mercantile and scientific circles. Both were fluent in English and gave eyewitness information to the curious about 'the state of the Eastern habitations' and of their own country, which no English person had yet visited.[17] Their acquaintances included William Barlowe, prebend of Lichfield Cathedral,* whose hobbies were mathematics and magnetics. When Barlowe met with Cavendish's 'Orientals', he questioned them about their navigational aids as well as their native land, and they astonished him with a practical demonstration of their science. 'Instead of our Compass,' he wrote, 'they use a Magnetical Needle of six inches long… upon a pin in a dish of white china earth filled with water: In the bottom whereof they have two cross lines, for the four principal winds.'[18] This novel practice may have been the 'valuable invention' mentioned by one of Philipp II's spies and moved Barlowe to redesign the English compass. After he published the fruits of his labour in his book *The Navigator's Supply*, his new *azimuth* compass, inspired by Cavendish, Christopher and Cosmus, became a standard instrument for English mariners.

While Cavendish was disposing of his private booty, he continued to grow in the public eye. Robert Greene, author of euphuistic romances and ironic repentances, included Cavendish as an example of heroism in his *Spanish Masquerado*. Writers, Greene declared, should 'eternalise with their pens' the deeds of this English paragon 'who so lately ventured with the farthest,

* Barlowe was a career cleric with the church in his blood. His father was a bishop, and his mother a former nun. All five of his sisters married bishops.

shewing great courage and fortune in bringing home from far so rich treasure'.[19]

Greene's advice was followed by other authors, including Leonard Wright, an essayist and pamphleteer specialising in morals and Protestant doctrine,[20] who dedicated a book of manners entitled *A Display of Duty decked with sage sayings, pithy sentences and proper similes: pleasant to read, delightful to hear, and profitable to practise*, to his 'childhood friend' the 'Right worshipful, most valiant, and famous Thomas Cavendish Esquire'. Wright declared in his dedication that he'd been moved by both the 'wonted courtesies' and 'friendly countenance' that Cavendish had shown when they were children to write his book 'as a true token and testimony of the faithful and hearty good will I have always born to you and your house and shall during life'.[21] Coincidentally, Wright was also parish priest of Kirketon-Shotley, across the Orwell Estuary from Grimston Hall, and perhaps was seeking patronage when he composed his dedication, which hints at the direction that Wright hopes Cavendish's mind will take with frequent, glowing references to generosity, and occasional examples of the evils that visit the parsimonious, as much as celebrating the achievements of his childhood friend.

The compliments Greene and Wright paid to Cavendish – as both a gallant and beneficent hero – were eclipsed by a new publication, which recorded his circumnavigation and deeds in the Americas and Asia for posterity. The *Principal Navigations* of Richard Hakluyt, cleric, diplomat, geographer and prophet of English colonies in America, was a behemoth of a book that contained every fragment of information Hakluyt could find – mythical, historical and factual – about English seafaring. Its purpose was to inspire his countrymen to undertake or invest in overseas voyages, and to give them both useful information and a taste for adventure. Hakluyt's work was encyclopaedic in its reach. Close to nine hundred pages long, its title alone took up ten lines of print, and began:

> *The Principal Navigations, voyages and discoveries of the English nation, made by Sea or over Lands to the most remote and furthest distant Quarters of the earth at any time within the compass of these 1500 years...*

Squeezed in at the bottom of the title page was the revelation that it included Cavendish's voyage – 'the last most renowned English Navigation round about the whole Globe of the Earth'.[22]

Hakluyt had a nose for vivid stories and eyewitness accounts, and the action in his compilation is terrific. There are wars, storms, incredible journeys, sometimes imaginary, mixed in with short practical entries such as how to recognise the anchorage at Roanoke should you sail to Virginia, and the Javanese names, courtesy of Cavendish's company, for rain ('endam') and beer ('aninage').[23]

Cavendish first appears in the *Principal Navigations* in accounts of the Virginia expedition of 1585, where he is pictured as one of its principal figures. His circumnavigation, performed 'with invincible courage, great good government, and incredible celerity; to the great admiration of all men of judgement', is covered in depth.[24] Hakluyt included Thomas Fuller's rutter, NH's journal, a description of the Great Map of China that Cavendish had brought back with him and the triumphant letter to Walsingham that he'd written when he reached Plymouth. It was a heady mixture of celebration and temptation. NH described the trials and rewards of the voyage in the language of a soldier, and Fuller gave precise instructions on how to repeat it. Latitudes were specified for hitherto secret places like St Helena.[25] Together, they challenged Englishmen to follow in Cavendish's footsteps, and England's enemies to do their best to stop them.

20

Gallant with a Pearl Earring

Lambeth, South London

AT THE SAME TIME THAT his daring was being praised all over England, Thomas Cavendish was making enemies as well as attracting admirers. Rather than paying the small sum he owed to Dr Julius Caesar, sole Judge of the Court of Admiralty and Commissioner for Piracy Causes, he'd treated him with contempt, meeting him, Caesar complained, 'dressed only in his robe' as if the judge were his servant.[1, 2] This cavalier attitude had consequences. The £2,000 bond Cavendish had paid on the *Desire* was confiscated under the orders of Caesar's court. Although there were grounds to justify the confiscation – a piracy claim had been made against the ship just after she'd left Plymouth in 1586, and there was plenty of evidence that Cavendish had 'broken bulk' by sharing out her cargo among her company before she was inspected by the Revenue – the authorities often turned a blind eye to such indiscretions. He was forced to come to terms with Caesar, repaying his initial investment, and converting the rest of the debt into a share in the new expedition that he'd started to plan.

Although Cavendish had returned from his circumnavigation rich – according to a contemporary, 'his great wealth was thought to have sufficed for him for his whole life'[3] – he was haunted by the even greater treasures he'd been forced to leave behind, especially the hundreds of tonnes of silk that his company had tossed overboard into the azure waters off Baja California. Rather than resting on his laurels, he decided to stake his fortune on another voyage – double or quits. This time, however, he'd take ships with bigger holds. He plotted his expedition-to-be with the same energy and attention to detail he'd demonstrated before setting off around the world. His first step was to accumulate all the charts, records and rutters covering parts of his proposed voyage that he could find. Plenty of new material had accrued since he'd left England in 1586, some of it published in Hakluyt's *Principal Navigations*. There was also a mass of handwritten material dispersed throughout England's merchant and privateering communities – drawings of recently discovered anchorages, accounts of encounters with foreign nations to both the east and west, information on the state of affairs in Sierra Leone and Brazil, and news of both the movements of Spanish treasure *flotas* carrying bullion and the tracks of Portuguese carracks laden with spices.

As part of his intelligence gathering, Cavendish visited Emery Molyneux, a mathematician and navigator who'd sailed with Drake around the world and who was building the first English terrestrial globe in Lambeth.[4] For the previous two years, Molyneux had been collecting the information that Cavendish was seeking. His globe would show the disposition of both the continents and oceans in accordance with the most recent observations. It would also function as a scientific instrument, which could be used to calculate distances between places as close together as London and Madrid and as far apart as Plymouth and Patagonia, using only the scale on its surface and a piece of string.

Terrestrial globes, which represented the Earth as a sphere that a person could hold in both hands, were an innovation of the era. Hitherto, when Europeans wrote of globes, they referred to the celestial variety, which depicted the planets and other astral bodies as they might appear from the focal point of a finite, spherical and geocentric universe. Celestial globes had first been made in Classical Greece, and were part of the iconography of antiquity, appearing on Imperial Roman coins and as motifs in the decorative arts.[5] Terrestrial globes, in contrast, did not exist before 1492, when Martin Behaim built the first example in Nuremberg. His globe was constructed from pasteboard covered in parchment, and showed the equator, tropics and polar circles, with an iron band marking the first meridian, which ran through Madeira. It was, according to Baron Nordenskiöld, 'the most important geographical' artefact 'since the atlas of Ptolemy had been produced in about 150 A.D.'[6] Innovation notwithstanding, Behaim's globe was out of date the year it was completed, when

Columbus returned to Spain with news of a new-found world. The name America was added to subsequent globes, and by 1520 enough of the continent had been charted to split it into two and add place names in precise locations, such as Florida and Acapulco.

Terrestrial globes were not only 'princely possessions' suitable, like unicorn horns, for gifts between monarchs, but also statements of power, used to assert territorial claims. A globe made by Euphrosinus Ulpius in 1542 in Rome, for instance, featured a prominent Tordesillas line close to the 46th Meridian showing where Spain and Portugal had divided the world between them, taking a hemisphere each to convert and exploit. Such partisan representations of the planet had to be countered and, when a copy of Gerard Mercator's globe from Louvain, which gave most of America beneath 'the Region of Cod-fish' to Spain, reached London it had been resolved that an English version, coloured with a Protestant world view and decorated with the feats of its navigators, should be built both to state the nation's global reach and assert Queen Elizabeth's claims to Virginia. The project had been entrusted to Molyneux, sponsored by William Sanderson, and announced in Richard Hakluyt's *Principal Navigations*.[7]

Molyneux followed his brief. He had rutters from both Cavendish's and Drake's circumnavigations, whose paths were to be marked on his globe, Cavendish's in blue, Drake's in red. These two bands would demonstrate that England had achieved more – in terms of circumnavigations – than all the other kingdoms in the world combined. Virginia, meanwhile, was mapped from information gathered on Raleigh's voyages, and some of the names John Davis had bestowed in Canada and Greenland were to be printed, together with the furthest point north that he'd reached.[8] A Northwest Passage, however, was hinted at rather than named on the new globe, whose poles Molyneux left vague.* In his opinion,

* Davis might perhaps have hoped for more. He was a longstanding friend of Molyneux, indeed had first introduced him to William Sanderson as a potential sponsor.

their form had yet to be seen by 'voyagers', i.e. known and trusted sources. He did, however, in a nod to the ancients, permit a massive hypothetical continent to be delineated with a dotted line around the South Pole, named Terra Australis Incognita.

Jodocus Hondius, a Dutch cartographer, had been recruited by Molyneux to decorate the new globe with place names, cartouches and compass roses once it had been shaped. When Cavendish visited, Hondius engraved his portrait.[9] He pictured Cavendish head on and from the waist up, dressed in an extravagant slashed doublet with puffed sleeves, and standing behind the eastern and western hemispheres of a globe, which were marked with the track of his circumnavigation. Cavendish, elegant as always, wore a single tear-drop pearl earring in his right ear.[10] This fashion, introduced by Sir Walter Raleigh, signified both his dedication to Queen Elizabeth (who'd adopted the pearl, symbol of chastity, as one of her emblems) and his achievements as a navigator. Hondius rendered Cavendish with large round eyes, and a neat, slender moustache above a sensual mouth. His cheeks are full, and his lips are pursed, as if about to issue a command. He looks fey – almost cherubic. A band encircles the engraving, which was printed for circulation, identifying its subject as THOMAS CANDYSSH NOBILIS ANGLUS AETA SUAE XXVIII ('the noble Englishman Thomas Cavendish at the age of twenty-eight').

Cavendish sat for another portrait, painted in oils by an anonymous artist, later that year.* This work brings the colour of his features to life – he had green eyes, chestnut hair and a slight beard and moustache, both a sandy shade of brown. Cavendish is depicted slightly sideways on, in a formal stance intended to demonstrate the courtly quality of *sprezzatura*, or nonchalance, so that he appears both at ease and poised for action. His right hand rests on his hip, his left on his sword. A cloak fit for a Spanish cardinal, embroidered with silver thread and seed pearls, is slung over his left shoulder, his peascod doublet is cut from vermillion

* Which now hangs in Longleat House.

velvet embroidered with gold thread, the velvet slashed to reveal puffs of golden silk and padded to resemble the pigeon-breast shape of a steel cuirass. The doublet is fastened with thirty-six hand-stitched gold buttons, and fourteen ropes of pearls hang like a sash from his shoulder to his waist. Below the doublet, Cavendish sports an embroidered set of trunk-hose and a spangled codpiece. He appears older than his representation in Hondius's engraving. The sickness that laid him low when he returned to England in 1588 shows in his pinched cheeks. His eyes, which had seen the wonders and the terrors of the world, are focused on some matter beyond the viewer.

His mind, indeed, was elsewhere. Over the same months that he'd been gathering information for his next voyage and sitting for portraits, Cavendish had been assembling a new fleet. His movements were followed by Spanish spies. They watched as the *Desire* was refitted in the Thames and reported to Mendoza (still fomenting discord in Paris) that Cavendish was making ready to 'go back to China'.[11] The spies also claimed that he'd commissioned a new pinnace, which had sunk with the loss of several men. The incident was magnified in subsequent communiques. Cavendish, wrote one spy, had lost a ship near Gravesend 'with 42 persons, none being saved'.[12] A week later, Mendoza received news from another informant that, when Cavendish's 'ship of 80 or 100 tonnes' 'was at anchor', his crew 'neglected to close her gun ports', and as the tide rose the sea poured in through them and sank her. She 'foundered so suddenly that only 15 out of the 70 persons on board were saved'. Two weeks later, the story, and casualty register, had grown even further. According to a third spy, 'Captain Cavendish' had set off for the South Seas 'with nine very well-armed ships. One of his ships foundered in the Thames, and all the crew were drowned except four men.'[13] No such human catastrophe or indeed expedition was recorded in England. Richard Hawkins later mentioned that Cavendish had lost a pinnace that had left her gunports open, but did not note any fatalities,[14] and the only death by drowning associated with the event recorded by the Gravesend coroners was that of a shepherd from Suffolk, who'd lost his flock and may have joined Cavendish as a privateer, hoping, perhaps, to repair his fortunes.

Once the *Desire* was back in trim, Cavendish turned to his Virginia connections to find him more ships. His first purchase was the *Roebuck*, acquired from Sir Walter Raleigh. At 240 tonnes, she was a step up both in size and potency from the *Desire* and had the reputation of being a fine sailing and fighting vessel. She'd been captained during the Armada campaign by Jacob Whitton, who Cavendish knew from Virginia. Whitton had managed to privateer as well as fight for his country during the campaign and his plunder had included ten bronze cannon, 'divers' muskets and pipes of wine,[15] which promised well for the voyage Cavendish had in mind.

Cavendish sent the *Roebuck* privateering in the Atlantic soon after he'd bought her. She was the first ship he'd owned that he hadn't commanded himself. However, William Battyn, the captain he retained for her shake-down voyage, showed none of his master's judgement once he was on the high seas. As soon as Battyn thought himself at a sufficient distance from the rule of law, he'd attacked a Dutch merchant ship, which he took to the Barbary Coast of Africa and sold to the Moslems, together with her crew.[16] However, she was not a legal prize; the Dutch accused Cavendish of piracy in the Admiralty Court, and Cavendish and the *Roebuck's* master were ordered to make restitution.

This setback didn't deter him. Cavendish replaced the over-enthusiastic Captain Battyn with John Cocke, his first cousin on his mother's side, who'd followed him into privateering, and increased his stake in the new venture that he was planning by buying a second ship, the *Galleon Dudley* (250 tonnes) from Sir Richard Grenville.[17] The *Dudley* had started life as the *Santa Marie de Vincente*, the Spanish galleon that Grenville had captured on his way back from Virginia in 1585. He'd refitted her as a privateer at Bideford in Devon and sent her out to raid, and afterwards to fight against the Armada. Like the *Roebuck*, she'd been tested in both action and heavy weather, and was an equally potent vessel.

Between the *Desire*, the *Roebuck* and the *Dudley*, Cavendish now had five times the carrying capacity of his circumnavigation fleet. Never again would he have to throw hundreds of tonnes of plunder into the sea. Nor would Spanish lancers decimate his men. His ships had space enough for over two hundred soldiers, which would give him sufficient firepower ashore to put his enemies to flight and ransack their towns.

Cavendish made the *Roebuck* and the *Dudley* earn their keep. He appointed John Clarke, another Virginia veteran, to manage the *Dudley*, and after taking out letters of reprisal for both ships and paying £2,000 bonds for each of them, he set them loose. The results were mixed. In February 1590, the *Dudley* attacked and plundered the *White Horse*, an English trading vessel laden with bullion, salt and other cargo. Her owners complained to the Privy Council about the 'outrage and insolency' of Captain Clarke, who'd given the *White Horse* a thorough going over. After being holed with cannonballs, she'd been boarded and robbed of her bullion, victuals, anchors and cables. She then sank with her cargo of salt, which dissolved back into the sea and Clarke had had to rescue her crew. The *Roebuck*, meanwhile, 'despoiled' two Irish fishing boats, and her actions prompted further complaints in the courts against Cavendish.

However, after these initial hiccoughs, both ships started to perform as expected. In July, the *Roebuck* brought a Portuguese prize laden with 550 tonnes of wine to Southampton;[18] and the *Dudley* returned to the same port with a Spanish prize carrying hides. A few months later, now under a new captain, Stephen Seaver, the *Dudley* took a Portuguese trader carrying sugar and cotton from Brazil and delivered her to Portsmouth. This prize was assessed at £1,340, close to the value of the privateer herself.[19]

Cavendish had chosen to land his ships in Southampton and Portsmouth rather than the usual western points of entry to England as a consequence of his budding friendship with Sir George Carey, the handsome, dashing and authoritarian Captain-General of the Isle of Wight. Thirteen years senior to Cavendish,

Carey had led an active life serving both the Crown and his own interests. He ran his island fiefdom with a firm hand. When some of its gentry had objected to him calling himself governor, he'd had their ringleader, Robert Dillington, summoned before the Privy Council and imprisoned. Carey is even reputed to have cleared the Isle of Wight of lawyers during his tenure. Sir John Oglander noted in his memoirs that 'in Sir George Carey's time an attorney coming to settle in the island was, by his command… hunted out of the island' and sent away with 'a pound of candles hanging at his breech lighted' and 'bells about his legs'.[20]

Carey had much in common with Cavendish. Both had been young achievers and believed in the maxim that the end justifies the means. Each considered privateering to be a sound way to take war to the enemy – and to make fortunes. Carey facilitated rather than indulged in the practice. He financed expeditions, offered privateers safe havens and rigged the courts to ensure they were biased in their favour. Privateering prospered in both Portsmouth and Southampton under his benign despotism. The merchants of Southampton in particular became major sponsors of voyages of reprisal. Both cities enrolled Cavendish as a burgess, which gave him the right to trade and other useful privileges that could be exploited when disposing of prizes. These new safe havens were part of Cavendish's planning for his forthcoming expedition. He wanted friendly home ports where he could break bulk before the revenue arrived.

While he trialled his new vessels and arranged havens for them, Cavendish considered the route he should take to China. Which way round the world should he travel? Should he follow in his own footsteps and sail via the Strait of Magellan and the Pacific, or might it be a safer bet to travel east, round the Cape of Good Hope at the tip of South Africa and across the Indian Ocean? Although his passage through the Strait had seemed easy, in hindsight this may have been unusually good luck. While Cavendish was considering his options, news arrived that the only English expedition to have attempted the Strait since 1587 had failed. In September 1590, four broken men appeared in Weymouth, passengers on a trading ship. They were the sole survivors of John Chidley's voyage to China by way of the great South Sea, which had attempted to repeat Cavendish's feats of navigation and robbery under licence.

Chidley had sailed from Plymouth in August 1589 with four ships, the *Wildman*, the *White Lion*, the *Delight* and the *Wildman's Cub*, and the highest expectations.[21] The City had been eager to finance him, and James Garet had sponsored Chidley's surgeon to build on Cavendish's botanical discoveries. In the event, the expedition was an outstanding disaster in an age where failure was commonplace. Chidley sickened and died aboard his flagship off the coast of Africa, and she immediately turned for home; the crews of two other ships became infected with the same fatal disease; and only the *Delight*, which had been separated from the rest of the fleet, reached the agreed rendezvous at Port Desire in Patagonia. She too had been struck by contagion and had lost sixteen of her men 'by God's visitation of sundry diseases' before she dropped anchor.[22]

The *Delight* was the first English ship to visit Port Desire since Cavendish had discovered it. It proved to be as fine a sanctuary as it had been in 1586. She graved her hull, took on water and fuel and topped up her provisions with 'good store of seals both old and young'. After this high point, her luck resumed its downward trend. William Magoths, who kept an account of the *Delight's* ill-starred voyage, detailed the decline. Her company lost another fifteen men and their landing boat on a penguin-hunting expedition soon after entering the mouth of the Strait. A storm then tore her off her mooring and carried her to Port Famine, where her company found the last man living of the garrison Sarmiento had planted in 1584. The other dozen who'd refused to leave with Cavendish had perished in the interim, and the survivor told Magoths that he'd since led a melancholy existence, living in a hut 'by himself a long time' and feeding himself by shooting game. This time he agreed to travel under a Protestant flag but died through sickness, malnutrition or delirium soon afterwards.[23]

As the *Delight* pushed on into the Strait, she lost five more of her crew to the Patagonians, who ambushed and murdered them. A further thirty-eight perished, 'partly by casualty, and partly by sickness'. After six weeks of butting against headwinds, and losing two out of three of her remaining anchors, the survivors had had enough. They presented a petition to the *Delight's* master, begging to return home and threatening a mutiny if they did not turn back at once. They also accused her captain, Hawlse, of carrying a pistol 'secretly under his gown, intending therewithal to have murdered Andrew Stoning and William Combe', who'd protested against his increasingly erratic command. They terminated their petition with the plea that 'we may (by God's help) return back into England, rather than die here among wild and savage People'.*

The petitioners got their way and the *Delight* sailed for Plymouth. However, the winds on the return voyage home were unfavourable, her rations ran out and, when she reached the Channel four months later, Captain Hawlse was dead and only six of her crew still lived. They steered for Cherbourg in France, where they dropped their last anchor. As a storm approached, they begged the governor of its port for the loan of a second, but he refused and 'suffered' the *Delight* 'miserably to be splitted, with desire to enrich himself by her wreck'. Magoths and three other survivors were finally shipped as passengers to Weymouth, the last of the ninety-one 'men and boys' who'd left England aboard the unfortunate *Delight* just over a year before.

Although it was unusual for a voyage to have had such comprehensive bad luck, the individual perils that had done for

* The petition was strikingly detailed: Captain Hawlse and Mr Street, the ship's mate, were alleged to have 'taken and seized upon 17. pots of butter, with certain cheese, and an hogshead of bread at a time, and have been thereof possessed to their own private uses And have not only immoderately spent the company's provision in butter, cheese, aquavitae, &c. but have also consumed those sweet meats, which were laid up in the ship only for the reliefs of sick persons'. See Hakluyt (Goldsmid) p.84.

Chidley's expedition were quotidian – shipwreck, violent storms, enduring calms, contagious and uncurable diseases, starvation, demented leaders and mutinous crews – and the odds against success were very long. But even failed endeavours brought back information that Cavendish could use – about ports, fortifications and conditions in Africa, the Azores and the Americas – and lessons to be learned. There was some good news buried in Magoth's tragedy: Port Desire was still an excellent haven for a small privateer (the *Delight* was the same size as the *Desire*), and the Spanish hadn't re-fortified the Strait of Magellan. There were also cautionary tales. The Gold Coast of Africa was rife with pestilence and to be avoided, and the penguins of Penguin Island in the Strait had to be 'eaten with speed' for the *Delight's* crew had 'found them to be of no long continuance' and had starved once they'd rotted.[24] On balance, Cavendish decided, after the obvious problems of Chidley's expedition, especially his failure to steer clear of Africa, had been stripped out, the Strait still seemed a sound bet. He was confident in the navigation, and could calculate with reasonable accuracy how long it might take to reach Port Desire and the provisions he'd need to carry. He'd learned how the currents flowed and the direction of the prevailing winds along the coast of South America during his circumnavigation, and where to catch these to carry him over the Pacific.

However, Cavendish continued to weigh up other options, including either sailing to or returning from China via the Northwest Passage. He paid a visit to Dr John Dee, the mathematician and necromancer who'd been its champion back in the 1570s. Dee had recently returned to England after five years' absence at various European courts, which he'd passed trying to converse with angels via an untrustworthy intermediary and a crystal ball. Cavendish was introduced to him by his uncle Richard Cavendish, a courtier who ran clandestine errands for the queen. Richard was fascinated by arcana and had been close to Dee for over a decade, even appearing in the doctor's dreams. Dee recorded one such encounter in his diary:

> France. Sept. 10th, [1579] 'my dream of being naked, and my skin all overwrought with work like some kind of tuft mockado*, with crosses blue and red... and another the same night of Mr. Secretary Walsingham, Mr. Cavendish, and myself'.[25]

Dee seems to have been star-struck when he met his friend's nephew. The 'most famous Mr. Thomas Cavendish', he wrote in his diary, who'd 'sailed round about the world, did visit me at Mortlake'.[26] Cavendish hadn't come for a horoscope. In addition to attempting communication with angels in his years abroad, Dee had kept up with developments in mathematics and cosmography, and Cavendish was there to pick his brains. How confident was Dee that the Northwest Passage *did* rather than *should* exist? Might it be easier to find its Pacific end, the Strait of Ainan, than its Atlantic entrance?

To counter whatever Dee told him, Cavendish had the evidence of the *Content*, the fly-boat on his circumnavigation, which had left him off Cabo San Lucas in 1587 to take the trans-polar route home, and hadn't been seen since. It was possible that she was still afloat, but, if so, the course she'd steered was no shortcut. He also had the evidence of Molyneux's globe, which was vague about the Northwest Passage, in contrast to the Strait of Magellan, which had been threaded with the red and blue tracks of English circumnavigators. Cavendish decided the passage was a bet he'd rather offer than take – the odds against it being navigable seemed too long. It was conceivable, however, that he could shepherd an expedition to find it at least part of the way there – a voyage within a voyage – and he was still considering the offer made to him in the preface to the *History of China* – that if he looked for the passage, with the assistance of John Davis, then the merchant William Sanderson would open his purse.

Cavendish rearranged his fleet while he considered his options, disposing of the *Dudley* and acquiring another, larger ship, the

* Imitation velvet made from wool.

Galleon Leicester from the sixteen-year-old Robert Dudley. Dudley was the illegitimate son of the Earl of Leicester, who'd been Queen Elizabeth's favourite of favourites for much of her reign, and had bequeathed the galleon to 'his well-beloved... base son' before his death in 1588.[27] The *Leicester* was an old vessel of 400 tonnes, built in the Hamble River in 1578, designed by the master shipwright Matthew Baker and framed by John Ady.[28] She'd served as Edward Fenton's flagship in his unfortunate voyage of 1582, and had proved herself in combat by sinking the Spanish galleon *Begonia*. She'd also seen action in the Armada campaign, when she was recorded as mounting forty-two guns and carrying one hundred and sixty men. Her broadside was powerful enough to batter down a fort, bring a ship of twice her tonnage to terms, or impress Asian potentates with English sea-power. Her hold, meanwhile, could accommodate nearly 300 tonnes of plunder.

Although the *Leicester* added an extra dimension to the forthcoming expedition, she was also a handicap. She was large for a privateer, with a draught of nearly twenty feet when fully laden, which was too great for shallow harbours on wild coasts where safe havens were few and far between. Cavendish compensated for diminished mobility by buying yet another ship, the *Black Pinnace*. She was a famous vessel – she'd recovered the body of Sir Philip Sydney, the 'peerless courtier', from Holland in 1586 and had played a part in the elaborate funeral celebrations that had preceded his burial. The *Black Pinnace* had since been relaunched as a privateer by Cavendish's fixer, Henry Seckford, and had notched up several prizes, including a large merchant vessel carrying salt cod to Lubeck.[29] She was a good sailer, well armed for her size and could be rowed into shallow havens where the *Leicester*, the *Roebuck* and the *Desire* couldn't venture.

Cavendish had his ships, and now he needed to prepare them for the voyage. He appointed Thomas Androwes, a gentleman who'd sailed on his circumnavigation, as his 'steward, overseer and paymaster of certain workmen doing divers things needful for their fitting out'.[30] Androwes had become a touch feral after sailing round the world and very quickly exceeded his authority, killing Edward Glasse, a working man who'd had the temerity to disagree with him, with a single punch 'of which' his victim 'died in a quarter-of-an-hour'. Androwes was locked in jail and charged with murder, leaving Cavendish's ships in limbo. Although he was acquitted after pleading self-defence, his imprisonment and trial had delayed preparations. Whenever Cavendish delegated, he seemed cursed to suffer for the wilfulness of his subordinates. The matter was much on his mind when he started to assemble a company for his ships.

21

Second Sons

London

ON 6 NOVEMBER 1590, A new romance entitled *Rosalynde: Euphues' Golden Legacy* was entered for publication in the Stationers' Register, whose author, Thomas Lodge, had just returned from serving as a gentleman-adventurer on a privateering expedition aboard Cavendish's *Galleon Dudley*. Lodge prefaced *Rosalynde* with two dedications in which he both explained its genesis and sought to establish a reputation for himself as a thinking man of action. Having 'made a voyage to the island of Terceira',* he told his first dedicatee, Lord Hunsdon, 'to beguile the time with labour I wrote this book; rough, as hatched in the storms of the ocean, and feathered in the surges of many perilous seas'. The second dedication was addressed to Lodge's 'Gentleman Readers', who he warned to 'make room for a soldier and a sailor, that gives you the fruits of his labours that he wrote in the ocean, when every line was wet with a surge, and every humorous passion counterchecked with a storm'. Lodge also cautioned his peers not to criticise his work, for, if any, metaphorically, were to board 'our barque to find fault with the tackling, when he knows not the shrouds', the author would react with equally metaphorical violence: 'I'll down into the hold, and fetch out a rusty pole-axe, that saw no sun this seven year, and either well baste him, or heave the coxcomb overboard to feed cods.'[1]

Despite the bombast in its dedications, *Rosalynde* was a pastoral romance, based on Chaucer's *Tale of Gamelyn*, most of whose action takes place in the semi-mythical Forest of Arden. Its style is euphuistic, with elaborate word play, labyrinths of metaphors and surreal mock pastoral scenes. Lodge clearly wasn't thinking about the sea raging and roaring around him while he wrote it, and *Rosalynde* is almost bare of maritime imagery. It does,

* In the Azores archipelago.

however, show the influences of a privateering voyage, including almost continuous heavy drinking and, against the tradition of the genre, an unhappy ending for Alinda, one of its princesses playing shepherdesses, whose father is killed on the last page.*

Thomas Lodge concluded his bibulous romance with a postscript to his Gentleman Readers, in which he told them his next project would be the 'Sailor's Calendar'. The title was tongue in cheek – mariners were known for being foul-mouthed and rowdy[2] rather than the natural poets and lovers who graced Edmund Spenser's *The Shepheardes Calender* or indeed *Rosalynde*, but it signalled that Lodge intended to build on his reputation as a man of action. He was true to his word and signed up for Thomas Cavendish's forthcoming expedition as a gentleman-adventurer aboard the *Leicester*.

Rosalynde inspired other gentlemen to follow Lodge into privateering. The novel had a second son as its hero, and Lodge had stressed that 'second and even third sons... yet may be superior to honours' to the firstborn. This notion appealed to many of his readers, themselves second, third, fourth or anything up to eleventh sons. The English law of primogeniture gave everything to their eldest brothers and forced them to make their own fortunes. Their caste prohibited them from participating in trade or indeed most types of work, and their paths to the wealth and fame they craved were limited. Their minds, moreover, had been shaped by Medieval concepts of honour and the chance, however slender, of winning fame (and money) by sailing around the world was irresistible.

Theoretically, gentlemen-adventurers were ideal recruits. They paid their own costs, brought their own servants and participated for a share of the profits, to be paid when the ship came home. Their ambition and willingness to treat themselves as expendable in the cause of honour, the hope of glory or the chance of

* William Shakespeare excised the scene when he turned *Rosalynde* into a play – *Love's Labour's Lost.*

paying off their debts blinded them to the high odds of dying on an intercontinental voyage. They flocked to Cavendish when they learned he was looking for volunteers, and over seventy of them signed up. His recruits included the nobly born and well-connected Edward Stafford, Henry Barwell, a member of the Norfolk gentry, Robert Arundell, kinsman to an admiral in the queen's fleet, and Anthony Knivet,[3] the illegitimate son of Sir Henry Charles Knivet. To these Cavendish added a similar number of military officers of a slightly lesser caste, who likewise participated for a share of the profits alone, brought their own arms and armour, and included veterans of the wars in the Low Countries such as Captains Morgan and Barker, and Lieutenant Royden.[4]

Mariners, in contrast, were reluctant to sign on for Cavendish's new voyage. Although even the apprentice Richard Casey had become rich on his circumnavigation, fewer than a third of his crew had survived it. Many of the missing were still unaccounted for, and some were assumed to be in the hands of the Inquisition. It was safer to ship coals from Newcastle or to go fishing or privateering in the English Channel than to join an expedition across the oceans. Chidley's voyage, for example, had achieved nothing and had lost hundreds of men, and there had been other expensive failures with long casualty registers over the years. Mariners' hearts were further hardened when Job Hortop, who'd been press-ganged to serve as a gunner aboard the *Jesus of Lubeck* on Sir John Hawkins's 1567 slaving voyage to Africa and the West Indies, returned to England in December 1590. Job had spent most of the intervening twenty-three years as a galley slave or a prisoner of the Inquisition, during which he'd endured sorrows to match those of his Biblical namesake. His troubles had only ended when Cavendish's *Dudley* had picked him up as a stowaway on a prize and set him down in Portsmouth.

Job's tale of woe spread through the ports, and a sensational version of his adventures was published in London two months later as *The travails of an Englishman*. His story made grim reading or listening for the average mariner. It included the highs as well as the lows of privateering, which made its author's losses all the keener. Hortop had lived through some of their worst fears, with every triumph succeeded by disaster. The expedition he'd been pressed on had had a prosperous start – Hawkins had enslaved five hundred Africans for the loss of only seventeen of his own men and had sold his victims to the Spanish in the Caribbean. Meanwhile, Job and his crewmates had accumulated parrots, monkeys and other exotica to peddle in England, including the skin of a giant alligator '23 foot by the rule, headed like a hog, in body like a serpent, full of scales as broad as a saucer', which they had stuffed with straw, 'meaning to have brought it home'.[5]

But the *Jesus of Lubeck* was old and rotting, and a few hard blows had opened her seams. Fish swam freely through gaps between her planking and darted among the ballast stones in her flooded bilges. Hawkins took her to San Juan de Ulloa in Mexico for repairs, where he was attacked by Spanish galleons. Caught in the crossfire of enemy cannon, he responded with the nonchalance of a courtier. Hawkins 'courageously cheered up his soldiers and Gunners and called to Samuel, his page for Beer, who brought it him in a silver cup'. Sir John toasted his crew, 'willed the Gunners to stand by their ordnance lustily' and emptied his cup. The instant he put it down, a cannonball crossed the deck and carried it overboard, 'which nothing dismayed our General, for he ceased not to encourage us, saying, fear nothing, for God who hath preserved me from this shot, will also deliver us from these traitors and villains'.[6]

God preserved Hawkins, although he had to abandon the *Jesus of Lubeck*, and cut and run after transferring her treasure and crew to the *Minion*, a smaller ship in his flotilla. The winds however were against him, his provisions were almost spent and, after a fortnight eating stewed leather, cats, dogs, rats and the parrots and monkeys his crew had hoped would make them rich at home, Hawkins returned to Mexico. Some of his men begged to be put ashore, claiming that they'd rather trust their luck as Spanish captives than starve at sea, and Hawkins told them to choose: those who wanted to stay should stand by the foremast, and those who wished to sail back to England with him should gather aft. Job went forwards and his decades of torment began. Captured by the Spanish and delivered to the Inquisition in Seville, Job watched two close friends being incinerated in front of a crowd chanting 'burn those heretics', before he too was hauled onto the scaffold and sentenced to ten years as a galley slave.[7] After he'd served his time, living on black biscuit and water and sleeping on 'the bare boards' of the rowing benches of the galley in extremes of both heat and cold, Job was returned to the Inquisition, who flung him into prison in Seville for four more years. He passed another seven working as a drudge for a Spanish bureaucrat, before escaping on a Flemish cargo ship carrying wine and oil from Spain to Holland. She had been intercepted by the *Dudley*, and Cavendish's ship took Job Hortop home.[8]

The timing of the publication of *The travails of an Englishman* was unfortunate. Cavendish had to pay over the odds to get the mariners he needed and offer up-front bounties in addition to the traditional inducements of free food and weapons and a share in the profits. By the time he had a basic complement for his ships, it was low on men who could manage them and top-heavy with officers and gentlemen.

Cavendish now had to arrange provisions for a year or more for his forthcoming expedition, which would cost as much as his fleet. There were rumours in London that he'd been gambling while putting his new venture together and had dissipated at cards much of the 'great wealth' he'd gained from his circumnavigation. He'd succumbed, it appeared, to the 'enchanting witchery' of gambling, 'an itching disease, that makes some scratch the head, while others, as if they were bitten by a Tarantula, are laughing themselves to death'.[9] He'd certainly made himself an attractive target for the wastrel companions of his pre-privateering days, happy to flaunt his sumptuous clothing and strands of pearls, as if he wished to tempt them to the gaming tables.

Whatever the cause, Cavendish was short of funds and turned to Henry Seckford, his privateering neighbour and fixer in Suffolk, who put Grimston Hall back into hock, together with 'Morston Hall, Stratton and other Trimley lands' that he owned nearby, which raised several thousand pounds.[10] Although Cavendish was opposed in principle to selling shares in his venture – he'd no wish to have to consider the demands and instructions of men in London when he was on the other side of the globe – he accepted several hundred pounds from small investors, including Carew Raleigh, Henry Seckford, Sir Henry Palmer, Richard Cocke, the Customer of Southampton, Master Heton, Eliot of Ratcliff and his cousin John Cocke, captain of the *Roebuck*.[11] Sir George Carey lent him an unspecified amount of money, secured on the *Desire*, together with a pair of fine bronze cannon.

Finally, Cavendish decided to admit William Sanderson, in addition to the voyage-within-a-voyage that had been proposed to him two years before. For the price of £1,100, John Davis would join the expedition, together with a barque named the *Dainty*, which had been loaned to him by Sir Adrian Gilbert.* According to Davis, the money was paid and the ship provided on the understanding that Davis would sail in convoy with Cavendish through the Strait of Magellan and into the Pacific. Once they reached California, Davis would break away with the *Dainty* and a pinnace that Cavendish would build for him and search for the Strait of Ainan – the eastern entrance to the Northwest Passage – 'upon those back parts of America'.[12] While he was keeping Cavendish company, the *Dainty* and her crew would participate in any privateering activities, and Davis would contribute his skills in navigation by captaining the *Desire* for the Atlantic part of the journey. It seemed a mutually beneficial

* A cousin of Sir Walter Raleigh famed for his rapaciousness.

arrangement, that would help Cavendish to balance his fleet and bring him an officer accustomed to sailing in stormy and frigid waters. It also gave him enough money to get over the line.

By mid-1591, all was ready and Cavendish applied to the queen for permission to leave England. On 24 June, she issued a 'Warrant for a writ of protection and assistance' to 'Thomas Cavendish esquire', which allowed him 'to take in hand a voyage by sea, for the service of the Realm, and to the increase of his own knowledge, whereby he shall be the better able hereafter to do service'; also granting him and his fellow adventurers the 'benefit of all prizes that may be taken by them'.[13] The writ constituted – in deliberately vague terms – a general royal licence to privateer.

Cavendish sailed from the Thames to Southampton, which was to be his new home port, where he was appointed Burgess on 9 July. He continued along the south coast of England to Plymouth, the assembly point for his fleet. He'd planned to recruit more mariners when he arrived but found it difficult to attract volunteers. Job Hortop's story was still news, the market was wary and he was forced to offer cash advances to recruit additional men. A number of those who signed up absconded with their advances, which enraged Cavendish. He complained to Sir Richard Hawkins, the eminent naval officer and privateer who was in Plymouth at the time, that deserters had cost him 'above a thousand and five hundred pounds'. Sir Richard noted afterwards that, within a few days of Cavendish's departure, he saw 'these varlets', 'walking the streets of Plymouth… without punishment' vaunting 'how they'd cozened' Cavendish 'some of five pounds, some of ten'.[14]

Rounding up the crew who did intend to sail took several days. Hawkins observed that he, his 'good friends and the justices of the town' were forced 'to search all lodgings, taverns, and ale-houses' for absentees. Some of the men they found were so drunk that they had to be carried aboard, 'they of themselves were not able to go one step'; others feigning illness were roused from their beds, and a number had become indebted to their landlords, 'and forced me to ransom them; one, his chest; another, his sword: another, his shirts'; another, his navigation instruments.[15]

Cavendish's final business before departure was to lade the expedition's victuals. Barrels filled with salt beef, salt pork and slabs of salted cod were unloaded from carts together with firkins of beer, rolled onto tenders and rowed out to the waiting ships, where they were hoisted aboard and stowed in their holds. Lading was slow and laborious. Barrels and other heavy items were manoeuvred with blocks and tackles, with several men hauling on each rope. Everything smaller was passed from hand to hand. There were sacks of dried peas and ship's bread, whole cheeses, kegs of butter, jars of sweet oil and vinegar, bricks of salt, live hogs and hens, and a cask or two of aquavit for invalids. At the same time, wood for the galley fire was loaded by the cord, together with sacks of charcoal, and the water casks were rowed ashore and filled.

While provisions were stowed, the fleet also took on its munitions. Cannon were shifted from wharf to ship and ship to ship and bedded in their carriages. They were accompanied with kegs of gunpowder, and boatloads of iron shot. Stores were taken on to build and repair as well as destroy. The timber to construct a pinnace, barrels of tar and nails, coils of rope, a forge and pigs of iron, spare spars and planks, and a second set of sails were stowed both above and below decks. Next, personal effects were added to the lading. Every man had his sea chest; the gentlemen packed theirs with finery – jaunty hats, their best shirts and doublets, and their personal weapons and armour. They also loaded private stores of food – pots of jam, casks of wine, haunches of venison and flitches of bacon. Finally, there were silver goblets and plates for the officers, trumpets, horns and drums for the musicians, and a few dogs and cats to be taken aboard.

On 26 August 1591, Cavendish sounded his trumpets, fired off a salute from his cannon and sailed his ships out of Plymouth harbour, the first man yet to attempt a second circumnavigation of the globe. His fleet comprised his flagship the *Leicester*, the

Roebuck, under John Cocke, the *Desire*, captained by John Davis, Davis's *Dainty* commanded by Randolph Cotton and the *Black Pinnace,* under its master, Tobias. Between them, they carried three hundred and fifty men.[16]

22

Through the Doldrums

Brazil

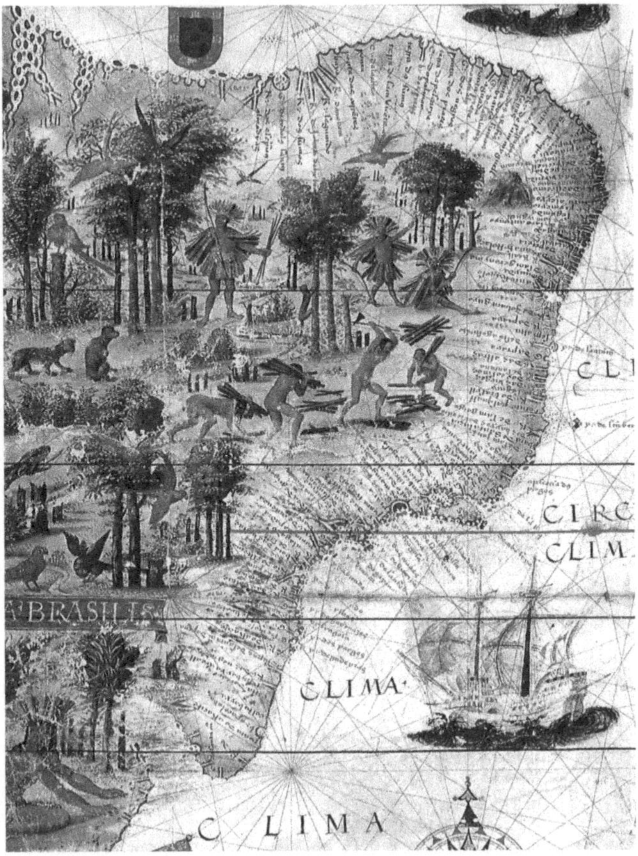

A FEW NIGHTS INTO ITS voyage, Cavendish's fleet 'met with nineteen sail' in the dark. The *Roebuck* immediately peeled off and attacked, 'not regarding who they were'. She captured one of the ships, which proved to be a foreign merchantman carrying salt. After the trader had been pillaged, three tonnes of her cargo were rowed over to the *Leicester*. The next morning, her master 'was brought before the General' and told Cavendish that his ship was a Flemish ship – an ally – showing him 'a license that he had to pass the sea, under Her Majesty's hand and seal'.[1] The *Roebuck* had committed an act of piracy when she took her, within sight of the eighteen other vessels in her convoy, which were only a week or so's sail away from their home ports. Cavendish immediately 'commanded that every man should return all such things as they had' pillaged. He then opened his own purse and 'he himself paid for the salt that he had taken'. This ostentatious gesture soothed hurt feelings and ensured the merchantman had no grounds for charging him with piracy. It would be ill luck indeed to get to China and back only to find himself on trial in the Admiralty Court over three tonnes of salt and the contents of a few mariners' sea chests. Diplomacy over, Cavendish departed from the mollified trader with a fair wind, holding his course 'from the coast of Portugal to the islands of Canary'.

He'd decided to head straight to Brazil rather than stopping in Sierra Leone, where Chidley's recent expedition had been ravaged by disease, and the Canaries were the first and only waypoint on his planned passage. His company knew the archipelago well – the *Roebuck*, with Thomas Lodge aboard, had been privateering off Terceira the year before – and when Cavendish reached the islands he paused his fleet just over the horizon, commanding 'the two smallest ships, the *Dainty* and the *Black Pinnace*, to be sent' inshore 'to see if they could espy any Caravels fishing, or any ships between the islands'.[2] The odds against picking up anything of value were long, but fresh fish and casks of wine were always welcome, as was news about the movements of enemy shipping. The *Dainty* and the *Black Pinnace* drew a blank, and Cavendish pushed on towards Brazil.

He was aiming for the port of Santos, in the Captaincy of Rio de Janeiro, which he intended to occupy and sack. He'd chosen to pursue a different strategy to the covert tactics he'd used on his circumnavigation. The research he'd conducted before leaving England had convinced him both that his fleet was likely to be more potent than any enemy he might meet in South American waters, and that he'd nothing to fear from launching an amphibious assault on a major settlement such as Santos. His course was south until he caught the trade winds, then west-southwest over the Atlantic to Brazil. However, he turned west too early and got caught in the doldrums, where his ships wallowed 'for seven and twenty days, driving to and fro without puff of wind'.[3] The tropical sun beat down from a cloudless sky, the air was hot and humid, and in these sweltering conditions the provisions started to rot. Cavendish discovered that he'd been dealt a bad hand back in Plymouth. He was only a month out of port, and his barrels of salted meats should have been proof against the elements for at least a year.

As the windless days turned into weeks, scurvy appeared. Its symptoms horrified any gentlemen-adventurers who hadn't seen it before. An ungallant listlessness was accompanied by spongy, bleeding gums, corpse breath and loose teeth. The extreme pain its victims suffered, as their cartilage wasted away and their joints disintegrated, was hard to disdain. The malady, moreover, seemed to strike at random, giving it a supernatural malevolence. Various theories of scurvy were voiced among Cavendish's company, including that it was triggered 'by the extreme heat of the sun and the vapours of the night'.[4] Whatever its cause, his surgeons were powerless against it and also suffered. One of their contemporaries summed up scurvy's symptoms, and his own efforts to cure himself:

> My thighs and lower legs were black and gangrenous, and I was forced to use my knife each day to cut into the flesh in order to release this black and foul blood. I also used my knife on my gums, which were livid and growing over my teeth. When I had cut away this dead flesh and caused much black blood to flow, I rinsed my mouth and teeth with my urine, rubbing them very hard.[5]

Morale fell as the weeks in the doldrums dragged on and the scurvy spread. Cavendish hadn't banked on being trapped for so long – if at all. He was irked by the delay and irritated by the speed at which the oppressive conditions had spawned divisions in his company.

One night while he was at dinner, Christopher and Cosmus, the 'two men of Japan', who he'd taken with him as interpreters, burst into his cabin 'telling their tale so loud that every one might hear the report (which was thus) that the Portugal of the ship' (a Portuguese pilot Cavendish had taken on for South American waters) 'was a Traitor, and that he had often given them counsel to run away with him at Brazil'.[6] Cavendish heard them out and, the more of the story he was told, the less he liked it. The 'Traitor', it seemed, had promised any deserters that, when they reached Brazil, he'd lead them across the continent to its Pacific coast, where they would be 'well rewarded for their intelligence'. Cavendish and his veterans knew that this was 'a thing impossible, for the Country is all Wilderness, and full of Savages'.[7] He realised that the promises were intended to entrap some of his men, who would be killed as soon as they travelled inland. The 'Portugal' had also known exactly where Cavendish was heading in Brazil, even naming Santos, suggesting that he'd been spying on him, for Cavendish hadn't disclosed his destination to his company. As punishment for his treachery, he had the pilot hanged from the main yard of the *Leicester*.

Cavendish's fleet finally slipped into the trade winds and, on 29 November, over three months after leaving Plymouth, 'we fell in with the Bay of Salvador' in Brazil, 'where we were becalmed until the second of December'.[8] While he waited for a breeze, Cavendish anchored his ships and sent their boats to reconnoitre the coast. They found a Portuguese barque – also becalmed – carrying bars of Peruvian silver and a cargo of African slaves, sugar and 'haberdash wares'.[9] They took the barque, named the *Marquina*, without a fight, and returned to Cavendish with their prize. The silver had vanished into his mariners' cloaks by the time they reached the *Leicester*, and Cavendish had no interest in the *Marquina's* human cargo. He allowed his company to pillage what they could, and they were amused to find 'a friar that hid himself in a Chest of meal' as they ransacked the hold.[10] Cavendish, meanwhile, summoned the barque's pilot, Jaspar Jorge, for interrogation.

Jorge claimed to know the coast of Brazil inside out, and Cavendish put him to the test immediately. The fleet needed fresh provisions – where was the best, nearest place to find them between their present location and Santos? Jorge piloted the *Leicester* to Ilha Grande, a fertile and lightly populated island fifty miles south of Rio de Janiero 'where we arrived the Fifth of December'.[11] Cavendish anchored and surveyed the shore. Large, isolated plantations showed up as cleared patches in the jungle, which rose up the faces of the steep hills behind them and cut them off by land from the rest of the island. Such remote settlements were usually self-sufficient, growing crops for their masters and slaves, rearing chickens, pigs and cattle, and maintaining large stores of wine and maize. If Cavendish was quick, he could load up on food and be on his way to Santos before news of his presence in Brazilian waters reached it. He sent a foraging party ashore to see what they could gather.

Antony Knivet was one of the foragers and wrote an eyewitness account. He was the illegitimate son of Sir Henry Knivet, a courtier who'd pursued a martial career and had shed 'both Limb and Blood' fighting for Queen Elizabeth. He'd inherited his father's strength, had had some military training and was in his late teens or early twenties when he'd joined Cavendish as an adventurer.* His account of his first footsteps on Brazilian soil is a mixture of wonder and disbelief. The planters and their slaves had fled into the jungle as soon as they caught sight of the foragers, leaving their houses empty and crops and livestock unprotected. Although ravenous himself, Knivet was shocked by the feeding frenzy that followed. Rather than collecting provisions for Cavendish in a calm and methodical fashion, his fellows rampaged through the plantations, with 'such disorder amongst ourselves that if any of the Portuguese had been of any courage, they might have killed many of us'. Gentlemen-adventurers fought each other for live chickens and chunks of the pigs and dogs they'd run down and ripped apart. Those that tore off the largest portions of flesh 'would get them into some hole, or into the wilderness under some tree, and there they would remain as long as they had meat'. The carnivorous orgy continued all day. Knivet joined in the 'sharking', grabbed 'a quarter of a hog' and withdrew into the woods with some friends, where 'we were merry for a night'. The next morning, they pilfered yams from a garden, which they carried to a house occupied by the 'General's Musicians',† who were 'dressing of eight young puppies for dinner'. They pooled their resources and feasted together before returning to the fleet, bellies full, but almost empty-handed.

Cavendish was exasperated by their failure. This was the first time his gentlemen-adventurers had been tested, and they'd proven to be wild and disorderly. If the simple task of looting a plantation was beyond them, how would they stand up to Spanish lancers? However, there was no time to send in further foragers. A trading vessel might spot his ships, or a *patache* be dispatched in search of the barque he'd captured, and it was possible that canoes were already carrying news of his arrival to the mainland. He had to strike before his intended victims could organise their defences. Before Cavendish sailed, the *Marquina* was looted of everything

* Knivet didn't know his own date of birth.

† Cavendish's company referred to him as their 'general'.

and anything of use or value, her cargo of slaves was emancipated, rowed ashore and abandoned, and the empty vessel was set ablaze. She was the only ship in the Americas to have known that he'd returned.

He now turned his fleet towards his target, the town of Santos. Founded in 1549, Santos was a flourishing settlement on San Sebastian Island that shipped sugar to Portugal and imported slaves from Africa. Trade each way was profitable, and Santos was graced with a handsome church, a hospital, a Jesuit college and library, and several minor chapels. The Jesuits had arrived in the town with its founders. Their fanatical asceticism* had won them respect among the indigenous Tupinambá, and their fortunes had flourished. Their college in Santos sent students to Lisbon and Rome to finish their educations, and its library had the finest collection of religious books in Brazil.

Cavendish had decided to attack this wealthy and secluded settlement before he left England. Santos had been charted by recent English visitors, inside information was available from an English merchant who'd settled there and Cavendish knew how to approach it, and where to land. He planned to take it, ransack it, replenish his victuals and use it as a base while his men built the pinnace that he'd promised to John Davis. Once the new vessel was complete, he'd sail for the Strait of Magellan.

As his ships closed in, Cavendish paused just over the horizon and sent the *Dainty* ahead to reconnoitre. She was fitted out as a trader, flew a false flag and sailed into Santos without mishap, where she bought a cargo of sugar from the ships anchored in its port. She returned with the news that the town was both prosperous, and poorly defended, confirming Cavendish's information, and Jaspar Jorge's advice that it 'was of no strength'.[12] Cavendish consulted

* '[I]f you could see Nobrega, their Superior, you would see a man who does not look like one: a man of skin and bones held together by hinges; a face of yellow wax, although always cheerful and full of smiles; sunken eyes;... bare feet flayed by the ground.' Hemmings, p. 97.

with his captains and decided that a hundred men would be enough to take it. These would go ashore in two large boats after dark on Christmas Eve, and attack on the morning of Christmas Day as soon as Mass was underway, when the Portuguese colonists and their families would have crowded into Santos's church. The landing party was to be led by Captain Cocke of the *Roebuck*.

When Cavendish announced his plan to his company, the gentlemen-adventurers stampeded for the boats. There was only room for half of them, and all were eager to exercise their swords and acquire some pillage for their sea chests. According to Knivet, 'there were so many of us that would have gone that we began to fight and cast one another overboard into the sea'.[13] In order to be sure of joining the raid, Knivet hid under a seat at the stern of the first boat and was trapped by the scramble for places. The press of bodies above him cut off his air supply and, the more he shouted, the quicker he used up what was left to him. As he was down to his last breath, 'William Waldren that was our Boatsman' heard his cries, 'tore up the boards and saved my life'.

The raiding party set off at ten at night, and by three in the morning were within sight of Santos, where Knivet's boat intercepted a canoe carrying a Portuguese couple, who were to be married in the town's church on Christmas Day. The wedding party were taken aboard and hushed, for Jorge had told the raiders to keep silent and stay out of sight until they heard the church's bell ring, 'for he knew by that Bell that they were in the middle of their Mass and at that instant the Friar was holding up the Bread of Sacrament for his congregation to venerate'.[14]

While Cavendish's boats waited off Santos, three hundred men and uncounted women and children, the cream of this affluent and oppressive settlement, fell to their knees in its church. The priest raised the Host to mark the instant of transubstantiation; the bell rang and Knivet and his fellow adventurers stormed ashore and attacked. Their first step was to bolt the church doors, and this simple measure gave them nominal control of the town. They collected swords from the congregation and waited for the rest of the assault party to arrive. The longboat, however, overloaded with gentlemen, had lagged far behind them and they were too few to achieve more than guarding the church and looting its immediate surroundings. Meanwhile, the faithful slaves of their Portuguese prisoners, who hadn't been admitted to Christmas Mass, carried their owners' valuables and provisions to safe havens. When the longboat finally reached shore, the advantage of surprise had been squandered.

The gentlemen-adventurers consoled themselves by sacking the town. The watching Jesuits bewailed their sacrilege. 'Those damned English', wrote Father Tolosa, made 'great assaults on the images, temples, relics', and even stole 'a holy head of one of the eleven thousand virgins which they threw into the sea'.[15] The Jesuits lost money as well as icons. Knivet joined in looting their college and, as he searched the cells of its priests, who were sworn to poverty, 'I looked under a bed, where I found a little chest fast nailed... I drew it forth, and finding it of great weight, broke it to pieces'. Glittering inside it were one thousand seven hundred solid golden coins.[16]

Cavendish brought the *Leicester* into Santos's port on Boxing Day 1590, together with the rest of his fleet. Davis had carried John Jane, his faithful accomplice and the chronicler of his arctic voyages, as part of his company on the *Desire*, and Jane once again kept a journal. Both the scale of Cavendish's venture, and its rapacious nature, were unfamiliar to him. He was used to celebrating landfalls with communal prayers, or a dance and a game of football with friendly heathens rather than looting public buildings and smashing statues of Catholic saints. Jane took a dim view of the disorder in Santos. It offended him most as a merchant. 'Such was the negligence,' he recorded, 'that the Indians were suffered to carry out of the town whatsoever they would in open view, and no man did control them.'[17] The following day, moreover, 'our prisoners were all set at liberty; only four poor old men were kept as pawns to supply our wants. Thus in three days the town that was able to furnish such another fleet with all kind of necessaries was left unto us nakedly bare, without people and provisions.' Jane's pessimism is at odds with Knivet's description of Santos, which recorded provisions aplenty. Cavendish had made contact with the local Tupinambá tribe, not all of whom were faithful to their Portuguese overlords, and the rebels among them had told him where he might find three hundred head of cattle, which were rounded up and 'served us all the time we were there'.[18]

Once he'd secured provisions, Cavendish detailed men to build the pinnace he'd carried over in kit form. Davis was to take ownership of her once they'd passed through the Strait of Magellan. She was completed within the month, fitted with masts, rigging and sails, and christened the *Crow*. She was a handy little craft of twenty tonnes, which could be either sailed or rowed, with ten oars per side.

While work on the pinnace was underway, Cavendish boarded his gentlemen-adventurers with him at the Jesuit college. The Tupinambá had warned him that the Portuguese had gathered soldiers around the town and would attack if they ventured out. Although Cavendish might have been happy to rid his company of some of its less disciplined members to a Portuguese ambush, it was safer to keep them under his eye. The writer Thomas Lodge was one of the gentlemen that Cavendish confined to the college, and he whiled away his time in its library, looking for inspiration for a new book. He found it in a 'history in the Spanish tongue, which as I read delighted me, and delighting me won me, and winning me, made me write it'.[19] Using the quills, paper and ink he'd carried over in his sea chest, supplemented by Jesuit supplies, he started work on a novel set in the Americas.

At the time, it seemed to Lodge that he might have months ashore to write it. After the delay in the doldrums, the word in the fleet was that it was getting too late in the year to attempt the Strait of Magellan. 'Many of our company,' Knivet recorded, 'counselled the General to winter at this town', arguing that it would be better to sit out the seasons than brave the Southern Ocean in late autumn.[20] Santos was renowned in Brazil for its fine weather all year round. According to the Franciscan friar Vincente Do Salvador, its climate was moderate 'like that of Iberia' as it was situated 'beyond the torrid zone at twenty-four degrees south latitude or more. This means that the land is very healthy and has good water'.[21] Why leave so pleasant a spot, where they could be sure of eating well and sleeping in comfortable beds? The prospect of returning to their cramped cabins, which they associated with hunger, discomfort and the dread of scurvy, for the long slog south to the Strait, grew less appealing every day they continued ashore.

However, Cavendish had resolved that 'he would not by any means' linger after the *Crow* was fit for sea. His company had had time enough to recuperate, and he was now racing the clock to get to the Strait before the seasons changed. The town was scoured for provisions, and the gentlemen were sent back to the ships. Thomas Lodge raided the library before he left, and said his goodbyes at the waterfront to Giuseppe Adorno, an elderly Genoese merchant and scholar who owned a sugar cane plantation mill near the town and had become a friend over his stay. At their parting, Adorno gave Lodge a valediction and prophesised that he would come to no harm on the journey ahead: 'Vale said he, mi fili, Deus te salvum reducat in domum tuam.' ('Farewell, my son, God will bring you home safely.')[22]

The fleet sailed from Santos on 22 January 1592. Just before he hauled anchor, Cavendish sent a party of men overland to sack the nearby hamlet of St Vincent, to be collected by the ships' boats once they'd performed their task. This gave some of the gentlemen who'd been cooped up for a month the chance to vent their aggression, and they wrecked St Vincent, its famous chapel (one of the first to have been built in Brazil) and burned 'five Engenios, or Sugar Mills' before linking back up with the ships. If Cavendish had hoped that the raid might have served as a safety valve, purging his company of its pent-up frustration and readying it for the journey south, he was to be disappointed. The raid ended, according to Knivet, in a similarly chaotic way to the action in Ilha Grande the month before: 'the disorder of our men was such at their embarking, that if the Portugals had been of any courage, they might easily have cut our throats.'[23]

Once Cavendish's fleet had passed over the horizon, the traumatised inhabitants of Santos and St Vincent emerged from the rubble to rebuild their settlements. The Spanish priest Martín del Barco Centenera visited shortly afterwards and witnessed the damage. Centenera was a high-living religious man who'd been disciplined and fined by the Inquisition for his scandalous lifestyle after it had been 'proved that he treated the people of his district like Jews and Moors, that he revenged himself on all that offended him', that 'At public banquets he drank to intoxication… talked openly of his successful amours' and 'kept a married woman as a mistress'.[24] His own lax standards notwithstanding, Centenera was shocked by what he saw. Stone walls had been smashed down, the church of Santos and various chapels had lost their facades and belfries, icons of the Holy Saints had been torn from their niches and shattered into pieces and even the alms boxes had been 'pillaged of their poor pence'. Door and window frames had been prised out of houses for firewood, and anything of any value in the houses, including furniture and bedsheets, had been stolen. Their owners, meanwhile, had had their rings ripped off their fingers and their clothing torn off their backs. 'Happy was the man,' Centenera observed, 'who found his home still standing, for all the rest / In smoking ruins blocked up every street.'[25]

In addition to listing Cavendish's atrocities, Centenera accused Machado, the Portuguese governor of Santos, of weakness and duplicity. If he'd summoned up his Tupinambá warriors at once he might have saved his town and its sacred icons and sent his enemies to hell. Centenera did, however, find something to celebrate amid the ashes and rubble of Santos. The faith of its inhabitants was intact, as was their belief in the power of prayer:

The folk,
Did with a thousand voices that sad day
Clamour to heaven; there the old men moan,
The youths upraise… imploring eyes,
Matrons and maidens wipe their streaming cheeks[26]

And, Centenera concluded, 'even tender infants by their sobs' begged God for vengeance on Thomas Cavendish.

23

The Gate to Hell

South Atlantic

CAVENDISH'S FLEET HAD FAVOURABLE WINDS for the first fortnight of its eighteen-hundred-mile journey to the Strait of Magellan. His ships cruised in sight of each other, the newly built *Crow* proved to be a good sailer and Cavendish entertained his masters and captains aboard the *Leicester*. En route to the southernmost part of the known world, he maintained the standards of an English gentleman and indulged in his favourite diversion of gambling. His musicians played, his guests dined off silver plate, the cards were shuffled and, according to Knivet, Cavendish 'won a great sum of money'.

On 7 February, the breeze died and, when Cavendish took observations, he found he was at the same latitude as the River Plate, which led to the Spanish city of Buenos Aires. The calm seemed fortuitous, and he decided to send his smaller ships – the *Dainty*, the *Black Pinnace* and the *Crow* – into the river to see what they could pick up. He gathered his captains together and gave them sailing instructions as to how to proceed if they became separated: they 'should use their endeavour', he told them, to reach Port Desire, where 'they should tarry a fortnight'. If no other ships appeared during that time, then 'they should leave some mark on the shore and go on their voyage' to the Strait.[1]

However, the still airs were the prelude to a *pampero*, a violent weather system from the southwest, triggered by cold air rushing up from the Antarctic to fill in an Atlantic low. It exploded over Cavendish's fleet before he could detach his three light ships on their raid. The *pampero* was the first true storm that Knivet had experienced, and he was astounded both by how quickly it had come on, and by its ferocity. The wind switched direction to southwest, the sea became 'very dark, swelling in waves so high that we could not perceive any of our accompanied ships, although we were very near to one another'. The wind kept rising and waves started breaking 'over the poop of our ship and washed our men astonished with fear into the scuppers'.[2] They hung on for their lives to stop themselves going overboard, grabbing at ropes, blocks and rails. As the *pampero* took hold, the *Roebuck* was driven into the *Leicester* and 'broke down all our gallery', while tumbling waves swept her deck clean. 'Here miserable Fortune began to frown on us all,' Knivet grieved, 'especially on me.' His sea chest was swept overboard 'and all that I had, both in clothes and money', including his horde of gold coins, 'were cast into the Sea.'[3]

The *pampero* blew for three days, and Cavendish lost sight of all his ships bar the *Crow*. At the height of the storm, the *Leicester's* sails were 'blown away from the yards' and the *Crow* sank within sight of her, drowning the thirteen souls aboard. Knivet was struck by Cavendish's poise amid the maelstrom. 'Our General showed himself to be of a noble courage,' he recorded, for Cavendish 'did nothing but run up and down, encouraging his men, who were all amazed, thinking that to be their last hour.' His exertions saved his flagship, but when the wind abated the seas were still huge, and she was 'not able to bear any sail'.[4]

While the *Leicester* was driven along under bare masts, her company, according to Knivet, 'wished themselves again at Santos'. They'd been frightened rather than inspired by Cavendish's 'noble courage', which had seemed more like obsession than valour. When he got wind of the grumbling, Cavendish 'came forth upon the half-deck', called his company together and commanded them to speak their minds. He gave them time to vent their fears, heard out their claims that the rest of the ships had already turned back for Brazil, then explained that he'd 'given directions to all the masters and captains of the fleet' to rendezvous at Port Desire. There would be no turning back. They might even meet their consorts en route and Cavendish promised a reward of £20 'to whomsoever could first spy a sail'. He'd calculated their mood very well, and 'every man was satisfied', heartened that there was a clear plan to follow. When the sea calmed down, they got underway again and, ten days later, the *Leicester* and her company 'safely arrived at our desired port', where Cavendish found the *Desire*, the *Black Pinnace* and the *Roebuck* waiting for him.[5]

Davis had reached the rendezvous nearly a fortnight before his general. The *Desire* had weathered the *pampero* relatively well, and by chance Davis had picked up the *Roebuck* en route, which he'd found in 'a very desperate case'.[6] She'd been damaged by her collision with the *Leicester*, and the storm had shredded her sails and ripped away her rigging. Her captain, John Cocke, had been convinced she might sink at any moment and had begged Davis 'to keep him company'. When the seas permitted, Davis had rowed over to her, assessed the damage 'and returning' instructed the master of the *Desire* and all her company 'to be careful in all their watches not to lose the *Roebuck*'.[7]

The ships had entered Port Desire together and, once they'd anchored, Davis and Cocke organised their companies into working and hunting parties. The workers, comprising carpenters and other skilled mariners, repaired the damage to their ships while the hunters collected seals, penguins and fresh water. They were joined ten days later by the *Black Pinnace*, and on 18 March, six weeks after the *pampero* had struck, 'Master Cavendish came into the harbour in a small boat which he had made at sea, for his longboat and light-horseman were lost'.[8]

Cavendish was spitting blood by the time he reached the *Desire* on his makeshift craft. According to Jane, he exploded in fury as soon as he stepped aboard 'and spoke most hardly of his company and of divers gentlemen that were with him' on the *Leicester*. He'd been shocked by their lack of spirit when it had been put to the test and voiced his pent-up rage at their weakness.

Once he'd let his anger run, Cavendish checked his ships. The *Desire* and *Black Pinnace* both seemed in good condition, and he was relieved to see the *Roebuck* at all – she'd looked ready to sink when they'd crashed together during the *pampero*. He told

Davis that the *Crow* had been lost, and asked Randolph Cotton, the master of the *Dainty* who was standing on the deck of the *Desire*, what had happened to *his* ship? The *Dainty's* company had been itching to sail back to England after she'd loaded up with sugar in Santos, so was she wrecked or had she run for home? Although Cotton couldn't answer his questions, Jane recorded that it was assumed throughout the fleet that the *Dainty* had used the storm to creep away. Cotton hadn't been able to hold her back as he'd been visiting Davis when the *pampero* struck and had been trapped on the *Desire* for its duration. Although disappointed by the news, Cavendish wasn't surprised that she'd deserted. Her owner, Sir Adrian Gilbert, was greed personified, and likely had given her company secret orders to return to England at the first opportunity if they found a worthwhile cargo.

Cavendish's next concern was to establish whether or not he could bring the *Leicester* safely into Port Desire. It had been four years since he'd christened the haven and written its name onto his chart. On that occasion it had been the perfect retreat, where he'd beached and graved his ships and stocked up with enough fresh provisions to carry him to Chile. This time, however, the sweeping tides that had been so useful for careening were a menace. When he asked his captains if they thought the *Leicester* would be secure in Port Desire, they said no. The tidal streams 'ran so violently' that the *Roebuck* and *Desire* were having trouble holding their anchors, and the larger, heavier *Leicester* didn't stand a chance. 'They told me,' Cavendish recorded, 'in any wise not to come in with my ship, for that if she should come on ground she would be utterly cast away.'[9] But should he trust them? He knew Port Desire from his last visit, and it was possible that his captains were exaggerating its hazards.

He weighed up the risk of running aground against the condition of both the *Leicester* and her company. The *pampero* had given her hull a beating, she'd had 'a new shift of sails clean blown away' and had come close to sinking three times. She needed urgent repairs, and if Cavendish could get her into the harbour she could be patched up in a week or two with the help of the mariners from the rest of his fleet. Her crew meanwhile were close to collapse. 'There were never men that endured more extremities of the sea,' Cavendish wrote, 'than my poor company had done.'[10] They'd had to pump and bail continually to stop the *Leicester* foundering and were in far worse health than those aboard the *Roebuck* and the *Desire*, who'd spent the past fortnight feasting on sealion and roasted penguins, supplemented by tapioca and other delicacies they'd looted at Santos.

A rest, fresh food and light work, Cavendish reasoned, might also restore morale aboard the *Leicester*. But, then again, too much rest could be counterproductive, feed his company's fears and render them unwilling to confront whatever terrors lay ahead. They might panic, mutiny and force him to return to Santos. Meanwhile the southern summer was nearly over. In 1587, he'd reached the Pacific end of the Strait of Magellan by 24 February, and the winds had already turned furious and contrary. It was now late March and, the longer he waited in Port Desire, the slimmer his chances of getting through. In the event, the risk of wrecking his lumbering flagship – which he was beginning to loathe – was the deciding factor: 'finding this to be no place for so great a ship without her utter ruin', he wrote, he kept the *Leicester* anchored outside Port Desire and commanded his fleet 'to make themselves ready to depart'.[11] It was imperative that his ships stayed together. The *Leicester* had proved to be useless for coastal work, the *Roebuck* was also restricted by her draught, both had lost their landing boats and Cavendish needed the *Desire* and *Black Pinnace* to carry out raids and collect provisions in shallow waters.

❧

The two-hundred-and-forty-mile journey to the mouth of the Strait of Magellan took eighteen long and turbulent days, with 'furious storms between Port Desire and the Strait'. The air chilled as the ships edged south and the sea turned a cold steel-grey, crested with whitecaps raised by the powerful and contrary winds.

Cavendish was alarmed by the continuing decline of his company, who 'were grown extremely weak'.[12] He'd taken a chance on a quick voyage and as the days ticked by his men faded. Few of them had been this far south before and their febrile imaginations had been nourished by horror stories of their destination – a channel between the oceans so deep that an anchor might be let out to the end of its cable and still swing over an abyss, blasted by storms and hemmed in by icy mountains whose flanks were populated with giant-footed, dog-faced cannibals. Santos seemed a paradise in comparison, and, as the journey wore on, more and more men aboard the *Leicester* wished they could turn back.

On 8 April 1592, Cavendish sighted the entrance to the Strait, and some of his company's imagined fears very quickly came to life. An intense cold descended and the sky turned black. As soon as his ships had nosed their way through the entrance, the wind ratcheted up against them until it blew a constant gale. 'Such was the adverseness of our fortunes,' Cavendish wrote, that we 'found in the Straits the beginning of a most extreme winter not durable to Christians.'[13] Hoping to change his luck, he drove his ships into the wind, fighting his way forward mile by mile. The *Leicester*, Knivet recorded, was 'forced to lie beating before the harbour of Port Famine three days ere we could double that cape'. When the ships tried to anchor 'in twenty fathoms of water' to stop being blown backwards, the current was so vicious that 'on a sudden' it 'would carry away the ships with cables and anchors afloat in the night'[14]

It took Cavendish three times as long to reach Port Famine, a sanctuary of sorts, as it had in 1587. He found the former city of King Philip, which had been filled with the 'noisome stench' of dead bodies on his last visit, to be dissolving into the landscape. Its buildings and gibbet had tumbled down, and the bones of its citizens had been picked clean by seabirds and had settled into the soil.

The winds held Cavendish captive in Port Famine for a week. The *Leicester's* company, like the Spanish before them, went ashore to pick 'mussels and fruits of the country to eat, and the bark of a tree that was like cinnamon'.[15] When they had signed up for the expedition, few of the gentlemen-adventurers had expected to spend their time on land dressed in rags and scavenging rock pools. Many, like Knivet, had lost their sea chests to the *pampero* and were forced to make do with what they'd been wearing when it struck. Even the best made clothes didn't last long on an expedition. Sir Walter Raleigh reckoned that 'a suit of apparel would be worn to shreds', in average conditions, 'within six months at sea'.[16] In the Strait of Magellan, wading through the seaweed and slipping against rocks studded with barnacles, its lifespan could be measured in days.

While Cavendish's fleet was weather-bound at Port Famine, the temperature dropped below zero. Snow covered the ships and whirled down their hatches. The men who'd been foraging had to sleep in the same sodden tatters that they'd worn all day, and many contracted frostbite. Knivet woke one morning so 'numbed that I could not stir my legs'. When he pulled off his stockings to wring them out, 'my toes came with them' and the remains of his feet 'were as black as soot and I had no feeling of them'.[17] Crippled by his injuries, Knivet lay shivering below deck. There was no room for him in a cabin, and he was laid out on a sea chest behind a bulwark.*[18]

As soon as a window in the weather appeared, Cavendish got his ships underway. He made steady progress for a few days. 'So long as we had ground to anchor in and tide to help us,' he wrote, 'we beat into the Straits some 50 leagues, having for the most part the winds contrary.'[19] Jane, aboard the *Desire*, ticked off the landmarks in his journal. On 14 April, 'we passed through the first strait. The 16 we passed the second strait, being ten leagues distant from the first. The 18 we doubled Cape Forward.' Three days later,

* This may have been a blessing. Cabins on long voyages were reckoned to be 'sluttish dens that breed sickness' where flesh killed by frostbite soon became gangrenous. See Dyer, p.135.

however, 'we were enforced by the fury of the weather to put into a small cove' on Tierra Del Fuego, 'where we remained until the 15th of May'.[20]

This sanctuary, an uncharted haven, was christened Tobias Bay after the master of the *Black Pinnace*. A broad river led inland from the bay, and Cavendish sent a boat to explore. Could it be an unknown channel to the Pacific? His crew 'found it to be very straight and deep' but of limited extent. It had, however, some value. 'On the sides thereof they found great mussels, and in them good store of pearls, and we named it the River of Pearls.'[21] None of the explorers had the strength to gather them. Conditions were apocalyptic. John Jane, a veteran of three arctic voyages, had never before experienced such brutal weather. 'We endured extreme storms,' he wrote, 'with perpetual snow, where many of our men died with cursed famine and miserable cold.'[22] Knivet, meanwhile, recorded that 'with the cold there died every day out of our ship eight or nine men'. Many of the survivors were maimed, like Knivet, by frostbite: 'Here one Harris a goldsmith lost his nose, for going to blow it with his fingers cast it into the fire.'[23]

Even Cavendish thought conditions exceptional. The month of May brought 'nothing but such flights of snow and extremities of frosts, as in all the time of my life I never saw none to be compared with them'.[24] He was losing men at an unprecedented rate. 'In seven or eight days', he recorded, 'there died forty men and sickened seventy, so that there was not fifty men who were able to stand upon the hatches.' Some of the sick – as was the custom – were carried onto land to recuperate, but in the circumstances this action was tantamount to murdering them. According to Jane, they 'were most uncharitably put ashore into the woods in the snow, rain and cold, where men of good health could scarcely endure it, where they ended their lives in the highest degree of misery'.

The *Leicester*, moreover, was falling apart. She'd lost her best sails in the *pampero*; Cavendish had given some of her spares to the *Desire* and had to force his way into the Straits with wholly inadequate canvas, for 'no ships carrieth three new shifts of sails'. Her rigging and tackle, meanwhile, had frozen over and were wearing out – the ropes were frayed and had been spliced again and again to repair snapped sections. She'd lost an anchor and anchor cable, was still leaking from the storm and was becoming impossible to steer. She'd almost run aground three times 'by reason of her unyarey working'.[25] If the weather didn't break soon, the *Leicester* might never escape Tobias Bay. But what were the chances of it breaking?

Cavendish decided to sound out Davis, 'because', in Jane's words, 'he was a man that had good experience of the Northwest parts in his several discoveries that way'. Did storms give way to calms in high latitudes? Should they turn back, or wait for change? Davis told him to bide his time. In his opinion, 'this snow was a matter of no long continuance'. However, Cavendish wasn't convinced. He'd seen what a Patagonian winter could do to a well-equipped venture in 1587, when he'd renamed the City of *Rey Felipe* Port Famine. He couldn't sit it out for much longer. The alternative was to spin around, exit the Strait, sail east across the Atlantic and reach Asia via Africa rather than the Americas. So major a change of course required his company's assent. He called them together aboard the *Leicester*, pulled out his charts and ran through their options.

Cavendish reminded them that their ultimate destination was China and told them that there were two ways to reach it. They could either continue to try to pass through the Strait and travel to it westwards across the Pacific, or they could turn back on their tracks and sail east towards the Cape of Good Hope in South Africa and from there to Asia, 'which course I showed them was as well-known to me' as the route through the Strait.[26] In his mind, the Cape was the best option. The wind would be with them, they would be sailing into warmth and sunshine, and Cavendish promised his company he had no doubt that together they would 'perform to their contents our intended voyage' if they took that route.[27]

However, most of his audience had forgotten the original intents of the voyage. They'd become focused on survival in the Strait, and visions of bloated galleons groaning with the limitless wealth of the Far East had lost their allure. After hearing Cavendish, they rejected the African option and 'plainly and resolutely determined never to give their willing consents' to setting course for the Cape of Good Hope.

John Davis was also opposed to the Cape route, which would entail sailing in the opposite direction from his private objective in the North Pacific, even though the agreement that he'd reached with Cavendish was now void. The *Crow* had been lost, the *Dainty* had run away and these had been the vessels allotted to him for his search for the Strait of Ainan. Davis, however, believed that events might offer opportunities to resurrect his ambitions, and advised Cavendish against sailing east. If 'it pleased him to consider', he told him, 'the great extremity of his estate, the slenderness of his provision, with the weakness of his men, it was no course for him to proceed in that new enterprise'. He added that the *Desire* too had suffered and that, though she carried seventy-five men, 'there is but the Master alone that can order the ship, and but fourteen sailors'.[28] Like the *Leicester*, she was top-heavy with gentlemen, who had not as yet made any effort to learn to sail.

With Davis on their side, Cavendish's company composed a 'Humble Supplication' to their general, which begged him not to risk his life, which was their 'Chiefest Care', nor indeed *their* lives by embarking on so long a voyage with broken-down ships and insufficient provisions. They suggested that they returned to Brazil instead, where his force 'was able to take any place'. They could choose their anchorages, repair their vessels, reprovision at leisure and 'at a seasonal time' return to the Strait 'and so perform our first objective.'[29]

Cavendish ran through the odds stacked against the alternatives to returning to Brazil, as if to prove to himself that honour sometimes had to bow to misfortune. He'd lost a fifth of his crew, and twice that many were too sick to stand upright. The

Leicester continued to deteriorate, and as she fell apart she became ever harder to sail. He'd taken stock of his provisions in Tobias Bay and calculated he'd enough for four months, which might not be sufficient to see his fleet past the Cape of Good Hope. Brazil was closer, and its settlements, from recent experience, were undefended. He could send in his smaller ships to pick up seals and penguins at Port Desire en route.

He told his company that he was ready to turn back on his tracks, on condition that they gave the Strait of Magellan one last try. They would 'put out of the harbour and beat to get through so long as the furious and westerly winds would suffer us but if they came upon us so as we could not hold it up – we would then... according unto their requests, go for the coast of Brazil which they so much seemed to desire, and which I so hated'.[30] Soon after his ships had raised anchor, the winds started howling in their faces, and on 15 May, Cavendish turned his fleet around. 'We were beaten out of the Strait,' he wrote, 'with a monstrous storm at west south-west from which place we continued together till we came in the latitude of 47 degrees south.'[31]

24

Betrayal

South Atlantic

THE WINDS DIED AFTER BLASTING Cavendish out of the Strait, and he paused at Penguin Island to collect fresh provisions. While gathering penguins and sealions, his men came across a group of Tehuelche tribesmen, one of them a shaman 'who cured with words'.[1] Cavendish called him aboard the *Leicester* when he heard about his skills. Any treatment, however strange, was worth trying if it might help heal his sick crew members.

The shamans of the Tehuelche peoples of Patagonia were supposed to have wondrous powers, granted to them by demons, who attended them in pairs and obliged them to dress as women. These powers included the ability to 'foretell future events; to discover what is passing, at the time present, at a great distance; and to cure the sick, by fighting, driving away, or appeasing' the fiends that tormented them. Shamans achieved their ascendancy over the forces of evil with no other magic than oral spells. After death, they themselves became demons.[2]

Knivet was a willing patient for the shaman. 'I was so ill in the Strait,' he confessed, 'that no man thought I would have lived; and twice I was brought up upon the Hatches to be cast into the Sea; but it was the will of God' that on both occasions 'I spoke, desiring them not to cast me overboard until I was dead.' Each time he'd been returned to his bed on the sea chest, where the lice 'lay in clusters' 'within my flesh'.[3]

The shaman's method of healing seemed very strange to Knivet. Rather than applying a poultice, or manipulating his injured limbs, 'this man', he recalled, 'said some words over my feet, and I had feelings in my legs and feet, which I had lost before for the space of a fortnight'. He was astonished at the change, not least of all because 'many times before' the shaman came 'I had hot irons laid to my feet, but I had no feeling were they ever so hot'.[4]

Although Knivet recovered sensation in his legs, he couldn't yet stand up and remained on his chest-bed while Cavendish, on the half deck overhead, gave sailing directions to the masters of his ships for the return journey to Brazil. They should follow him out to sea until midnight and, when he showed two lights at the *Leicester's* stern, they were to tack back towards the coast. It was crucial that they stayed together, in so far as the weather permitted. If separated, they were to rendezvous off Santos.

The fleet split that night. The *Leicester* and the *Roebuck* tacked inshore, but the *Desire* and *Black Pinnace* either did not see, or chose not to follow, their General's signal at the agreed time. They continued out into the Atlantic, and at dawn the next day were nowhere in sight. Rather than heaving to and waiting for his missing vessels, Cavendish continued north, expecting that they would realise their error and catch up with him soon. He made steady progress up the coast, covering, by his own calculations, over five hundred miles until he reached 'the latitude of 36', close to the mouth of the River Plate, still without any sight of his missing ships.[5] It was a good point on the coast to pause, where their tracks might converge, and the season for *pamperos* was thought to have passed. But 'three or four days after this', Cavendish 'encountered the most grievous storm that ever any Christians endured upon the seas to live' 'in the which the *Roebuck* lost her main mast, and we lost her'.[6] It was a mirror image of a *pampero*. Equally intense, it blew from the north instead of south, and once again into his face.

As waves tumbled the *Leicester* about, Knivet's chest-bed broke loose from its lashings and slid sideways over the gun deck each time the ship rolled, accompanied by loose barrels and cannonballs. If Knivet was dislodged or the chest tipped over, he was doomed. He prayed as his chest rumbled across the deck, and his prayers were answered. The finger of the Almighty steered it into a gap between a gun carriage and the 'carpenter's cabin on one side' of the *Leicester*, and when she rolled the other way to a niche between another cannon and the surgeon's cabin on the opposite side of the ship. It 'was the will of God that the chest never turned over', he concluded, 'for if it had, I could not have escaped death'.[7]

The storm blew itself out within a few days. The *Leicester's* mariners were shattered and crept below hatches to sleep. Some refused to take orders 'and would not come up' to help manage the ship.[8] Their disobedience infuriated Cavendish. The *Leicester* was still a long way from safety, and it seemed self-evident to him that there was no time yet for sleep. His character was changing as the pressure on him built. He'd lost faith in his company and realised that the odds of achieving his own dreams or indeed preserving his honour were subject to the whims of cowards and buffoons who needed to be shocked into their senses. According to Knivet, Cavendish seized 'the end of a rope as big as my arm', descended to the gun deck and lashed out at the malingerers.[9] As he aimed his knout at a mariner hiding behind Knivet's chest, he hit the invalid instead and knocked him out. Cavendish's fury and strength soon quelled the revolt, and the men returned to their duties. Knivet, however, was taken for dead for a third time on the voyage. He was carried to a gun port and his feet pointed overboard, when God once again prompted him to speak, and the sea-burial party restored him to his chest.

After subduing his men, Cavendish continued towards Brazil. He had other worries on his mind. The *Roebuck* hadn't been seen since the storm. If she was lost, it would be a double tragedy as she carried most of his expedition's provisions. She also had a serviceable landing boat, whereas the *Leicester* was limited to a scratch vessel pieced together from sugar chests and barrel boards. Even if he found the *Roebuck* as a floating wreck, she could be of use to him. The weather however kept driving him north, and Cavendish nursed his ship towards the Tropic of Capricorn 'with most extreme labour and great danger'.[10]

Meanwhile, rumours that Davis had deserted him were flying round the *Leicester* and ringing in his head. They seemed true.

When the fleet had been trapped in the Strait of Magellan by foul winds and the cold had laid waste to his crew, Davis had argued that they should sit it out and had been wrong when he'd promised that the snows would end soon. And when Cavendish had suggested they went for the Cape of Good Hope, Davis had demurred. Rather than accepting that his sub-venture to the Strait of Ainan was now impossible, he'd backed the mariner's petition for Brazil, claiming the *Desire* was suddenly in need of a quiet place to refit. If Cavendish had turned for Africa, Davis's chance of breaking away from the fleet to search for the Northwest Passage would have been lost. These suspicions hardened into the conviction that he'd been betrayed. Davis knew that the *Leicester* was useless for coastal raids. She drew too much water to get into many anchorages, including Port Desire, was hard to control in narrow channels like the Strait and – as Davis also knew – had lost both of her landing boats. Moreover, Davis appreciated that, if he split the *Desire* and the *Black Pinnace* from the fleet, he was condemning the larger ships to almost certain ruin, and their crews to starvation, if they persisted in the expedition rather than turning for home, yet he'd ignored both Cavendish's sailing instructions and his signal.

Cavendish had to put Davis from his mind while he focused on his immediate need for a safe anchorage where he could patch up the *Leicester*. When he sighted the Brazilian coast, he navigated north until ten leagues short of Santos. He halted off the island of Santo Amaro, whose crest of hills hid him from the town. Santo Amaro's Atlantic coast was sparsely settled, with a few plantations and sugar mills backed by jungle and precipices.

The moment the *Leicester* had set her anchor, Cavendish was mobbed by his gentlemen for permission to launch a raid on a sugar mill that was visible from her decks. His needs were pressing, but the mill was isolated and the risk of a raiding party being ambushed seemed small. Cavendish agreed to let them go on condition that they stayed within a mile of their landing place. A handful of gentlemen climbed into the *Leicester's* patchwork tender, rowed for shore and struck lucky. They took the mill without firing a shot and found it to be crammed with provisions, including pigs, chickens and sacks of guinea wheat. The gentlemen also seized a longboat that had been moored near the mill, which they loaded with some of their loot and sent out to the *Leicester*. The new boat was a godsend to Cavendish, more important than the fresh food it carried. Like a pinnace, it could be either sailed or rowed, and it was large enough to accommodate two dozen armed men. It restored his ability to work in shallow waters and harbours and tilted the odds a little way back in his favour.

The success of this initial raid prompted his company to ask for another. A Tupinambá tribesman, who'd shipped on the *Leicester* in Santos, stepped forward supported by Captain Barker, a veteran mercenary, to tell Cavendish that there was a substantial farm just out of sight around a point, which possessed huge stocks of food. The Tupinambá seemed credible, Cavendish trusted Barker 'in the Conduction of men', believing him to be 'the most careful in such matters of service', and he gave the proposed raid his blessing. He told Barker to pick 'some 20 or 30 men', and gave him explicit orders on how to proceed, willing him that if 'he had any Respect or regard of my commandment' he must not linger and 'return quickly' whether he found 'anything or nothing'.[11]

The scratch boat was prepared and twenty-five of the 'most principal men' on the *Leicester* crowded into it, including Captain Edward Stafford. Stafford was Cavendish's close friend, and of equal social status. They had a distant family connection and Cavendish felt responsible for the younger man. The boat left at four in the morning. Nine hours later it was sent back with a part load of victuals – 'Guinea wheat, six hens, and a small hog', and the message that they would provide more by and by. This leisurely style of looting for no great reward 'very much aggrieved' Cavendish. Why hadn't they obeyed his command to get in and out as quickly as possible? Cavendish knew the dangers of landing a small party beyond the protection of his ship's guns – he'd lost a fifth of his crew that way on his circumnavigation. He sent a message back that he 'much marvelled that they would tarry at a place so long with so few men' for so little reward: 'it was not a hog and six hens that could relieve us' and 'charged them straightly to come aboard'.[12]

The raiders didn't return that night. Cavendish suspected the worst but had no way of sending them reinforcements. He'd posted the boat taken at the sugar mill up the coast to look out for the *Roebuck* and his other missing ships, and the wind was blowing offshore, preventing him from moving the *Leicester* any closer to land. On the second day, the wind swung round and Cavendish tacked into the bay. He anchored 'within musket-shot' of the shore, as close as he dared to approach, and waited out a third night.

The Portuguese had been preparing for Cavendish's return ever since he'd sacked Santos. Salvador Correia de Sá, the governor of Rio de Janeiro, had ordered the men and ports under his command to look to their arms and organise their defences. If Cavendish came back, de Sá and his forces would be ready. And the odds suggested that he would return. No one had succeeded in passing west through the Strait of Magellan during winter, and Sarmiento, Fenton and Chidley, all known to de Sá, had failed in kinder conditions.

De Sá was a conquistador of the old school, cold, hard and daring. He'd emigrated from Portugal to Brazil in 1557 at the age of twenty and was responsible for much of Rio de Janeiro's prosperity. He'd first served as its governor between 1567 and 1572, when he'd encouraged immigration from his homeland, 'stimulated the installation of sugar mills', 'promoted the construction of the city's defences' and encouraged the slave trade with Africa.[13] During his second term as governor, which had commenced in 1578, de Sá had sponsored searches for gold, diamonds and slaves in the hinterlands of his captaincy and set himself up as a warlord. Friendly tribes sold 'their Wives and Children' to his expeditions for 'knives and hatchets' and provided him warriors for his slaving raids against their enemies.[14] The Tupinambá tribesmen who supported him were potent allies, bred from infancy to combat, who wouldn't flinch at the sight of a steel sword or twitch at the sound of gunfire. Their bows were as powerful as English longbows and their aim so accurate that they could shoot birds, however small, out of the sky; their preferred weapons for close combat were clubs heavy enough to crush skulls and spatter brains; and their tribal customs expected them to fight to the death, not just for glory, but also for pleasure.[15]

De Sá sent a force of eighty Portuguese and three hundred Tupinambá to ambush Cavendish's shore party as soon as he learned of its whereabouts. According to Centenera (the philandering Argentinian priest and poet), whose details came from eye-witnesses, a massacre resulted. Captain Barker's prudence had deserted him the instant he'd landed. He and his men had behaved like schoolboys on holiday, stretching their 'ship-cramped legs' and strolling up and down the beach while De Sá's force moved into position on the hill above them.[16] As Cavendish's men ambled towards the ambush, Tupinambá crept in to surround their landing point and a 'vigorous youth of Santos' swam out to their boat, hauled up its anchor and set it on fire. The trap was sprung, and Barker's company were forced back to the tideline, where the tribesmen rained arrows on them. Once they'd been incapacitated, their enemies rushed in and bludgeoned the wounded to death with their 'studded battle-mauls'. Those who put up any resistance were 'Hacked into a hundred gobbets in a trice'.[17]

After the victory, trophies were carried back to Santos and put on show. Centenera recorded that a Tupinambá displayed a finger he'd cut off one of his victims that 'Bore a gold ring, set with a costly gem'.[18] The ring was for sale, with or without the finger. This event was taken as proof of divine favour: God had seen the tears of frustration trickling down the faces of the town's young men, frustrated at their impotence during Cavendish's last visit, had heard the sobs of its infants and had given them the revenge they'd prayed for.

Cavendish learned of the tragedy four days after his shore party had left him. The Indian who had proposed the raid alongside Captain Barker was seen signalling to the *Leicester* from the shore. When no boat came to pick him up, he paddled out on a log. He was badly wounded, 'having one arrow shot through his neck and another in his mouth and out through the pole', and told Cavendish that all his men 'had been slain'. When Cavendish asked why his men had disobeyed his orders to return at once, the Indian replied that 'some were unwilling' and 'the rest did nothing else but eat hens and hogs'. Cavendish was furious at their fatal idiocy and grief-stricken to 'see twenty-five of my principal men thus basely and wilfully cast away'.[19] His anger was compounded by frustration. De Sá's men had destroyed his last boat, and the long boat captured from the sugar mill was scouting for the rest of his ships. He was forced to wait at anchor for a week until she returned, followed shortly afterwards by the *Roebuck*.

The *Roebuck* was, Cavendish recorded, 'in the most miserable' condition, 'having spent all her masts' bar her mizzen, with her 'sails blown clean away'. However, while her masts were broken, her soldiers were alive, her landing boat was intact and Cavendish determined 'to be revenged of' the 'base dogs' who'd massacred Captain Barker and his party, by attacking Santos and beating it 'to the ground'.[20] Although he'd occupied the town without bloodshed back in December, this time he wouldn't scruple to spare lives.

He took the *Leicester* and *Roebuck* into the *Canal de Bertioga*, a narrow channel that offered a back route to Santos. This was a gamble – heavy vessels avoided the *Canal*. Less than a mile across at its widest point, it was dotted with shoals and hemmed in by mangrove swamps, and its winds were few and fickle under the lee of the island's spine. As Cavendish led his ships into the channel, it shoaled, revealing beds of 'ooze' along both banks. At the sight of this hazard, familiar to many of his mariners from home waters, panic spread through the *Leicester*. The 'Company affirmed plainly' to Cavendish that 'it was both desperate and most dangerous' to push on. If they grounded, they would be lost. The gelatinous ooze would swallow an anchor, and if it bound to the *Leicester's* hull would hold the ship in place by suction, making it impossible to tow her free. The small tidal range, meanwhile, wasn't enough to refloat her if she became stranded. Their fears seemed realised when the *Leicester's* keel grounded and, according to Knivet, 'we had much ado to get her clear again'.[21] Nothing larger than a pinnace could have reached Santos through the *Canal*. Cavendish was forced 'to let our Revenge pass', and 'determined to part from thence'.[22] He couldn't make a frontal attack on Santos without the *Desire* and *Black Pinnace*, and there was no sign as yet of Davis.

Necessity, moreover, compelled him to move on rather than wait for his missing ships and the chance of revenge. 'Our great wants did constrain us to seek some course of relief', he confessed and he sailed for the island of San Sebastian, sixty miles to the north.[23] San Sebastian was large and lightly populated, with good anchorages and plenty of firewood and drinking water. Before he set sail, Cavendish dispatched a raiding party to loot the plantations bordering the *Canal*. This foray was a success and the raiders returned with 'great store of Mandiora Roots, Potatoes, Plantains and Pineapples'.[24] Cavendish also made a last attempt to recover his friend and cousin Edward Stafford, sending a letter to the governor of Santos demanding his release, and threatening 'vengeance dire, with fire and sword' if he failed to comply.[25]

According to Centenera, the letter arrived in Santos on 'St Peter's Eve' and was received by its residents as 'a very jocund and amusing hap'.[26] Stafford had been one of the twenty-three men killed in the ambush and mutilated by Tupinambá warriors. It might have been his finger and ring that had been exhibited round Santos. Let Cavendish threaten as he wished. He couldn't reach them, and nothing larger than a finger remained of his friend.

Their schadenfreude was stimulated by Cavendish's confession in his letter that he dared not return to England 'without this youth' for fear that his noble father would kill him for so great a breach of honour.

25

The Petition

South Atlantic

After sailing away from Cavendish, John Davis had been struck by the same anti-*pampero* that had beaten up his General's ships. The winds blew so hard that the *Desire*, according to John Jane, was 'enforced to hull, not being able to bear sail' and let the sea carry her along under bare masts. 'And in this night,' he continued, 'we perished our main trestle trees, so that we could no more use our main topsail, lying most dangerously in the sea.' The *Black Pinnace*, meanwhile, had sprung 'a great leak' and was 'enforced to seek the next shore'. Both vessels were also running out of food and 'because famine was like to be the best end', Davis was forced 'to go for Port Desire'.[1]

According to Jane, their safe arrival in this sanctuary was a blessing. God had directed them to a snug anchorage, with a self-regenerating pond of sweet water close by, from which 'we fetched more than forty tuns of water, and yet we left the pool as full as we found it'. The Almighty had also guided an 'abundance of smelts' to the ships, 'so that with hooks made of pins every man caught as many as he could eat'.[2] The giant tides, meanwhile, uncovered rich mussel beds, and the islands in the harbour yielded seals and penguins.

Davis knew that Cavendish wouldn't make for Port Desire in the *Leicester* – the tides had been too much for her in February. The company of the *Desire* knew this too and besides were underwhelmed by the bounteous provisions Jane recorded. 'We live only upon seals and mussels,' they protested, 'having but five hogsheads of pork within board, and meal three ounces for a man a day.' Worst of all, there was only water to drink. Angry that they'd lost touch with Cavendish, concerned about both the condition of the *Desire*, whose shrouds were 'all rotten, not having a running rope whereto we may trust', and the absence of 'any pitch, tar, or nails' to repair her, they wanted to seek their General off Brazil rather than hang on in bleak Patagonia.[3]

Davis was alert to the discontent but didn't want to miss his chance. He now had the ships he needed for his quest for the Strait of Ainan. The *Desire* and the *Black Pinnace* were an altogether better hand than the missing *Dainty* and the sunken *Crow*, the vessels that had been allotted to him for exploration. Davis needed a ruse to distract his crews from looking for Cavendish and proposed a compromise to them. He would take the *Black Pinnace* north, manned with the 'best of the company' to find their General and collect naval stores from him so that they could carry out essential repairs. The *Desire* could stock up on seals and smelts and refit in his absence. Her men 'utterly misliked' the suggestion. Rumours quickly spread aboard the *Desire* that Davis intended to abandon them 'to be devoured by the cannibals'. This was the last straw and, according to John Jane, they plotted to assassinate him. Led by Charles Parker and Edward Smith, 'the whole company joined in secret in a night to murder our captain' together with Jane and 'all those which they thought' were Davis's friends. The proto-mutineers scratched marks on the walls of the captain's cabin so that they could 'kill him with muskets' fired 'through the ship's side', and – an occult touch – cast 'bullets made of silver for [his] execution'.[4]

Davis got wind of the conspiracy and faced down the *Desire's* company before they could carry out their plan. He spoke humbly when he addressed them. In 'danger of being murdered', Jane noted, he was 'constrained to use lenity, and by courteous means to pacify this fury'.[5] He also changed his story, telling the company that he wanted to send the *Black Pinnace* in search of Cavendish because he knew that his leader 'could not be without her, because he was fearful of the shore in so great ships' rather than to collect provisions and stores. But the men didn't believe him. If that was the case, then why didn't they all go? Besides, how could such a celebrated navigator have made so elementary a mistake as losing contact with his flagship, unless it had been on purpose? Davis might pretend to want to do the right thing, but they suspected he had ulterior motives. The company 'all cried out with cursing and swearing that the pinnace would not go unless the ship went' too. Their blasphemous language gave Davis an opening, and he launched into a sermon. He seems to have been a mesmerising preacher, and he trusted his powers of persuasion when appealing to men via their faith. Why, he asked the company, were they not thanking God for their deliverance from hunger and storms? Davis offered 'many examples of God's sharp punishment for such ingratitude', and concluded with pious barbs at the ringleaders of the insurrection against him, telling them that 'the Lord' would 'judge between you and me'. According to Jane, the sermon pacified the crew, who agreed that the ships would stay together and wait at Port Desire for Cavendish. However, the company insisted that they put their version of events on record and drew up a petition, which they delivered to Davis. It was clear to them that he'd broken away on some private mission, and they wanted no part of it. The petition set out the company's past torments and present wants, and their version of how the fleet had become separated off Patagonia. When Cavendish had turned 'for Brazil', it stated, 'there to winter and procure victuals', the whole fleet had followed him, the *Desire* 'coming under his lee shot ahead of him, and so framed sail fit to keep company'. However, 'This night we were severed, by what occasion we protest we know not, whether we lost them or they us. In the morning we only saw the *Black Pinnace*.'[6] The petitioners' protest was studied ignorance: they'd kept the course that Davis had set – it was for him to explain why he'd chosen it. Storm damage and the threat of famine, the petition continued, had since forced them to make for Port Desire. Now they wanted to sail back to Brazil to look for Cavendish, or to Plymouth if they couldn't find him.

The petition was signed, or marked, by thirty-nine men, mostly drawn from the ship's officers and mariners. Some were identified by their titles – 'The Boatswain', 'The Boatswain's mate' – rather than their names, and a number of individuals were represented by a single name – Fisher, Leonard, Benjamin – and 'his mark' i.e. a cross rather than a signature. The list was headed by John

Perry, master of the *Desire* who'd served under Cavendish on his circumnavigation, and the petitioners demanded that Davis sign it too. They wanted to ensure that their resistance had been documented and their behaviour justified – to their General, if the fleet was reunited, or to an English court if they returned home.

Davis signed, harmony returned and, according to Jane, 'we began to travail for our lives'.[7] The company dug a charcoal pit, and built a forge where they made 'nails, bolts and spikes'. The mariners unbraided an anchor cable and used its strands to plait new rigging. Those not engaged in remedial work collected mussels, fished for smelts and killed seals. The marine bonanza enabled Davis to conserve the ship's stores, and they 'spent not any' during their stay at Port Desire. After two months of make and mend, Davis announced that it was time to move on. Instead of heading north to his rendezvous with Cavendish in Brazil, he told his crews that he was now 'fully persuaded that the General might go directly for the Straits', rather than waiting for the southern hemisphere summer to arrive, and without looking in on Port Desire. The harbour, it seemed, had gone from the most likely place to find Cavendish to the last place he would visit.[8] The General, Davis argued, had had plenty of time to resupply in Brazil, might even have sailed by while they were holed up in Patagonia and, if they were to find him now, they should hurry south. His disingenuous advice was accepted, and on 6 August Davis sailed for Penguin Island, where the crews of the *Desire* and the *Black Pinnace* 'salted twenty hogsheads of seals', then turned for the Strait of Magellan in high hopes.[9]

As a reminder, however, that winter lingered, Davis met with 'a sore storm' shortly after taking on his seals, and the *Desire* was forced to drop all her canvas and drift with the wind and waves.[10] The storm forced them east, deep into the Atlantic and, on 14 August 1592, they were 'driven in among certain isles never before discovered by any known relation, lying fifty leagues or better from the shore, east and northerly from the straits'.[11] These were the Falkland Islands, and Davis and his men were possibly the first humans to set eyes on them. The winds spun around before they were wrecked against the Falklands and blew Davis back to the South American coast and the entrance to the Strait, where he anchored on 18 August in dense fog.

The air soon cleared, the wind turned fair, Davis raised anchor and sailed into the Strait. Three days later, he reached Cape Froward, a journey that had taken ten days in April. The nights were now longer, the days colder and, as the *Desire* and *Black Pinnace* zig-zagged west, south, then west again through the silent and sinister landscape, their companies waited in dread for the storms that had turned them back four months previously. Meanwhile the mountains rose up on both sides of the Strait with snow on their peaks and flanks, glaciers in their valleys and clouds boiling over their summits. After passing the ruins of Port Famine, haunted by 'the sinister grey *Carnero*', a carrion-eating bird that 'picks out the eyes of shipwrecked sailors', they rounded Cape Froward and turned northwest.[12]

As the Strait narrowed, the mountains crowded in on them, often seeming to block the way, the only suggestion that there might be open water ahead a narrow V between the precipitous slopes on either side. The ships sailed in shadows during the short hours of daylight, and in this hallucinatory landscape it appeared that the sea beneath them was draining away, back into the Atlantic, its previous high-water mark delineated by patches of stunted birch trees clinging to the lower slopes of the hills like seaweed, and cascade waterfalls pouring out of apertures around them. By 25 August, Davis was 'within fourteen leagues' of the Pacific Ocean.[13] This was the closest he'd been to the exit from the Strait, he didn't know the route ahead and he had to trust the navigation to the ship's master, John Perry. However, before he could proceed any further, the weather checked him. He found shelter from the headwinds in a cove and, once the *Desire* was safely at anchor, made the most of this setback by telling her company that it was the best place to wait for their General, 'for the strait in this place is scarce three miles broad'. It would be impossible to miss the *Leicester* and *Roebuck* – should they come that way.

The excuse wore thin after Davis had been pinned in place for ten days by freezing winds. Meanwhile, the seals his company had collected at Port Desire were rotting and 'stunk most vilely'. There was little else to eat, the temperature was sub-zero all day every day and, according to Jane, 'our men died pitifully through cold and famine, for the greatest part of them had not clothes to defend the extremity of the winter's cold'. Their weakness was to Davis's advantage. They were now so close to the Pacific that he could argue that their best option was to continue rather than to turn back and wait for Cavendish. They were more likely to find food ahead. When the winds became fair on 13 September, Davis set off northwest and, Jane recorded, 'came in sight of the South Sea' the same day.[14]

However, the break in the weather was brief. The clouds rolled down from the mountain tops and formed a black lid overhead that shut out the sky. The winds ratcheted up to gale force in this daylight darkness, and Davis had to take shelter just nine miles short of the Pacific. When the storm eased, Davis tried to break out again, and was almost clear, before 'furious weather' rose up and headed him once more. He put out two anchors on the *Desire*, but the high winds and turbulent seas snapped the hawser on her main anchor, and though the company sweated to recover it their efforts were futile as 'it lay so deep in the water', embedded in the dreaded ooze. Happily, Jane recorded, God was watching over them and on 1 October the winds eased. The *Desire* raised her remaining anchor, which was found to be attached to its cable by a single strand of rope. Another twitch and it would have parted.

The *Desire* was towed off into the Strait by her boat, but, before Davis could get her underway, her company forced another council. They had waited for Cavendish without success, and now it was time to let the winds they'd been fighting against take them back to Port Desire, where the seals were fresh and men did not freeze to death. Davis recognised that the company no longer trusted him and, by a clever piece of subterfuge, got John Perry to argue his case that they should continue towards the Pacific. Davis first warmed up his audience with a liberal portion of godliness, filled with digs against Cavendish. 'And because I see in reason that the limits of our time are now drawing to an end,' he told them:

> I do in Christian charity entreat you all, first to forgive me in whatsoever I have been grievous unto you; secondly, that you will rather pray for our General than use hard speeches of him, and let us be fully persuaded that not for his cause and negligence but for our own offences against the Divine Majesty we are presently punished.[15]

Davis concluded his softening-up process with an appeal for forgiveness, accompanied by maudlin reflections on mutability. 'Lastly, let us forgive one another,' he said to them, 'and be reconciled as children in love and charity, and not think upon the vanities of this life.' If they died they would all go to 'live with our glorious redeemer', and if they lived they would 'find favour with God'.[16]

His words resonated with his audience. In the present circumstances, the vanities of this life were easy to scorn. The company were focused rather on necessities – on staying warm and eking out their diminishing stock of rations. The sombre surroundings, with the route back to the Atlantic hidden behind Cape Froward, and the way ahead represented by a thin and distant strip of daylight between the mountains, also encouraged reflections on their own insignificance. If they were ever to return home, the crews of these weather-beaten ships, with frayed sails and brittle rigging, would need the blessing, if not the outright assistance, of a greater power.

Davis now turned to John Perry and asked his advice as to which course they should take. Perry was unequivocal. 'If you think good to return,' he told Davis in front of the company, 'I will not gainsay it; but this I assure you, if life be preserved by any means, it is in proceeding.' Once they were through the Strait, he explained, there would be provisions in abundance in Chile. At 'the Isle of Santa María I do assure you of wheat, pork and roots enough. Also I will bring you to an isle where Pelicans be in great abundance' and, when they reached Peru, 'we shall have meal in great plenty'. There was also a fair chance of intercepting Spanish ships along the way. 'But if we return,' he continued, 'there is nothing but death to be hoped for.' Perry's points were confirmed by other circumnavigators in the crew; the promises of fresh food swayed the minds of the rest 'and there was a general consent of proceeding'.[17]

'And so, on the second of October,' Jane recorded, 'we put into the South Sea.' The *Desire* and the *Black Pinnace* were through the Strait of Magellan, 'free of all land' and riding Pacific swells.[18]

26

Dark Star

Brazil

WHILE DAVIS WAS FIGHTING HIS way through the Strait, Cavendish navigated the *Leicester* and the crippled *Roebuck* along the coast of Brazil towards the island of San Sebastian. He'd built his pinnace there in 1586 and knew it offered a secluded anchorage. It was far enough offshore to protect him from a surprise attack by the Portuguese and had the timber and water he needed to repair his ships and replenish his casks.[1] Moreover, Cavendish still held the faint hope that Davis might reappear, and San Sebastian was ideally positioned to keep a lookout for him. Finally, he could keep his company under his eye on the island and get his sick men ashore to recuperate. Once his situation was stable, Cavendish's plan was to strip the *Roebuck* of her crew, provisions, guns and any useful fittings, and then scuttle her.[2] This would give him a full complement for the *Leicester*, with two serviceable boats, and, once the southern summer arrived, he could attempt the Strait of Magellan again.

The plan would only work if he could win his company round. They'd encountered more terrors than wonders in their fourteen months away from England, and many wanted simply to sail for home. All the gentlemen-adventurers, Cavendish learned, 'had taken an oath upon the Bible to die rather than ever yield their consents to go back' to the Strait, such were the 'miseries and torments they had endured'. In consequence, Cavendish kept his plan 'most secret for fear of some mutiny'. When he gathered his company on the half deck, he told them instead that, once they'd refitted in Brazil, they'd sail east across the Atlantic to St Helena, which he showed them on his chart. There, they 'should meet the Portuguese carracks' loaded with spices and Chinese porcelain.[3]

However, even this course, which would take them in the direction of England, was too much for their shattered nerves. They 'desired nothing more than returning home',[4] Cavendish recorded, and it would be his will against theirs unless he could convert them to his way of thinking. When he pressed his company for reasons, he learned that 'their greatest grief was the want of the small ships, without which they all affirmed (and that truly) that we were able to do nothing for the ports where their towns stand were all barred harbours'.[5] Cavendish remained impassive when they voiced his own fears. Davis had his small ships and, unless these had foundered, he'd betrayed him for certain. Changing the subject, Cavendish comforted 'their despairing minds as well as I might' and promised that 'we would presently seek some place of relief' in San Sebastian 'with all speed'.[6]

However, en route to the island, Jaspar Jorge, the Portuguese pilot Cavendish had taken off Santos, suggested a different option. In his opinion, they should make for Espírito Santo, two hundred leagues further north where, Jorge claimed, a deep-water channel led right up to the town. Cavendish could anchor his ships and batter it into submission with his demi-culverins and, Jorge told him, 'without danger we might take many sugar mills and good store of cattle'.[7]

Cavendish knew Espírito Santo only from his charts, which showed a sand bar across the entrance to its harbour. Before altering his course, he charged Jorge 'upon his life to tell me truly' whether the *Leicester* might pass safely over the bar. Jorge willed Cavendish 'to take his life if ever the ships came in less water than five fathom'. He also swore that 'he desired not to live if he should not perform this'.[8] These were dangerous promises to make to a gambler on the edge, who was struggling to control his fortunes. Cavendish took Jorge at his word and staked his luck on Espírito Santo.

Lying on his sea-chest bed on the *Leicester's* gun deck, Anthony Knivet counted off the days as they progressed up the Brazilian coast. They were creeping into the Tropic of Capricorn. The nights grew warmer, the winds gentle. At twilight on the eighth day, they arrived abreast of their target, whose lights sparkled in the distance. Cavendish's ships anchored out of sight, and when night fell he sent the *Leicester's* boat to the entrance to Espírito Santo's harbour to check the depth of water over its bar. Jorge was made to travel in the boat so that he could witness the soundings. The lead-line was lowered, and they found 'sixteen or seventeen feet' – just under three fathoms – far less than the five fathoms that Jorge had staked his life on – and too shallow for the *Leicester* to cross in safety at low tide.

When Jorge returned to the ship, Cavendish 'demanded of him why he had so lied to me'? Jorge confessed that he had never sounded the bar before but had crossed it previously 'in ships of an hundred tuns' and, as far as he could judge, there had 'not been less water than 5 fathoms' each time. Cavendish was incandescent. His company had wasted eight painful days to get to Espírito Santo, which had been promised to be the solution to all his problems, only to find another harbour he couldn't enter without his missing ships. Perhaps Jorge had intended to betray him? Cavendish held him to his promise, made on his life, that the water would be deeper and 'without any trial caused him to be hanged, which was done in a trice'.[9]

Meanwhile, the *Roebuck's* boat had been exploring and had crept over the bar towards Espírito Santo. It returned with the news that there were three Spanish ships anchored in the harbour, which transformed the mood aboard the *Leicester*. Cavendish was astonished by the change in sentiment. 'The company seemed much to rejoice,' he recorded, 'and all affirmed that they would go with our boats' and capture the ships. He sought to capitalise on their enthusiasm while it lasted, calling them together and explaining 'how much the taking' of the ships 'imported to us'. Since the anchored vessels were light enough to cross Espírito Santo's bar, if they were captured, they could be substitutes for the *Desire* and *Black Pinnace*, and remove what his company had claimed to be their principal objection to continuing the expedition. Speed, however, was of the essence. Cavendish told his men that, 'although the day was spent', he 'thought the night not to be altogether inconvenient if they would put on mind to perform it resolutely'. If they set out at once they would have the advantage of surprise, which would be lost when daylight returned.[10]

However, the suggestion of a raid in total darkness spooked his company. Although a handful readied their weapons and armour, Cavendish found most of them 'utterly unwilling to go that night'. He promptly lost his temper, giving them 'bitter words'. 'Our case was not to prognosticate,' he said, 'but to take that opportunity which was offered to us and not to fear a night more than a day.'[11] Time was not on their side, 'over the bar we could not go', their present anchorage was hazardous, and they could see that the countryside had been burned clear around any landing points, indicating that the Portuguese expected an attack. They either had to go now or not at all. When the silent and sullen faces around him told him their choice, Cavendish resolved 'to depart the next morning from that place' and sail for his original destination, San Sebastian.

To Cavendish's amazement, 'there was an uproar among them' at dawn the next day when he gave the order to raise anchors, 'the most of them swearing that if I would not give them leave' to launch a raid on Espírito Santo, 'they would take the boats and bring away' the ships in its harbour themselves. Cavendish couldn't believe his ears. He 'began to reprehend them for their rashness', for 'now all opportunity was past'. The ships might look tempting in daylight, but the *Leicester* and the *Roebuck* were also visible, silhouetted against the rising sun, and 'now they must be contented, for go they should not'.[12]

When bluster failed to move their General, the gentlemen and soldiers begged him instead. 'Some of the chiefest among them,' Cavendish wrote, 'desired me with tears in their eyes that they might go,' promising that they would be cautious and would return at once if they couldn't cut out the ships in the harbour. To their tears, they added the argument that, if they sailed away 'without attempting to do this', it would be a stain on their honour, 'a thing that most greatly grieved them'.[13]

Although Cavendish neither trusted nor respected his supplicants, he reasoned that a successful raid might stabilise them, and, as long as they stayed away from dry land, they should be safe. The sea was flat calm and they'd be able to row their way out of trouble if they came under fire from shore. He was also swayed by his contempt for the capabilities of the local shipping. In his experience, 'no ships useth Brazil that be able to defend themselves from a cock-boat'. Cavendish agreed to the raid and chose Captain Morgan, his best surviving officer, to lead it. He gave him explicit orders for the action. First and foremost, 'upon pain of his life', Morgan 'should not land at all, what opportunity soever there was offered'. If Morgan doubted that his General was ready to take a life that had been pledged to him, he could look to the example of the late Jaspar Jorge. Finally, Morgan was ordered to return immediately if he spotted any 'danger in coming to these ships in the harbour'.[14]

After receiving his commands, Morgan assembled the raiding party, loading both the *Leicester* and *Roebuck's* boats with 'as many musketeers as could sit one by another'. Knivet, hearing the stamp of feet and clank of armour on the deck above his head, detected a similar energy to the raid on Santos a year before, when he'd been so eager to participate that he'd nearly suffocated beneath the helmsman's seat. Full of hope that the raid might turn his fortunes round, 'my boats departed from me', Cavendish wrote, 'having some eighty men as well furnished with weapons as it is possible'.[15]

Their target, Espírito Santo, was tough as well as rich.[16] Many of its first settlers (and the first bishop of Brazil) had been killed and eaten by the indigenous Caeté tribe, whom even the Tupinambá acknowledged to be fierce. Once the Caeté had been subdued by Mem de Sá, uncle of the warlord of Rio, both colonists and indigenous had been struck by wave after wave of diseases. In 1551, a mystery ailment appeared, which caused 'bloody fluxes', usually fatal; the plague was imported from Lisbon in 1562, and again the next year in what seems to have been a sinister new variant.* Next came smallpox, which wiped out most of the remainder of the indigenous community, so that by 1582 the Portuguese were forced to send slaving trips into the hinterlands to repopulate their plantations. Hardened by war, winnowed down by sickness, and vigilant through experience, the people of Espírito Santo were ready to defend their town. Cavendish had been sighted before he'd dropped anchor, and they prepared to receive him.

Overnight, while the timid gentlemen-adventurers on the *Leicester* slept, the colonists moved the ships in their harbour closer to shore, and manned trenches and ramparts on either side of the channel leading into it. The fortifications, sited at the narrowest point, where the channel was only a 'bird bolt shot' (a couple of hundred yards) wide, were armed with light cannon, and packed with musketeers and Tupinambá archers. There were also natural defences: one bank of the channel was overhung by a precipice, whose summit was topped with loose boulders, which its defenders 'might but tumble' down and 'beat away a thousand men'.[17]

When Captain Morgan's raiding party approached the channel, he spotted the defences ahead, remembered Cavendish's instructions and ordered that they turn back at once. But then a gentleman-adventurer in his boat called Morgan a coward, and other voices added that he always had been, and was now demonstrating his shameful weakness as he 'durst not attack a bauble ditch' – a toy fortification. This grave insult to his honour demanded that he efface it with an act of senseless bravery. Morgan ignored his orders and directed the *Roebuck's* boat to assault the

* 'The disease began with serious pains inside the intestines, which made the liver and the lungs rot. It then turned into pox that were so rotten and poisonous that the flesh fell off its victims in pieces full of evil smelling maggots.' Hemmings, p.142.

defences on the west side of the channel immediately while he engaged the larger and more dangerous fort on the opposite bank. The *Leicester's* boat, weighed down by men, grounded a distance from shore and he and his detachment jumped overboard and waded into action.

The 'bauble ditch' was protected by a stone wall ten feet tall, which Morgan scaled, 'more resolute than discreetly', accompanied by his bravest men. Their enemies were waiting for them, hidden in a trench on the precipice above. Once they'd struggled over the wall in their armour, boulders were rolled onto their heads, killing six of them, including Morgan, whose honour was cleansed by his exemplary death.[18]

The survivors of the assault were all badly wounded and ran back towards the *Leicester's* boat under a flurry of arrows. The men aboard the boat were sitting targets, and 'there escaped not eight of them unhurt, some having three arrows sticking in them'. In their haste to get out of range, they 'put the boat from the shore, leaving the bodies of their dead and wounded on land, 'a spoil for the Indians' and their studded clubs.[19]

The raiders aboard the *Roebuck's* boat had better luck on the east side of the channel, whose fort was less of an obstacle and whose defenders ran away as soon as they landed. They occupied its strongpoint and shot up a vessel full of Portuguese soldiers sent to relieve the fort. However, these minor triumphs were followed by calamity. The *Leicester's* boat rowed across the channel, and its shell-shocked company yelled at the *Roebuck's* men to evacuate immediately. Their agitation, and bleeding wounds, made as strong an impression as their words and their colleagues rushed to their own boat, which they all tried to board together, but the tide had fallen and they grounded her. Ten of her 'lustiest' men jumped overboard and slowly dragged her clear. When the Tupinambá saw them retreating, they reoccupied the fort and rained arrows on them. Once the boat was afloat, she was rowed into the channel and the men who'd freed her were left behind. She was commanded by Robert Tharlton, master of the *Roebuck*, in Cavendish's opinion the 'most cowardly villain that was ever born of woman'. Even though the forsaken soldiers 'waded up to their necks in the water to them… these merciless villains in the boat would have no pity on them'.[20] The men they'd abandoned had their heads smashed in plain sight, or were seized, bound and dragged away.

Cavendish was incandescent when the survivors returned. He'd lost forty men, and most of the rest had been gravely wounded. When they struggled aboard the *Leicester*, he demanded 'the cause of all their mishaps, and how they durst land, considering my straight commandment to the contrary?' They gave him the unsatisfactory explanation that Captain Morgan had been goaded beyond endurance and added that every single one of the men who had provoked him to disobedience had received their just deserts, perishing beside him, crushed by boulders. Although Cavendish did not believe the second part of their story, he bridled his fury and sent the wounded below deck to keep Knivet company, who noted that 'there came not one without an arrow or two in his body, and some had five or six'.[21]

Cavendish took a headcount on the *Leicester* and found he had less than 'fifty sound men' left – barely enough to hoist her anchor and get her under way. He wanted to put some miles between his ships and the scene of this latest calamity, but the calm weather continued and the *Leicester* was 'constrained to come to anchor again'. While he waited for a fair wind, Cavendish 'comforted these distressed poor men what I might'. He sounded them out at the same time as he soothed them – had their spirit been broken? The answer seemed to be yes: 'I found most of their desires,' he wrote, were 'to return again to England.' However, it would have been suicide to sail for home in their current condition. Cavendish therefore told them they would make for San Sebastian, where they could take counsel and, once they'd refitted the ships, together 'make a resolute determination of the rest of our proceedings.'[22]

Although Cavendish had succeeded in pacifying the *Leicester's* company – 'this course seemed to like them very well', he noted – the company of the *Roebuck* were up in arms after he'd spoken. It was common knowledge on the *Leicester* that Cavendish, as Knivet put it, 'meant to burn one of our ships' after she'd been cannibalised, and they'd got wind of his plans.[23] The *Roebuck's* company protested 'that it was a pity such a ship should be cast off'.[24] She'd fought well against the Armada, had taken many times her own value in prizes and, although battered, she was by no means broken beyond repair. Cavendish, however, didn't believe that they objected to her sacrifice out of a love for their vessel. In his opinion, 'it was not of any care of the ship, but only of a most cowardly mind of the master and chiefest of the company to return home' that motivated their protestations. He didn't give them much weight. He was certain that the *Roebuck* was too badly damaged to make it back to England. She'd been jury-rigged since losing her masts and had become 'the most laboursome ship that ever did swim in the sea'. Indeed, Cavendish wrote, 'in the sense and Judgement of any man living', 'such was the case of that ship' that not even the 'desperate minded men in the world… would have ventured to have sallied in her half so far as England'.[25] With such long odds, he reasoned, there was no need to take precautions against her deserting him, even though most of his fleet's provisions were stowed on her, and all her sick and wounded including her captain, his cousin John Cocke and the men wounded by arrows in the last engagement, had been transferred to the *Leicester*. Confident that she could not run away, Cavendish left the *Roebuck* under the charge of her master Robert Tharlton, the same villain who'd abandoned ten of his crew in the attack on Espírito Santo. Although Cavendish knew that Tharlton lived without scruples, he underestimated his determination. He may too have overlooked the possibility that Tharlton had dressed his ship in rags to hide her true condition from him.

The wind returned, the ships hauled anchor and the *Roebuck* stole away that night, leaving Cavendish 'in the most greatest distress that ever one Christian left another in'. He didn't dare risk hunting her down, lest the *Leicester's* company mutinied too, and he continued towards San Sebastian, shaken by yet another instance of treachery.[26]

❧

Espírito Santo's colonists celebrated once Cavendish's ships had disappeared over the horizon. They sent immodest letters to Lisbon, Madrid and Rome boasting of their triumphs. The English Jesuit John Yates, writing to Rome from Brazil, rejoiced that Cavendish 'seeing water and earth fighting against him' had fled, 'but whither no man knoweth', having been 'well whipped with the scourge of God, for the irreverence he committed against His Divine Majesty and His saints, especially against a holy head of one of the 11,000 virgins of England'.[27]

The poet-priest Centenera also recorded the victors' version of events. Although he inflated English casualties to a hundred and ten, he agreed with Cavendish that he'd been undone by the folly of his men and pictured him stalking the deck of the *Leicester* like a lion at bay, roaring 'Now all is lost!' at the survivors, before hanging four of them for disobeying orders and launching a tirade against the zodiac that had hexed him:

> Cursed be the day when my sad mother's womb
> Opened to cast me into this world of woe,
> And doubly cursed be the dark, malevolent star
> That oversaw my Birth.[28]

27

'A heart made of flesh'

Coast of Brazil

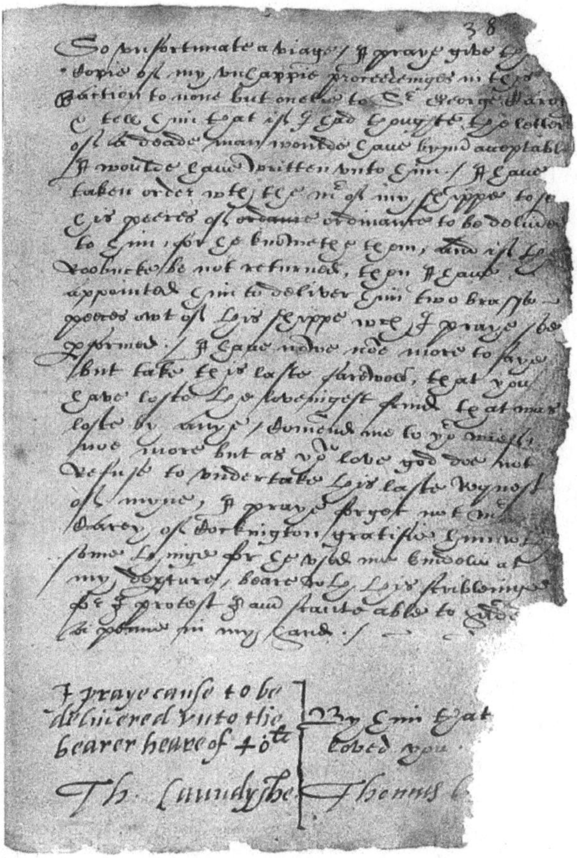

I praye cause to be delivered unto the bearer heare of 40 li

By him that loved you

Th. Caundyshe

Thomas C

Cavendish's journey from Espírito Santo to San Sebastian was slow and hard. The *Leicester* was down to her last cask of drinking water when she arrived, and her company were 'most extremely pinched' by thirst. She was also running out of food. The *Roebuck* had been carrying three-quarters of the expedition's provisions when she'd deserted – in Cavendish's estimate, 'six months' victual for 120 men at large' – despite having only forty-six men aboard. Moreover, both of the expedition's surgeons had run away with her, and Cavendish was left without anyone who knew 'how to lay a plaster to a wound, much less to cure by any salves'.[1] Unable to heal his sick on board, and unwilling to risk them spreading diseases to his healthy men, he put twenty of the worst cases ashore straight after dropping anchor.

Anthony Knivet was one of the sick to be stranded. He expected to die soon. The remains of his toes were raw flesh and bone, his body had turned black and, although the shaman had restored feeling to his legs, he couldn't yet stand on them.[2] Knivet dozed in the sand on the beach where he'd been set down, until the heat of the sun woke him up and he found himself surrounded by corpses, and dying men clutching their throats with agonised expressions on their faces. Some of the more mobile invalids who'd been landed with him had foraged along the shore and eaten 'a kind of peas which did poison them'. The 'peas' were the fruits of the manchineel tree, known to the Portuguese as the *Arvore da Morte* (the 'Tree of Death'). Every part of it is toxic and any external contact results in instantaneous and excruciatingly painful blisters. If eaten, the blisters form internally and a single fruit can cause death by asphyxiation, as its victim chokes on their screams of pain.

The shock of this *danse macabre* revived Knivet and he dragged himself on his elbows to the tideline. Ravenous, he dug mud crabs from their holes with his bare hands, stuffed them in one of his stockings, dragged his catch back to the fire that smouldered on beside the bodies of his friends and broiled it over the coals. He recuperated over the next week on a diet of crabs and river water, and the mud that he crawled through healed his feet so quickly that soon he was able to walk upright again. However, the stench of his shipmates' bodies rotting in the sunshine became so nauseating that he decided to seek another sanctuary. Knivet limped along the coast of San Sebastian until he chanced upon the sun-bleached carcass of a whale, 'lying on the shore like a ship with the keel upwards'. He made his home beside it, gorging on its withered flesh, drinking from a nearby stream and, day by day, recovering his strength. A week later, he returned to the spot where he'd been laid ashore to die and was amazed to find that Cavendish had established a thriving camp of forty men there in his absence. Trees had been felled and planks shaped to convert the *Leicester's* landing boat into a pinnace, casks were being filled, firewood cut and the men had 'a net continually a-fishing' under the direction of John Chambers, Cavendish's cook.[3]

Although the new camp appeared to be a picture of both harmony and industry to Knivet, Thomas Cavendish had had to face down a mutiny while Knivet had been wandering. After putting his sick men ashore, Cavendish had moored the *Leicester*, assembled his company on her half deck and explained his plan for the months ahead. His first aim, he told them, was to beach the boat they'd taken in Santo Amaro and convert her into a working pinnace. His audience objected immediately and 'forthwith openly began to murmur and mutiny, affirming plainly that I need not mend the boat, for they would go home, and then there should be no use of her'.[4]

Cavendish bit his tongue and changed tack. He'd counted up his supporters aboard the *Leicester* and, by his own reckoning, only her master Stephen Seaver and his cousin John Cocke (who was seriously ill) could be relied upon to back him up.

His opponents meanwhile numbered in the dozens. Rather than telling them outright that he wouldn't turn for England, Cavendish asked instead if they had any sense of honour left and, if so, why did they not want to 'cheerfully go forward to attempt either to make themselves famous in resolutely dying, or in living to perform that which will be to their perpetual reputations?' The alternatives of famous deaths or fame eternal gave the mutineers food for thought. They were wary of their General, who seemed to have little respect for human life. Was he willing to drive them to their deaths in pursuit of a glory they no longer cared about?

Once he had calmed – or distracted – his company, Cavendish explained the rest of his plan. As soon as he had converted the boat into a pinnace, they would return to the Strait of Magellan when the seasons changed, stock up on seals and penguins, 'which they very well did know we might do in greater quantity than our ship could carry', and 'if we got through the Strait, which we might now easily perform considering we had the chiefest part of summer before us, we could not but make a rich voyage'.[5] Cavendish also held up the prospect of meeting 'with the two small ships which were gone from us'. The company knew that the *Desire* and the *Black Pinnace* could change their fortunes, and Cavendish hoped the faint chance that his small ships might reappear would stiffen their resolve. He concluded his speech by pointing out that the Strait was only six hundred leagues away, whereas England was over two thousand. What gentleman would run from such a challenge? They would be despised by the world if 'being so close to the place which we so much desired', they'd made the 'most infamous and beggarly' choice to retreat a far greater distance.[6]

But the very mention of the Strait made the company mutinous. Tempers flared and, rather than hinting that they were fixed on sailing home, as they had when Cavendish had told them his plan for rebuilding the boat, the rebellious members of his company 'most boldly affirmed' that they had sworn never to return to the

Strait of Magellan. To reinforce their point to Cavendish, 'one of the chiefest of their faction most proudly and stubbornly uttered these words to my face in the presence of the rest'.[7]

This challenge to his authority and insult to his honour made Cavendish wild. 'I took this bold companion by the bosom,' he confessed, 'and with my own hands put a rope around his neck, meaning resolutely to strangle him.'[8] Before Cavendish could throttle his victim, the mutineers broke. The makeshift noose reminded them of the summary executions they'd already witnessed on the voyage, and they crowded round Stephen Seaver, the master of the *Leicester*, begging him to stop their General. In return, they promised instant and total submission, crying out to Cavendish that 'they would be ready to take any course he should think good'.

With his company obedient, Cavendish 'stayed' himself and 'let the fellow go'. Having 'somewhat pacified' the rebels with the speed and violence of his reactions, he told them point-blank 'that by no means would I take any other course than to go for the Strait'. He then marched on with his plans. 'Leaving aboard all my sailors and the rest to rig the ship and mend sails and do other business,' Cavendish landed on San Sebastian with a shore party of 'thirty soldiers and my carpenters, carrying fourteen days' victuals', and 'haled up my boat to new build her in such sort as she might be able to abide the seas'.[9] He set up camp at the river mouth beside those invalids who'd survived their encounter with the *Arvore da Morte*, and buried his dead.

Cavendish slept ashore while the boat was being converted into a pinnace. The mainland, where 'the Portingals had continual watch over us, looking but for a fit opportunity to set upon us', was less than a mile away from San Sebastian. His enemies were more likely to attack the camp than the *Leicester*, and Cavendish did not trust his men to keep a proper look out after dark. He also worried that malcontents might desert the instant they were out of his sight and reasoned that his presence among them was the only sure deterrent. The decision, however, left the door open for those still aboard the *Leicester* to desert and, after Cavendish landed, some started 'making rafts to go over to the main'. He spent a nervous fortnight ashore, among men he neither respected nor trusted, 'always expecting the coming of the Portingals, against whom I could have made small resistance, and further the treachery of some of my company, which desired nothing more than to steal over so to betray me'. 'I protest,' he admitted, 'I lived hourly as he that still expecteth death.'[10]

Private fears notwithstanding, Cavendish kept his poker face. His carpenters and soldiers worked assiduously while he watched over them, and the boat was reconfigured quickly. By the time that Knivet had returned to the camp from his wanderings, she was being made ready for sea, and Cavendish had been rowed back to the *Leicester*. The shore parties were now ordered to return to the ship every evening, leaving only the invalids, who were in no fit state to run away, on San Sebastian. Cavendish could not, however, monitor the movements of every member of his company and, despite his precautions, 'an Irishman, a noble villain' slipped away from the *Leicester* one night. 'Having made a raft,' he 'got over to the main and told the Portingals' 'that if they would go over in the night they would find most of our men ashore without weapon, and that they might do by them what they would.'[11]

Salvador de Correa de Sá, warlord of Rio, had prepared for action as soon as he'd learned that Cavendish had landed again in his territory. Once his scouts had given him details of both his enemies' numbers and their vulnerability, he sent his illegitimate son, Martim de Sá, with a pinnace, a company of musketeers and a mass of Tupinambá warriors to obliterate them. Martim landed his force on the north point of San Sebastian, 'hard by' Knivet's whale. As his men fanned out along the shoreline, they chanced upon three of Cavendish's company and caught two of them. The sole survivor ran back to the camp, where he found his crewmates seated around the fire, feasting on a 'great tortoise' that they had roasted in its shell.[12]

Rather than panicking at the news that their foes were at hand, Knivet and his fellow invalids bid the escapee 'to be of good cheer, for if it were true, it was the better for us'. Surrendering to the Portuguese seemed to be their least worst course of action. Some were convinced that Cavendish would sail away without them, others that he would carry them to the Strait and certain death. In these melancholy circumstances, 'We all commended ourselves to God', Knivet recorded, and 'toasted our friends with river water'.[13] They agreed to wait until morning, then march along the shore towards the Portuguese, waving a white shirt as a flag of truce. However, when dawn broke, the weather was against them, and the sea was running too high for men in their condition to risk the coast. It was also too rough for the *Leicester* to send her boat to the camp, and the invalids stayed by their fire, waiting for deliverance.

After nightfall, they stood watches. They had to stay awake to ensure they could make a formal surrender to Martim's force, rather than be murdered as they slept. Knivet took the first watch. When his four-hour stint was over, he shook another man awake to take his turn. But this individual refused to get up, telling Knivet that he considered standing watches to be a waste of time. Knivet countered that they knew the Portuguese were on the island, but the man answered, 'Tut, tis a lie.' Too worn out to argue, Knivet lay down beside his companions.

Before he'd drifted into sleep, 'the Portugals' arrived in force. Their Tupinambá auxiliaries dragged the sleepers from their circle round the fire and marched them to the beach, where they were 'knocked on the head with firebrands'. A warrior grabbed Knivet and 'struck twice or thrice' at him with a club. But, as he fended off the blows, a Portuguese officer strode past and Knivet threw his arms around his legs, begging for mercy and shouting out in

Portuguese that he was a Catholic. The officer handed Knivet over to a 'Cannibal', who carried him away on his back.[14]

The following morning, after the sea had subsided, Cavendish sent his boat to re-establish contact with the camp, and the massacre was discovered. The corpses included five 'healthful' men who'd stayed ashore against orders. He was appalled by the evident cruelty – 'sick men not able to stir to help themselves' had had their skulls smashed open and their bodies beaten to a pulp. The landing party, meanwhile, came under fire. Martim de Sá had posted archers in the jungle behind the beach and around the watering place, who 'shot at and hurt' some of them. Although Cavendish knew that it would be best to get his fragile company away from the scene of this latest calamity, he couldn't simply cut and run: the *Leicester* wasn't yet ready to sail. He still needed to fill her water casks and prepare more timber to finish off the new pinnace. He sent another shore party for water, but they were also driven off by the Tupinambá, who were too well camouflaged to locate and shoot down with arquebuses. Their failure persuaded Cavendish to change his mind: 'I could do nothing there without more loss of men.' The *Leicester's* company was now down to 'ninety… or a little over', only thirty of whom were mariners. 'I was forced to depart,' he mourned, 'fortune never ceasing to lay her greatest adversities upon me.'[15]

After weighing anchor, Cavendish set a course south. He was determined to make one last attempt on the Strait of Magellan. However, as soon as his company had recovered from their shock, and realised they were sailing towards the Strait, they confronted him. Cavendish tried to reason with them, but they were adamant in their opposition. 'Know this', he wrote, 'that for the Straits I could by no means get my company to give their consents to go.' The massacre at San Sebastian had been one horror too many – the last act in a tragic voyage to the New World on a quest for glory and gain. The *Leicester's* company blamed their lack of heart on the condition of her sails, telling Cavendish she had only three left to attempt the dangerous and stormy waters ahead, and 'the loss of one of these was death'. Although he acknowledged in private that they were right on this point, Cavendish found their weakness nauseating. He would rather, he stated, 'die in going forward than basely returning backward again'.[16]

Cavendish still had the force of character to impose his will on his men. He told them 'plainly that to England I would never give my consent to go, and that if they should not take such courses as I intended, that then I was determined that ship and all should sink in the seas together'. His threat cowed them. They had seen how quickly Cavendish's fury could escalate into violence. If he said he was ready to scuttle the *Leicester*, they believed he meant it.[17]

Once his company had become 'more tractable', Cavendish decided to meet them halfway and adjusted his plans again. He told them that they would instead make for the South Atlantic island of St Helena, which lay in the general direction of their route back to England, 'there either to make ourselves happy', he told them, 'by mending or ending'. However, 'this course in truth pleased none of them' and Cavendish had to assert himself again. Although he didn't specify his methods, he regained control over his company: 'seeing my determination and supposing it would be more danger to resist me than in seeming to be willing, they were at quiet.'[18]

St Helena was a feasible objective. It was about two and half thousand miles to the northeast, or twenty days' sailing with fair winds. Cavendish knew from his visit in 1588 that the island, which Pretty and his companions had believed to be a kind of Eden, could provide him with all the provisions, fresh water and fuel that he needed to continue his expedition. He now had a working boat for boarding and landing and still had plenty of gunpowder and shot for his cannon, which had yet to be fired against an enemy. Moreover, the Portuguese carracks from Asia – each of which carried a fortune – were due to arrive in St Helena within a few months. The island offered him a last chance to save his expedition, his honour and his fortune.

The winds were constant, if contrary, and the *Leicester* slowly beat her way across the Atlantic until she reached twenty degrees south, where Cavendish had found a favourable breeze for St Helena on his circumnavigation. However, the trade winds at that point on his course were seasonal and had switched direction during the southern summer. Rather than carrying him to his destination as he'd expected, they now blew into his face. He realised his only chance of recovering the winds was to turn back on his tracks. Cavendish ordered his company 'to tack about the ship to the southward', but they 'all plainly made answer that they would not, and that they had rather die… than be starved in seeking an island which they thought that way we should never get'. Once again, Cavendish subdued them. The force still flickered inside. 'What means I used to stand again to the southward,' he wrote to his executor, 'I leave you to enquire of themselves.'[19]

The *Leicester* pushed south into 'such contrary winds as I suppose never man was troubled with'. Progress was tortuously slow and Cavendish became seriously ill. 'I am grown so weak and faint,' he wrote, 'as I am scarce able to hold the pen in my hand.'[20] Meanwhile, he'd been tending to his kinsman, John Cocke, now on the edge of death and shaking with pain, which was aggravated by the jolting movement of the ship and the 'continual disquietedness' of the crew.

Cocke's illness was likely to have been typhus, a bacterial infection spread through close contact with other victims and via parasites, including fleas and lice, which abounded aboard privateers. Its symptoms included fever, exhaustion, skull-splitting headaches and delirium. When typhus took hold, it caused blood clots and gangrene as it progressed. Cavendish realised he was suffering from the same symptoms as Cocke, and that the disease that was eating its way through his cousin had now infected him.

Cocke's agonies not only distressed him but also demonstrated the suffering he himself could soon expect to face.

Thomas Cavendish had controlled his company through willpower as much as dynamism. But his aura diminished as he sickened and, as its light faded, the shadows crept in. The *Leicester's* helmsman changed course in the night while he slept when they were only sixty leagues from St Helena, letting the wind carry her away from the island and towards England. When Cavendish awoke, he had the strength for one last attempt to rule his ship. He took stock of the *Leicester's* provisions and found there were only 'eight weeks' victuals' left. He assembled his company and gave them a choice: would they 'venture like good minded men to beat to the south… to get this island, where we should not only relieve ourselves, but also be in full assurance either to sink or take a carrack, and by this means we should have a sufficient revenge of the Portingals for all their villainies done to us'; or would they rather 'pinch and bate' on half rations 'and so go for England'? 'They all answered me,' Cavendish recorded, 'that they would pinch to death rather than go again to the southward', and when he ordered them to change course, they mutinied and refused.[21] This time he could not overrule them, and he lost control of his ship.

The revolt coincided with the death of John Cocke. Cavendish was too heartsick and too ill to face down his company once more. 'What with the grief for' his cousin, he confessed, 'and the continual trouble I endured amongst such hell hounds… my spirit was clean spent, wishing my place upon any desert place in the world, there to die, rather than thus basely to return home again.'[22] Cavendish was now a passenger – or prisoner – on the *Leicester*. However, he still had a hand in her navigation and found a 'desert place' – Ascension Island – on one of his charts. This solitary volcanic peak, eight degrees south of the equator, had been discovered by the Portuguese nearly a century before. They'd seeded the island with goats and, every few years when one of their vessels passed that way, harvested them together with the turtles that nested on its beaches. Cavendish nudged his course towards it. His force was spent but his pride lingered. Ravaged by disease, he'd rather be put ashore like a common mariner, and there end his 'unfortunate life', rather than return to England as the dying prisoner of his mutinous company of 'hell hounds'. 'But God suffered no such happiness to light on me', he admitted. Try as he may, Cavendish 'could by no means find' Ascension. He'd thrown the dice one last time – and lost.

The mutineers took the *Leicester* north, across the equator, while Thomas Cavendish shook with fever. His ship juddered and creaked as he wrote his will and a narrative of his final weeks in the stifling tropical air of his cabin. He addressed it to Tristram Gorges Esquire, who'd been a close friend in his days as a courtier. Gorges had long since married an heiress, settled down at the family manor of Butshead in Devon and fathered ten children. Although Gorges remained well connected at court through his elder brothers, Cavendish chose him out of affection rather than for his influence. Death was approaching and perhaps he cast his mind back to his spendthrift years and circle of friends at court, when he'd yet to encounter adventure beyond what he found in tales of chivalry, and thrills had been limited to laying wagers and playing games of chance.

'Most loving friend,' Cavendish wrote to Gorges, 'there is nothing in this world that makes a truer trial of friendship than at death to show mindfulness of love' and begged him 'to hold my love as dear, dying poor, as if I had been most infinitely rich.'[23] Cavendish was, he confessed, weighed down by the 'bitter torments' of failure, which were as agonising as his illness and 'all the adverse happs that hath befallen me on this voyage, the least of which is my death'. He advised Gorges that he'd 'made a simple will wherein I have made you sole and only disposer of such little which is left', giving him ownership of the *Roebuck*, should she reach England, and brief instructions on the disposal of his other possessions. When he turned to the *Desire*, however, his rage exploded on the page: 'And now to come to that villain that hath been the death of me and the decay of the whole Action, I mean

Davis, whose treachery in Running from me hath been An utter Ruin of all.' Cavendish begged Gorges, 'as ever you love me', to make sure that Davis didn't profit from his treachery, should the *Desire* return home.[24]

Cavendish collected himself to finish his bequests, before providing a narrative of the last months of his expedition, breathing his dying rage into every line. He told Gorges how fortune had cursed him with an abject company of mutinous villains and endless bad luck, how flawed individuals like Captain Morgan – whose pride in his own honour had led to dozens of needless deaths – had compromised the expedition, and how extreme weather, beyond his previous experience, had forced him to change his plans time after time. When he reached the point in his narrative where Davis had deserted him, he spelled out his subordinate's treachery and concluded: 'the short of all is this Davis his only intent was utterly to overthrow me which he hath well performed.'[25] He hoped that his executor would ensure that justice was done.

However, the recollection of such duplicity forced Cavendish to let his emotions slip. 'Consider,' he asked Gorges, 'whether a heart made of flesh be able to endure so many misfortunes all falling on me without intermission?' He'd made his dreams real when he'd sailed around the world. He knew what could be achieved by men who believed in willpower, with luck on their side. And now, as he wasted away, racked with fever and surrounded by his enemies, Cavendish begged his friend to forgive him for his weakness in complaining that fate could be cruel as well as kind. Death would be a release from his torments. 'I thank my God,' he told Gorges, 'that in ending of me he hath pleased to rid me of all further trouble and mishaps.'[26] As a valediction, Cavendish added: 'I have no more to say, but take this last farewell, that you have lost the lovingest friend that was lost by any.'[27]

The will and narrative were bound up and addressed to Gorges, with the instruction that their bearer was to be paid £40 – more than a year's wages for a master shipwright. The will was witnessed by Steven Seaver, Thomas Hammond and the Oxford mathematician Robert Hues. No record exists of the manner and hour of Cavendish's death. English privateers gave their dead, whether gentleman or commoner, to the sea. Like the other men who'd sailed and died with him on his ventures, Cavendish's body was probably sewn into a canvas shroud with a cannonball at his feet and pushed overboard, as the watchers prayed.

28

Lockdown

Surrey, England

On 1 July 1593, Queen Elizabeth's Privy Council met at Oatlands Palace, one of her minor residences, to discuss the plague that was raging through London. Situated in the hunting grounds of Hampton Court, Oatlands had been commissioned by her father, Henry VIII, for his fourth wife, Anne of Cleves. It was built from new-baked bricks and stones quarried from the ruins of Chertsey Abbey, which had been abandoned after Henry had commanded its dissolution. When the palace was completed, it featured cloistered walks, elaborate gatehouses and a prospect tower, whose spiral staircase led to a polygonal viewing chamber offering panoramic views of the surrounding park. Henry married his fifth wife, Catherine Howard, in its chapel on 28 July 1540. Oatlands had since become a favourite summer retreat for Elizabeth, who'd inherited her father's love of the chase. On this occasion, however, matters of state brought her and her privy councillors to the palace. Bubonic plague* had been flaring up in London all year, and it seemed that an epidemic was about to erupt. Her councillors had been trying to control it without success since January, when they'd imposed a partial lockdown, closing playhouses, bear-baiting pits, bowling alleys and other places of public entertainment. In February, the opening ceremonies of Parliament had been abridged, and the queen had travelled to Westminster on the Royal Barge to avoid contact with crowds; and in May the Justices of Surrey, where Elizabeth planned to spend the summer, were commanded to impose travel restrictions on the county. They were 'not to receive any child born in London, the suburbs and confines thereto adjoining, to be nursed in any of their houses, nor any inhabitants

* The principal cause of the Black Death, which had killed over one-third of the population of England in the fourteenth century.

within the said places to come to make their dwelling... upon pain of imprisonment and her Majesty's grievous displeasure'.[1]

Londoners, however, were frantic to escape the capital. The speed at which the plague advanced could be measured by the number of houses with red crosses splashed on their front doors, and day by day the crosses multiplied. The Parish of All Hallows London Wall, for example, had to pay an extra twenty pence to its painter 'for making red crosses... where the infection of the plague was'.[2] Meanwhile, those trapped in the city found solace in pamphlets predicting the end of days. These included a popular collection of 'godly meditations' gathered during the plague of 1563, which was reprinted for 'the like present visitation of God's heavy hand for our manifold sins'.[3]

The queen had retreated to Oatlands from Nonsuch Palace, her previous residence, after one of Lord Lumley's maids had died there, disfigured by stinking buboes in her groin and armpits. The plague was now 'dangerously dispersed' in the towns and villages surrounding London. Further interventions were required to prevent it spreading at the 'common assemblies of people at fairs', which were customary in late summer. Her Privy Council, comprising five barons and three knights, sat in their robes at table in Oatlands and addressed the matter, dictating their resolutions to scribes. They decided to close the fairs down and issued a prohibition in Elizabeth's name that combined tender sentiments with strict limitations on the freedom of assembly. The queen, her councillors declared, out of her 'princely care for the preservation of Her loving subjects' was cancelling most of the country's festivals, many of which had been running for hundreds of years.[4] The list of prohibited fixtures included Saint Bartholomew's fair at Smithfield (first staged in 1133), and the ale-sodden extravaganzas celebrated in Croydon (1276) and Southwark (1462).

After restricting freedom of assembly, the privy councillors turned from public to private matters. A 'writing written with his own hand sealed up by master *Thomas Candish* in a Certain Packet with his will' had been passed to them by Cavendish's executor, Tristram Gorges, and they considered its contents.[5]

The Council had already looked into Cavendish's affairs twice since the *Leicester* had returned to England in February 1593 without his body. The *Leicester* had moored in Portsmouth alongside the *Roebuck*, which, despite her makeshift masts, had made it back over the Atlantic. Cavendish's sister Anne, who in the absence of any other evidence would be his beneficiary, and her husband Robert Dudley had moved quickly to secure letters of administration and had applied to the Privy Council for the powers to seize both ships, which it had granted on 18 March. Letters were sent to the Mayor and officers of Portsmouth, commanding them to deliver the *Leicester* and the *Roebuck* to Dudley and confirming him as the administrator 'of the goods of Thomas Cavendish, esquire, lately deceased at the seas'.[6] There was no curiosity expressed as to the cause of death. Many of England's sea knights perished in their sea-boots, and Cavendish joined a long list of Elizabethan heroes whose bodies had been buried in foreign soil or launched overboard mid-ocean, the victims of gangrenous wounds, fatal accidents, starvation, scurvy, typhus, murder and the many other occupational hazards of privateering.

Not long after the Privy Council had appointed Anne and Dudley as administrators, the packet containing Cavendish's will, and its promise of a forty pound reward, had reached his executor, Tristram Gorges. Cavendish had told Gorges in his narrative – a voice from beyond the grave – that he'd 'appointed some of the most sensible men that I left behind me to make discourse unto you' of his last days, and Gorges had perhaps received eyewitnesses' reports of their general's demise when the narrative was delivered to him.[7] Cavendish had chosen the right man to protect his memory.[8] Gorges' brothers, Sir Edward and Sir Arthur, were senior courtiers, and access to the Privy Council was arranged. Tristram was granted control of Cavendish's affairs on the strength of his word as a gentleman, and his first act was to have the *Leicester* put under armed guard in Portsmouth.

Six weeks later, the Council was again petitioned about Cavendish, this time by 'Robert Russel, William Harrison, Gabriel North and other soldiers to the number of twelve', who complained that Gorges had wronged them by seizing the *Leicester*, for they deserved a share of whatever plunder it carried.[9] The Council, which had yet to see Cavendish's narrative, sided with the soldiers and declared that Gorges should not have impounded 'their parts and shares of such goods, ordinance and spoil as by their endeavour and valour was obtained and brought home in the ship called the Galleon Leicester'.[10] The fact that the petitioners were veterans of the war in Flanders played in their favour. The Privy Council declared that: 'Forsomuch as there is good report of the service of some of these done her Majesty in the Low Countries, and that it is thought this ship and goods had not been brought home but by their special industry'; and directed Gorges 'to yield the said Theobald and the rest such reasonable satisfaction ... for their comfort and relief out of the ship and goods, &c'. This, the Council concluded, would both stop their complaints and might inspire them to join similar voyages 'hereafter as occasion shall be offered'.[11]

However, by July 1593, Gorges had passed them Cavendish's narrative with its accusations of both treachery against Davis and of revolt against his 'abject and mutinous company', and the Council realised that the matter involved more than apportioning goods between executors and survivors. They also noted that the *Desire* and the *Black Pinnace* were as yet unaccounted for. Could Davis, even now, be on his way home from the Pacific where 'prizes of great value and riches are oftentimes taken'?[12] Might the *Desire* have intercepted another Manila galleon, or a coaster ballasted with silver ingots from Peru? And if Davis had found the Northwest Passage and was bringing his prizes home that way, his return was imminent.

Letters were sent to admirals around the English coast, commanding them that, if the *Desire* put into any port or harbour, she was to be boarded, 'her hatches nailed down and a just inventory taken'. All valuables were to be removed ashore and placed in safe keeping, and her officers and crew were to be detained and examined 'upon such interrogatories as you shall think good'. When the news that the *Desire* had indeed returned reached Oatlands a week later, the Privy Council sent Bryan Chamberlen, a Messenger of the Chamber, to Devon with instructions 'to apprehend one captain Davis and to bring him before their lordships'.[13]

29

The End of Desire

The Strait of Magellan

John davis had indeed returned from the Pacific, although his foray into the 'Spanish Lake' had been short-lived. The *Desire* and the *Black Pinnace* had been battered by storms as soon as they'd broken out of the Strait of Magellan, and giant waves had forced them back towards the rock reefs and uncharted granite islands that stretched north from its mouth. The *Desire* had faced Pacific swells before, but the *Black Pinnace* hadn't been built to ride their motion. She crept under the lee of the *Desire* and Tobias, her master, shouted over to Davis that his ship had 'received many grievous seas, and that her ropes did every hour fail her' and that 'he could not tell what shift to make'.[1] The *Black Pinnace* was breaking up, and Tobias wanted to save her crew by transferring them to the *Desire*. Davis yelled back that there was nothing he could do, as he and his company were also in trouble and 'expecting our ruinous end'.[2] The following day, the Pacific tempest grew 'beyond all furious' and Jane saw the *Black Pinnace* 'strake suddenly a hull, so that we thought she had received some grievous sea or sprung a leak, or that her sails failed her'.[3] Rather than going to help the doomed ship, Davis left her to her fate. The *Black Pinnace* sank that night and took her company with her.

Davis fought the same storm for a further week as it kept him pinned against the Chilean coast. It was the worst tempest that Jane had ever seen, 'without all reason in fury, with hail, snow, rain', and a wind 'so mighty that in nature it could not possibly be more'. The waves meanwhile were equal prodigies, their peaks fracturing into avalanches of foam that washed over the *Desire* and 'many times we were doubtful whether our ship did sink or swim'. Some of her company, including Jane, gave up on any hope of survival and 'yielded ourselves to death'. Jane went to Davis's cabin to say his farewells, where he found the arctic explorer 'so 'cold that he could scarcely move a joint'. As the ship shook and groaned and slammed around them, Jane fixed his captain a cup of spiced brandy, which 'comforted' his heart, and inspired him, for the 'ease of his conscience', to make his confession to God – with Jane his witness – of the sins of his 'forepassed time'. After praying for absolution, Davis begged God for 'some merciful sign of Thy love and our preservation', and Jane believed that his prayer had been heard, for the sky had immediately cleared of clouds, allowing Davis to take a sun-sight and fix his position.[4]

The clear air also revealed the hazards that had been hidden by the storm. Blue mountains of water with tumbling white crests detonated against the jagged pinnacles lining the coast, raking their faces as they withdrew. The boom of each collision carried to the ship over the roar of the wind. Amid this maelstrom, Davis sighted Cape Deseado, which marked the bottom jaw of the mouth of the Strait of Magellan and realised that the *Desire* was being forced closer and closer to land. His last hope of survival was to slip back into the Strait he'd spent six weeks fighting to escape. He consulted John Perry who told him that he didn't think they'd make it. Davis replied that it was their only chance: 'either we must double it or before noon we must die. Therefore loose your sails and let us put it to God's mercy.'

The sails were unfurled from their yards, and the *Desire* turned and ran with the sea. Waves broke over her stern, 'flying into the sails with such violence' that Jane feared they would be shredded by the weight of water. Worse still, the added canvas didn't seem to have the required effect on the *Desire's* course, and she continued to point at the rocks. 'We perceived,' wrote Jane, 'that we fell still more and more to leeward.' The *Desire* was now so close to the shore that the backwash from breaking waves 'would rebound against the ship's side, so that we were much dismayed with the horror of our present end'. Just as Jane thought he was 'at the very pinch of death, the wind and seas raging beyond measure', Perry eased the *Desire's* mainsail and she 'quickened her way and shot past that rock where we thought she would have shored'. Jane credited this narrow escape to 'some current, or 'the wonderful power of

God', rather than Perry's expertise. He chalked it up as the second miracle of what he'd expected to have been his last day.[5]

The *Desire* wasn't out of danger yet. After driving her out of the Pacific, the storm pursued her into the Straits. Its enormous swells concertinaed as they pressed into the narrow channel, and as they crowded together their faces grew steeper. Although Perry ordered her sails furled, the *Desire* was blown along at a furious rate under her bare masts, pitching and rolling as she tore down waves and wallowed in their troughs while three men strained at her whipstaff, 'not being able to guide the helm'.[6] She travelled the remarkable distance of seventy-five miles in six hours before the storm left her and Davis could get her under control. After the wind abated, her exhausted mariners pumped her dry. They held up until they had anchored her in a sheltered cove, then collapsed, 'not able to move', for 'their sinews were stiff and their flesh dead'.[7]

Davis had been shaken both by the fury of the Pacific, and his narrow escape from being wrecked. He may also have grown wary of asking God for too many favours. He had indeed been saved, but only just – a sign, perhaps, that his Maker intended him to turn back from his quest. These considerations, as well as the wretched condition of his company, persuaded him to give up – this time at least – his dream of discovering the Northwest Passage. The obsession had inspired him to treachery and had lost him both the *Black Pinnace* and the confidence of his men, who were no longer willing to follow his demon. On 21 October 1592, he hoisted anchor and sailed for home.

Once Davis had given up on the impossible, he was in his element. Provisions were low, the navigation ahead was tricky, but he'd twice before brought a small boat back to England through dangerous seas with an understrength crew on short rations. He could also rely on the expertise and strong nerves of John Perry. However, the storm that had driven the *Desire* out of the Pacific and into the Strait had been waiting for her to emerge from shelter and, within a few hours of setting sail, she was hit by mounting winds from the northwest. Soon she was pitching horribly, she could neither anchor nor turn around, and Davis and Perry had to pilot the *Desire* through the Strait's twists and turns in both daylight and darkness. There were no fires or lamps ashore to mark the edges of the channel – they had to navigate blind, using a chart that Davis had drawn on his outbound journey – but through the 'hell-dark night... without any doubting they conveyed the ship through that crooked channel'.[8] The *Desire* was spat into the Atlantic by tailwinds on 27 October, just under a month after breaking into the Pacific.

Now the breezes blew strong and fair, racing Davis up the coast of Patagonia to Port Desire, where he planned to reprovision and refit before sailing for England. He'd given up any pretence to his crew that he was looking for Cavendish. It was every man for himself, and Davis focused on the logistics of the long voyage home. Before entering Port Desire, he sent a boat to Penguin Island, which returned loaded with birds and eggs and the news that 'the penguins were so thick upon the isle' that 'they could not go without treading on' them, 'whereat', Jane recorded, 'we greatly rejoiced'. Jane remembered the following weeks as a time of ease and plenty, waxing lyrical in his journal about the penguins whose bodies were mounting up in the hold, and sketching out their attractions both anatomical and gastronomic. The penguins were supplemented by other coastal fauna including young gulls and baby seals, which Jane accepted as 'manna from heaven'. The wildlife was served with 'an herb called scurvy grass', which was fried with penguin eggs in seal oil. 'This herb did so purge ye blood,' Jane noted, that it restored both he and his companions 'to perfect health of body, so that we were in as good case as when we came first out of England.'[9]

Jane was optimistic about his prospects of returning home. By late December, the *Desire's* crew had killed and cured twenty thousand penguins, which seemed enough to sustain them over the eight-thousand-mile voyage ahead. Davis left Port Desire for

England on 22 December, hoping 'that within six months we might recover our country, though our sails were very bad'.[10] He tallied up his stores and set rations. Each man was to have five ounces of flour, nine spoonfuls of oil and half a pint of dried peas per week, and one-and-a-quarter fat penguins every day. Although the beer had long since run out, and the spiced brandy was reserved for Davis and any invalids aboard, there was enough sweet water for a daily allowance of six pints per man, assuming the casks remained sound.

However, as soon as he'd put out to sea, the *Desire's* casks had leaked at a tantalisingly slow, yet agonisingly steady rate, forcing Davis to divert to Isla Grande in Brazil, which he'd visited with Cavendish the previous year. The journey took more than a month, while the drinking water seeped and dribbled away. On arrival, he found the Portuguese had burned their fields, a sure sign that they expected to be attacked. Isla Grande was part of the territory of Salvador Correa de Sá, who'd mobilised the instant his lookouts reported that yet another English ship had appeared off the coast. By the time that Davis had moored the *Desire*, de Sá had evacuated Isla Grande's plantations, torched their fields and was preparing an ambush.

Davis failed to read the warning signs, as did Jane, who regretted the wasteful practice of burning standing crops and the consequent lack of fresh provisions for enemy ships. Davis meanwhile was absorbed with his water casks. His obsessive attention to detail, which had served him so well in his arctic crises, blinded him to evident danger. The casks were rowed ashore with carpenters and coopers to stave and hoop them. Davis also sent out foraging parties to dig up cassava roots from the abandoned farms and, when they returned, they reported that the island seemed eerily empty of men.

That night, after the shoregoers had returned to the *Desire*, 'many of the men in our ship', Jane reported, dreamed of seeing their friends murdered. In the morning, they described their dreams, 'one saying to another, "this night I dreamed that thou were slain", and this was general through the ship'. Davis 'likewise had dreamed very strangely himself'.[11] When he sent out the shore party the next day, he ordered the men to carry firearms and detailed some to stand guard while the others worked.

The foragers laboured until ten in the morning, when the heat of the day became too intense. They laid down their tools in the shade of a boulder at the edge of the jungle, boiled up cassava and ate. Their guards put down their weapons and joined them and, when they finished their meal, some ambled along the shore and washed in the sea, 'all being stripped to their shirts and no man keeping watch', while their less active fellows returned to their reveries.

De Sá's men were watching from their hiding places. 'Suddenly,' according to Jane, 'as they were thus sleeping and sporting... there came a multitude of Indians and Portugales upon them', who slew them, stripped them of their weapons, armour and clothes and melted away, leaving thirteen corpses 'laid naked on a rank, one by another, with their faces upwards.'[12] Only three of the shore party survived the massacre. Andrew Towers, a genuine Catholic, was taken prisoner,[13] one man, horribly wounded, was left for dead and the third swam back to the *Desire*, where he raised the alarm.

Davis sent a boat ashore, but its crew panicked when they saw the bodies of their friends, blood seeping from their wounds, their clouded eyes staring at the sky, a cross planted in the sand beside them. They turned and ran back to the boat, too terrified to stay and bury their dead. Their ragged nerves were shredded further when two Portuguese pinnaces, loaded with soldiers that De Sá had dispatched from Rio, rounded the headland and sailed straight at them. The *Desire* was moored by cables to trees, within easy musket range of the shore. Unless she cut and ran, she would be caught by De Sá's pincer movement, under attack from both the sea and land. Davis made for the open ocean, while the *Desire's* gunners loaded her swivel-mounted sakers and trained them on the jungle, electing, according to Jane, 'rather to fall into the hands of the Lord than into the hands of men; for of His exceeding mercies we had tasted, and of the other's cruelty we were not ignorant'. God seemed to oblige, sending a 'small gale of wind' that whisked the ship away from Isla Grande and out into the Atlantic.[14]

The gale carried the *Desire* a hundred miles before she ran into headwinds off Cabo Frio, which so 'vexed' her course that she scarcely progressed over the following three weeks. She had only twenty-seven men left out of an initial compliment of seventy-six. Davis had lost proportionally more of his company than Cavendish, without once attacking an enemy. As the *Desire's* meagre supply of drinking water dwindled, the survivors proposed to Davis that, rather than die of thirst, they turn towards the Brazilian port of Bahia and place themselves at the mercy of the Portuguese. However, Davis, 'with fair persuasions' and a liberal dose of piety, snuffed out dissent. His eloquence, Jane recorded, was supported by a coincidental miracle: 'In this distress it pleased God to send us rain in such plenty' that the company slaked their thirsts and filled their casks and were 'well-watered and in good comfort' to return to England.[15]

Divine favour is absent in Jane's description of the next stretch of the voyage. As the *Desire* progressed through the torrid zone towards the equator, the penguins in her hold decomposed. Chidley had warned that they did not last, and they were the mainstay of the *Desire's* rations. As the birds rotted, 'loathsome and ugly' worms hatched in their putrid meat and crawled out of their carcasses to infest the ship. With rising dread, Jane confessed his fear that he might be 'devoured by these wicked creatures' before he had the chance to starve to death. The worms were omnivorous and, with the exception of iron, there was 'nothing that they would not eat'. They attacked the men's 'clothes, boots, shoes, hats, shirts, stockings; and for the ship they did so eat the timbers as that we greatly feared they would undo us by gnawing through the ship's side'. Davis organised attempts to exterminate them, 'but the more we laboured to kill them the more they increased so that at the last we could not sleep for them, but they would eat our flesh'.[16]

The worms were accompanied by a mysterious and fatal illness, which spread through the *Desire's* company shortly after she'd crossed the equator. One by one, Jane recorded, they succumbed to 'such a monstrous disease as I think the like was never heard of'. Its first symptoms were swollen ankles, followed within two days by an inability to breathe. In its third, most dangerous stage, the disease descended to the genitals, and its victims' 'cods and yards did swell most grievously, and most dreadfully to behold'. Davis himself was struck with this inflammatory malady and his meekness in suffering impressed Jane, as did his words of comfort to his fellow victims. Although his captain 'was in such woeful case that he desired only a speedy end and scarce able to speak for sorrow, yet he persuaded them to patience, and to give God thanks, and like dutiful children to accept of His chastisements'. His piety was of little consolation. Many of the sick 'grew raving mad, and some died in most loathsome and furious pain'.[17]

After the disease had run its course, only sixteen men were left alive, 'of which there were but five able to move'. The five included Davis and Perry, who managed the ship between them. 'The Captain and the Master,' Jane recorded, 'would take in and heave out topsails', climbing the rigging to perform this arduous manoeuvre that usually required half a dozen skilled mariners. When they grew too weak to go aloft, they left the *Desire's* canvas to the mercy of the winds and her 'topsails and spritsails were torn all in pieces by the weather'. In this ragged condition, serenaded by 'the most woeful lamentation of our sick men', Davis and Perry steered the ship homewards, both 'mightily distressed and monstrously grieved'.[18]

On 11 June 1593, these 'lost wanderers upon the sea' made landfall at Berehaven on the southwest coast of Ireland. It offered a protected anchorage, but Davis had cut the cable to his last anchor in Brazil and was forced to run the *Desire* onto the shore. Irish labourers from the fields came aboard to help take down her sails and make her fast. Jane (who had not lost his merchant's soul) noted that they charged Davis £10 for their 'slender pains'. He forgot to account for danger money – it took a brave man to board a ship that stank of death.[19]

Five days after tying up in Berehaven, Davis and Jane found a fishing boat to take them to Padstow in Cornwall. The *Desire* was left with a skeleton crew under Perry. From Padstow, Davis continued overland to his house in Stoke Gabriel in South Devon. He had a disappointing homecoming. First, he discovered that his wife, Faith, had cheated on him; then, shortly afterwards, Bryan Chamberlen arrived to arrest him.

30

Aftermath

London, England

THE *DESIRE* WAS THE LAST of Cavendish's ships to reach home, and brought the final, ill-starred venture of an Elizabethan maritime hero to its close. However, details of its events were disputed for decades after his death. Realpolitik and false witnesses obscured the truth. After being taken to London and interrogated by the Privy Council, Davis was released rather than being gaoled and executed as a traitor. He was too skilled a navigator and pilot to waste. Parliament had been summoned once again in 1593 to grant fresh subsidies for war, and John Puckering (who'd risen since his debut as speaker in 1584 to become Lord Keeper of the Great Seal) had highlighted the 'great malice of the King of Spain', who was 'again preparing for invasion' in his opening oration.[1] Until the present crisis had abated, Davis was of more use to his country at sea than divided into quarters and displayed, in pieces, on the spikes of London Bridge.

A free man, Davis published his version of the events of the last voyage of Thomas Cavendish a year later in his *The Seamen's Secrets*, a treatise on navigation.[2] Rather than letting the matter that had so nearly cost him his neck go to rest, Davis went on the offensive, convinced that he had a wrong to right. He wasn't ready to draw a curtain over the expedition. Although Cavendish's narrative had yet to be circulated and his accusations of treachery against Davis weren't yet public knowledge, Davis aired them in his *Secrets*, which he dedicated to Lord Howard of Effingham, Lord High Admiral and Privy Councillor, victor of the Armada campaign. He started by restating his belief in a Northwest Passage ('Undoubtedly, there is a passage navigable, and easy to be performed'), and explained how his determination to find it had induced him 'to go with Mr Cavendish in his second attempt at the South Seas', on the strength of Cavendish's 'constant promise' to Davis that, once they reached California, 'I should there have his pinnace with my own barque... to search that northwest discovery upon those back parts of America'.[3]

Davis then gave Howard a précis of the voyage, beginning with the fleet's arrival at the Strait of Magellan, 'where M. Cavendish, being halfway through... and impatient of the tempestuous fury of that place... returned for Brazil'. Having pictured Cavendish as fickle and implied that he ran from foul weather, Davis followed up these insults with *his* version of how they'd lost contact in the South Atlantic. Separated 'in a fret of weather', the dismal condition of the *Desire* had forced him to run for Port Desire, where he had waited in vain for his General, 'there staying four months in most lamentable distress' before making three attempts at the Strait, all thwarted by furious storms. Davis concluded his summary by launching a counteraccusation against an accusation that he'd made public for the first time. While, Davis claimed, Cavendish had been 'content to account me to be the author of his overthrow, and to write with his dying hand that I ran from him, his own ship was returned many months before me'. It had been *Cavendish* who had run away, and he, Davis, was no traitor. He acknowledged that this was a bold claim and told Howard he'd made it 'only to satisfy your Honour' of his sincerity; 'for were I guilty of so foul a crime, I were worthy of ten thousand torments in presuming to present this treatise to your lordship'.[4]

Davis would receive his 'ten thousand torments' in due course. Although he was never appointed captain on an expedition again, his nautical skills found him work as a pilot. After several voyages to Asia with the Dutch East India Company, he joined an expedition in the same direction under Sir Edward Michelbourne, consisting of the *Tiger* and the *Tiger's Whelp*, which sailed from Cowes in December 1604 for Sumatra. Just over a year after leaving England, the expedition came across a junk off Penang, which was crammed with Japanese pirates whose own vessel had been wrecked. The captain of the *Tiger* sent a boat to look it over and found its 'men and furniture very unproportionable for such a ship as they were in', which was 'not above seventy tonnes in burthen, and they were ninety men, and most of them in too gallant a habit for Sailors'.[5] These men in 'gallant' clothing were *Wako*, sea-going samurai feared across Asian waters for their brutality and banned from going ashore throughout Indonesia.

The *Tiger's* master decided to entertain the *Wako* aboard his ship and pump them for information about when and where prizes could be taken 'on the coast of China'. At the same time, he sent a party under John Davis to search the junk, to find if anything had been hidden under her cargo of rice. Davis was ordered to confiscate the 'Japonians' weapons and make them stand before the mast while his men searched. But 'Davis being beguiled with their humble semblance, would not possess himself of their weapons', even after the master had 'sent twice' to command him to do so. Instead, he left the search party at work in the middle of an armed mob of *Wako* and returned to the *Tiger*.[6]

At sunset, when they judged the searchers on their junk to be defenceless and their hosts on the *Tiger* to be off guard, the *Wako* attacked 'resolutely in both ships'. The Englishmen on the junk were killed or driven overboard, and the pirates in the captain's cabin on the *Tiger* armed themselves with the swords they found hanging on its walls and charged out. The first man they met on deck was John Davis, who 'they pulled into the Cabin, and giving him six or seven mortal wounds, they thrust him out'. As Davis bled to death on deck, the master of the *Tiger* rallied his men, drove his enemies back, loaded two demi-culverins with 'Cross-bars, Bullets, and Case-shot', placed their muzzles against the cabin's bulkhead and fired. The 'legs, arms, and bodies' of the *Wako* were 'so torn', declared an eyewitness, 'as it was strange to see, how the shot had massacred them'. Only one of the 'Japonians' survived, begging 'that he might be cut in pieces' rather than live on in shame as a captive.[7]

Thomas Lodge was the next to open a window onto the last voyage of Thomas Cavendish and he added a macabre lustre to its events. The novel that had budded in his mind aboard the *Leicester* during her wild journey to the Strait in 1592 had bloomed into *A Margarite of America*, which was published in London four years later. If Lodge's fans had expected a sequel to *Rosalynde* featuring boozy swains and princesses disguised as shepherdesses, they were to be disappointed. *A Margarite* is a blood-soaked tragedy with revenge as its theme. Lodge dedicated it to both Lady Russel, and to his Gentlemen Readers, and these dedications went some way towards explaining his state of mind when he'd composed his slaughter-fest. 'Touching the place where I wrote this,' he told Lady Russel, with a dash of melodrama, 'it was in those straits christened by Magellan; in which place to the southward, many wondrous isles, many strange fishes, many monstrous Patagons… many bitter and extreme frosts at midsummer.' 'It might be marvelled', he continued, 'that in such scanty fare, such causes of fear, so mighty discouragements and many crosses, I should deserve or eternise anything.'[8]

Lodge gave his Gentlemen Readers a little more background. He'd been inspired to write *A Margarite*, he told them, while 'being at sea with M. Cavendish (whose memory if I repent not, I lament not)'. 'The place where I began my work was a ship,' he explained, and 'the time I wrote in was when I had rather will to get my dinner than to win my fame.' Lodge had thought it more likely that 'the fish should eat both me writing and my paper written, than fame should know me, hope should acquaint her with me, or any but misery should hear my ending.'[9]

The scars never healed. Having laid down a marker with *A Margarite* for the Tragedy of Blood genre that followed, Lodge gave up writing, converted to Catholicism, took up medicine and achieved some recognition in his new profession before dying of the plague in 1625 while tending to its victims.[10]

Whereas Lodge had cast a dark, sometimes surreal pall over Cavendish's pandemonic final expedition, John Jane, faithful accomplice of Davis and the next to appear in print, sought to resurrect his master's slurs. Jane's account of his experiences aboard the *Desire* appeared in the 1600 edition of Richard Hakluyt's *Principal Navigations* and, like Lodge, he seems to have been traumatised by his experiences. Although most of Jane's suffering had occurred after Davis had deserted and could only be blamed on his friend, his narrative is haunted by the General he'd despised and feared, who looms in the background like an angry ghost. The story of his last months aboard the *Desire* becomes increasingly morbid as Jane describes their horrors. He loses count of the days, no longer records either the ship's position or her course, and the hand of God chastises rather than saves. Jane never went to sea again.

However, both Jane's insults and Davis's accusations against Cavendish fell on deaf ears. Their *bête noire* remained as famous and respected after death as he'd been when he'd sailed the *Desire* up the Thames to Greenwich in 1588 to entertain his queen. No new voyages had since matched or eclipsed his achievements and his memory was honoured by the men who'd known him, including the merchant William Sanderson, who christened one of his sons Cavendish Sanderson after the departed hero. Although Sanderson fathered six other sons, including Raleigh Sanderson and Drake Sanderson, none were named after John Davis, whose voyages he'd sponsored.

Thomas Cavendish was also recognised as an inspiration by the men who'd sailed with him. His acolytes included Randolph Cotton, captain of the *Dainty*, 'whose courage in midst of all broils never quailed'. Cotton attested that he'd learned his valour from 'that most renowned and forward Gentleman Thomas Candish Esquire… the remembrance of whose death; with grief he often times bewailed'. Cotton resolved to imitate his idol and 'to gain fame which before wealth he prized'. He succeeded in winning his reward through an exemplary death, killed in Brazil while still in his twenties but fighting like a lion 'in right of country and our Queen'.[11]

Cavendish's international reputation as a navigator also flourished after his death. His vision of direct trade with China and his discovery of potential allies in Southeast Asia had inspired the Dutch to set up their East India Company, which used his charts and employed his veterans – including Davis, John Buteres and Timothy Shotten, one of the first Englishmen to reach Japan – on its trading voyages. Meanwhile the compass that Cavendish's Japanese interpreter had demonstrated to William Barlowe was adapted, perfected and introduced to English ships, where it became a standard navigational instrument.

Although Davis and Jane's slights against Cavendish had been discounted both by his friends and by the English public, it was a matter of posthumous honour that they were quashed. However, it wasn't until 1625, twenty-eight years after the *Leicester* had appeared in Portsmouth without Cavendish's body, that his narrative of his last months and its charge of treachery against Davis appeared in print. The narrative was published by the Reverend Samuel Purchas, who'd picked up where Hakluyt had left off after his death in 1616, collecting stories of English ventures overseas under the title of *Hakluytus Posthumus or Purchas his Pilgrims*.

Purchas, both as editor and cleric, had a taste for the Old Testament and its stirring examples of the Wrath of God, and he warmed up his readers with a preface. 'Here,' he declaimed, 'mayest thou read that dismal and fatal voyage of Master Thomas Cavendish, in which he consummated his earthly peregrination.' Cavendish had achieved wonders on his circumnavigation – 'no man ever having in near so little time' 'compassed that huge circumference' of the globe, 'or taken his choice of so much more wealth than he could bring home, or revisited his native soil with greater pomp and triumph'. However, these accomplishments had been followed by an unhappy ending, for 'where it is said ye are Gods, it is added, ye shall die like men'.[12]

When Purchas turned to Cavendish's narrative itself, he explained that, while he'd redacted 'some passionate speeches of Master Candish against some private persons not employed in this action', he'd 'let pass' others, notably the accusations against Davis. If Davis 'did deal treacherously', Purchas pointed out, 'treachery found him out',[13] and he referred his readers to Davis's bloody end off Penang, which was included elsewhere in his *Pilgrims*. His sympathies evidently were with the circumnavigator.

In keeping with his ecclesiastical status, Purchas concluded his preface with a sermon that explained, in Christian terms, why Thomas Cavendish had failed. He'd been undone by sin as well as treachery and, in the publishing style of the time, a note in the margin identified the adjacent text as 'The moral of this and other Historical Tragedies'. The moral was to beware of pride, that invidious and mortal sin. Cavendish had presumed that his luck would run forever, and God had punished him accordingly. 'Let not prosperity poison the soul, with the sting of the old Serpent,' Purchas thundered. 'Let not any magnify himself in whatsoever exploits, or trust in uncertain riches, or promise to himself the perpetual smiles of the world.' Pride was 'a Witch which transformeth men into Swine'.[14]

Purchas included Anthony Knivet's account of Cavendish's final, fatal voyage in his *Pilgrimes* (under the title of *The Admirable Adventures and Strange Fortunes of Master Anthony Knivet which went with Master Thomas Candish in his second voyage to the south sea*) as evidence to support his conviction that Cavendish had been right to claim that Davis had been a turncoat.[15] Knivet's adventures had barely started when he was captured by the Portuguese on the island of San Sebastian in 1592 and carried away on a cannibal's back. He'd spent the following eight years as the slave of various colonists, including both Salvador Correa de Sá and his son Martim, who sent him on slaving expeditions into the Brazilian interior. When Knivet escaped to England in 1601, his father, Sir Henry, found him a post at the Royal Mint. He met up in London with other survivors from the *Leicester*, including Cesare Ricasen and John Chambers, Cavendish's cook, and used their memories to corroborate his account of the last voyage. These enabled Knivet to supply details such as Harris the goldsmith blowing his frostbitten nose into the fire at Port Famine in February 1592, and hard evidence that Davis had deserted the expedition. Moreover, during his time as a slave, Knivet had met Andrew Towers,[16] a fellow captive from the last voyage, but taken from the *Desire* rather than the *Leicester*, who'd confirmed that Davis had always intended to run away. Cavendish *had* given orders to rendezvous in Brazil, and Davis *had* deserted him. Knivet spoke out against Davis for personal reasons rather than from admiration for his General, who he believed had put him ashore at San Sebastian to die rather than to recover. Cavendish, through Knivet's eyes, was a whirlwind of activity, cheering men on when storms threaten to sink his ship and beating them when they fail to live up to his standards. He was careless of both his own life and those of others, but a gentleman nonetheless. Davis, in contrast, was a turncoat pure and simple, who'd cost Knivet nearly nine years of pain.[17]

By the time that Purchas published his *Pilgrimes*, Cavendish's adventures belonged to a past era. Elizabeth I had been succeeded by James I, who'd declared peace with Spain in 1604 and ended patriotic privateering. However, *Purchas his Pilgrims* was the new monarch's favourite bedtime reading, and its author's assessment of Thomas Cavendish – as an English hero whose feats had yet to be repeated or surpassed – prevailed throughout his reign. Cavendish's portraits were copied and hung in stately homes, and engravings, based on the work of Hondius, were circulated. A 1601 example, for instance, features an angel's hand emerging from a cloud, offering Cavendish a fistful of pearl necklaces under the motto 'Fortune favours the Brave'. The detail is reminiscent of the imprese in the portrait by John Bettes the Younger, painted before the circumnavigation, when Cavendish hoped to carry out deeds that would stun the world. Fire would erupt from the clouds and blaze across the history of his age.

Cavendish was commemorated by poets as well as historians and artists, including Michael Drayton, who summed up his public persona:

Courageous Cavendish, a second Neptune here,
Whose fame filled every mouth, and took up every ear...
Who through the South Seas passed, about this earthly Ball...
And with his silken sails, stained with the richest Ore,
Dared anyone to pass where he had been before.[18]

He continued to receive personal as well as public tributes in the decades after his death. Robert Hues, the navigator and stargazer who'd both sailed round the world with him and had been a witness to his will on the last voyage, singled out the circumnavigation as the most important event of his own long and fruitful life. Years after the controversies surrounding Cavendish had subsided, the memory of the man and his achievements still shone bright. Hues spent his final sixteen years at Christ Church College, Oxford where he was celebrated for his academic genius, and where he died – unlike most of his shipmates from either the *Desire* or the *Leicester* – of old age in bed, 'his body exhausted, but with a lively spirit on 24 May, in the year of our salvation 1632'.[19] Hues was buried in Christ Church Cathedral and was commemorated with a brass plaque listing his accomplishments. Although he'd been a notable theologian, scholar and philosopher, and a famous mathematician, the plaque proclaimed that the primary achievement Hues wished to record for posterity was that he'd sailed around the world with Thomas Cavendish.*

* 'Primum Thomæ Candishio conjunctissimi, cujus in consortio, explorabundis velis ambivit orbem' Hues, p.xxxvii.

Acknowledgements

At Head of Zeus, I would like to thank Richard Milbank for his wholehearted support for this book at every turn and for helping me to reshape it into its present form; and Megan Harris for seeing it through the editorial process. At the University of Southampton, where this book began its life as the thesis for my PhD, my particular thanks to Carole Burns and Dr Jakub Boguszak for their support and guidance over the years, which has enabled me to bring a neglected Elizabethan hero back into the limelight; to Philip Hoare, for his expert feedback on the work in progress; and to Dr Alice Hunt, for reintroducing me to Elizabethan literature.

I am grateful to Dr Paul Hunneyball at the History of Parliament online, for information on Cavendish's time as an MP; to Susan Maxwell, for sources for his gambling debts; to Dr Thomas Lockley for information on the Japanese men Cavendish brought to England; to Dr Florike Egmond, for new sources on Cavendish's time in London between his major voyages; to Professor Stephen Gunn, for guiding me through Tudor coroners' reports; and to Elania Pieragostini for advice on Cavendish's portrait.

Finally, I would like to thank both Fiona Gately and Nick Pitt for reading an early version of the manuscript and giving me invaluable advice as to how to revise it.

Notes

Chapter 1

[1] Reginald J. Fletcher, Ed., *The Pension Book of Gray's Inn* (London: Chiswick Press, 1901).

[2] See *The winning of Calais by the French*, by George Ferrers, the Poet, in *Tudor Tracts*, 1532–1588, introduction by A.F. Pollard, Archibold Constable and Co., LTD, Westminster, 1903, pp.289–293.

[3] Gabriel Harvey, *Speculum Tuscanismi*, quoted in de Vere, Edward, Seventeenth Earl of Oxford, Nelson, Alan H., Oxford Dictionary of National Biography, https://doi.org/10.1093/ref:odnb/2820 [accessed 7 July 2025].

[4] Violet A. Wilson, *Queen Elizabeth's Maids of Honour* (London: John Lane the Bodley Head Limited, London, MCMXXII) p.148–149.

[5] Alnwick Castle archives, S H Mss at AC Y III, I Bundle 5: Recognisance Cavendish, Skipwith & Perrott to George Gifford, 2 September 1581.

[6] Sir Robert Naunton, *Fragmenta Regalia, or Observations on the Late Queen Elizabeth, Her Times and Favorits*, Ed. E. Arber (1653); repr. (1870) (Oxford Text Archive) p.31.

[7] See Anna Whitelock, *Elizabeth's Bedfellows, An intimate History of the Queen's Court* (London: Bloomsbury, 2013).

[8] See Kenneth R. Andrews, 'Elizabethan Privateering' in *Privateering and Colonization in the Reign of Elizabeth I: Raleigh in Exeter 1985* Ed. by Joyce Youings (Exeter, England: University of Exeter Press, 1985) p.9.

[9] See Andrews, PHD, p.16: 'investment in war for booty was an honoured tradition, easily transposed from land to sea in Tudor times.'

[10] David Beers Quinn, Ed., *The Roanoke Voyages 1584–1590, Volumes I and II* (New York: Routledge, 2016) p.82.

[11] Quinn (2016) p.94.

[12] Quinn (2016) pp.96–97.
[13] Quinn (2016) pp.98–99.
[14] Quinn (2016) p.108.
[15] Quinn (2016) p.106.
[16] Quinn (2016) pp.111–113.

Chapter 2

[1] See Maxwell, ODNB.
[2] Sir Simonds D'Ewes, *The Journals Of All The Parliaments During The Reign Of Queen Elizabeth, Both Of The House Of Lords And House Of Commons, Collected By Sir Simonds D'Ewes*, Printed for John Starkey at the Mitre in Fleet Street near Temple-Bar. 1682, EEBO.
[3] Houses of Parliament online, Puckering, John, 1544–1596.
[4] Quinn (2016) p.117. It's possible that the placeholder was chosen to throw the Spanish spies listening to Parliament's proceedings off the scent.
[5] Quinn (2016) p.126.
[6] D'Ewes, p.356.
[7] D'Ewes, p.357.
[8] BL, Lansdowne MS 43, fol. 127.
[9] Tonnes were used as a measure of the volume of a ship's hold, based on the size of a large barrel or tun of wine. The largest warships and cargo vessels could be rated at 1,400 tonnes; oceanic privateers ranged from pinnaces rated at 20 tonnes to medium-sized warships of 300–500 tonnes.
[10] Gwyneth Dyke (1958), 'The Finance Of A Sixteenth-Century Navigator, Thomas Cavendish Of Trimley in Suffolk', *The Mariner's Mirror*, 44:2, 108–115, DOI: 10.1080/00253359.1958.10658384, p.110.
[11] Quinn (2016) p.148.
[12] Quinn (2016) pp.130–139. The authorship of the notes has not been established, but Smythe is considered to be the most likely candidate.
[13] Quinn (2016) p.173.

Chapter 3

[1] Now Tallaboa Bay.
[2] Quinn (2016) p.182.
[3] John Donne, *The Storm*, Poems (1633) (Bristol: Shearsman Books Ltd, 2015), p.52.

4 Jan Huyghen van Linschoten *The Last Fight of the Revenge at Sea*, Edward Arber, Ed., (London: Southgate, 1871). https://ia601306.us.archive.org/10/items/lastfightofrevenooarbeuoft/lastfightofrevenooarbeuoft.pdf [accessed 23 January 2025].

5 R. Pearse Chope, New Light on Sir Richard Grenville, Report and Transactions of the Devonshire Association, Barnstaple, July, 1917, p.232, https://archive.org/stream/ReportTransactionsOfTheDevonshireAssociationVol491917/TDA1917vol49_djvu.txt.

6 Quinn (2016) p.174.

7 Quinn (2016) p.184.

8 Quinn (2016) p.184.

9 Quinn (2016) p.184.

10 Quinn (2016) p.186.

11 Quinn (2016) p.186.

12 Quinn (2016) p.186.

13 Quinn (2016) pp.186–187

14 Quinn (2016) p.744.

15 Quinn (2016) pp.740–742.

16 Geoffrey Parker, *Imprudent King, a New Life of Philip II* (Newhaven and London: Yale University Press, 2014) p.76.

17 Parker (2014) p.282.

18 Parker (2014) p.282.

19 Parker (2014) p.86.

Chapter 4

1 Quinn (2016) p.188.

2 Quinn (2016) pp.188–189.

3 Quinn (2016) p.188–189.

4 Quinn (2016) pp.176–177.

5 Quinn (2016) p.139.

6 Quinn (2016) p.192.

7 Only eight miles by two. Manhattan Island, in contrast, is 13.4 miles long by 2.3 miles at its widest.

8 As per the terms of his patent. See Quinn (2016) p.83.

9 Quinn (2016) p.211.

10 Quinn (2016) p.193.

[11] Quinn (2016) p.203.
[12] Quinn (2016) pp.211–213.
[13] Quinn (2016) p.230.

Chapter 5

[1] Kenneth R. Andrews, *Elizabethan Privateering* (Cambridge: Cambridge University Press, 1966) p.70.
[2] Sir Julian Stafford Corbett, *Drake and the Tudor Navy, With a History of the Rise of England as a Maritime Power* (2 vols.) (New York: Burt Franklin, 1899) p.217.
[3] See Felipe Fernandez Armesto, *Straits, Beyond the Myth of Magellan* (London: Bloomsbury, 2023).
[4] Inspired by Sir Humphrey Gilbert and Dr John Dee. See Margaret Small, *From Thought to Action: Gilbert, Davis, And Dee's Theories behind the Search for the Northwest Passage* Author(s): The Sixteenth Century Journal, Winter 2013, Vol. 44, No. 4 (Winter 2013), pp.1041–1058 Published by: Sixteenth Century Journal www.jstor.org/stable/24246301.
[5] See Corbett (1899).
[6] Francis Pretty, *Sir Francis Drake's Famous Voyage Round the World*, www.gutenberg.org/files/2991/2991-h/2991-h.htm [accessed 1 June 2025].
[7] Private Diary of Richard Madox, in E.G.R. Taylor, Ed., *The Troublesome Voyage of Captain Edward Fenton 1582–1583* (London and New York: The Syndics of the Cambridge University Press, 1959) Document 38, p.163.
[8] Domesday Book: www.domesdaybook.co.uk/suffolk3.html.
[9] See Susan Maxwell (1996), 'HENRY SECKFORD: Sixteenth-Century Merchant, Courtier And Privateer' in *The Mariner's Mirror*, 82:4, 387–397, DOI:10.1080/00253359.1996.10656613.
[10] See Dyke (1958).
[11] See www.mhs.ox.ac.uk/staff/saj/thesis/baker.htm#note9.
[12] Quoted in Johnson p.33.
[13] Blatcher, Margaret, *Chatham Dockyard and a Little Known Shipwright, Matthew Baker (1530-1613)*, Kent Archaeological Society, http://kentarchaeology.org.uk/research/archaeologia-cantiana/. [accessed 30 January 2025].
[14] N.A.M. Rodger, *The Safeguard of the Sea* (London: Penguin, 2004) pp.214–216.

[15] Roger (2004) p.217.
[16] Robert Hues, *Tractatus De Globis* (London: Haklyut Society, 1889).
[17] Dyke (1958) p.70.
[18] Corbett (1899) p.245.
[19] See Kenneth R. Andrews, 'The Elizabethan Seaman' in *The Mariner's Mirror*, 68:3, 245–262, DOI: 10.1080/00253359.1982.10655868, 2013, p.251.
[20] Rogers (2004) p.235.
[21] Rogers (2004) p.236.
[22] Dyke (1958) p.69.
[23] Andrews (1951).
[24] Francis Pretty, *The Admirable and Prosperous Voyage of the Worshipfull Master Thomas Cavendish, Haklyut, Richard, The Principal Navigations Voyages Traffiques and Discoveries of the English Nation*, Goldsmid, Ed. (Edinburgh: I & G Goldsmid, 1890) p.5.

Chapter 6

1 Pedro Sarmiento de Gamboa, *CONCISE NARRATIVE BY Pedro Sarmiento de Gamboa, Governor and Captain-General of the Strait of the Mother of God, formerly called the Strait of Magellan, and of the settlements made and which may be made for his Majesty*, translated by Clements Markham (London: Hakluyt Society, 1895) p.340.
2 Hakluyt, Blackwood, Vol. VII.
3 Raleigh paid off his crews when they reached Southampton.
4 Hakluyt, Beazley, p.282.
5 Hakluyt, Beazley, p.281.
6 On 25 August 1586.
7 Pretty (1890) p.6.
8 Hakluyt, Goldsmid, p.59.
9 Cada Mosto, *Original Journals of the Voyages of Cada Mosto and Piedro de Cintra to the Coast of Africa, the former in the years 1455 and 1456, and the latter soon afterwards*, reprinted in R. Kerr, *A General History of Voyages and Travels to the End of the 18th Century* Vol. 2 (Edinburgh: Blackwood, 1811). https://books.google.co.uk/books?id=YVjm2VmuOlgC&pg=PA200&redir_esc=y#v=onepage&q&f=false p.221.
10 See Sir John Hawkins, Second Voyage to the West Indies, 18th Oct., 1564, 20th Sept., 1565 in Hakluyt, Beazley p.40.

[11] Andrews (1984) p.105.
[12] Andrews (1984) p.110.
[13] See E.G.R. Taylor, Ed. *The Troublesome Voyage of Captain Edward Fenton 1582–1583* (London and New York: The Syndics of the Cambridge University Press, London and New York, 1959).
[14] Pretty (1890) p.7.
[15] Pretty (1890) p.7.
[16] Cotton MS., fol. 23 in Hair, p.211.
[17] Pretty (1890) p.7.
[18] Pretty (1890) p.8.
[19] Dyke (1970) p.77.

Chapter 7

[1] Las Casas, Bartolomeo, *Brief Account of the Destruction of the Indies, www.gutenberg.org/ebooks/20321* [accessed 15 January 2025].
[2] André Thevet, Thomas Hacket (1568). *The New found worlde, or Antarctike, wherein is contained wonderful and strange things, as well of humane creatures, as beastes, fishes, foules, and serpents, trees, plants, mines of golde and siluer: garnished with many learned authorities. Imprinted at London, in Knight-rider strete*, by Henry Bynneman, for Thomas Hacket: OCLC 977063449.
[3] Pretty (1890) p.9.
[4] Ibid.
[5] Burghley and Leicester (29/6/1583) in Taylor (1959), p.266.
[6] Samuel Eliot Morison, *The European Discovery of America, The Southern Voyages 1492–1616* (New York: Oxford University Press, 1974) p.362.
[7] Fenton's expedition didn't trust Drake's chart but did not travel far enough south to confirm their doubts as to its accuracy. See Taylor (1959), p.189.
[8] 1st Cs p.22.
[9] Pretty (1890) p.5.
[10] Corbett (1899) p.247.
[11] Spelled 'Porte Desier' on his chart. See Quinn (1975) p.156.
[12] Pretty (1890) p.10.
[13] See Richard Barker, Careening: Art And Anecdote, Mare Liberum No. 2, 1991, pp.177–207.
[14] Voyages and Travels, Introduction C. Raymond Beazley, Archibald, Constable and Co., Ltd., Westminster, 1903 (NH) p.283. See also Richard

Hakluyt, *The Principal Navigations Voyages Traffiques and Discoveries of the English Nation*, Imprinted at London by George Bishop and Ralph Newberie, 1589, EEBO, for a facsimile of the original.

15 Pretty (1890) p.11.

16 Reproduced in Quinn (1975) p.159.

17 Pretty (1890) p.11.

Chapter 8

1 De Gamboa (1895) p.363.

2 Pedro Sarmiento De Gambóa, *Concise Narrative by Pedro Sarmiento de Gamboa, Governor and Captain-General of the Strait of the Mother of God, formerly called the Strait of Magellan, and of the settlements made and which may be made for his Majesty*, Translated Clements Markham, (London: Hakluyt Society, M.DCCC.XCV) p.328.

3 De Gambóa (1895) p.364.

4 NH (1903) p.283.

5 De Gambóa (1895) p.362.

6 Pretty (1890) p.63.

7 Written as 'Pt Famin'. See Quinn (1975) p.156.

8 Pretty (1890) p.13.

9 NH (1903) p.283.

10 Pretty (1890) p.13.

11 Pretty (1890) p.19.

12 De Gambóa (1895) p.373.

13 Pretty (1890) p.19.

14 Pretty (1890) p.13.

15 NH (1903) p.284.

16 Pretty (1890) p.15.

17 NH (1903) p.284.

18 Pretty (1890) p.16.

19 Pretty (1890) p.16.

Chapter 9

1 William Lytle Schurz, *The Manila Galleon* (New York: Dutton Paperback Edition, E.P. Dutton & Co., Inc., 1959) p.196.

2 Schurz (1959) p.210.

[3] See Schurz (1959) p.32 et seq.

[4] The musk had been collected from musk deer, deer-like creatures the size of a dog with a pair of dagger-like tusks and no antlers, native to the forests of Southeast Asia.

Civet was extracted from the perineal glands of Indian Civet Cats – solitary, nocturnal species of Viverrids. Civets excrete a few grams each week of aromatic oil, and use it to mark their territories by raising their tails and rubbing the scent glands beneath them against strategic points along their boundaries. Both musk and civet are still ingredients of expensive perfumes.

[5] 28 June.

[6] Schurz (1959) p.253.

[7] Schurz (1959) p.221.

[8] Schurz (1959) p.222.

[9] Schurz (1959) p.236.

[10] Schurz (1959) p.230.

[11] Schurz (1959) p.238.

[12] Schurz (1959) p.267.

[13] Schurz (1959) p.267.

[14] Pedro Sarmiento was the first to use the Lunar method of calculating longitude at sea. See De Gambóa (1895) p.164, fn.

[15] Schurz (1959) p.239.

[16] Schurz (1959) p.239.

[17] Schurz (1959) pp.272–273.

[18] Schurz (1959) p.254.

Chapter 10

[1] Pretty (Drake) www.gutenberg.org/files/2991/2991-h/2991-h.htm. The Spanish confessed to losing less. See José María Moreno Madrid & David Salomoni (2022), 'Nuno Da Silva's Third Relation: An Unknown Report on Francis Drake's Voyage (1577–1580)', *Terrae Incognitae*, 54:1, 64–82, DOI: 10.1080/00822884.2022.2048246, p74, where the total is recorded as '12… thousand gold pesos'.

[2] Pretty (1890) p.17.

[3] Pretty (1890) p.18.

[4] See de Góngora Marmolejo, Alonso, Historia de Chile desde su descubrimiento hasta el año 1575, Biblioteca Virtual Miguel de Cervantes.

www.cervantesvirtual.com/obra/historia-de-chile-desde-su-descubrimiento-hasta-el-ano-1575--0/ [accessed 19 January 2025]

5 Pretty (1890) p.18.

6 NH (1903) p.284.

7 'El capitan Gaspar de la Barrera, / Don Gonzalo, el de Cuevas i Molina, / Campofrio, Pasten i el de Herrera / … with Valor en gran manera / Descubre cada cual es la marina, / Derribando cabezas enemigas / Cual diestro segador cortando espigas' *Los Lisperguer y La Quintrala* (Valparaiso: por B. Vicuña Mackenna, 1877) p.89. www.memoriachilena.gob.cl/archivos2/pdfs/MC0031769.pdf [accessed 21 January 2025]. From Alonso de Ovalle. Histórica relación del Reyno de Chile. Francisco Cavallo, Roma, 1646, libro 6, caps.III–VIII, pp.221, 229, 237, 238.

8 NH (1903) p.284.

9 Pretty (1890) p.20.

10 NH (1903) p.284.

11 www.worldhistory.org/article/2049/the-silver-of-the-conquistadors/

12 Angela Schottenhammer, Connecting China with the Pacific World, ORIENTIERUNGEN *FRANKFURT* Zeitschrift zur Kultur Asiens Vol. 31 No. 2019, pp.111–171, (2020).

13 Pretty (1890) p.20.

14 Pretty (1890) p.21.

15 Pretty (1890) p.21.

16 Centenera p.443.

17 Pretty (1890) p.21.

18 See NH (1903) p.285.

19 Pretty (1890) p.25 (on 27-4-1587).

20 NH (1903) p.285.

21 Pretty (1890) p.22.

22 NH (1903) p.285.

23 Pretty (1890) p.24.

24 NH (1903) p.285.

25 Pretty (1890) p25.

26 Pretty (1890) p.25.

Chapter 11

1 Pretty (1890) p.25.

[2] Cavendish's troubles in Puna are analysed in Susan Maxwell (2017), 'Thomas Cavendish's Visit to Puná Island in 1587', *The Mariner's Mirror*, 103:2, 136–149, DOI: 10.1080/00253359.2017.1317134.

[3] Pretty (1890) p.25.

[4] Pretty (1890) p.25.

[5] Pretty (1890) p.25.

[6] Pretty (1890) p.28.

[7] Pretty (1890) p.26.

[8] Pretty (1890) p.27.

[9] See Lane, Quito p.205.

[10] See Pretty (1890) p.29.

[11] Kris Lane, *Quito 1599, City and Colony in Transition* (University of New Mexico Press, 2002) p.200.

[12] Pretty (1890) p.29.

[13] NH (1903) p.286.

[14] Pretty (1890) p.30.

[15] NH (1903) p.286.

[16] Pretty (1890) p.30.

[17] NH (1903) p.286.

[18] NH (1903) p.286.

[19] Pretty (1890) p.30.

[20] 'Michael Sancius' (Pretty).

[21] NH (1903) p.287.

[22] NH (1903) p.287.

[23] Pretty (1890) p.31.

[24] Pretty (1890) p.31.

[25] Pretty (1890) p.32.

[26] Pretty (1890) p.32.

[27] Pretty (1890) p.33.

[28] Pretty (1890) p.34.

[29] NH (1903) p.288.

[30] Pretty (1890) p.34.

[31] Pretty (1890) p.34.

[32] Pretty (1890) p.35.

[33] Pretty (1890) p.35.

Chapter 12

[1] Pedro Unamuno, *The Voyage of Pedro to California in 1587* Author(s): H.R. Wagner and Pedro de Unamuno, California Historical Society Quarterly, Vol. 2, No. 2 (Jul., 1923), pp.140–160 Published by: University of California Press in association with the California Historical Society. <www.jstor.org/stable/25177703> [accessed 14 July 2025] pp.145–148.
[2] Unamuno (1923) p.146.
[3] Unamuno (1923) p.149.
[4] Unamuno (1923) p.155.
[5] Unamuno (1923) p.156.
[6] Unamuno (1923) p.156.
[7] Unamuno (1923) p.158.
[8] Unamuno (1923) p.159.
[9] W. Michael Mathes, *The capture of the Santa Ana, Cabo San Lucas, November, 1587: The accounts of Francis Pretty, Antonio de Sierra, and Tomás de Alzola* (Los Angeles: Dawson's Book Shop) p.36.
[10] Mathes (1969) p.37.
[11] Pretty (1890) p.35.
[12] Pretty (1890) p.35.
[13] Mathes (1969) p.38.
[14] Mathes (1969) p.46.
[15] Mathes (1969) p.39.
[16] Pretty (1890) p.35.
[17] Mathes (1969) p.39.
[18] Pretty (1890) p.35.
[19] Mathes (1969) p.48.
[20] Pretty (1890) p.36.
[21] Pretty (1890) p.36.
[22] Pretty (1890) p.36.

Chapter 13

[1] Mathes (1969) p.49.
[2] Pretty (1890) p.36 et seq.
[3] Virginia Benitez Licuanan, and José Llavador Mira, eds., *The Philippines under Spain: A compilation and translation of original documents, Book IV*

(1583–1590) (Philippines: National Trust for Historical and Cultural Preservation of the Philippines, 1993) p.459.

[4] Licuanan (1993) p.460.

[5] Licuanan (1993) p.462.

[6] Licuanan (1993) p.462.

[7] Pretty (1890) p.37.

[8] Mathes (1969) p.50.

[9] NH (1903) p.288.

[10] Pretty (1890) p.37.

[11] Ibid.

[12] Mathes (1969) p.51.

[13] Mathes (1969) p.51.

[14] Pretty (1890) p.38.

[15] Mathes (1969) p.50.

[16] Licuanan (1993) p.462.

[17] Pretty (1890) p.38.

[18] Mathes (1969) p.41.

[19] Antonio de la Ascensión, *Father Antonio de la Ascension's Account of the Voyage of Sebastián Vizcaíno*, Spanish Voyages to the Northwest Coast in the Sixteenth Century, Chapter XI: Henry R. Wagner, California Historical Society Quarterly, Vol. 7, No. 4 (Dec., 1928) www.jstor.org /stable/25177964 p.310.

[20] Mathes (1969) p.41.

[21] Mathes (1969) p.52.

[22] Mathes (1969) p.41.

[23] General Archive of the Indies, CONTRACT DOCUMENTS, 484, N.2, R.5.

[24] NH (1903) p.288.

Chapter 14

[1] Hakluyt, Fuller, p.69.

[2] Carta de Santiago de Vera sobre el corsario inglés Cavendish y otros asuntos, Archivo General de Indias, Pares, ES.41091.AGI/24// FILIPINAS,34,N.79.

3 Antonio de Pigaffeta, *The First Voyage Round the World, by Magellan*, with notes and an Introduction by Lord Stanley of Alderney (London: Hakluyt Society, 1874) pp.69–70.

4 Polynesia George French Angas, *A Popular Description Of The Physical Features, Inhabitants, Natural History, And Productions Of The Islands Of The Pacific. With An Account Of Their Discovery, And The Progress Of Civilisation And Christianity Amongst Them* (London: Society For Promoting Christian Knowledge, 1866) p.405.

5 Pretty (1890) p.39.

6 Pretty (1890) p.39.

7 NH (1903) p.289.

8 Pretty (1890) p.39.

9 Pretty (1890) p.39.

10 Pigafetta p.65.

11 Pigafetta p.68.

12 Capul, *Before and Now, a History of Capul Island* (Manila, Summer Institute of Linguistics, Philippines, Inc., 1983) p.89.

13 Pretty (1890) p.40.

14 Pretty (1890) p.41.

15 Pretty (1890) p.42.

16 Pretty (1890) p.42.

17 Pretty (1890) p.43.

18 Licuanan (1993) p.464.

19 Pretty (1890) p.43.

20 *Letter of the Bishop of the Philippines to His Majesty, 27 June 1588*, Licuanan (1993) pp.305–312.

21 Pretty (1890) p.43.

22 Pretty (1890) p.45.

23 Licuanan (1993) p.480.

24 Bishop of the Filipinas, to Philip II, 27 June 1588, in Licuanan (1993) p.506.

25 Licuanan (1993) p.507.

26 Licuanan (1993) p.507.

27 Lemos, Ibid.

Chapter 15

1 Pretty (1890) p.75.

[2] Pretty (1890) p.51.
[3] Corbett (1899) p.302.
[4] Pretty (1890) p.51.
[5] Pretty (1890) p.47.
[6] Pretty (1890) p.47.
[7] Pretty (1890) p.47.
[8] Pretty (1890) p.48.
[9] Pretty (1890) p.48.
[10] Pretty (1890) p.48.
[11] Pretty (1890) p.49.
[12] Pretty (1890) p.49.
[13] Blair & Robertson, Vol. VII, p.79.
[14] Blair, Excerpt of a Letter from the Viceroy of India.
[15] Pretty (1890) p.50.
[16] Pretty (1890) p.50.
[17] Pretty (1890) p.51.
[18] NH (1903) p.291.
[19] Pretty (1890) p.52.
[20] Pretty (1890) p.54.
[21] See Quinn (1975) p.152.
[22] NH (1903) p.290, fn., Account of Jan Huyghen van Linschoten 'who reached St Helena… on the 12th May 1589'.
[23] NH (1903) p.191.

Chapter 16

[1] See Froude, p.23.
[2] Charles Howard, Second Baron Howard of Effingham and first Earl of Nottingham (1536–1624), James McDermott, Oxford Dictionary of National Biography, 2004, https://doi.org/10.1093/ref:odnb/13885.
[3] Robert Hutchinson, *The Spanish Armada* (London: Weidenfeld & Nicolson, London, 2013) p.122.
[4] Hutchinson (2013) p.125.
[5] Sir George Carey, Letter to Sussex, 25 July 1588, in Laughton, p.323.
[6] Garrett Mattingly, *The Defeat of the Spanish Armada* (London: Pimlico Edition, 2000) p.285.
[7] Quoted in Hutchinson (2013) p.158.

[8] Froude, p.56.

[9] Froude, p.56

[10] Hutchinson (2013) p.164.

[11] Hutchinson (2013) p.177.

[12] John Knox Laughton, *State Papers relating to the Defeat of the Spanish Armada, anno 1588* (Vols. 1–2) ([London]: Naval Records Society, 1894) p.95.

[13] Laughton (1894) p.96.

Chapter 17

[1] John Harvey, 'A discoursiue probleme concerning prophesies how far they are to be valued, or credited, according to the surest rules, and directions in diuinitie, philosophie, astrologie, and other learning: deuised especially in abatement of the terrible threatenings, and menaces, peremptorily denounced against the kingdoms, and states of the world, this present famous yeere, 1588, supposed the greatwonderfull, and fatall yeere of our age. By I.H. physition.' In the digital collection Early English Books Online. https://name.umdl.umich.edu/A02779.0001.001 University of Michigan Library Digital Collections. [accessed 17 July 2025]

[2] Fuller in Goldsmid, p.75.

[3] Hakluyt (1589) p.808 (also in Goldsmid pp.81–82).

[4] Trevelyan Papers, Camden Society, London, 1872, p.21 in Folgerpedia, 1588.

[5] Calendar of State Papers Foreign 22 f. 392.

[6] See Mattingly (2000) pp.318–325.

[7] 'Simancas: November 1588', in Calendar of State Papers, Spain (Simancas), Volume 4, 1587–1603 (London, 1899) pp.474–492. British History Online www.british-history.ac.uk/cal-state-papers/simancas/vol4/pp474-492 6 Nov. Paris Archives, K. 1567.

[8] Simancas: November 1588.

[9] [Ven.viii.403]

[10] British Library, Harleian MS286, fol 161 – reproduced in Quinn, Cavendish, p.4.

[11] Ibid.

[12] Calendar of State Papers (Simancas) p.478.

[13] Calendar of State Papers (Simancas) p.476.

[14] Calendar of State Papers (Simancas) p.484.

[15] Calendar of State Papers (Simancas) p.481.

[16] Hyder E. Rollins, *The Black Letter Broadside Ballad*, PMLA, 1919, Vol. 34, No. 2 (1919), pp.258–339, www.jstor.org/stable/457063 p.272.

[17] Transcript of the Registers of the Company of Stationers of London 1554–1640 A.D. II. 505–509, London, 1875, in Hakluyt (1904) p.294.

[18] Rollins (1919) p.310.

[19] Rollins (1919) p.324.

[20] Thomas Fuller, *The Worthies of England,* John Freeman, Ed. (London: George Allen & Unwin, 1952), p.346.

[21] Gamini Salgado, *The Elizabethan Underworld* (London: the Folio Society, 2006) p.9.

[22] Calendar of State Papers (Simancas). Queen Elizabeth left a hint to posterity as to how its value might have diminished when she'd dined on the *Desire*. An unquantified portion of the 'silver and gold from the Indies' had been delivered to her.

[23] 27 Nov. Paris Archives, K. 1569, in Calendar of State Papers (Simancas).

[24] Cheryl Fury, *Tides in the Affairs of Men: The Social History of Elizabethan Seamen 1580 – 1603*, Thesis, McMaster University, Ontario August 1998, p.77.

[25] Calendar of State Papers (Simancas) 10 Nov. Paris Archives, K. 1567.

[26] https://folgerpedia.folger.edu/mediawiki/media/images_pedia_folgerpedia_mw/archive/1/15/20170609170646!ECDbD_1588.pdf – Elizabeth jewel book.

[27] Dyke (1970) p.154.

[28] Herbert Cescinsky and Ernest. R. Gribble, *Early English Furniture & Woodwork* (London: George Routledge And Sons Limited, 1922) Wood Panellings and Mantels, Part 20.

[29] A literary language used in parts of northern Italy from the mid-thirteenth century to the fifteenth.

[30] Certeine notes or references taken out of the large map of China, brought home by M. Thomas Candish 1588, in Goldsmid p.84.

[31] Pretty (1890) p.40.

[32] R. Parke, *The Historie Of The Great And Mightie Kingdome Of China, And The Situation*, Translated out of Spanish, Hakluyt Society, 1854, Project Guttenberg edition www.gutenberg.org/files/39009/39009-h/39009-h.htm [accessed 15 July 2025].

[33] Parke (1854) p.2.

Chapter 18

[1] Albert Hastings Markham, *Collected Voyages of John Davis* (London: Hakluyt Society, 1880) p.ii.

[2] See Rory Rapple, *Gilbert, Sir Humphrey*, Oxford Dictionary of National Biography, 2012 https://doi.org/10.1093/ref:odnb/10690.

[3] Gilbert, Sir Humphrey, 'A discourse of a discouerie for a new passage to Cataia. VVritten by Sir Humfrey Gilbert, Knight.' In the digital collection Early English Books Online. https://name.umdl.umich.edu/A01749.0001.001. University of Michigan Library Digital Collections. [accessed 16 July 2025].

[4] Small (2013) p.1050.

[5] Small (2013) p.1057.

[6] Small (2013) p.1056.

[7] See Markham (Davis, 1880) pp.15–30.

[8] See William Cotton, *An Elizabethan Guild of the City of Exeter, An Account of the Proceedings of The Society of Merchant Adventurers During the Latter Half of the 16th Century* (Exeter: Printed for the Author by William Pollard, 1873) pp.81–84.

[9] Markham (Davis, 1880) p.30.

[10] Cotton, p.84.

[11] Markham (Davis, 1880) p.40.

[12] Markham (Davis, 1880) p.39.

[13] Markham (Davis, 1880) p.39.

[14] Markham (Davis, 1880) p.40.

[15] Markham (Davis, 1880) p.40.

[16] 14 June 1587.

[17] Suggesting they might have had previous contact with a French-speaking visitor?

[18] Markham (Davis, 1880) p.42

[19] Markham (Davis, 1880) p.44.

[20] Gilbert, Discourse.

[21] Markham (Davis, 1880) p.44.

[22] See Markham, (Davis, 1880) pp.45–53; and p.45 (Jane).

[23] Markham (Davis, 1880) p.46.

[24] Markham (Davis, 1880) p.46.

[25] Markham, (Davis, 1880), p.55.

[26] Markham (Davis, 1880) p.48.
[27] Markham (Davis, 1880) p.59.
[28] Markham letter to Sanderson, 14 October 1586 p.32.

Chapter 19

[1] See Browne Willis LLD, *Notitia Parliamentaria* (London: Printed for the Author in the Year MDCCL) https://archive.org/details/bim_eighteenth-century_notitia-parliamentaria-_willis-browne_1750 [accessed 15 July 2025].
[2] Sir Simonds d'Ewes, *The Journals Of All The Parliaments During The Reign Of Queen Elizabeth, Both Of The House Of Lords And House Of Commons*, Collected By Sir Simonds d'Ewes, Printed for John Starkey at the Mitre in Fleet Street near Temple-Bar. 1682, EEBO, p.420.
[3] See www.historyofparliamentonline.org/volume/1558-1603/parliament/1589.
[4] D'Ewes (1682) p.423.
[5] Maxwell (Seckford, 1996) p.390.
[6] See Dyke (1970) p.51. Writing in 1970, she states: 'it was buried muzzle down on the south side of Gun Corner Lane, Trimley St Martin… about four feet of the barrel formed the corner post of an adjacent cottage. Recently it was moved to the opposite side of the lane during road widening.'
[7] Which lived until at least 1735 when it was recorded by Kirby in the 'Suffolk Traveller'. See Dyke (1970) p.160.
[8] Hugh Morgan, John Bennell, Oxford Dictionary of National Biography, 2008, https://doi.org/10.1093/ref:odnb/61062.
[9] Quoted in Florike Egmond, 'Clusius And Friends: Cultures Of Exchange In The Circles Of European Naturalists', in *Carolus Clusius. Towards a cultural history of a Renaissance naturalist*, edited by Florike Egmond, Paul Hoftijzer and Robert Visser (Amsterdam, 2007).
See also Elgood, Cyril, A Treatise on the Bezoar Stone, Mahmud Bin Masud, The Imad-Ul Din The Physician of Ispahan, www.ncbi.nlm.nih.gov/pmc/articles/PMC7942278/pdf/annmedhist147397-0083.pdf.
[10] Eggmond (2007) p.154.
[11] Cassandra Auble, 'The Cultural Significance of Precious Stones in Early Modern England' (2011). Dissertations, Theses, & Student Research,

Department of History. 39. https://digitalcommons.unl.edu/historydiss/39 p.18.

[12] See Florike Egmond, and Deborah E. Harkness, *Elizabethan London's Naturalists and the work of John White*, European Visions: American Voices, Ed. Kim Sloan (London: British Museum Research Publication, 2009) p.46.

[13] See https://powo.science.kew.org/taxon/urn:lsid:ipni.org:names:821337-1/general-information.

[14] Egmond (2007) p.206.

[15] Egmond, p.195

[16] Pretty (1890) p.37.

[17] Lockley, p.13.

[18] Lockley, p.13.

[19] Robert Greene the Spanish Masquerado London 1589, EEBO.

[20] Wright, Leonard, by Sidney Lee, Dictionary of National Biography, 1885–1900, V. 83. Wright took the side of the Bishops in the Martin Marprelate debate, which won him transient fame and the anathemas of his opponents.

[21] Leonard Wright, *A Display of Duty decked with sage sayings, pithy sentences and proper similes: pleasant to read, delightful to hear, and profitable to practise* Printed by John Wolfe, London, 1589, EEBO, www.proquest.com/books/display-dutie-dect-vvith-sage-sayings-pythie/docview/2248572483/se-2.

[22] Richard Haklyut, *The principal nauigations, voyages, traffiques and discoueries of the English nation. [vols. 1–3] made by sea or ouer-land, to the remote and farthest distant quarters of the earth, at any time within the compasse of these 1600. yeres: deuided into three seuerall volumes, according to the positions of the regions, whereunto they were directed. The first volume containeth the worthy discoueries, &c. of the English... The second volume comprehendeth the principall nauigations... to the south and south-east parts of the world... By Richard Hakluyt preacher, and sometime student of Christ-Church in Oxford.* In the digital collection Early English Books Online. https://name.umdl.umich.edu/A02495.0001.001 University of Michigan Library Digital Collections [accessed July 16, 2025], title page.

[23] Ibid p.813.

[24] NH (1903) pp.809–813.

[25] This openness contrasted with Hakluyt's account of Drake's circumnavigation, details of which were suppressed.

Chapter 20

[1] Dyke (1970).

[2] See David B. Quinn and David R. Ransome (1997), 'Economic and Political Profit-Taking in the Aftermath of Thomas Cavendish's Circumnavigation of the Globe, 1588–1589', *Terrae Incognitae*, 29:1, 22–34, DOI: 10.1179/tin.1997.29.1.22.

[3] John Hooker, Exeter City Record Office, Book No. 51 (*sub anno* 1588).

[4] Ana Maria Crino and Helen Wallis, *New Researches On The Molyneux Globes*, Der Globusfreund, JUNI 1987 (für 1987/88/89), Nr. 35/37, REPORT on the VIth International Symposium Of Coronelli Society (JUNI 1987 (für 1987/88/89)) p.12 (Crino).

[5] See Robert Hues, *Tractatus De Globis* (London: Haklyut Society, 1889) pp.xii–xiii.

[6] Hues (1889) p.xvi.

[7] The history of terrestrial globes is summarised in Hues (1899) pp.xv–xxv.

[8] Hues (1889) p.xxviii.

[9] See https://exhibits.stanford.edu/ruderman/catalog/mc237sx9606.

[10] See www.npg.org.uk/collections/search/portrait/mw80753/Thomas-Cavendish.

[11] Calendar of State Papers, Spanish (1587–1603) London, 1899, pp.504–564 www.cambridge.org/core/books/abs/calendar-of-letters-and-state-papers-relating-to-english-affairs/calendar-of-state-papers-spanish-elizabeth-15871603-pages-504-to-564/BCE36D57E660EEEF99FEF9DAF3CE513E.

[12] CSP Spanish, p.516.

[13] CSP Spanish, p.522.

[14] Richard Hawkins, Observations, N.17 p.11.

[15] See Armada Papers p.186, 289.

[16] British Library, Landsdowne MS145 fol. 83v.

[17] Quinn (1975) pp.18–19, provides a summary of Cavendish's purchases.

[18] Andrews (1966) p.248.

[19] Andrews (1966) p.263.

[20] George Carey, Second Lord Hunsdon, Thompson Cooper, ODNB, 1886, https://doi.org/10.1093/odnb/9780192683120.013.4645.

[21] Andrews (1966) pp.67–8.

[22] See John Chidley, *A briefe relation of a voyage of The Delight a ship of Bristoll one of the consorts of M. John Chidley esquire and M. Paul Wheele, made unto the Straight of Magellan: with divers accidents that happened unto the company, during their 6. weekes abode there: Begun in the yeere 1589.* Written by W. Magoths, in Hakluyt (Goldsmid) pp.381–384.

[23] Ibid.

[24] Magoths p.85.

[25] Dee p.l6 (8 August 1578).

[26] Dee p.34 (15 May 1590).

[27] See Arthur Gould Lee, *The Son of Leicester* (London: Victor Gollancz Ltd, 1964) pp.26–35.

[28] Fenton Madox, p.158 (at the time she was called the *Galleon Oughtred*).

[29] Andrews (1966) p.248.

[30] See Dyke (Finances, 1958) p.114.

Chapter 21

[1] Thomas Lodge, Rosalynde. Euphues golden legacie, By T.L. Gent., Imprinted by Thomas Orwin for T.G. and John Busbie, London, 1590, Project Gutenberg Edition, www.gutenberg.org/ebooks/17181.

[2] See F. Beaumont and J. Fletcher, 'The Scornful Lady', in A. Glover Ed. *The Worlds of Francis Beaumont and John Fletcher,* Vol. 1 (Cambridge: Cambridge University Press) p.255.

[3] See Richard Hitchcock, 'Samuel Purchas as Editor: A Case Study: Anthony Knyvett's Journal', *The Modern Language Review*, Apr. 2004, Vol. 99, No. 2 (Apr. 2004), pp.301–312 Modern Humanities Research Association, www.jstor.org/stable/3738747.

[4] See R.F. Hitchcock (1994), 'Cavendish's Last Voyage: The Charges Against Davis', *The Mariner's Mirror*, 80:3, 259–269,<https://doi.org/10.1080 /00253359.1994.10656503> p.7.

[5] Job Hortop, *The Rare Travails of Job Hortop, an Englishman*, London, 1591, in Haklyut (1904) p.226.

[6] Hortop (1591) p.230.

[7] Hortop (1591) p.240.

[8] Hortop (1591) p.241.

[9] Charles Cotton, *The Complete Gambler*, J. Issacs, Ed., *Games and Gamesters of the Restoration* (1930), http://hdl.handle.net/1880/454 [accessed 15 July 2025] p.1.

[10] Dyke (Finances, 1958) p.114.

[11] Dyke (Finances, 1958) p.114.

[12] Philip Edwards, Ed., *Cavendish, Hudson, Raleigh, Last Voyages, the Original Narratives* (Oxford: Clarendon Press, 1988) p.97.

[13] Dom. Eliz., Vol. 237, ff. 53–4.

[14] See Sir Richard Hawkins, *The Observations of Sir Richard Hawkins Knight, In His Voyage into the South Sea, London, 1622*, University of Michigan Library Digital Collections [accessed 16 July 2025], pp.108–111.

[15] Hawkins (Observations) p.108.

[16] See Knivet (Edwards, 1988) p.81 and Jane (Edwards, 1988) p.98.

Chapter 22

[1] Knivet (Edwards, 1988) p.81.

[2] Ibid.

[3] Ibid.

[4] Vivien Kogut Lessa De Sá, Ed. *The Admirable Adventures and Strange Fortunes of Master Anthony Knivet* (New York: Cambridge University Press, 2015), p.46.

[5] Florence E. Dyer, 'The Elizabethan Sailorman', *The Mariner's Mirror*, 10:2, 133–146, DOI: https://doi.org/10.1080/00253359.1924.10655268 pp.135–136 and www.sciencehistory.org/stories/magazine/the-age-of-scurvy/.

[6] Knivet (Edwards, 1988) p.81.

[7] Ibid.

[8] Knivet (Edwards, 1988) p.98.

[9] See Centenera, p.452.

[10] Knivet (Edwards, 1988) p.82.

[11] Jane (Edwards, 1988) p.98.

[12] De Sá, p.47.

[13] De Sá (2015) p.47.

[14] De Sá (2015) p.48.

[15] Quoted in De Sá (2015) p.33. See also p.61 fn 34 and p.62 fn 37 (letter of Marcal Beliarte). The statue is said to have been dredged up centuries later and found to be encrusted with pearls – a natural tribute to its sanctity.
[16] De Sá (2015) p.48.
[17] Jane (Edwards, 1988) p.99.
[18] De Sá (2015) p.49.
[19] A Margarite of America (1596) Donald Beecher (introduction) Henry D. Janzen (editing and annotations) (Toronto, Barnabe Riche Society Publications Volume 17, 2005) p.75.
[20] De Sá (2015) p.49.
[21] Hemming p.45.
[22] Lodge, Margarite p.59.
[23] De Sá (2015) p.50.
[24] H.C. Lea, PERU, in The Inquisition in the Spanish Dependencies: Sicily, Naples, Sardinia, Milan, the Canaries, Mexico, Peru, New Granada (Cambridge, Cambridge University Press, 2010) <www.cambridge.org/core/books/abs/inquisition-in-the-spanish-dependencies/peru/3D2C75139368AC093C66B87F44EDE356> [accessed 15 July 2025] p.336.
[25] Centenera p.471.
[26] Centenera p.471.

Chapter 23

[1] De Sá (2015) p.50.
[2] Ibid.
[3] Ibid.
[4] Ibid.
[5] De Sa (2015) p.51.
[6] On 6 March 1592.
[7] Jane (Edwards, 1988) p.100.
[8] Ibid.
[9] Quinn, Cavendish, p.58. Note that Cavendish's manuscript can be viewed at: Cavendish, Thomas, Account of the last voyage of Thomas Cavendish, 1592 (Manuscript): https://collections.britishart.yale.edu/catalog/orbis:9595091.
[10] Ibid.
[11] Quinn (1975) p.58.

[12] Quinn (1975) p.60.
[13] Ibid.
[14] De Sá (2015) p.51.
[15] Ibid.
[16] Fury (1998) p.354.
[17] De Sá (2015) p.51.
[18] Fury (1998) p.358.
[19] Quinn (1975) p.60.
[20] Jane (Edwards, 1988) p.100.
[21] De Sá (2015) p.52.
[22] Edwards (1988) p.101.
[23] De Sá (2015) p. 52.
[24] Quinn (1975) p.60.
[25] Quinn (1975) p.66.
[26] Quinn (1975) p.62.
[27] Ibid.
[28] Jane (Edwards, 1988) p.101.
[29] Quinn (1975) p.64.
[30] Quinn (1975) p.68.
[31] Ibid.

Chapter 24

[1] Edwards (1988) p.90.
[2] Thomas Falkner, *A Description of Patagonia* (London: Printed by C. Pugh MDCCLXXIV, 1774) p.116.
[3] De Sá (2015) pp.52–53.
[4] De Sá (2015) p.53.
[5] Quinn (1975) p.70.
[6] De Sá (2015) p.53.
[7] Ibid.
[8] De Sá (2015) p.53.
[9] Ibid.
[10] Quinn (1975) p.70.
[11] Quinn (1975) p.72.
[12] Quinn (1975) p.74.

[13] See De Sá, Salvador Correia, BRAZILHIS Database, https://brasilhis.usal.es/en/node/480 [accessed 17 July 2025].
[14] De Sá (2015) p.66.
[15] Hemmings p.26.
[16] Centenera p.462.
[17] Centenera p.463.
[18] Centenera p.464.
[19] Edwards (1988) p.46.
[20] Quinn (1975) pp.77–78.
[21] De Sá (2015) p.54.
[22] Edwards (1988) p.65.
[23] Quinn (1975) p.80.
[24] De Sá (2015) p.54.
[25] Centenera, p.464.
[26] Ibid.

Chapter 25

[1] Jane (Edwards, 1988) p.105.
[2] Jane (Edwards, 1988) p.103.
[3] Jane (Edwards, 1988) p.106.
[4] Jane (Edwards, 1988) p.103.
[5] Jane (Edwards, 1988) p.104.
[6] Jane (Edwards, 1988) p.105.
[7] Jane (Edwards, 1988) p.107.
[8] Ibid.
[9] Ibid.
[10] Ibid.
[11] Ibid.
[12] Morrison, p.391.
[13] Jane (Edwards, 1988) p.108.
[14] Ibid.
[15] Jane (Edwards, 1988) p.109.
[16] Ibid.
[17] Jane (Edwards, 1988) p.110.
[18] Ibid.

Chapter 26

[1] Quinn (1975) p.102.
[2] See Quinn (1975) p.80 'have caste of the Roebuck'.
[3] Quinn (1975) p.80.
[4] Ibid.
[5] Edwards (1988) p.66.
[6] Ibid.
[7] Edwards (1988) p.92.
[8] Edwards (1988) p.66.
[9] Ibid.
[10] Edwards (1988) p.68.
[11] Ibid.
[12] Edwards (1988) p.69.
[13] Ibid.
[14] Ibid.
[15] Ibid.
[16] Capital of the Brazilian Captaincy of the same name.
[17] Edwards (1988) p.70.
[18] Ibid.
[19] Ibid.
[20] Ibid.
[21] Edwards (1988) p.93.
[22] Edwards (1988) p.72.
[23] Edwards (1988) p.93.
[24] Edwards (1988) p.72.
[25] Quinn (1975) p.104.
[26] Edwards (1988) p.73.
[27] John Vincent (alias John Yates) to Sir Francis Englefield (PRO, S.P. 12/245,33).
[28] Centenera, p.468.

Chapter 27

[1] Edwards (1988) p.73.
[2] Edwards (1988) p.93.
[3] Edwards (1988) p.94.

[4] Quinn (1975) p.110.
[5] Edwards (1988) p.75.
[6] Ibid.
[7] Ibid.
[8] Ibid.
[9] Edwards (1988) p.75–76.
[10] Edwards (1988) p.76.
[11] Ibid.
[12] Edwards (1988) p.95.
[13] De Sá (2015) p.56.
[14] Edwards (1988) p.95.
[15] Edwards (1988) p.77.
[16] Ibid.
[17] Ibid.
[18] Ibid.
[19] Quinn (1975) p.124.
[20] Quinn (1975) p.126.
[21] Ibid.
[22] Quinn (1975) p.126.
[23] Quinn (1975) p.52.
[24] Quinn (1975) pp.52–53.
[25] Quinn (1975) p.70.
[26] Quinn (1975) p.128.
[27] Quinn (1975) p.132.

Chapter 28

[1] Jan 28, Privy Council to the Lord Mayor and Aldermen of London, concerning the number of plague-deaths in London, Folgerpedia, 1593. https://folgerpedia.folger.edu/mediawiki/media/images_pedia_folgerpedia_mw/1/1a/ECDbD_1593.pdf.
[2] Folgerpedia, 1593.
[3] Ibid.
[4] Ibid.
[5] Quinn (1975) p.36.

[6] Acts of the Privy Council of England Volume 20, 1590–1591, Ed. John Roche Dasent (London, 1900), British History Online www.british-history.ac.uk/acts-privy-council/vol20 [accessed 17 July 2025].

[7] Quinn (1975) p.50.

[8] See Raymond Gorges, *The Story Of A Family Through Eleven Centuries, Illustrated by Portraits and Pedigrees, Being A History of the Family of Gorges* (Boston, 1944), pp.49–51.

[9] Probably from Santos. If other members of the *Leicester's* company had been as lucky as Knivet in finding gold coins in the town, the pillage may have been considerable, and perhaps a motive to Cavendish's gentlemen-adventurers to return home. The *Leicester* may, however, have taken a prize on her way back to England.

[10] APC V.20 p.233.

[11] Ibid.

[12] APC V.20 p.346.

[13] Ibid.

Chapter 29

[1] Jane (Edwards, 1988) p.110.

[2] Jane (Edwards, 1988) p.111.

[3] Ibid.

[4] Ibid.

[5] Jane (Edwards, 1988) p.112.

[6] Jane (Edwards, 1988) p.111.

[7] Ibid.

[8] Jane (Edwards, 1988) p.113.

[9] Jane (Edwards, 1988) p.114.

[10] Jane (Edwards, 1988) p.117.

[11] Jane (Edwards, 1988) p.118.

[12] Ibid.

[13] See De Sá (2015) p.97.

[14] Jane (Edwards, 1988) p.119.

[15] Ibid.

[16] Ibid.

[17] Jane (Edwards, 1988) p.120.
[18] Ibid.
[19] Ibid.

Chapter 30

[1] D'Ewes (1682) p.419.
[2] In Markham (Davis, 1880) p.229.
[3] Edwards (1988) p.97.
[4] Ibid.
[5] In Markham, pp.347–366.
[6] Ibid.
[7] Ibid.
[8] Lodge, Thomas, A Margarite of America (1596) Donald Beecher (introduction) Henry D. Janzen (editing and annotations) (Toronto: Barnabe Riche Society Publications Volume 17, 2005), p.72.
[9] Lodge (Beecher) p.73.
[10] See Lodge (Beecher) pp.62–63.
[11] LANCASTER his Allarums, honorable Assaultes, and supprising of the Block-houses and Store-houses belonging to Fernand Bucke in BRASILL, 1595, 1595, EEBO, www.proquest.com/eebo/docview/2240926187/citation/EB86F9D694DF4486PQ/3?accountid=13963&sourcetype=Books.
[12] Purchas, p.146.
[13] Purchas, p.148.
[14] Purchas, pp.148–9.
[15] Purchas, pp.177–195.
[16] Towers had prospered since being captured. After establishing himself as a good Catholic and a capable physician who 'did many cures', he'd revealed occult skills. According to Knivet, the Portuguese thought he was 'a Sorcerer, for he would prognosticate many things'. Towers had lost one of his eyes in his privateering days and they believed that a demon had occupied its empty socket. See de Sa (2015) p.97.
[17] See Hitchcock (Knyvett, 1994), and De Sá (2015) Appendix 1, pp.161–172.
[18] Drayton (1622), *Poly-Olbion*, Song XIX.
[19] Hues, p.xxxvii.

Bibliography

References are set out in accordance with MHRA guidelines, with the exception of sources where the style of citation has been prescribed by the publisher.

A

Acts of the Privy Council of England Volume 20, 1590-1591, ed. John Roche Dasent (London, 1900), Web: British History Online https://www.british-history.ac.uk/acts-privy-council/vol20 [accessed 17 July 2025].

Alnwick Castle archives, S H Mss at AC Y III, I Bundle 5: 'Recognisance Cavendish, Skipwith & Perrott to George Gifford, 2nd Sept 1581'.

Andrews, K.R., *The Economic Aspects of Elizabethan Privateering*, A Thesis submitted for the Degree of Doctor of Philosophy in the University of London, September, 1951.

Andrews, Kenneth R., *Elizabethan Privateering* (Cambridge: Cambridge University Press, 1966).

Andrews, Kenneth R., *Trade, Plunder and Settlement, Maritime Enterprise and the Genesis of the British Empire*, 1480 – 1630 (Cambridge: Cambridge University Press, 1984).

Andrews, Kenneth R., 'Elizabethan Privateering' in *Privateering and Colonization in the Reign of Elizabeth I: Raleigh in Exeter 1985* Joyce Youings, ed., (Exeter, England: University of Exeter Press, 1985).

Arber, Edward ed., *A Transcript of the registers of the Company of Stationers of London, 1554 - 1640 5 vols*, (London and Birmingham, 1875-94).

Auble, Cassandra, *The Cultural Significance of Precious Stones in Early Modern Englan*d (2011) Dissertations, Theses, & Student Research, University of Nebraska, Lincoln, Department of History. 39. <https://digitalcommons.unl.edu/historydiss/39>.

Aubrey, John, *Aubrey's Brief Lives*, Andrew Clark ed., (London: Clarendon Press, 1898) https://www.gutenberg.org/files/47787/47787-h/47787-h.htm [accessed 21 July 2025].

B

Bacon, Francis, *The Project Gutenberg eBook of the Advancement of Learning*, by Francis Bacon. [n.d.]. Gutenberg.org <https://www.gutenberg.org/files/5500/5500-h/5500-h.htm?> [accessed 11 January 2025].

Bailey, Amanda, *Flaunting: Style and the Subversive Male Body in Renaissance England*, (Toronto: University of Toronto Press, 2007).

Ballads: Transcript of the Registers of the Company of Stationers of London 1554-1640 A.D. II. 505-509, London, 1875.

Barker, Richard, *Careening: Art And Anecdote*, Mare Liberum No. 2, 1991, pp 177 – 207.

Blair, Emma Helen and Robertson, James Alexander, *The Philippine Islands, 1493-1898, Vol VII*, Project Gutenberg, <https://www.gutenberg.org/ebooks/13701>[accessed 21 July 2025].

Blatcher, Margaret Chatham Dockyard and a little known Shipwright, Matthew Baker (150 – 1616), Kent Archaeological Society, <http://kentarchaeology.org.uk/research/archaeologia-cantiana/.> [accessed 30 January 2025].

C

Calendar of State Papers, Spanish (1587-1603) London, 1899, <https://www.cambridge.org/core/books/abs/calendar-of-letters-and-state-papers-relating-to-english-affairs/calendar-of-state-papers-spanish-elizabeth-15871603-pages-504-to-564/BCE36D57E660EEEF99FEF9DAF3CE513E>. [accessed 11 January 2025].

Capul: *Before and Now, a History of Capul Island* (Manila, Summer Institute of Linguistics, Philippines, Inc., 1983).

Castiglione, Baldassare, *The Book of the Courtier*, ed. by Daniel Javitch, trans. by Charles S. Singleton (New York, NY: WW Norton, 2002).

Carey George, Second Lord Hunsdon, Thompson Cooper, ODNB, 1886, https://doi.org/10.1093/odnb/9780192683120.013.4645 [Accessed 27th June 2025].

Cavendish, Thomas, 1560 – 1592, *Account of the last voyage of Thomas Cavendish, 1592*, web: https://collections.britishart.yale.edu/catalog/orbis:9595091 [Accessed 27th June 2025].

Centenera, Martin del Barco, *The Argentine and the Conquest of The River Plate*, translated Walter Owen (Buenos Aires: Instituto Cultural, 1965).

Centenera, Martin del Barco, *La Argentina o La Conquista del Rio de la Plata*, web: https://www.cervantesvirtual.com/obra-visor/la-argentina-o

-la-conquista-del-rio-de-la-plata-poema-historico--0/html/ [accessed 1st August 2025].

Chapter Book 1 of Corpus Christi College, Cambridge https://www.corpus.cam.ac.uk/sites/default/files/downloads/chapter-book-1.pdf [accessed June 2025].

Cescinsky, Herbert, and Gribble Ernest. R., *Early English Furniture & Woodwork*, (London: George Routledge And Sons Limited, 1922) Wood Panellings and Mantels, Part 20.

Corbett, Sir Julian Stafford, *Drake and the Tudor Navy, With a History of the Rise of England as a Maritime Power* (2 vols.), (New York: Burt Franklin, 1899).

Cotton, William, *An Elizabethan Guild of the City of Exeter, An Account of the proceeding The Society of Merchant Adventurers During the Latter Half of the 16th Century*, (Exeter: Printed for the Author by William Pollard, 1873).

Cotton, Charles. *The Complete Gambler*, J. Issacs, ed., *Games and Gamesters of the Restoration* (1930), http://hdl.handle.net/1880/454 [accessed 15 July 2025].

Crino, Ana Maria and Helen Wallis, *New Researches On The Molyneux Globes*, Der Globusfreund , JUNI 1987 (für 1987/88/89), Nr. 35/37, REPORT on the VIth International Symposium Of Coronelli Society (JUNI 1987 (für 1987/88/89)).

D

Davis, John, *Voyages and Works of John Davis, the Navigator*, Albert Hastings Markham, ed., (London: Hakluyt Society, No LIX, MDCCCLXXX).

Davis, John, Michael Hicks, Oxford Dictionary of National Biography, January 2008, https://doi.org/10.1093/ref:odnb/7326

de Góngora, Marmolejo, Alonso, *Historia de Chile desde su descubrimiento hasta el año 1575*, Biblioteca Virtual Miguel de Cervantes. https://www.cervantesvirtual.com/obra/historia-de-chile-desde-su-descubrimiento-hasta-el-ano-1575--0/. [accessed 20 January 2025].

De Sa, Vivien Kogut Lessa, ed. *The Admirable Adventures and Strange Fortunes of Master Anthony Knivet*, (New York: Cambridge University Press, 2015).

de Vera, Santiago, Carta de Santiago de Vera sobre el corsario inglés Cavendish y otros asuntos, Pares, ES.41091.AGI/24//FILIPINAS,34,N.79.

D'Ewes, Sir Simonds, *The Journals Of All The Parliaments During The Reign Of Queen Elizabeth, Both Of The House Of Lords And House Of Commons, Collected By Sir Simonds D'Ewes*, Printed for John Starkey at the Mitre in Fleet street near Temple-Bar. 1682, EEBO.

De Cuellar, Francisco, *Letter from One Who Sailed with the Spanish Armada and Tells the Story of the Enterprise of England*, in Gallagher, P. and Cruikshank, D.W. eds., *God's Obvious Design, Papers for the Spanish Armada Symposium, Sligo*, (London: Tamesis Books Limited, 1988).

de la Ascension, Antonio, *Father Antonio de la Ascension's Account of the Voyage of Sebastian Vizcaino*, in Spanish Voyages to the Northwest Coast in the Sixteenth Century, Chapter XI: trans. Henry R. Wagner, California Historical Society Quarterly, Vol. 7, No. 4 (Dec., 1928), Web: <https://www.jstor.org/stable/25177964>.

de Pigaffeta, Antonio, T*he First Voyage Round the World, by Magellan*, with notes and an Introduction by Lord Stanley of Alderney, (London: Hakluyt Society 1874).

De Gamboa, Pedro Sarmiento, *CONCISE NARRATIVE BY Pedro Sarmiento de Gamboa, Governor and Captain-General of the Strait of the Mother of God, formerly called the Strait of Magellan, and of the settlements made and which may be made for his Majesty*, Translated Clements Markham (London: Hakluyt Society 1895).

De Toledo, Fernando Alvarez, *Puren Indomito*, Poema por el Captaine *FERNANDO ALVAREZ DE TOLEDON* A. Franck, Leipzig 1862, Web: https://books.google.co.uk/books?id=47AGAAAAQAAJ&printsec=frontcover&source=gbs_ge_summary_r&cad=0#v=onepage&q&f=false [accessed 25 August 2025].

de Los Rios, Dona Catalina, *Los Lisperguer y La Quintrala* (Valparaiso: por B. Vicuna Mackenna, 1877). Web <https://www.memoriachilena.gob.cl/archivos2/pdfs/MC0031769.pdf> [accessed 21 January 2025].

de Unamuno, Pedro, *The Voyage of Pedro to California in 1587* Author(s): H. R. Wagner and Pedro de Unamuno, California Historical Society Quarterly, Vol. 2, No. 2 (Jul., 1923), pp. 140-160 Published by: University of California Press in association with the California Historical Society. https://www.jstor.org/stable/25177703 [accessed 14 July 2025].

Dee, John, The Private Diary of John Dee, Project Gutenberg Edition, Web < https://www.gutenberg.org/files/19553/19553-h/19553-h.htm> [accessed August 2025].

Donne, John, The Storm, *Poems* (1633) (Bristol: Shersman Books Ltd, 2015).

Drayton, Michael, Poly-Olbion, Song XIX (1622) <https://poly-olbion.exeter.ac.uk/the-text/full-text/song-19/> [accessed 12 January 2024].

Duffy, Eamon, F*ires of Faith, Catholic England Under Mary Tudor* (London: Yale University Press 2009.)

Dyer, Florence E., The Elizabethan Sailorman, *The Mariner's Mirror*, 10:2, 133-146, DOI: < https://doi.org/10.1080/00253359.1924.10655268>.

Dyke, Gwyneth, *The Proud Fortune*, MS, Ipswich, HD1643/3/9, 1970.

Dyke, Gwyneth, *Thomas Cavendish and the Roanoke Voyage, 1585, Notes on some recently discovered documents,* Suffolk Review 1, No 2, (1956).

Dyke, Gwyneth (1958) The Finance Of A Sixteenth-Century Navigator, Thomas Cavendish Of Trimley In Suffolk, *The Mariner's Mirror*, 44:2, 108-115, DOI: 10.1080/00253359.1958.10658384.

E

Edwards, Philip, ed., *Cavendish, Hudson, Raleigh, Last Voyages, the Original Narratives*, (Oxford: Clarendon Press, 1988).

Egmond, Florike, *Clusius And Friends: Cultures Of Exchange In The Circles Of European Naturalists,* In: Carolus Clusius. Towards a cultural history of a Renaissance naturalist, edited by Florike Egmond, Paul Hoftijzer and Robert Visser (Amsterdam, 2007).

Egmond, Florike, and Harkness, Deborah E., *Elizabethan London's Naturalists and the work of John White*, European Visions: American Voices, ed Kim Sloan, (London: British Museum Research Publication, 2009).

F

Falkner, Thomas, *A Description of Patagonia*, (London: Printed by C. Pugh MDCCLXXIV, 1774).

Ferrers, George, *The winning of Calais by the French*, in Tudor Tracts, 1532 – 1588, introduction by A.F Pollard, (Westminster: Archibold Constable and Co., LTD, 1903).

Fletcher, Reginald J., ed., *The Pension Book of Gray's Inn,* (London: Chiswick Press, 1901).

Forster, E.M., *Aspects of the Novel* (New York: Harcourt Brace and Company, Inc., 1927).

Foxe, John, *Actes and Monuments of these Latter and Perillous Days, Touching Matters of the Church, 1593*, Exclassics.com: https://www.exclassics.com/foxe/foxe268.htm [accessed 11 January 2025].

Freil, Iain, E*lizabethan Merchant Ships and Shipbuilding*, Gresham College Lecture, London, 29 September 2009, https://www.gresham.ac.uk/sites/default/files/transcript/Elizabethan%20Merchant%20Ships%20and%20Shipbuilding.pdf [accessed 11 January 2025].

Froude, James Anthony, *English Seamen in the Sixteenth Century, Lectures Delivered at Oxford Easter Terms 1893-4*, (London: New Edition, Longmans, Green and Co., 1896).

Fuller, Thomas, *The Worthies of England,* John Freeman, ed. (London: George Allen & Unwin, 1952).

Fury, Cheryl, *Tides in the Affairs of Men: The Social History of Elizabethan Seamen 1580 – 1603*, Thesis, McMaster University, Ontario August 1998.

G

Garet, J., letter to Carolus Clusius, University Library Leiden MS Vulc 101 https://clusiuscorrespondence.huygens.knaw.nl/edition/entry/877. [accessed 5 July 2025].

Gilbert, Sir Humphrey, Dictionary of Irish Biography, October, 2009, DOI: https://doi.org/10.3318/dib.003467.v1 [accessed 5 July 2025].

Gilbert, Sir Humphrey, Rapple, Rory, Oxford Dictionary of National Biography, 2012 https://doi.org/10.1093/ref:odnb/10690.

Gilbert, Sir Humphrey, *"A discourse of a discouerie for a new passage to Cataia. VVritten by Sir Humfrey Gilbert, Knight."* Imprinted at London by Henry Middleton for Richarde Ihones, 1576. In the digital collection Early English Books.https://name.umdl.umich.edu/A01749.0001.001. University of Michigan Library Digital Collections. [accessed July 16, 2025].

Gorges, Raymond, *The Story Of A Family Through Eleven Centuries, Illustrated by Portraits and Pedigrees, Being A History of the Family of Gorges*, (Boston, 1944).

Robert Greene, the Spanish Masquerado, (London: EEBO, 1589).

Griggs, David , *The World of Christopher Marlowe* (London: Faber and Faber, 2004)

Gunn, Steven (2017). Sixteenth-century English accident inquests. [Data Collection] Colchester, Essex: UK Data Archive.10.5255/UKDA-SN-852155.. Colchester, Essex: UK Data Archive.10.5255/UKDA-SN-852155.

Goodman, Ruth, *How to be a Tudor, A Dawn-to-Dusk View of Tudor Life*, (London: Penguin, 2017).

H

Hakluyt, Richard , *The Principal Navigations Voyages Traffiques & Discoveries of the English Nation, etc.* (Glasgow: Hakluyt Society; Extra Ser., nos. 1–12]: James MacLehose & Sons for the Hakluyt Society. 12 vols, 1904).

Haklyut, Richard, *The Principal Navigations Voyages Traffiques and Discoveries of the English Nation*, Goldsmid (editor) (Edinburgh: I & G Goldsmid, 1890).

Haklyut, Richard, T*he principal nauigations, voyages, traffiques and discoueries of the English nation. [vols. 1-3] made by sea or ouer-land, to the remote and farthest distant quarters of the earth, at any time within the compasse of these 1600. yeres: deuided into three seuerall volumes, according to the positions of the regions, whereunto they were directed. The first volume containeth the worthy discoueries, &c. of the English ... The second volume comprehendeth the principall nauigations ... to the south and south-east parts of the world ...* By Richard Hakluyt preacher, and sometime student of Christ-Church in Oxford." In the digital collection Early English Books Online. https://name.umdl.umich.edu/A02495.0001.001. [accessed July 17, 2025].

Harvey, John *"A discoursiue probleme concerning prophesies how far they are to be valued, or credited, according to the surest rules, and directions in diuinitie, philosophie, astrologie, and other learning: deuised especially in abatement of the terrible threatenings, and menaces, peremptorily denounced against the kingdoms, and states of the world, this present famous yeere, 1588, supposed the greatwonderfull, and fatall yeere of our age. By I.H. physition."* In the digital collection Early English Books Online. https://name.umdl.umich.edu /A02779.0001.001 University of Michigan Library Digital Collections. [accessed July 17, 2025].

Hawkins, Sir Richard, *The Observations of Sir Richard Hawkins Knight, In His Voyage into the South Sea, London, 1622*, University of Michigan Library Digital Collections. [accessed July 16, 2025].

Hemming, John, *Red Gold, The Conquest of the Brazilian Indians* (London: PAPERMAC, Macmillan London Limited, 1987).

Hitchcock, R. F, (1994) Cavendish's Last Voyage: The Charges Against Davis, *The Mariner's Mirror*, 80:3, 259-269.

Hitchcock, R. F, (2001) Cavendish's Last Voyage: Purposes Revealed and Concealed, *The Mariner's Mirror*, 87:1, 5-14.

Hitchcock, R. F. (2003) CAVENDISH'S LAST VOYAGE: JOHN JANE'S NARRATIVE OF THE VOYAGE OF THE DESIRE , *The Mariner's Mirror*, 89:1, 4-16, DOI: 10.1080/00253359.2003.10659270.

Hitchcock, Richard, *Samuel Purchas as Editor: A Case Study: Anthony Knivet's Journal*, The Modern Language Review , Apr., 2004, Vol. 99, No. 2 (Apr., 2004), pp. 301- 312 Modern Humanities Research Association, https://www.jstor.org/stable/3738747.

Hooker, John, Exeter City Record Office, Book No. 51 (*sub anno* 1588).

Hortop, Job, *The Rare Travails of Job Hortop, an Englishman*, London, 1591, in Haklyut (1904)

Howard, Charles, second Baron Howard of Effingham and first earl of Nottingham (1536 – 1624), James McDermott, Oxford Dictionary of National Biography, 2004, https://doi.org/10.1093/ref:odnb/13885

Hutchinson, Robert, The Spanish armada, (London: Weidenfeld & Nicolson, 2013).

Hues, Robert, *Tractatus De Globis*, (London: Haklyut Society, 1889).

J

Johnston, Stephen Andrew, 1994. "*Making Mathematical Practice : Gentlemen, Practitioners and Artisans in Elizabethan England*" (Apollo - University of Cambridge Repository) https://doi.org/10.17863/CAM.19773 pp. 107-165.

Jowitt, Claire, *The Hero and the Sea: Sea Captains and Their Discontents*, L'Empire, 74, 2017 https://doi.org/10.4000/1718.888.

K

Keen, Maurice, *Chivalry* (New Haven and London: Yale University Press, 1984).

Kingsley, Charles, Vance, Norman, Oxford Dictionary of National Biography,2019, https://doi.org/10.1093/ref:odnb/15617.

L

Lane, Kris, *Quito 1599, City and Colony in Transition*, (New Mexico: University of New Mexico Press, 2002).

"Lancaster his allarums, honorable assaultes, and supprising of the block-houses and store-houses belonging to Fernand Bucke in Brasill With his braue attempt in landing in the mouth of the ordinaunce there, which were cannons culuering, cannon periall and sacres of brasse, with other sundry his most resolute and braue attempts in that country. From whence he laded of their spoyles and rich commodities he there found fifteene good ships, which was sinemon, sugar, pepper, cloues, mace, calloco-cloth and brassel-wood with other commodities. With the names of such men of worth hauing charge within this most honorable attempt lost their liues. Published for their eternall honor. by a vvelvviller." In the digital collection Early English Books Online. https://name.umdl.umich.edu/A10810.0001.001. University of Michigan Library Digital Collections. [accessed January 17, 2025].

Las Casas, Bartolomeo, *A Brief Account of the Destruction of the Indies*, Project Gutenberg edition: <https://www.gutenberg.org/ebooks/20321. [accessed 15 January 2025].

Laughton, John Knox ed., *State Papers Relating to the Defeat of the Spanish Armada, Anno 1588* (London: Naval Records Society, 1894).

Lea, H.C., PERU, in *The Inquisition in the Spanish Dependencies: Sicily, Naples, Sardinia, Milan, the Canaries, Mexico, Peru, New Granada* (Cambridge, Cambridge University Press, 2010) <https://www.cambridge.org/core/books/abs/inquisition-in-the-spanish-dependencies/peru/3D2C75139368AC093C66B87F44EDE356> [accessed 15 July 2025].

Lee, Arthur Gould, *The Son of Leicester*, (London: Victor Gollancz Ltd, 1964).

Lemos, Manuel, *Carta de Manuel Lorenzo de Lemos sobre corsario inglés*, 1588-06-30, Archivo de Indias, FILIPINAS,34,N.80, ES.41091.AGI/26//FILIPINAS,34,N.80.

Linschoten, Jan Huygen Van, in *The Last Fight of the Revenge at Sea*, Edward Arber, ed., (London: Southgate, 1871). https://ia601306.us.archive.org/10/items/lastfightofrevenooarbeuoft/lastfightofrevenooarbeuoft.pdf [accessed 23 January 2025].

Lockley, T. (2019). 'Yong lads of very good capacitie.<i>'</i> Christopher and Cosmus, Anglo-Japanese pioneers. Japan Forum, 31(1), 86–109. https://doi.org/10.1080/09555803.2018.1488760

Lodge, Thomas, *A Margarite of America* (1596) Donald Beecher (introduction) Henry D. Janzen (editing and annotations) (Toronto: Barnabe Riche Society Publications Volume 17, 2005).

Lodge, Thomas, *Rosalynde., Euphues golden legacie*, By T.L. Gent., (London: Imprinted by Thomas Orwin for T.G. and John Busbie 1590, Project Gutenberg Edtion, <https://www.gutenberg.org/ebooks/17181>. Also available at https://quod.lib.umich.edu/e/eebo/A06173.0001.001/1:3?rgn=div1;view=fulltext>

M

Madox, Richard, *Private Diary of Richard Madox*, in E.G.R Taylor, ed., *The Troublesome Voyage of Captain Edward Fenton 1582 - 1583*, (London and New York: The Syndics of the Cambridge University Press, 1959).

Magoths, W., *A briefe relation of a voyage of The Delight a ship of Bristoll one of the consorts of M. John Chidley esquire and M. Paul Wheele, made unto the Straight of Magellan: with divers accidents that happened unto the company, during their 6. weekes abode there: Begun in the yeere 1589. Written by*

W. Magoths, in Hakluyt (Goldsmid) and at https://www.perseus.tufts.edu/hopper/text?doc=Perseus%3Atext%3A1999.03.0070%3Anarrative%3D933 [accessed 28 June 2025].

Markham, Albert Hastings, *Collected Voyages of John Davis*, (London: Hakluyt Society, 1880).

Marshall, Peter, *Heretics and Believers, A History of the English Reformation* (London: Yale University Press, 2017).

Marvell, Andrew , *Britannia and Raleigh*, 1674, [Web: https://dn720002.ca.archive.org/0/items/satiresofandrewmo0marvuoft/satiresofandrewmo0marvuoft.pdf.

Mathes, W. Michael, *The Capture of the Santa Ana, Cabo San Lucas, November, 1587* (Los Angeles: Dawson's Book Shop, 1969).

Mattingly, Garrett, *The Defeat of the Spanish Armada*, (London: Pimlico Edition, 2000).

Maxwell, Susan M., Cavendish, Thomas, Oxford Dictionary of National Biography, 2004, <https://doi.org/10.1093/ref:odnb/4942> [Accessed 12 January 2025].

Maxwell, Susan (2017) 'Thomas Cavendish's Visit to Puná Island in 1587', *The Mariner's Mirror*, 103:2, 136-149, DOI: 10.1080/00253359.2017.1317134.

Maxwell, Susan, 'The Philippines, A link between Thomas Cavendish (1560–1592) and Sir Robert Dudley (1574–1649)', Journal of the International Map Collectors' Society, December 2018 No. 155 ISSN 0956-5728, pp 26 – 39.

Maxwell, Susan (1996) HENRY SECKFORD: Sixteenth-Century Merchant, Courtier And Privateer, *The Mariner's Mirror*, 82:4, 387-397, DOI:10.1080/00253359.1996.10656613.

Morgan, Hugh, by John Bennell, Oxford Dictionary of National Biography, 2008, https://doi.org/10.1093/ref:odnb/61062

Moreno, José María Madrid & David Salomoni (2022) 'Nuno Da Silva's Third Relation: An Unknown Report on Francis Drake's Voyage (1577–1580)', Terrae Incognitae, 54:1, 64-82, DOI: 10.1080/00822884.2022.2048246.

Mosto, Cada, *Original Journals of the Voyages of Cada Mosto and Piedro de Cintra to the Coast of Africa, the former in the years 1455 and 1456, and the latter soon afterwards*, reprinted in R. Kerr, 1811, A General History of Voyages and Travels to the end of the 18th century, vol. 2, (Edinburgh: Blackwood, 1811).

Morgan, Hugh, Letter to Carolus Clusius, 22nd July 1590, Web: https://clusiuscorrespondence.huygens.knaw.nl/edition/entry/1203.

Morison, Samuel Eliot , *The European Discovery of America, The Southern Voyages 1492 - 1616*, (New York: Oxford University Press, 1974).

N

N.H., *The worthy and famous Voyage of Master Thomas Cavendish made round about the Globe of the Earth; in the space of two years, and less than town months*, in Hakluyt, Richard, *The Principal Navigations Voyages Traffiques & Discoveries of the English, Nation, etc.* (Glasgow: Hakluyt Society; Extra Ser., nos. 1–12]: James MacLehose & Sons for the Hakluyt Society. 12 vols, 1904).

"Haue vvith you to Saffron-vvalden. Or, Gabriell Harueys hunt is vp Containing a full answere to the eldest sonne of the halter-maker. Or, Nashe his confutation of the sinfull doctor. The mott or posie, in stead of omne tulit punctum: pacis fiducia nunquam. As much to say, as I sayd I would speake with him." In the digital collection Early English Books Online. https://name.umdl.umich.edu/A08003.0001.001. University of Michigan Library Digital Collections [accessed September 2, 2025].

Naunton, Sir Robert, *Fragmenta Regalia, or, Observations on the Late Queen Elizabeth, Her Times and Favorits Written by Sir Robert Naunton ...* (1641) (Proquest, Eebo Editions. 2011).

P

Parke, R.: *The Historie Of The Great And Mightie Kingdome Of China, And The Situation, Translated out of Spanish*, Haluyt Society, 1854, Project Guttenberg edition, https://www.gutenberg.org/files/39009/39009-h/39009-h.htm [accessed 15 July 2025].

Parker, Geoffrey (1996) The Dreadnought Revolution Of Tudor England, *The Mariner's Mirror*, 82:3, 269-300, DOI: 10.1080/00253359.1996.10656603.

Parker, Geoffrey, *Imprudent King, a New Life of Philip II,* (Newhaven and London: Yale University Press, 2014).

Pearse Chope, R, 'New Light on Sir Richard Grenville', Report and Transactions of the Devonshire Association, Barnstaple, July, 1917. P232 , https://archive.org/stream/ReportTransactionsOfTheDevonshireAssociationVol491917/TDA1917vol49_djvu.txt.

Licuanan, Benitez Licuanan and Jose Llavador Mira, eds., T*he Philippines Under Spain, a compilation and translation of Original Documents*, Book IV (1583 – 1590) (Philippines: National trust for Historical and Cultural Preservation of the Philippines, 1993).

Pretty, Francis, *Sir Francis Drake's Famous Voyage Round the World*, Web: https://www.gutenberg.org/files/2991/2991-h/2991-h.htm [accessed 1st June 2025].

Pretty, Francis, *THE ADMIRABLE AND PROSPEROUS VOYAGE OF THE WORHSIPFULL MASTER THOMAS CAVENDISH*, Haklyut, Richard, The Principal Navigations Voyages Traffiques and Discoveries of the English Nation, Goldsmid, ed. (Edinburgh: I & G Goldsmid, 1890)

Purchas, Samuel, *Hakluytus Posthumus, or, Purchas his Pilgrimes*, 20 bks in 4 vols., repr.20 vols., (London: Hakluyt Society, extra ser., 14–33, 1905–7).

Q

Quinn, David Beers, *The Last Voyage of Thomas Cavendish 1591 - 1592*, (Chicago and London: University of Chicago Press, 1975).

Quinn, David Beers, *The Roanoke Voyages 1584 - 1590, Volumes I and II*, (New York: Routledge, 2016).

Quinn, David B. & David R. Ransome, (1997) 'Economic and Political Profit-Taking in the Aftermath of Thomas Cavendish's Circumnavigation of the Globe', 1588–1589, Terrae Incognitae, 29:1, 22-34, DOI: 10.1179/tin.1997.29.1.22.

R

Rodger, N.A.M, *The Safeguard of the Sea*, (London: Penguin, 2004).

Rodger, N.A.M, The Development of Broadside Gunnery, 1450–1650, *The Mariner's Mirror*, 82:3, 301-324, DOI: 10.1080/00253359.1996.10656604.

Rollins, Hyder E, '*The Black Letter Broadside Ballad*', PMLA , 1919, Vol. 34, No. 2 (1919), pp. 258-339, https://www.jstor.org/stable/457063.

S

Sacks, David Harris 'The Religious Beliefs of Richard, Oliver and Edmond Hakluyt: The Word of the Cross', The Journal of the Hakluyt Society June 2025.

Salgado, Gamini, *The Elizabethan Underworld* (London: The Folio Society, 2006).

Saul, Nigel, *For Honour and Fame, Chivalry in England, 1066 – 1500*, (London: Pimlico, 2012).

Schottenhammer, Angela, 'Connecting China with the Pacific World?', ORIENTIERUNGEN Zeitschrift zur Kultur Asiens 31 (2019).

Schurz, William Lytle, *The Manila Galleon*, (New York, Dutton Paperback Edition, E.P. Dutton & Co., Inc., 1959).

Small, Margaret, 'From Thought to Action: Gilbert, Davis, And Dee's Theories behind the Search for the Northwest Passage', Author(s): The Sixteenth Century Journal , Winter 2013, Vol. 44, No. 4 (Winter 2013), pp. 1041-1058 Published by: Sixteenth Century Journal < https://www.jstor .org/stable/24246301> p 1050

Strong, Roy *The Cult of Elizabeth, Elizabethan Portraits and Pageantry* (London: Pimlico, 1999).

Strong, Roy, *The Elizabethan Image* (New Haven and London: Yale University Press, 2021).

The practice, proceedings, and lawes of armes described out of the doings of most valiant and expert captaines, and confirmed both by ancient, and moderne examples, and præcedents, by Matthevv Sutcliffe." In the digital collection Early English Books Online 2. https://name.umdl.umich.edu /A13173.0001.001. University of Michigan Library Digital Collections [accessed July 4, 2025].

T

Taylor, E.G.R, ed., *The Troublesome Voyage of Captain Edward Fenton 1582 - 1583* (London and New York: The Syndics of the Cambridge University Press, London and New York, 1959).

Thevet, André; trans. Hacket, Thomas (1568). *The New found worlde, or Antarctike, wherein is contained wonderful and strange things, as well of humaine creatures, as beastes, fishes, foules, and serpents, trees, plants, mines of golde and silver: garnished with many learned authorities. Imprinted at London; Imprinted at London, in Knight-rider street, by Henry Bynneman, for Thomas Hacket.* OCLC 977063449.

https://www.proquest.com/eebo/docview/2240926187/99846156/C5133A79B9D44205PQ/1?accountid=13963.

V

Vincent, John (alias John Yates) to Sir Francis Englefield (PRO, S.P. 12/245,33).

W

Warner William, *Albions england a continued historie of the same kingdome, from the originals of the first inhabitants thereof: And most the chiefe alterations and accidents there hapning: Vnto, and in, the happie raigne of our now most gracious soueraigne queene elizabeth. VVith varietie of inuentiue and historicall intermixtures* (London: 1597) www.proquest.com/books/albions-england-continued-historie-same-kingdome/docview/2240941836/se-2 .

Webster, John, "Monuments of honor Deriued from remarkable antiquity, and celebrated in the honorable city of London, at the sole munificent charge and expences of the right worthy and worshipfull fraternity, of the eminent Merchant-Taylors. Directed in their most affectionate loue, at the confirmation of their right worthy brother Iohn Gore in the high office of His Maiesties liuetenant ouer his royoll [sic] chamber. Expressing in a magnificent tryumph, all the pageants, chariots of glory, temples of honor, besides a specious and goodly sea tryumph, as well particularly to the honor of the city, as generally to the glory of this our kingdome. Invented and written by Iohn Webster Merchant-Taylor." In the digital collection Early English Books Online. https://name.umdl.umich.edu/A14871.0001.001. University of Michigan Library Digital Collections [accessed July 10, 2025.

Whitelock, Anna, *Elisabeth's Bedfellows, An intimate History of the Queen's Court*, (London: Bloomsbury, 2013).

Willis, Browne LLD, *Notitia Parliamentaria*, (London: Printed for the Author in the Year MDCCL)https://archive.org/details/bim_eighteenth-century_notitia-parliamentaria-_willis-browne_1750 [accessed 15 July 2025].

Wilson, Violet A. , *Queen Elizabeth's Maids of Honour*, (London: John Lane the Bodley Head Limited, London, 1922).

Wirth, Edward , *Certain Errors in Navigation*, Web: https://archive.org/details/bim_early-english-books-1475-1640_errors-in-navigation_wright-edward_1599.

Wright, Leonard, '*A Display of Duty decked with sage sayings, pithy sentences and proper similes: pleasant to read, delightful to hear, and profitable to practise*' (London: Printed by John Wolfe, 1589) EEBO. https://www.proquest.com/books/display-dutie-dect-vvith-sage-sayings-pythie/docview/2248572483/se-2.

Image Credits

p.1 Portrait of a Gentleman, thought to be Thomas Cavendish; Christie's Images / Bridgeman Images
p.7 Engraving from *The Roxburghe Ballads*; The Reading Room / Alamy
p.15 Interior of the House of Commons, *c.*1640; Pictorial Press Ltd / Alamy
p.23 Illustration of Cabo Rojo Fort *c.*May 1585; Rye Hobie / Alamy
p.35 Panel from *A Cheife Herowans Wyfe* by John White depicting an Algonquian child holding an English doll; Print Collector / Contributor / Getty Images
p.47 Drawing of a Ship by Matthew Baker (1530–1613); Eagen Archive / Alamy
p.61 1563 Map of West Africa; Pictorial Press Ltd / Alamy
p.71 *Sailors Hunting Seals* by Theodor de Bry; Artefact / Alamy
p.79 Illustration of the Strait of Magellan, *c.*1603; From the British Library Archive / Bridgeman Images
p.89 *Armed Three-Master* by Frans Huys, 1561–5; Harris Brisbane Dick Fund, 1928 / The Metropolitan Museum of Art
p.97 Woodcut of Potosi, Peru; Lakeview Images / Alamy
p.111 Fleet of Ships at Puna; Library of Congress Prints and Photographs Division Washington, D.C. 20540 USA
p.125 Map of the Coast of 'New Spain'; Pares Archive / Archivo General de Indias, MP-MEXICO, 518
p.135 Section of Cavendish's Sea Chest; Courtesy of Christchurch Mansion, Ipswich
p.145 Reception of a Manila Galleon by Theodor de Bry *c.*1590; Granger – Historical Picture Archive / Alamy
p.157 Map of St Helena, *c.*1603; Antiqua Print Gallery / Alamy
p.169 Map of English and Spanish Fleets; Library of Congress, Rare Book and Special Collections Division

Index

Illustrations are indicated by numbers in italics.

D

T